Nigerian Taxation

Multiple-Choice and Short-Answer Questions with Solutions

Fourth Edition

By the same author:

Personal Income Tax in Nigeria
Companies Taxation in Nigeria
Petroleum Profits Tax in Nigeria
Foundations of Group Accounts
CITN Practice & Revision Kits:
- Principles of Taxation
- Income Taxation
- International Taxation
- Tax Audit & Investigation
- Oil & Gas Taxation

ICAN Practice & Revision Kit:
- Taxation & Advanced Taxation

Nigerian Taxation

Multiple-Choice and Short-Answer Questions with Solutions

Fourth Edition

Offiong U. Bassey

Internal Audit Department

Central Bank of Nigeria

First edition 2015
Second edition 2016
Third edition 2018
Fourth edition 2019

ISBN: 978-978-57181-0-2

Distributed by
Best Brain Bookshops
No. 16 Adedoyin Street,
Kosofe, Ketu, Lagos, Nigeria
P.O. Box 6461, Marina, Lagos
E-mail: bassey64@yahoo.com
Phone: 08091091666, 08025294928, 08036722720

Published & Printed in Nigeria by
The CIBN Press Ltd
A. A. Plaza, 4 Araromi Street,
Shomolu, Lagos, Nigeria. Tel: 09093624958

About the Author

Offiong Udo Bassey is a Chartered Accountant (FCA) and has a Master's degree in Banking & Finance and a doctorate in Business Administration. He is also a Fellow of the Chartered Institute of Taxation of Nigeria (FCTI) and a Member of the Nigerian Institute of Management (Chartered) (MNIM).

He was a Senior Lecturer in the Department of Accountancy, Akwa Ibom State Polytechnic, where he taught Advanced Financial Accounting, Taxation and Auditing & Investigation. He has taught at the Federal Polytechnic, Auchi, Akanu Ibiam Federal Polytechnic, Uwana as well as satellite campuses of the University of Jos and the Polytechnic, Calabar. While employed in the industry, he held senior managerial positions in a number of reputable companies, including Consolidated Breweries Plc. Offiong also served as a Bank Examiner in the Banking Supervision Department, Central Bank of Nigeria for a number of years. He is an Examiner to the Chartered Institute of Taxation of Nigeria.

Offiong has written over ten books, including Personal Income Tax in Nigeria, Companies Taxation in Nigeria, Petroleum Profits Tax in Nigeria and Foundations of Group Accounts. He is widely acknowledged as a best-selling author and his books are highly recommended for professional examinations.

He resides in Lagos with his lovely wife, Frances, and children, Edidiong, Eno and Idara. To communicate with him, please send your letters to P. O. Box 6461, Marina, Lagos or e-mail bassey64@yahoo.com.

Dedicated to
Edidiong Offiong Bassey
for passing the final examinations of the Chartered Institute of Taxation of Nigeria and the Institute of Chartered Accountants of Nigeria in 2013 and 2015 (few months to his 16th and 18th birthday anniversaries) respectively and for emerging as the overall best graduating student of Lead City University in 2014 with B.Sc (First Class Honours) in Accounting at the age of seventeen.

Contents

Preface to the Fourth Edition		ix
Preface to the First Edition		x
Acknowledgements		xi
1	Introduction to Taxation	1
2	Nigerian Tax System and National Tax Policy	9
3	Administration of Personal Income Tax	21
4	Federal Capital Territory Internal Revenue Service Act, 2015	31
5	Federal Inland Revenue Service (Establishment) Act, 2007	55
6	Persons and Income Chargeable	81
7	Residence and Relevant Tax Authority	91
8	Employment Income and Pay As You Earn	99
9	Investment Income and Withholding Tax	113
10	Ascertainment of Profits	127
11	Basis of Assessment	145
12	Capital Allowances	159
13	Loss Reliefs	187
14	Partnership Assessment	197
15	Estates, Trusts and Settlements	203
16	Tertiary Education Tax and National Information Technology Development Levy	209
17	Taxation of Specialized Companies	219
18	Pioneer Companies	227
19	Tax Returns, Assessments, Objections, Appeals and Collection	243
20	Tax Clearance Certificate	261
21	Tax Evasion, Tax Avoidance, Tax Offences and Penalties	265
22	Presumptive Taxation and Tax Amnesty	269
23	Stamp Duties	281
24	Value Added Tax	289
25	Capital Gains Tax	307
26	Petroleum Profits Tax	327
27	Double Taxation Relief and Taxation of Non-residents	355

28	Transfer Pricing, Thin Capitalization and Electronic Commerce	373
29	Merger, Acquisition, Tax Incentives and Tax Planning	391
30	Tax Implications of Leasing	407
31	Taxation of Non-Governmental Organisations (NGOs)	411
32	Tax Audit and Investigation	415
Solutions to Multiple-Choice and Short-Answer Questions		425

Preface to the Fourth Edition

In this fourth edition, every effort has been made to bring the book up-to-date to include recent amendments to the Nigerian tax laws and developments in the Nigerian taxation scene. Three new chapters and 124 additional questions and answers have been included to make the book totally comprehensive. The book now contains thirty-two chapters and 1,692 multiple-choice and short-answer questions with solutions based on the Nigerian tax laws as contained in the Laws of the Federation of Nigeria 2004 and subsequent amendments up to 31st July, 2019 as known to the author.

The book will continue to be useful to a wide range of readers including the members of staff of the Federal Inland Revenue Service and State tax authorities who are preparing for their promotion examinations as well as students reading Financial Studies, Accountancy, Taxation and related courses in the Nigerian universities and polytechnics. The book will be a good companion to the students preparing for the Accounting Technicians Scheme West Africa (ATSWA), the Institute of Chartered Accountants of Nigeria (ICAN), the Chartered Institute of Taxation of Nigeria and other professional examinations that include multiple-choice questions and/or short-answer questions in their examination papers. The book will also be of tremendous assistance to lecturers, professional accountants, tax practitioners and others who need a book of this nature for whatever reason.

It is recommended that students should use this book for revision after they have studied the relevant Taxation textbooks such as Personal Income Tax in Nigeria, Petroleum Profits Tax in Nigeria and Companies Taxation in Nigeria by the same author.

O. U. Bassey
E-mail: bassey64@yahoo.com
August 2019

Preface to the First Edition

Following the publication of Personal Income Tax in Nigeria, Companies Taxation in Nigeria and Petroleum Profits Tax in Nigeria in 2013, many of the users of the books requested that I should make available to the public the solutions to the 1,490 multiple-choice and short-answer questions contained in the three books. In view of the fact that the questions are meant to be given out to the students as class work and assignment, the answers could only be released to lecturers on demand. However, I was encouraged to write this book to satisfy the needs of students, tax practitioners, lecturers, etc who are looking for a book with questions and answers.

This book contains 1,095 multiple-choice and short-answer questions with solutions covering personal income tax, companies income tax, pioneer industries, education tax, information technology development levy, stamp duties, value added tax, capital gains tax, double taxation and taxation of non-residents, tax incentives, tax planning, transfer pricing, thin capitalization, e-commerce, tax audit and investigation, etc.

The book will be useful to a wide range of readers particularly students reading Financial Studies, Accountancy, Taxation and related courses in the Nigerian universities and polytechnics and students preparing for professional examinations in Accounting and Taxation. The book will be of great assistance to the staff of the Federal Inland Revenue Service and State tax authorities who are preparing for their promotion examinations. The book will also serve the needs of lecturers, professional accountants, tax practitioners and others who need a book of this nature for whatever reason.

This book is based on the Nigerian tax laws as contained in the Laws of the Federation of Nigeria 2004 and subsequent amendments up to 31st December, 2014 as known to the author. In using the book, it should be borne in mind that tax laws are not static. Changes are made to some of the provisions of our tax laws from time to time. It is recommended that students should use this book for revision after they have studied the relevant taxation textbooks.

O. U. Bassey
E-mail: bassey64@yahoo.com
January 2015

Acknowledgements

I wish to profusely thank the almighty God for His generosity in giving me life, good health, knowledge, wisdom and understanding. I am heavily indebted to my parents, late Chief Udo Akpan Bassey and Mrs Affiong Udo Akpan for their parental care and sacrifice. I am grateful to my elder brother, Mr Edem Bassey, FCA, for showing me the way to the accounting profession and my sisters for their spiritual support. I gratefully acknowledge the training, instructions, guidance, encouragement and support I received from my teachers in Christ Church Primary School and African Church Secondary Commercial School, Oku Iboku, Akwa Ibom State and my lecturers in the Department of Accountancy, the Polytechnic, Calabar. A special debt of appreciation is due to Elder B. T. Udoete, who was my lecturer in Taxation at the Polytechnic, Calabar and the Head of Department of Accountancy, Akwa Ibom State Polytechnic when I was a lecturer at the Polytechnic.

I wish to acknowledge and thank lecturers, tax practitioners, professional accountants, tax officials, students and other readers of the first, second and third editions of this book for their encouragement, comments and useful suggestions. I owe special thanks to Messrs Monday Abutu (ACA) and Niyi Fowobaje (ACA) of the Federal Inland Revenue Service and Broadmind Intellectual Resources respectively for their encouragement and support. I am also greatly indebted to all other individuals who have contributed in one way or the other to the publication of this book. I hope that they will not be offended by my inability to mention all their names.

As always, I wish to thank my family members for their support, understanding and forbearance.

I eagerly look forward to your comments and suggestions.

1 Introduction to Taxation

Part I Multiple-Choice Questions

1. Which of the following statements is not true?
   - A. A taxpayer receives a specific and direct quid pro quo from the government for paying tax.
   - B. Tax is levied according to predetermined criteria.
   - C. Tax is paid to the government.
   - D. Tax is a compulsory payment.
   - E. Tax is usally backed by law.

2. The reasons for the imposition of taxes include all the following except ...
   - A. to raise revenue for the government.
   - B. to reduce inequality in the distribution of income and wealth.
   - C. to discourage the consumption of harmful goods (e.g. alcohol).
   - D. to boost inflation.
   - E. to protect home industries from foreign competition.

3. Which of the following statements is not true?
   - A. Fines are compulsory payment like taxes.
   - B. Fines are mostly levied in return for specific benefits or services.
   - C. Fines are imposed as punishment for some offences or crimes committed.
   - D. The primary objective of imposing fines may not necessarily be to collect revenue like taxes.
   - E. Fines are imposed on those who contravene the provisions of the law while taxes are imposed on taxable persons.

4. One of the following is not a canon or principle of taxation and that is …

A. equity.
B. arbitrariness.
C. certainty.
D. convenience.
E. economy.

5. A good tax system should ensure that both administration and compliance costs are kept lower than the tax revenue raised. This is referred to as the principle of …
A. convenience.
B. economy.
C. fiscal adequacy.
D. simplicity.
E. diversity.

6. The principle of equity says that ....
A. every taxpayer should be taxed according to his ability to pay.
B. a tax should be levied at the time and in the manner most likely to suit the convenience of the taxpayer.
C. the amount of tax each taxpayer ought to pay, the date for payment and the manner of payment should be certain and very clear to the taxpayer.
D. there should be a variety of taxes (both direct and indirect taxes) in the economy to ensure that as many people as possible are made to contribute to the government revenue.
E. the tax system should be capable of being quickly adjusted to meet the changing needs of the economy.

7. The principle of fiscal adequacy advocates that ….
A. people with equal abilities to pay should pay the same amount of tax while people with different abilities to pay should pay different amount of tax.
B. the government should be able to estimate with a high degree of certainty the amount of tax revenue expected to be realized and the time they are expected to flow in.

C. the cost of tax collection should be as low as possible when compared with the tax revenue.

D. there should be a multiplicity of taxes in the economy to ensure that as many people as possible are brought into the tax net.

E. a tax should yield sufficient revenue to cover the government expenditure.

8. The final resting place of the burden of a tax is referred to as the
   A. impact of a tax.
   B. effect of a tax.
   C. incidence of a tax.
   D. tax base.
   E. tax rate.

9. All the following are direct taxes except ...
   A. personal income tax.
   B. companies income tax.
   C. value added tax.
   D. petroleum profits tax.
   E. capital gains tax.

10. All the following are indirect taxes except ...
   A. tertiary education tax.
   B. excise duties.
   C. import duties.
   D. sales tax.
   E. export duties.

11. Direct taxes payable by individuals in Nigeria include ...
   i. personal income tax.
   ii. capital transfer tax.
   iii. capital gains tax.
   iv. inheritance tax.
   A. i only
   B. i and iii only
   C. i, ii and iii only

D. i, ii and iv only
E. All of the above
Which of the options A to E is correct?

12. Direct taxes payable by companies in Nigeria include ...
i. companies income tax.
ii. excise duties.
iii. capital gains tax.
iv. tertiary education tax.
A. i only
B. i and ii only
C. i and iii only
D. i and iv only
E. i, iii and iv only
Which of the options A to E is correct?

13. Taxes levied on imports and exports are referred to as ...
A. value added tax.
B. excise duties.
C. customs duties.
D. sales tax.
E. customs drawback.

14. Taxes imposed on locally manufactured goods within a country are referred to as ...
A. value added tax.
B. excise duties.
C. customs duties.
D. sales tax.
E. export duties.

15. Which of the following is not an advantage of direct taxes?
A. Direct taxes can be used to checkmate inflation as the tax rates can be increased to reduce the disposable income of taxpayers.
B. Direct taxes can be used as an instrument for the reduction of inequality in the distribution of income and wealth.

C. There is certainty as the taxpayer knows how much tax he ought to pay and the time for payment.
D. Direct taxes are equitable as they are based on the ability to pay principle.
E. The degree of voluntary compliance is high.

16. Which of the following is not a disadvantage of direct taxes?
A. The scope is narrow as many citizens are not covered under direct taxes.
B. Disincentive to work where a high income is taxed at a higher rate than a lower income.
C. Direct taxes can be imposed to reduce the consumption of harmful or non-essential commodities.
D. The rate of tax evasion is high as many taxpayers may not declare their true incomes or profits to the tax authorities.
E. Direct taxes are unpopular as people know exactly how much they are being taxed and can feel the pains.

17. Which of the following statements is not true of indirect taxes?
A. Indirect taxes are levied on goods and services or expenditure.
B. Indirect taxes are not paid directly to the tax authority by the taxpayer on whom it is imposed.
C. The tax burden of indirect taxes can be passed on to others by the individuals or businesses that initially paid the taxes.
D. Indirect taxes can increase inflation as they are levied on goods and services.
E. The individual or business that is being taxed bears the impact and the incidence of indirect taxes.

18. Which of the following is not an advantage of indirect taxes?
A. Government raises substantial revenue from indirect taxes due to wider tax base.
B. Indirect taxes are cheaper and easier to collect as there are many unpaid agents collecting them on behalf of the government.

C. Indirect taxes take into account the taxpayer's ability to pay tax.
D. Indirect taxes can be used to discourage the consumption of harmful or non-essential commodities.
E. The degree of voluntary compliance is high.

19. Which of the following is not a disadvantage of indirect taxes?
A. Government cannot estimate in advance with a fair degree of accuracy how much revenue indirect taxes will yield.
B. Indirect taxes are regressive.
C. Indirect taxes end up increasing the prices of some goods and services and can accelerate the rate of inflation.
D. Indirect taxes are progressive in nature.
E. Loss of revenue due to many intermediaries involved in the collection of indirect taxes as some of them may not account for all the taxes collected.

20. The object which is being taxed (e.g. income, profit, expenditure, value of property,etc) is referred to as the ...
A. tax base.
B. tax rate.
C. tax incidence.
D. tax impact.
E. tax effect.

21. The process of transferring the burden of a tax wholly or partially to others by the person who initially paid the tax to the tax authority is referred to as ...
A. tax avoidance.
B. tax evasion.
C. tax incidence.
D. tax planning.
E. tax shifting.

22. A tax system in which each taxpayer pays the same rate of his income as tax is referred to as...

A. progressive taxation.
B. proportional taxation.
C. regressive taxation.
D. retrogressive taxation.
E. ad varolem tax.

23. A tax system in which the rate of tax increases as the income of the taxpayer increases is known as…
A. progressive taxation.
B. proportional taxation.
C. regressive taxation.
D. retrogressive taxation.
E. specific tax.

24.

Taxable Income	Rate of Tax	Tax Paid
₦	%	₦
50,000	40	20,000
100,000	25	25,000
150,000	15	22,500
200,000	10	20,000

Which type of tax system is exhibited above?
A. Progressive taxation
B. Proportional taxation
C. Regressive taxation
D. Retrogressive taxation
E. Ad varolem tax

Part II Short-Answer Questions

25. Define a tax in one sentence.

26. In one sentence, define the term indirect taxes.

27. Mention one advantage of direct taxes.

28. State one disadvantage of direct taxes.

29. The person who pays direct tax does not bear the incidence of the tax. True or false?

30. Most direct taxes are imposed on income. True or false?

31. Distinguish between specific tax and ad varolem tax.

32. In one sentence, explain one of the theories of taxation known to you.

2 Nigerian Tax System and National Tax Policy

Part I Multiple-Choice Questions

1. The National Tax Policy (NTP) was first published in …
   A. 2017.
   B. 2015.
   C. 2014.
   D. 2013.
   E. 2012

2. The revised National Tax Policy (NTP) was published in …
   A. 2017.
   B. 2015.
   C. 2014.
   D. 2013.
   E. 2012

3. Which of the following seeks to provide a set of guidelines, rules and modus operandi to regulate Nigeria's tax system and provide a basis for tax legislation and tax administration in Nigeria?
   A. Federal Inland Revenue Service (Establishment) Act, 2007
   B. Income Tax Management Act, 1961
   C. Tax Administration (Self Assessment) Regulations, 2011
   D. Nigerian tax laws compendium
   E. National Tax Policy 2017

4. The National Tax Policy is expected to achieve the following specific objectives except …
   A. provide a level playing field between multinational enterprises and independent enterprises doing business within Nigeria.
   B. guide the operation and review of the tax system.

C. provide the basis for future tax legislation and administration.
D. serve as a point of reference for all stakeholders on taxation.
E. provide clarity on the roles and responsibilities of stakeholders in the tax system.

5. According to the National Tax Policy, all existing and future taxes are expected to align with the following fundamental features or principles except …
A. equity and fairness.
B. simplicity, certainty and clarity.
C. inflexibility.
D. convenience.
E. low compliance and administration cost.

6. The challenges mentioned in the National Tax Policy as being responsible for the inability of the Nigerian tax system to achieve its objectives include all the following except …
A. insufficient information available to taxpayers on tax compliance requirements.
B. transfer pricing and thin capitalization.
C. fragmented database of taxpayers.
D. inordinate drive by all tiers of government to grow internally generated revenue.
E. lack of clarity on taxation powers of each level of government

7. Despite the potentials of taxation as a dynamic tool for sustainable national development, the Nigerian tax system has been unable to achieve its objectives due to a number of challenges. According to the National Tax Policy, these challenges include all the following except …
A. unwillingness of religious organisations to honour their tax obligations.
B. poor accountability for tax revenue.
C. use of aggressive and unorthodox methods for tax collection.

D. failure by tax authorities to honour refund obligations to taxpayers.
E. the non-regular review of tax legislation.

8. The National Tax Policy has highlighted the challenges responsible for the inability of the Nigerian tax system to achieve its objectives. These challenges include all the following except…
A. lack of robust framework for the taxation of informal sector and high network individuals.
B. lack of strict adherence to tax policy direction and procedural guidelines for the operation of the various tax authorities.
C. weak infrastructural facilities.
D. insufficient capacity which has led to the delegation of powers of revenue officials to third parties.
E. weak structure for exchange of information by and with tax authorities.

9. The key stakeholders in the Nigerian tax system include all the following except …
A. government.
B. taxpayers.
C. revenue agencies.
D. international financial institutions.
E. tax practitioners, consultants and agents.

10. Which of the following has the primary responsibility for tax policy matters, including initiating proposals for amendments to tax laws?
A. Central Bank of Nigeria
B. National Planning Commission
C. Ministry of Finance
D. Ministry of Justice
E. Ministry of Economic Planning

11. The relevant levels and arms of government, ministries, extra-ministerial departments and agencies shall …
    - A. act in accordance with professional code of conduct and ethics of the Chartered Institute of Taxation of Nigeria.
    - B. implement and regularly review tax policies and laws.
    - C. provide information on all revenue collected on a quarterly basis.
    - D. ensure adequate funding of tax authorities.
    - E. ensure administrative and operational autonomy of tax authorities.

    Which of the options A to E is incorrect?

12. The National Tax Policy provides that relevant levels and arms of government, ministries, extra-ministerial departments and agencies shall ensure a reasonable transition period of … before implementation of a new tax.
    - A. between three and six months
    - B. between six and eighteen months
    - C. between three and twelve months
    - D. between six and twelve months
    - E. between twelve and eighteen months

13. A taxpayer shall consider tax responsibility as a civic obligation and constant duty that must be discharged as and when due. On the other hand, the taxpayer shall be entitled to …
    - A. representation by an accredited tax practitioner free of charge.
    - B. relevant information for the discharge of tax obligations.
    - C. receive prompt, courteous and professional assistance in dealing with tax authorities.
    - D. raise objections to decisions and assessments and receive response within a reasonable time.
    - E. self-representation or by any agent of choice, provided an agent acting for financial reward shall be an accredited tax practitioner.

    Which of the options A to E is not correct?

14. Any agencies responsible for the collection and administration of revenue shall …
    A. treat the taxpayer as a customer.
    B. ensure efficient implementation of tax policies, laws and international treaties.
    C. facilitate inter-agency co-operation and exchange of information.
    D. undertake tax awareness and taxpayers' education.
    E. establish a disciplinary committee to detect and punish recalcitrant taxpayers.

    Which of the options A to E is not correct?

15. Tax practitioners, consultants and agents are expected to …
    i. act in accordance with professional code of conduct and ethics.
    ii. facilitate inter-agency co-operation and exchange of information.
    iii. aid and abet tax gap.
    iv. actively promote effective tax compliance.

    A. i and iv only
    B. i and iv only
    C. i, ii and iv only
    D. i and ii only
    E. ii, iii and iv

16. The roles of the media and advocacy groups in the Nigerian tax system include all the following except …
    A. to promote tax education and awareness.
    B. to articulate, protect and advance taxpayers' right.
    C. to advance accountability and transparency in the utilization of tax revenue.
    D. to ensure accurate, objective and balanced reporting in accordance with their professional code of conduct and ethics.
    E. to ensure adequate funding, administrative and operational autonomy of tax authorities.

17. In order to enhance efficiency in tax administration, the National Tax Policy recommends that …
    A. tax consultants could be engaged to assess and collect taxes and to account for the taxes collected.
    B. tax authorities shall develop an efficient framework for cooperation and sharing of information with other tax authorities and relevant local and international agencies.
    C. tax authorities shall ensure the enforcement of civil and criminal sanctions as provided under the various tax laws.
    D. government shall provide adequate funding for tax authorities.
    E. governments shall ensure a reasonable level of financial and administrative autonomy for their respective tax authorities.

18. In order to enhance efficiency in tax administration, the National Tax Policy recommends that tax authorities shall ensure …
    A. the deployment of technology to aid all aspects of tax administration.
    B. the integrity and regular update of the database.
    C. that states are empowered to make laws with regards to the imposition, collection and administration of stamp duties and tax on incomes/profits and capital gains.
    D. a workable and secure structure for intelligence and information gathering.
    E. that payment procedures and documentation are convenient and cost effective.

    Which of the options A to E is incorrect?

19. In order to improve voluntary compliance, the relevant authorities should ensure …
    A. the use of unorthodox means of tax collection such as military personnel and sealing up business premises without formal trial.
    B. that the option for self-assessment is in place and the process and procedures are simple.
    C. the development of frameworks for tax amnesty in order to expand the tax net.

D. constant tax education and enlightenment.

E. the establishment of a system to recognize and honour compliant taxpayers.

Which of the options A to E is incorrect?

20. The tripartite constituents of tax system include the …

i. tax policy.

ii. tax amnesty.

iii. tax laws.

iv tax administration.

A. i, ii and iii only

B. ii, iii and iv only

C. i, iii and iv only

D. i and ii only

E. ii and iv only

21. Which of the following taxes is not imposed on corporate entities in Nigeria?

A. Companies income tax

B. Petroleum profits tax

C. Personal income tax

D. Tertiary education tax

E. National information technology development levy

22. Taxes may be direct or indirect and may be imposed on individual basis, on entities, on assets and on transactional basis. All the following are imposed on transaction basis except …

A. value added tax.

B. stamp duty.

C. excise duty.

D. import duty.

E. development levy.

23. All the following are sources of internally generated revenue (IGR) to state government except …

A. fees.

B. rates.

C. excise duties.
D. penalties/fines.
E. development levy.

24. All the following are sources of revenue to the federal, state and local governments in Nigeria except ...
 A. income from the sale of government services.
 B. rents received from private-owned properties.
 C. interest income from government investments.
 D. loans, grants and donations given to the government.
 E. profits or surpluses from government-owned enterprises.

25. Which of the following is not a major source of federal government revenue in Nigeria?
 A. Petroleum profits tax
 B. Companies income tax
 C. Value added tax
 D. Capital gains tax
 E. Customs and excise duties

26. State governments in Nigeria are financed mostly through the monthly statutory allocations from the federation account. Which of the following states can finance its activities to a great extent using its internally generated revenue?
 A. Sokoto State
 B. Ondo State
 C. Niger State
 D. Katsina State
 E. Lagos State

27. All the following taxes are collectible by the federal government except ...
 A. value added tax.
 B. withholding taxes on companies.
 C. tertiary education tax.
 D road taxes.
 E. companies income tax.

28. All the following are approved taxes and levies to be collected by a state government except ...
    A. development levy.
    B. personal income tax.
    C. withholding tax.
    D. tenement rate.
    E. capital gains tax.

29. Which of the following taxes and levies is not collectible by the local government?
    A. Business premises registration fee
    B. Birth registration fees
    C. Motor park levies
    D. Merriment and road closure levy
    E. Domestic animal licence fees

30. Which of the following taxes and levies is not collectible by the state government?
    A. Vehicle radio licence fees
    B. Right of occupancy fees
    C. Naming of streets registration fees in the state capital
    D. Pools betting and lotteries, gaming and casino taxes
    E. Stamp duties

31. All the following taxes and levies are collectible by the local government except ...
    A. shops and kiosks rates.
    B. naming of street registration fees in the state capital.
    C. public convenience, sewage and refuse disposal fees.
    D. slaughter slab fees.
    E. on and off liquor licence fees.

32. What is the penalty for the mounting of road block in any part of Nigeria for the purpose of collecting any tax or levy as contained in the Taxes and Levies (Approved List for Collection) Act.
    A. A fine of ₦5,000 or imprisonment for 5 years or both
    B. A fine of ₦50,000 or imprisonment for 3 years

C. A fine of ₦500,000 or imprisonment for 3 years or both
D. A fine of ₦500,000 or imprisonment for 5 years
E. A fine of ₦50,000 or imprisonment for 3 years or both

33. Tax authority, as defined in the Taxes and Levies (Approved List for Collection) Act, includes all the following except ...
A. tax consultants.
B. Federal Inland Revenue Service.
C. State Board of Internal Revenue.
D. Local Government Revenue Committee.
E. any government body charged with the responsibility for assessing and collecting the particular tax.

34. Tax consultants can be engaged by the relevant tax authorities to carry out all the following assignments except …
A. computerization of the tax system.
B. training and re-training of personnel of tax authorities.
C. assesing, collecting and accounting for taxes and levies.
D. researching into specific areas where improvement in tax administration may be required.
E. reviewing of tax laws from time to time and helping to simplify difficult interpretations where necessary.

35. Sources of Nigerian tax laws include all the following except …
A. the Nigerian Constitution.
B. the tax Acts issued by the National Assembly.
C. court judgements on tax cases.
D. oral tradition.
E. official statements or pronouncements and the practices of tax authorities.

36. The rules governing tax matters in Nigeria are embodied in a number of tax Acts enacted by the National Assembly. The main tax statutes currently in force include all the following except …
A. Capital Transfer Tax Act, 1979.
B. Stamp Duties Act, Cap. S8, LFN 2004.
C. Personal Income Tax Act, Cap. P8, LFN 2004.

D. Petroleum Profits Tax Act, Cap. P13, LFN 2004.
E. Tertiary Education Trust Fund (Establishment, Etc) Act, 2011.

37. The tax laws in Nigeria currently in force include all the following except…
A. Value Added Tax Act, Cap. VI, LFN 2004.
B. Capital Gains Tax Act, Cap. C1, LFN 2004.
C. Companies Income Tax Act, Cap. C21, LFN 2004.
D. Federal Capital Territory Internal Revenue Service Act, 2015.
E. Income Tax Management (Uniform Taxation Provisions) Act, 1975

38. All the following are challenges faced by the tax authorities in the assessment and collection of taxes in Nigeria except ...
A. long delays by the court in hearing tax cases or enforcing tax payment.
B. difficulty in locating or tracking down self-employed taxpayers.
C. difficulty in ascertaining the taxpayers' incomes.
D. lack of co-operation from employers and MDAs to allow for free flow of information about taxpayers and their incomes.
E. quick passage of tax proposals into law.

Part II Short-Answer Questions

39. State whether the federal government, state government or local government has powers to legislate on (a) customs and excise duties, (b) export duties, (c) stamp duties and (d) taxation of incomes, profits and capital gains.

40. State the levels of government empowered to collect taxes and levies in Nigeria.

41. Which tier of government is responsible for collecting signboard and advertisement permit fees?

42. State three taxes collectible by the federal government.

43. State three taxes/levies collectible by the state government.

44. Mention three taxes/levies collectible by the local government.

45. State one problem encountered by tax authorities in Nigeria in the assessment and collection of taxes.

3 Administration of Personal Income Tax

Part I Multiple-Choice Questions

1. The tax administrative machinery currently existing in Nigeria includes all the following except …
   A. Local Government Revenue Committee.
   B. State Board of Internal Revenue (whose operational arm is the State Internal Revenue Service).
   C. Revenue Mobilization Allocation and Fiscal Commission.
   D. Federal Inland Revenue Service (under the supervision of the Federal Inland Revenue Service Board).
   E. Federal Capital Territory Board of Internal Revenue (whose operational arm is the Federal Capital Territory Internal Revenue Service).

2. Who is the Chairman of the Joint Tax Board?
   A. Federal Minister of Finance
   B. Accountant-General of the Federation
   C. Chairman of thc Federal Inland Revenue Service
   D. Director-General appointed by the Federal Civil Service Commission
   E. Legal Adviser to the Federal Inland Revenue Service

3. Which of the following is not a function of the Joint Tax Board?
   A. Exercising powers and performing duties conferred on it by any enactment of the Federal Government imposing tax on the income and profits of companies.
   B. Collecting taxes and penalties due to the Federal Government.
   C. Adjudicating in a case of dispute over an individual's residence.
   D. Advising the Federal Government on taxation matters.
   E. Promoting uniformity in the application of the Personal Income Tax Act.

4. The Secretary to the Joint Tax Board is appointed by the ...
   A. Federal Civil Service Commission.
   B. State Civil Service Commission.
   C. Joint Tax Board.
   D. Minister of Finance.
   E. President of the Federal Republic of Nigeria.

5. How many members can form a quorum at any meeting of the Joint Tax Board?
   A. $^2/_3$ of the total members
   B. $^1/_2$ of the total members
   C. 24 members
   D. 12 members
   E. 7 members

6. All the following are members of the State Board of Internal Revenue except ...
   A. the Legal Adviser to the State Internal Revenue Service.
   B. a Director from the State Ministry of Finance.
   C. the Directors within the State Internal Revenue Service.
   D. the Legal Adviser to the State Internal Revenue Service.
   E. the Supervisor for Finance from each Local Government Area of the State.

7. Which of the following is an ex-officio member of the State Board of Internal Revenue?
   A. Legal Adviser to the State Internal Revenue Service
   B. Secretary to the State Internal Revenue Service
   C. A Director from the State Ministry of Finance
   D. A representative of each Senatorial District appointed by the State Governor
   E. the Chairman of the State Internal Revenue Service

8. One of the following is a member of the State Board of Internal Revenue and that is ...

A. the Executive Head of the State Internal Revenue Service.
B. the Local Government Chairmen in the State.
C. a representative of the Chairman of the Revenue Mobilization, Allocation and Fiscal Commission.
D a representative of the Attorney-General of the State.
E. A representative of the Minister of Finance.

9. How many members are needed to form a quorum at any meeting of the State Board of Internal Revenue?
A. Five members
B. Seven members
C. Ten members
D. Eight members
E. Six members

10. The State Board of Internal Revenue is responsible for all the following except …
A. carrying out oversight functions over all taxes and levies accruable to the Government of the Federation.
B. making recommendations, where appropriate, to the Joint Tax Board on tax policy, tax reform, tax legislation, etc.
C. generally controlling the management of the State Internal Revenue Service on matters of policy.
D. appointing, promoting, transferring and imposing discipline on employees of the State Internal Revenue Service.
E. ensuring the effectiveness and optimum collection of all taxes and penalties due to the State Government.

11. The Personal Income Tax Act provides that an amount of not less than ... as may be approved by a State House of Assembly shall be retained by State Board of Internal Revenue to defray cost of tax collection and administration.
A. 15 per cent of revenue collected
B. 10 per cent of revenue collected
C. 5 per cent of revenue collected

D. 1 per cent of revenue collected
E. 20 per cent of revenue collected

12. Which of the following statements is not true?
    A. The State Internal Revenue Service is responsible for the taxation of businesses located within the state whether or not they are incorporated.
    B. The Personal Income Tax Act provides for the establishment of the Joint State Revenue Committee for each state of the federation.
    C. The State Internal Revenue Service is the operational arm of the State Board of Internal Revenue.
    D. The State Internal Revenue Service is established under the Personal Income Tax Act.
    E. The SBIR is autonomous in the day-to-day running of the technical, professional and administrative affairs of the State Internal Revenue Service.

13. One of the following is not a member of the Technical Committee of the State Board of Internal Revenue and that is ...
    A. the Director from the State Ministry of Finance.
    B. the Chairman of the State Board of Internal Revenue.
    C. the Directors within the State Internal Revenue Service.
    D. the Legal Adviser to the State Internal Revenue Service.
    E. the Secretary to the State Internal Revenue Service.

14. Members of the Joint State Revenue Committee include the following except ...
    A. the Chairman of the State Internal Revenue Service.
    B. the Chairman of the Local Government Revenue Committee.
    C. the Legal Adviser to the State Internal Revenue Service.
    D. a representative of the Bureau on Local Government Affairs.
    E. the Heads of Departments within the State Internal Revenue Service.

15. Functions of the Joint State Revenue Committee include all the following except ...
    A. implementing decisions of the Joint Tax Board.
    B. harmonising tax administration in the State.
    C. carrying out such other functions as may be assigned to it by the Joint Tax Board.
    D. approving pension or other retirement benefits scheme.
    E. enlightening the public on State and Local Government revenue matters.

16. The Joint State Revenue Committee for each state of the federation consists of ...
    A. seven members.
    B. eight members.
    C. four members.
    D. five members.
    E. six members.

17. Which of the following advises the Joint Tax Board and the State and Local Governments on revenue matters?
    A. Technical Committee of the SBIR
    B. Local Government Revenue Committee
    C. Federal Inland Revenue Service
    D. Technical Committee of the FIRS Board
    E. Joint State Revenue Committee

18. Which of the following is responsible for the taxation of individuals resident in each State of the Federation?
    A. Joint Tax Board
    B. State Board of Internal Revenue
    C. Federal Inland Revenue Service
    D. Joint State Revenue Committee
    E. Local Government Revenue Committee

19. The Chairman of the State Board of Internal Revenue is appointed by the ..

A. State Governor.
B. Commissioner of Finance.
C. State House of Assembly.
D. Joint State Revenue Committee.
E. the State Governor subject to confirmation by the State House of Assembly.

20. How many persons are appointed to the State Board of Internal Revenue on their personal merits to represent the Senatorial Districts in the State?
A. Two
B. Three
C. Four
D. Five
E. Six

21. The Local Government Revenue Committee for each Local Government Area of a State consists of …
A. seven members.
B. eight members.
C. four members.
D. five members.
E. six members.

22. Two members experienced in revenue matters are appointed to the Local Government Revenue Committee on their personal merits by the …
A. State Governor.
B. Commissioner of Finance.
C. Supervisor for Finance of the Local Government.
D. Joint State Revenue Committee.
E. Local Government Chairman.

23. One person from each state is nominated by … to be a member of the Joint Tax Board.
A. State Governor.
B. State Commissioner of Finance.

C. State House of Assembly.
D. Joint State Revenue Committee
E. Joint Tax Board.

24. Which of the following advises the federal government on rates of capital allowances and other taxation matters having effect throughout Nigeria?
A. Joint Tax Board
B. National Assembly
C. Joint State Revenue Committee
D. Federal Inland Revenue Service
E. Federal Inland Revenue Service Board

25. Which of the following is not a tax authority?
A. Local Government Revenue Committee
B. State Board of Internal Revenue
C. Joint State Revenue Committee
D. Federal Inland Revenue Service
E. Federal Capital Territory Internal Revenue Service

26. Who is the Chairman of the Joint State Revenue Committee?
A. A representative of the Revenue Mobilization, Allocation and Fiscal Commission
B. The Chairman of the Local Government Revenue Committee
C. The Secretary to the State Internal Revenue Service
D The Chairman of the State Internal Revenue Service
E. State Commissioner of Finance

27. Who is the Chairman of the Technical Committee of the State Board of Internal Revenue?
A. The Legal Adviser to the State Internal Revenue Service
B. The Secretary of the State Internal Revenue Service
C. One of the Directors of the State Internal Revenue Service
D The Chairman of the State Board of Internal Revenue
E. State Commissioner of Finance

28. One of the following is a member of the Joint Tax Board and that is
    A. one member from each state nominated by the Governor of the State.
    B. a representative of the Attorney-General of the Federation.
    C. a representative of the Minister of Finance.
    D. the Chairman of the Revenue Mobilization, Allocation and Fiscal Commission or his representative
    E. the Chief Executive Officer of the National Planning Commission or his representative.

29. The three components of the Nigerian tax system are ...
    i. tax concession
    ii. tax policy
    iii tax laws
    iv. tax administration.
    A. ii and iii only
    B. i, ii and iii only
    C. i, iii and iv only
    D. ii, iii and iv only
    E. all of the above.

30. In the Nigerian context, a tax regime under which different tiers of government (or different tax authorities) within Nigeria impose identical or substantially similar taxes or levies on the same taxpayer or on the same income or profit is referred to as …
    A. tax concurrent.
    B. presumptive taxation.
    C. regressive taxation.
    D. adjudication.
    E. multiple taxation.

31. The Schedule to the Personal Income Tax Act which specifies the income exempted from tax is the ....
    A. First Schedule.
    B. Second Schedule.
    C. Third Schedule.

D. Fourth Schedule.
E. Fifth Schedule.

32. Which of the following Schedules to the Personal Income Tax Act deals with capital allowances?
A. First Schedule
B. Second Schedule
C. Third Schedule
D. Fourth Schedule
E. Fifth Schedule

33. Which of the following is not a Schedule to the Personal Income Tax Act?
A. First Schedule – Determination of residence
B. Second Schedule – Income from settlements, trusts and estates
C. Sixth Schedule – Income tax table
D. Eighth Schedule – Warrant and authority to enter premises
E. Ninth Schedule – Taxes and levies (approved list for collection)

Part II Short-Answer Questions

34. ... is responsible for the administration of personal income tax laws in each State

35. Mention any two functions of the Technical Committee of the State Board of Internal Revenue.

36. State two duties of the Inspector of Taxes.

37. ... is responsible for assessing, collecting and accounting for Local Government taxes and levies.

38. Mention three members of the Local Government Revenue Committee.

39. A notice to be served on an individual or body of individuals must be addressed to ...

40 When is a notice sent by registered post deemed to have been served?

4 Federal Capital Territory Internal Revenue Service Act, 2015

Part I Multiple-Choice Questions

1. Which of the following is true of the Federal Capital Territory Internal Revenue Service?
   A. FCT Internal Revenue Service is responsible for the taxation of members of the Armed Forces.
   B. FCT Internal Revenue Service is the tax authority for corporate entities located within the FCT.
   C. FCT Internal Revenue Service is not a body corporate with perpetual succession.
   D. FCT Internal Revenue Service is under the supervision of the FIRS Board.
   E. None of the above.

2. The Federal Capital Territory Internal Revenue Service …
   i. is responsible for the administration of the different taxes and laws specified in the First Schedule to the Federal Inland Revenue Service (Establishment) Act.
   ii. may specify the form of returns, claims, statements and notices necessary for the due administration of the powers conferred on it.
   iii. is under the overall supervision of the Technical Committee of the FCT Internal Revenue Service Board.
   iv. is responsible for the collection of revenue accruable to the FCT.

   Which of the above statements are correct?
   A. ii, iii and iv only
   B. i, iii and iv only
   C. ii and iv only.
   D. iii and iv only.
   E. i, ii and iv only.

3. Who is the Chairman of the Federal Capital Territory Internal Revenue Service Board?
   - A. Minister of Finance
   - B. Minister of the Federal Capital Territory
   - C. Permanent Secretary of the Federal Ministry of Finance
   - D. Federal Capital Territory Director of Treasury
   - E. Chairman of the Federal Capital Territory Internal Revenue Service

4. The Chairman of the FCT Internal Revenue Service Board is appointed by the ...
   - A. President.
   - B. Minister of Finance subject to the approval of the National Assembly.
   - C. National Assembly.
   - D. Minister of the FCT subject to the approval of the National Assembly.
   - E. President subject to the confirmation of the Senate.

5. The Secretary to the FCT Internal Revenue Service Board is appointed by the ...
   - A. FCT Internal Revenue Service Board.
   - B. Minister of Finance subject to the approval of the National Assembly.
   - C. Federal Civil Service Commission.
   - D. Minister of the FCT subject to the approval of the National Assembly.
   - E. President subject to the confirmation of the Senate.

6. Which of the following is an ex-officio member of the FCT Internal Revenue Service Board?
   - A. Chairman of the FCT Internal Revenue Service Board
   - B. FCT Director of Treasury
   - C. Secretary to the FCT Internal Revenue Service
   - D. Director of Legal Services of the FCT Administration
   - E. Chairman of the Federal Inland Revenue Service Board

7. Who is the Deputy Chairman of the FCT Internal Revenue Service Board?
   A. Director of the Department of Economic Planning, Research and Statistics of the FCT Administration
   B. FCT Director of Treasury
   C. Secretary to the FCT Internal Revenue Service
   D. Director of Legal Services of the FCT Administration
   E. Chairman of the FCT Administration

8. All the following are members of the FCT Internal Revenue Service Board except ...
   A. six persons from six geopolitical zones of the Federation.
   B. the FCT Director of Treasury.
   C. the Chairman of the FCT Internal Revenue Service.
   D. a representative of the Federal Inland Revenue Service.
   E. the Director of Public Enlightenment of the FCT Administration.

9. One of the following members of staff of the FCT Administration is not a member of the FCT Internal Revenue Service Board and that is
   A. the Director of the Department of Legal Services.
   B. the Director of the Department of Lands, Planning and Survey.
   C. the Director of the Department of Area Councils.
   D. the Director of Public Enlightenment.
   E. the Director of Human Resources.

10. The Chairman and other members of the FCT Internal Revenue Service Board, other than ex-officio members, shall each hold office for a term of ……… years renewable once only.
    A. four
    B. five
    C. six
    D. three
    E. seven

11. Six members with relevant professional qualifications and knowledgeable in tax members are appointed to the FCT Internal Revenue Service Board to represent each of the six-geographical zones. Who is responsible for the appointment of these six members?
    A. The Minister of Finance
    B. The Chairman of the FCT Internal Revenue Service Board
    C. The President of the Federal Republic of Nigeria
    D. The Minister of the Federal Capital Territory
    E. The Joint Tax Board

12. Six members with relevant professional qualifications and knowledgeable in tax members are appointed to the FCT Internal Revenue Service Board to represent each of the six geographical zones. How many of them are expected to be women?
    A. One
    B. Two
    C. Three
    D. Four
    E. Five

13. The FCT Internal Revenue Service Board is required to hold its meetings at least .....
    A. three times in each year.
    B. four times in each year.
    C. five times in each year.
    D. six times in each year.
    E. seven times in each year.

14. All the following members of the FCT Internal Revenue Service Board are part-time members except the ...
    A. six persons from the six geopolitical zones of the Federation.
    B. FCT Director of Treasury.
    C. Chairman of the FCT Internal Revenue Service.
    D. Secretary to the FCT Internal Revenue Service.
    E. representatives from the FCT Administration.

15. The Chairman of the FCT Internal Revenue Service Board can convene a meeting of the Board if he is required to do so by notice given to him by not less than ...
   A. six other members of the Board.
   B. five other members of the Board.
   C. four other members of the Board.
   D. three other members of the Board.
   E. seven other members of the Board.

16. The FCT Internal Revenue Service Board shall, in the exercise of its powers and duties under the FCT Internal Revenue Service Act, 2015, be subject to the general directives of the
   A. Senate.
   B. Chairman of the FCT IRS Board.
   C. National Assembly.
   D. Minister of Finance.
   E. Minister of the FCT.

17. Who among the following is not a member of the Area Council Revenue Committee?
   A. Head of the Legal Department of the Area Council
   B. A member of the public nominated by the Legislative Arm of the Council
   C. Chaiman appointed by the FCTA
   D. Head of Treasury of the Area Council
   E. Chaiman appointed by the Minister of the FCT

18. A member of the FCT Internal Revenue Service Board shall cease to hold office as a member of the Board if …
   A. he resigns his appointment as a member of the Board.
   B. he is guilty of misconduct in relation to his duties.
   C. he is removed from office by the Minister of the FCT.
   D. he becomes a member of a professional body.
   E. he becomes bankrupt.

   Which of the options A to E is not correct?

19. A member of the FCT Internal Revenue Service Board shall cease to hold office as a member of the Board if …
    A. he becomes of unsound mind.
    B. he becomes incapable of carrying on the functions of his office.
    C. he is convicted of felony or any offence involving dishonesty or corruption.
    D. he is removed from office by the Minister of Finance.
    E. he has been found guilty of contravening the Code of Conduct Bureau and Tribunal Act.

    Which of the options A to E is not correct?

20. Members of the FCT Internal Revenue Service Board are entitled to emoluments, allowances and benefits as may be approved by the …
    A. Revenue Mobilization, Allocation and Fiscal Commission.
    B. President of the Federal Republic of Nigeria.
    C. Federal Civil Service Commission.
    D. Minister of the FCT.
    E. National Wages, Incomes and Salaries Commission.

21. If the Chairman of the FCT Internal Revenue Service Board is requested to convene a meeting of the Board by notice given to him by not less than seven other members of the Board, he shall convene the meeting to be held within ...
    A. thirty days from the date on which the notice was given.
    B. seven days from the date on which the notice was given.
    C. fifteen days from the date on which the notice was given.
    D. fourteen days from the date on which the notice was given.
    E. twenty-one days from the date on which the notice was given.

22. The FCT Inland Revenue Service is responsible for the taxation of ..
    A. members of the Armed Forces of the Federation.
    B. residents of the Federal Capital Territory.
    C. members of the Nigeria Police.
    D. officers of the Nigerian Foreign Service.
    E. non-residents individuals.

23. All the following are specifically stated in the FCT IRS Act, 2015 as the powers and functions of the FCT Internal Revenue Service except to …
    A. assess, collect, account and enforce payment of taxes due to the FCT.
    B. adopt measures to identify, trace, freeze, confiscate or seize the proceeds of tax fraud or evasion.
    C. stipulate remuneration, allowances and benefits of employees in consultation with the Minister of the FCT.
    D. collaborate and facilitate rapid exchange of information with relevant national or international agencies or bodies on tax matters.
    E. issue taxpayer identification number to every person taxable in the FCT.

24. The Chairman of each Area Council Revenue Committee is appointed by the ...
    A. FCT Internal Revenue Service.
    B. Federal Capital Territory Authority (FCTA).
    C. FCT Internal Revenue Service Board.
    D. Joint Tax Board.
    E. Chairman of the FCT Joint Revenue Committee.

25. Members of the FCT Joint Revenue Committee include all the following except ...
    A. the Chairman of the FCT Internal Revenue Service.
    B. the Chairman of each Revenue Committee in the FCT.
    C. the Legal Adviser to the FCT Internal Revenue Service.
    D. a representative of the FIRS.
    E. the Secretary to the FCT Joint Revenue Committee.

26. Functions of the FCT Joint Revenue Committee include all the following except ...
    A. enlightening the public on Federal, State and Local Government revenue matters.
    B. advising the Joint Tax Board, FCT and Area Councils on revenue matters.

C. harmonising tax administration in the FCT.
D. dealing with revenue matters of common concern to the FCT and Area Council.
E. enlightening members of the public generally on FCT and Area Council revenue matters.

27. All the following are specifically stated in the FCT Internal Revenue Service Act, 2015 as the powers and functions of the FCT Internal Revenue Service Board except ...
A. assessing, collecting and accounting for taxes due to the FCT.
B. reviewing and approving the strategic plans of the FCT Internal Revenue Service.
C. employing and determining the conditions of service of the employees of the FCT Internal Revenue Service.
D. providing the general policy guidelines relating to the functions of the FIRS.
E. managing and superintending the policies of the FCT Internal Revenue Service on matters relating to the administration of the revenue assessment, collection and accounting system.

28. Which of the following is not specifically stated in the FCT Internal Revenue Service Act, 2015 as the function of the FCT IRS?
A. Reviewing and approving the strategic plans of the Service.
B. Making, from time to time, a determination of the extent of financial and other losses by the FCT arising from tax waivers, fraud or evasion.
C. Maintaining up-to-date data and information on taxable persons within the FCT to enhance tax administration.
D. Carrying out and sustaining public awareness and enlightenment campaigns on the benefits of tax compliance within the FCT.
E. Administering, collecting and enforcing payment of property tax in the FCT.

29. The penalty prescribed in the FCT IRS Act, 2015 for any person who obstructs, hinders, molests or assaults any authorized officer in the performance of any function or the exercise of any power under the Act is a fine not exceeding …
    - A. ₦500,000 or imprisonment for not more than 3 years or both.
    - B. ₦600,000 or imprisonment for not more than 3 years or both.
    - C. ₦200,000 or imprisonment for not more than 3 years or both.
    - D. ₦300,000 or imprisonment for not more than 3 years or both.
    - E. ₦400,000 or imprisonment for not more than 3 years or both.

30. The penalty prescribed in the FCT IRS Act, 2015 for any person who counterfeits or falsifies any document required for tax purposes or knowingly accepts, receives or uses counterfeited or falsified document is a fine not exceeding …
    - A. ₦200,000 or imprisonment for not more than 3 years or both.
    - B. ₦300,000 or imprisonment for not more than 3 years or both.
    - C. ₦400,000 or imprisonment for not more than 3 years or both.
    - D. ₦500,000 or imprisonment for not more than 3 years or both.
    - E. ₦600,000 or imprisonment for not more than 3 years or both.

31. What is the penalty stipulated in the FCT IRS Act, 2015 for any person, who in commission of any offence against the Act, is armed with any offensive weapon?
    - A. Imprisonment for a term of 10 years.
    - B. Imprisonment for a term of 8 years.
    - C. Imprisonment for a term of 6 years.

D. Imprisonment for a term of 5 years.
E. Imprisonment for a term of 4 years.

32. If a person contravenes any provisions of the FCT IRS Act, 2015 for which no penalty is specifically prescribed, he shall be liable on conviction to a fine of …
A. ₦500,000 or imprisonment for not more than 6 months or both.
B. ₦200,000 or imprisonment for not more than 6 months or both.
C. ₦50,000 or imprisonment for not more than 6 months or both.
D. ₦5,000 or imprisonment for not more than 6 months or both.
E. ₦500 or imprisonment for not more than 6 months or both.

33. Members of the Tax Appeal Committee established under the FCT Internal Revenue Service Act, 2015 are appointed by the …
A. Chairman of the FCT Internal Revenue Service Board.
B. Chairman of the Federal Inland Revenue Service Board.
C. Minister of the Federal Capital Territory.
D. Minister of Finance.
E. President of the Federal Republic of Nigeria.

34. All appointments into the Area Council Revenue Committee in the FCT is subject to the approval of the …
A. Charman of the Council
B. FCT Joint Revenue Commitee
C. National Assembly
D. Legislative Arm of the Council
E. FCT IRS Board

35. The remuneration of the Tax Appeal Commissioners are determined by the …
A. Revenue Mobilization, Allocation and Fiscal Commission.
B. President of the Federal Republic of Nigeria.
C. Federal Civil Service Commission.

D. Minister of the FCT.
E. National Wages, Incomes and Salaries Commission.

36. What is the number of members that can form a quorum at any sitting of the Tax Appeal Committee established under the FCT Internal Revenue Service Act, 2015?
A. Any three Tax Appeal Commissioners
B. Any five Tax Appeal Commissioners
C. Any two Tax Appeal Commissioners
D. Any six Tax Appeal Commissioners
E. Any four Tax Appeal Commissioners

37. The Chairman of the Tax Appeal Committee for each zone must be a legal practitioner who has been qualified to practice for a period of not less than …
A. 5 years with cognate experience in tax legislation and tax matters.
B. 10 years with cognate experience in tax legislation and tax matters.
C. 15 years with cognate experience in tax legislation and tax matters.
D. 20 years with cognate experience in tax legislation and tax matters.
E. 25 years with cognate experience in tax legislation and tax matters.

38. The Tax Appeal Committee established under the FCT IRS Act, 2015 has power to adjudicate on disputes and controversies arising from the following tax laws except the …
A. Value Tax Act.
B. Personal Income Tax Act.
C. Capital Gains Tax Act.
D. Stamp Duties Act.
E. FCT Property Tax Regulation.

39. Which of the following statements is not true?
    A. The FCT IRS is a body corporate with perpetual succession and a common seal.
    B. The FCT IRS may sue and be sue in its corporate name.
    C. The FCT IRS may acquire, hold or dispose of any property.
    D. The FCT IRS have the power to administer any law on. taxation in respect of which the National Assembly may confer power on it.
    E. The FCT IRS can borrow money in foreign currency without the prior approval of the Minister of the FCT.

40. Which of the following statements is not true of the Tax Appeal Committee?
    A. Members of the Committee shall be persons with considerable experience and knowledge in tax matters.
    B. A member of the FCT IRS Board can be a member of the Committee.
    C. Members of the Committee are appointed by the Minister of the FCT on a part-time basis.
    D. None of the members of the Committee shall be a public officer.
    E. A member of the Committee can resign his appointment by notice in writing addressed to the Minister of the FCT.

41. What is the period of notice required to be given by the Secretary to the TAC to the FCT IRS Board and the appellant of the date and place fixed for the hearing of an appeal?
    A. Thirty clear working days
    B. Twenty-one clear working days
    C. Fourteen clear working days
    D. Ten clear working days
    E. Seven clear working days

42. A certified copy of the decision of the TAC shall be supplied to the appellant and the FCT IRS Board by the Secretary to the TAC, on a request within ... of the decision.

A. three months
B. thirty days
C. two months
D. fifteen days
E. twenty-one days.

43. No further appeal by the taxpayer shall lie from the decision of the TAC except with the consent of the FCT IRS Board if the tax chargeable on an appellant for a year of assessment in accordance with the decision of the TAC does not exceed ...
A. ten thousand Naira.
B. twenty thousand Naira.
C. fifty thousand Naira.
D. one hundred thousand Naira.
E. one million Naira.

44. After the determination of an appeal (notwithstanding that a further appeal may be pending), the tax chargeable as so determined by the TAC is payable within ....of notification of the taxpayer of the amount of the tax payable.
A. three months
B. fifteen days
C. two months
D. one month
E. twenty-one days.

45. All appeals before the Tax Appeal Committee shall be held
A. in camera.
B. in secret.
C. in public.
D. behind closed doors.
E. in private.

46. An award or judgment of the Tax Appeal Committee shall be enforced as if it were a judgment of the …
A. Magistrate Court.
B. Supreme Court.

C. Federal High Court.
D. Sharia Court.
E. Court of Appeal.

47. If a taxpayer or the FCT IRS Board is dissatisfied with the decision of the TAC he or it may appeal against that decision upon giving notice in writing to the other party to the appeal within ...
A. 30 days after the date on which the decision was given.
B. 15 days after the date on which the decision was given.
C. 60 days after the date on which the decision was given.
D. 21 days after the date on which the decision was given.
E. 7 days after the date on which the decision was given.

48. The FCT IRS is required to submit to the Minister of the FCT an estimate of its income and expenditure for the next succeeding year not later than …
A. 30th September in each year.
B. 31st December in each year.
C. 1st December in each year.
D. 31st October in each year.
E. 30th June in each year.

49. The accounts of FCT IRS are to be audited by the auditors not later than
A. three months after the end of each year.
B. four months after the end of each year.
C. five months after the end of each year.
D. six months after the end of each year.
E. nine months after the end of each year.

50 The FCT IRS is required to submit to the Minister of the FCT a report of its activities during the immediately preceding year together with its audited accounts not later than …
A. three months after the end of each year.
B. four months after the end of each year.
C. five months after the end of each year.

D. six months after the end of each year.
E. nine months after the end of each year.

51. All the following are specifically stated in the FCT IRS Act, 2015 as the powers and functions of the FCT Internal Revenue Service except to
    A. carry out examination and investigation with a view to enforcing compliance with the provisions of the tax Act.
    B. collate and continually review all policies of the FCTA relating to taxation and revenue generation and undertake a systematic and progressive implementation of such policies.
    C. undertake and support research on tax matters and make appropriate recommendations to the government.
    D. establish and maintain a system for monitoring international dynamics of taxation in order to identify suspicious transactions and the persons involved.
    E. promote uniformity in the application of tax laws in Nigeria.

52. The FCT IRS Board shall establish and maintain a fund to be applied towards the discharge of its functions which shall be credited with an amount not more than ... of all revenues collected by the FCT IRS in the preceding year as administrative charge or cost of collection.
    A. 5%
    B. 10%
    C. 15%
    D. 20%
    E. 25%

53. The FCT IRS has power to administer the following enactments except ...
    A. Companies Income Tax Act.
    B. Personal Income Tax Act.
    C. Capital Gains Tax Act.
    D. Stamp Duties Act.
    E. FCT Property Tax Regulation.

54. The FCT IRS is required to prepare a list of taxable persons assessed to income tax. The assessment list should contain all the following information except …
    A. evidence of payment of the whole or part of the tax due into a bank designated for the collection of tax.
    B. the names and addresses of the taxable persons assessed to income tax.
    C. the amount of the assessable, total or chargeable income on which the tax is computed as the case may be.
    D. the amount of the income tax charged.
    E. the name of the income assessed.

55. The FCT IRS may prescribe the form in which an employer should maintain a record for PAYE tax deduction and the form in which the tax so deducted should be accounted to the tax authority. The FCT IRS may give a notice to the employer to produce the record for examination within ….. from the date of notice given by the tax authority.
    A. twenty-one days
    B. thirty days
    C. seven days
    D. fourteen days
    E. sixty days

56. A taxable person who is not satisfied with any assessment made on him by the FCT IRS may send a notice of objection to the … to review and revise the assessment.
    A. Joint Tax Board.
    B. Tax Appeal Tribunal.
    C. Federal Inland Revenue Service Board.
    D. High Court.
    E. FCT IRS Board.

57. What is the time limit within which a taxable person can raise a notice of objection against the Federal Capital Territory Internal Revenue Service's assessment?

A. Within thirty days from the date of service of the notice of assessment.

B. Within twenty-one days from the date of service of the notice of assessment.

C. Within seven days from the date of service of the notice of assessment.

D. Within sixty days from the date of service of the notice of assessment.

E. Within fifteen days from the date of service of the notice of assessment.

58. What is the time limit within which an appeal can be made to the Tax Appeal Committee after the date of service of the FCT IRS Board's notice of refusal to amend the assessment as desired by the taxpayer?

A. Twenty-eight days

B. Thirty days

C. Sixty days

D. Ninety days

E. Seven days

59. A notice of appeal against an assessment should contain all the following except …

A. the name and address of the appellant.

B. the official number and the date of the relevant notice of assessment.

C. the quantum of withholding tax which the taxpayer suffered during the year..

D. the date on which the appellant was served with notice of refusal by the FCT IRS Board to amend the assessment as desired.

E. the precise grounds of appeal against the assessment.

60. An authorised officer of the FCT IRS shall between the hours of .... have free access to all lands, building and places and to all books and documents, whether in the custody or under the control of a public officer, institution or any other person whatsoever, for the

purpose of inspecting any book or document which he considers necessary for the purpose of carrying out any function lawfully conferred on the tax authority.

A. 8 a.m. and 4 p.m.
B. 8.30 a.m. and 4.30 p.m.
C. 8 a.m. and 5 p.m.
D. 8.30 a.m. and 3.30 p.m.
E. 9 a.m. and 4 p.m.

61. A written authorization to enter a private dwelling issued to an authorised officer by the Chairman of the FCT IRS is valid for a period of .... from the date of its issue or such lesser period as the Chairman considers appropriate.

A. 6 months
B. 5 months
C. 4 months
D. 3 months
E. 2 months

62. Under the FCT IRS Act, 2015, if any tax is not paid within the period prescribed, a sum equal to ......of the amount of the tax payable shall be added and the tax due shall carry interest at the prevailing commercial rate of the Central Bank of Nigeria from the date when the tax becomes payable until it is paid.

A. 5 per cent
B. 10 per cent
C. 15 per cent
D. 20 per cent
E. 25 per cent

63. The FCT IRS can exercise its power to seize and sell the goods, securities, land, premises, etc of a tax defaulter to recover the tax due but not paid. Things distrained by the tax authority may be kept at the expense of the tax defaulter for a maximum of ….. before disposal?

A. Sixty days
B. Thirty days

C. Fifteen days
D. Fourteen days
E. Twenty-one days

64. An immovable property distrained cannot be sold by the FCT IRS without an order of …
A. the Tax Appeal Committee.
B. the Joint Tax Board.
C. the Federal High Court.
D. the Minister of the Federal Capital Territory.
E. the Federal Capital Territory Authority.

65. The FCT IRS Board may issue a tax clearance certificate to a taxpayer within … of receipt of an application for the certificate.
A. twelve weeks
B. three weeks
C. four weeks
D. two weeks
E. six weeks

66. A tax clearance certificate is usually issued to cover a period of … immediately preceding the current year of assessment.
A. one year
B. six years
C. two years
D. five years
E. three years

67. Which of the following information is not contained in a tax clearance certificate?
A. Chargeable income of the taxpayer concerned
B. Tax payable
C. Tax paid
D. Tax outstanding
E. The rights of the taxpayer

68. A tax clearance certificate is demanded as a pre-condition for transacting the following businesses except …
    A. application for Minister's consent to real property transaction.
    B. application for admission into a University.
    C. application for approval of building plans.
    D. application for allocation of market stalls.
    E. application for certificate of occupancy.

69. The presentation of a tax clearance certificate is not a requirement for one of the following transactions and that is
    A. application for employment.
    B. registration for distributorship.
    C. application for any government licence or permit.
    D. application for award of contracts by registered companies.
    E. application relating to establishment or conduct of business.

70. Unauthorized communication of confidential information by any member or former member of the FCT IRS Board or any employee or former employee of the FCT IRS shall attract a fine of …
    A. ₦300,000 or imprisonment for not more than 3 years.
    B. ₦200,000 or imprisonment for 3 years or both.
    C. ₦100,000 or imprisonment for 5 years or both.
    D. ₦1,000,000 or imprisonment for not more than 3 years.
    E. ₦50,000 or imprisonment for 5 years or both.

71. No suit against the Chairman or a member of the FCT IRS Board or any employee of the FCT IRS for any act done in the pursuance or execution of the FCT IRS Act, 2015 shall lie or be instituted in any court unless it is commenced within …
    A. one month after the act, neglect or default complained of.
    B. two months after the act, neglect or default complained of.
    C. three months after the act, neglect or default complained of.
    D. four months after the act, neglect or default complained of.
    E. five months after the act, neglect or default complained of.

72. No suit shall be commenced against the Chairman or a member of the FCT IRS Board or any employee of the FCT IRS before the expiration of a period of … after a written notice of the intention to commence the suit shall have been served on the Service by the intending plaintiff or his agent.
    A. one month
    B. two months
    C. three months
    D. four months
    E. six months

73. In any action or suit against the FCT IRS, no execution or attachment of process in the nature thereof shall be issued against the Service unless not less than … notice of the intention to execute or attach has been given to the Service.
    A. six months
    B. two months
    C. one months
    D. four months
    E. three months

74. Which of the Schedules to the Federal Capital Territory Internal Revenue Service Act specifies the legislations to be administered by the Service?
    A. First Schedule
    B. Second Schedule
    C. Third Schedule
    D. Fourth Schedule
    E. Fifth Schedule

75. The Schedules to the Federal Capital Territory Internal Revenue Service Act include all the following except ...
    A. Second Schedule – Supplementary provisions relating to the Board
    B. Third Schedule – Form of authorisation to access lands, buildings, books and documents
    C. Fourth Schedule – Form of warrant of distraint

D. Fifth Schedule – Establishment, jurisdiction, authority and procedure of the tax appeal committee

E. Sixth Schedule – Capital allowances

Part II Short-Answer Questions

76. The Tax Appeal Committee established under the FCT IRS Act, 2015 consists of .... members.

77. What is the function of the Area Council Revenue Committee?

78. Which of the tax authorities has exclusive powers to control, administer and impose taxes and levies within the Federal Capital Territory .....

79. How many members can form a quorum at any meeting of the FCT Internal Revenue Service Board?

80. Who is responsible for the appointment of the Auditors to the FCT Internal Revenue Service?

81. A tax Appeal Commissioner is to hold office for a term of ..... renewable once only.

82. What is the penalty prescribed in the FCT IRS Act, 2015 for any tax official who demands more tax than the authorized tax assessment, misappropriates or embezzles a portion of the tax collected, renders false return of the amount of tax collected by him, defrauds any person or uses his position to deal wrongfully with any money accruable to the FCT IRS Board?

83. What is the penalty prescribed in the FCT IRS Act, 2015 for any person who makes an incorrect return or statement by omitting or understating any income chargeable to tax under the Act?

84. What is the penalty prescribed in the FCT IRS Act, 2015 for any person who fails to comply with any notice or summons served on

him in respect of any proceedings of the FCT IRS Board or that of the Tax Appeal Committee?

85. What is the penalty prescribed in the FCT IRS Act, 2015 for failure to deduct withholding tax or failure to pay withholding tax deducted to the FCT IRS within 30 days from the date the amount was deducted or the time the duty to deduct arose?

86. … has responsibility for the overall supervision of the FCT Internal Revenue Service.

87. The Secretary to the Tax Appeal Committee is appointed by …..

88. State two reasons under which the Tax Appeal Commissioners may adjourn the hearing of an appeal against a tax assessment and order the appellant to make a deposit an account of tax charged before the day of the adjourned hearing?

89. The Tax Appeal Committee may adjourn the hearing of an appeal against a tax assessment and order the appellant to make a deposit with the FCT IRS before the day of the adjourned hearing. What is the amount of deposit that the appellant may be required to make?

90. The Tax Appeal Committee may adjourn the hearing of an appeal against a tax assessment and order the appellant to make a deposit with the FCT IRS before the day of the adjourned hearing. What will happen if the appellant fails to comply with the order?

91. The Tax Appeal Committee may dismiss an appeal against a tax assessment on the hearing of the appeal. State two grounds for dismissing an appeal.

92. Give one reason why the Minister of the FCT may remove a Tax Appeal Commissioner from office before the expiration of his tenure.

93. An appeal against the decision of the Federal High Court shall lie with the ... and thereafter to the ...

94. The FCT IRS Board is subject to the general directives of the .... in the exercise of its powers and duties under the FCT IRS Act, 2015.

95. Who are the members of the Technical Committee of the FCT IRS Board?

96. State any two functions of the Technical Committee of the FCT IRS Board.

97. For the purpose of levying any distrain, an officer duly authorized by the Chairman of the FCT IRS Board may apply to .... for the issue of a warrant of distrain.

98. The power which the FCT IRS has to sell a taxpayer's goods, chattels or other properties and effects in the possession, use or found on the premises or on the land of the taxpayer for the purpose of enforcing or recovering the tax overdue for payment is referred to as .....

99. State the sequence for the utilization of the proceeds of sale of any property distrained by the FCT IRS.

100. What is the time limit within which the FCT IRS can raise an assessment or additional assessment on a taxpayer where the assessment relates to fraud, wilful default or neglect on the part of the taxpayer?

5 Federal Inland Revenue Service (Establishment) Act, 2007

Part I Multiple-Choice Questions

1. In exercise of the powers conferred on the Board of the FIRS by the Federal Inland Revenue Service (Establishment) Act, 2007, the Board with the approval of the Minister of Finance issued …
   A. Income Tax (Transfer Pricing) Regulations, 2018.
   B. Tax Administration (Self Assessment) Regulations, 2011.
   C. Pioneer Status Incentive Regulations, 2014.
   D. Operation of Pay As You Earned (PAYE) Regulations 2002.
   E. Personal Income Tax (Amendment) Act, 2011.

2. Which of the following statements is not true of the Federal Inland Revenue Service and the Federal Capital Territory Internal Revenue Service?
   A. FIRS collects the taxes due to the Federal Government while FCT IRS collects the revenue accruable to the FCT.
   B. FIRS is the tax authority of the federal government while FCT IRS is the tax authority of the FCT.
   C. FIRS is responsible for the taxation of companies and non-resident individuals while FCT IRS is responsible for the taxation of individuals resident in the FCT.
   D. FIRS is established under the Federal Inland Revenue Service (Establishment) Act while FCT IRS is established under the Federal Capital Territory Internal Revenue Service Act.
   E. The day-to-day operations of the FIRS are subject to the supervision of the Minister of Finance while that of the FCT IRS are under the purview of the Minister of the FCT.

3. Who is the Chairman of the Federal Inland Revenue Service Board?

A. Federal Minister of Finance

B. Executive Chairman of the FIRS

C. Permanent Secretary of the Federal Ministry of Finance

D. Director-General appointed by the Federal Civil Service Commission

E. Accountant-General of the Federation

4. The Chairman of the Federal Inland Revenue Service Board is appointed by the

   A. President.

   B. Minister of Finance.

   C. National Assembly.

   D. Joint Tax Board.

   E. President subject to the confirmation of the Senate.

5. The Secretary to the Federal Inland Revenue Service Board is appointed by the

   A. Federal Civil Service Commission.

   B. Federal Inland Revenue Service Board.

   C. Federal Ministry of Finance.

   D. Joint Tax Board.

   E. Revenue Mobilization, Allocation and Fiscal Commission.

6. All the following are members of the Federal Inland Revenue Service Board except

   A. one member from each State nominated by the Governor of the State.

   B. a representative of the Attorney-General of the Federation.

   C. the Governor of the Central Bank of Nigeria or his representative.

   D. a representative of the Minister of Finance.

   E. the Chairman of the Revenue Mobilization, Allocation and Fiscal Commission or his representative.

7. One of the following is not a member of the Federal Inland Revenue Service Board and that is ...

A. the Group Managing Director of the Nigerian National Petroleum Corporation or his representative.
B. the Comptroller-General of the Nigeria Customs Service or his representative.
C. the Registrar-General of the Corporate Affairs Commission or his representative.
D. a representative of the Minister of Petroleum Resources.
E. the Chief Executive Officer of the National Planning Commission or his representative.

8. How many members can form a quorum at any meeting of the Federal Inland Revenue Service Board?
A. Seven members
B. Five members
C. Nine members
D. Four members
E. Six members

9. For a quorum to be formed at any meeting of the Federal Inland Revenue Service Board, at least ... present must be outside the FIRS.
A. four members
B. three members
C. two members
D. one member
E. five members

10. Six members with relevant qualifications and expertise are appointed to the FIRS Board to represent each of the six-geographical zones. Who is responsible for the appointment of these six members?
A. The Minister of Finance
B. The Chairman of the FIRS Board
C. The President of the Federal Republic of Nigeria
D. The Senate
E. The Accountant-General of the Federation

11. All the following are members of the Technical Committee of the Federal Inland Revenue Service Board except
    A. the Secretary to the FIRS Board.
    B. the Executive Chairman of the FIRS.
    C. all the Directors and Heads of Departments of the FIRS.
    D. a representative of the Minister of Finance.
    E. the Legal Adviser of the FIRS.

12. In every calendar year, the FIRS Board is expected to hold at least
    A. twelve ordinary meetings.
    B. three ordinary meetings.
    C. four ordinary meetings.
    D. five ordinary meetings.
    E. six ordinary meetings.

13. The Chairman of the FIRS Board can convene a meeting of the Board if he is requested to do so by notice given to him by not less than
    A. six other members of the Board.
    B. five other members of the Board.
    C. four other members of the Board.
    D. three other members of the Board.
    E. seven other members of the Board.

14. The FIRS Board is subject to the authority, direction and control of the ... in the exercise of the powers and duties conferred on it.
    A. Senate
    B. House of Representatives
    C. Accountant-General
    D. Minister of Finance
    E. Auditor-General

15. A member of the FIRS Board shall cease to hold office as a member of the Board if ...
    A. he resigns his appointment as a member of the Board.
    B. he becomes incapable of carrying on the functions of his office.

C. he is removed from office by the President.
D. he becomes a member of a professional body.
E. he has been found guilty of contravening the Code of Conduct Bureau and Tribunal Act.

Which of the options A to E is not correct?

16. Members of the FIRS Board are entitled to emoluments, allowances and benefits as may be approved by the …
A. Revenue Mobilization, Allocation and Fiscal Commission.
B. President of the Federal Republic of Nigeria.
C. Federal Civil Service Commission.
D. The Ministry of Finance.
E. National Wages, Incomes and Salaries Commission.

17. If the Chairman of the FIRS Board is requested to convene a meeting of the Board by notice given to him by not less than four other members of the Board, he shall convene the meeting to be held within
A. thirty days from the date on which the notice was given.
B. seven days from the date on which the notice was given.
C. fifteen days from the date on which the notice was given.
D. fourteen days from the date on which the notice was given.
E. twenty-one days from the date on which the notice was given.

18. A member of the FIRS Board shall cease to hold office as a member of the Board if
A. he becomes bankrupt.
B. he becomes of unsound mind.
C. he has served for two terms of five years each.
D. he is convicted of any offence involving corruption.
E. he has been found guilty of gross misconduct in relation to his duties.

Which of the options A to E is not correct?

19. The administration of companies income tax is vested in the

A. Joint Tax Board.
B. State Board of Internal Revenue.
C. Federal Inland Revenue Service.
D. Joint State Revenue Committee.
E. Technical Committee of the SBIR.

20. The Federal Inland Revenue Service is responsible for the taxation of the following persons except
A. members of the Armed Forces of the Federation.
B. residents of the Federal Capital Territory.
C. Federal Civil Servants residents in the States.
D. officers of the Nigerian Foreign Service.
E. non-residents individuals.

21. All the following are specifically stated in the FIRS (Establishment) Act, 2007 as the powers and functions of the Federal Inland Revenue Service except to
A. assess, collect, account and enforce payment of taxes due to the Federal Government.
B. adopt measures to identify, trace, freeze, confiscate or seize proceeds derived from tax fraud or evasion.
C. stipulate remuneration, allowances, benefits and pensions of staff and employees.
D. collaborate and facilitate rapid exchange of information with relevant national or international agencies or bodies on tax matters.
E. issue taxpayer identification number to every taxable person in Nigeria in collaboration with States Boards of Internal Revenue and Local Government Councils.

22. The FIRS is required to submit to the Minister of Finance a report of its activities during the immediately preceding year together with its audited accounts not later than
A. 31st March in each year.
B. 30th June in each year.
C. 31st July in each year.

D. 30th September in each year.
E. 31st December in each year.

23. Where the FIRS gives a notice to any person calling for further returns, books, documents, information, etc, the period stipulated in the notice for compliance must be at least ... from the date of service of the notice.
A. twenty-one days
B. fourteen days
C. seven days
D. thirty days
E. sixty days

24. Every bank is required to prepare a return indicating the names and addresses of new customers of the bank and deliver the return to the FIRS not later than
A. seventh day of the following month.
B. sixth day of the following month.
C. tenth day of the following month.
D. seventeenth day of the following month.
E. fifth day of the following month

25. All the following are specifically stated in the FIRS (Establishment) Act, 2007 as the powers and functions of the Federal Inland Revenue Service Board except
A. assessing, collecting and accounting for taxes due to the Federal Government.
B. reviewing and approving the strategic plans of the FIRS.
C. employing and determining the conditions of service of the employees of the FIRS.
D. providing the general policy guidelines relating to the functions of the FIRS.
E. managing and superintending the policies of the FIRS on matters relating to the administration of the revenue assessment, collection and accounting system.

26. Which of the following is not specifically stated in the FIRS (Establishment) Act, 2007 as the functions of the Federal Inland Revenue Service?
    A. Employing and determining the terms and conditions of service of the employees of the service.
    B. Making, from time to time, a determination of the extent of financial and other losses by government arising from tax fraud or evasion.
    C. Maintaining database, statistics, records and reports on persons, organizations, proceeds, properties, documents or other items or assets relating to tax administration.
    D. Carrying out and sustaining rigorous public awareness and enlightenment campaign on the benefits of tax compliance within and outside Nigeria.
    E. Carrying out oversight functions over all taxes and levies accruable to the Government of the Federation.

27. The penalty prescribed in the FIRS (Establishment) Act, 2007 for any person who obstructs, hinders, molests or assaults any authorized officer in the performance of any function or the exercise of any power under the Act is a fine not exceeding
    A. ₦500,000 or imprisonment for not more than 3 years or both.
    B. ₦600,000 or imprisonment for not more than 3 years or both.
    C. ₦200,000 or imprisonment for not more than 3 years or both.
    D. ₦300,000 or imprisonment for not more than 3 years or both.
    E. ₦400,000 or imprisonment for not more than 3 years or both.

28. The penalty prescribed in the FIRS (Establishment) Act, 2007 for any person who counterfeits or falsifies any document required for tax purposes or knowingly accepts, receives or uses counterfeited or falsified document is a fine not exceeding

A. ₦200,000 or imprisonment for not more than 3 years or both.
B. ₦300,000 or imprisonment for not more than 3 years or both.
C. ₦400,000 or imprisonment for not more than 3 years or both.
D. ₦500,000 or imprisonment for not more than 3 years or both.
E. ₦600,000 or imprisonment for not more than 3 years or both.

29. What is the penalty stipulated in the FIRS (Establishment) Act, 2007 for any person armed with offensive weapon who causes injury to any officer of the FIRS in the performance of any function or duty under the Act?
A. Imprisonment for a term not exceeding 10 years.
B. Imprisonment for a term not exceeding 8 years.
C. Imprisonment for a term not exceeding 6 years.
D. Imprisonment for a term not exceeding 5 years.
E. Imprisonment for a term not exceeding 4 years.

30. If a person contravenes any provisions of the FIRS (Establishment) Act, 2007 for which no penalty is specifically prescribed, he shall be liable on conviction to a fine not exceeding
A. ₦500,000 or imprisonment for not more than 6 months or both.
B. ₦100,000 or imprisonment for not more than 6 months or both.
C. ₦50,000 or imprisonment for not more six months or both.
D. ₦5,000 or imprisonment for not more six months or both.
E. ₦500 or imprisonment for not more six months or both.

31. Members of the Tax Appeal Tribunal (referred to as Tax Appeal Commissioners) are appointed by the ...
A. Chairman of the State Board of Internal Revenue.
B. Chairman of the Federal Inland Revenue Service Board.
C. Chairman of the Joint Tax Board.

D. Minister of Finance.
E. President of the Federal Republic of Nigeria.

32. The Tax Appeal Tribunal established under the Federal Inland Revenue Service (Establishment) Act, 2007 consist of
    A. seven members.
    B. ten members.
    C. twelve members.
    D. five members.
    E. fifteen members.

33. The terms and conditions of service (including salary and allowances) of a Tax Appeal Commissioner are determined by the
    A. Revenue Mobilization, Allocation and Fiscal Commission.
    B. President of the Federal Republic of Nigeria.
    C. Federal Civil Service Commission.
    D. Ministry of Finance.
    E. National Wages, Incomes and Salaries Commission.

34. What is the number of members that can form a quorum at any sitting of the Tax Appeal Tribunal?
    A. Any three Tax Appeal Commissioners
    B. Any five Tax Appeal Commissioners
    C. Any two Tax Appeal Commissioners
    D. Any six Tax Appeal Commissioners
    E. Any four Tax Appeal Commissioners

35. The Chairman of the Tax Appeal Tribunal for each zone must be a legal practitioner of not less than ...
    A. 5 years' post call experience.
    B. 10 years' post call experience.
    C. 15 years' post call experience.
    D. 20 years' post call experience.
    E. 25 years' post call experience.

36. Within how many days can an appeal be made to the Federal High Court against the decision of the Tax Appeal Tribunal after the date on which the decision was given?
    A. Thirty days
    B. Sixty days
    C. Ninety days
    D. One hundred and twenty days
    E. Twenty-one days

37. A member of the Tax Appeal Tribunal cannot continue to hold office as a Tax Appeal Commissioner after attending the age of …
    A. 65 years
    B. 80 years
    C. 50 years
    D. 60 years
    E. 70 years

38. An appeal to the Tax Appeal Tribunal must be filed within … from the date on which a copy of the order or decision which is being appealed against was made or deemed to have been made by the FIRS.
    A. 30 days
    B. 15 days
    C. 45 days
    D. 21 days
    E. 7 days

39. All appeals before the Tax Appeal Commissioners shall be held
    A. in camera.
    B. in secret.
    C. in public.
    D. behind closed doors.
    E. in private.

40. Within how many days can an appeal be made by a company or the FIRS to the Federal High Court against the decision of the Tax Appeal Tribunal after the date on which the decision was given.

A. 30 days
B. 15 days
C. 60 days
D. 21 days
E. 7 days

41. The FIRS is required to prepare an estimate of its income and expenditure for the succeeding year not later than …
A. 30th September in each year.
B. 31st December in each year.
C. 1st December in each year.
D. 31st October in each year.
E. 30th June in each year.

42. The accounts of FIRS are to be audited by the auditors not later than
A. three months after the end of each year.
B. four months after the end of each year.
C. five months after the end of each year.
D. six months after the end of each year.
E. nine months after the end of each year.

43. The FIRS is required to submit to the Minister of Finance a report of its activities during the immediately preceding year together with its audited accounts not later than 30th September in each year. The Minister is required to present a copy of the report to the Federal Executive Council and a copy to the National Assembly within …
A. fifteen days of receipt of the report.
B. thirty days of receipt of the report.
C. ten days of receipt of the report.
D. seven days of receipt of the report.
E. twenty-one days of receipt of the report.

44. All of the following are specifically stated in FIRS (Establishment) Act, 2007 as the powers and functions of the Federal Inland Revenue Service except to
A. carry out examination and investigation with a view to enforcing compliance with the provisions of the tax Act.

B. collate and continually review all policies of the Federal Government relating to taxation and revenue generation and undertake a systematic and progressive implementation of such policies.

C. liaise with the relevant government agencies and financial supervisory institutions in the enforcement and eradication of tax related offences.

D. establish and maintain a system for monitoring international dynamics of taxation in order to identify suspicious transactions and the perpetrators and other persons involved.

E. promote uniformity in the application of PITA and in the incidence of tax on individuals throughout Nigeria.

45. The Federal Inland Revenue Service (Establishment) Act empowers the Accountant-General of the Federation to deduct at source from the budgetary allocation to any ministry or government agency the unremitted taxes due from such ministry or government agency to the FIRS. The amount deducted is to be remitted to the FIRS not later than ...

A. twenty-one days after deduction.
B. fourteen days after deduction.
C. thirty days after deduction.
D. seven days after deduction.
E. sixty days after deduction.

46. Every bank is required to prepare upon demand by the FIRS, quarterly returns and deliver the returns to the FIRS specifying the names and addresses of all customers of the bank connected with transactions involving ... million and above in the case of an individual.

A. ₦5 million Naira
B. ₦10 million Naira
C. ₦15 million Naira
D. ₦20 million Naira
E. ₦1 million Naira

47. The penalty prescribed in the FIRS (Establishment) Act, 2007 for any unauthorized person assuming the name, designation or impersonating the character of an authorized officer for the purpose of obtaining admission to any building or other place, or of doing or procuring to be done any act which he would not be entitled to do or procure to be done of his own authority or for any other unlawful purpose is a fine not exceeding
    A. ₦500,000 or imprisonment for not more than 3 years.
    B. ₦200,000 or imprisonment for not more than 3 years.
    C. ₦20,000 or imprisonment for not more than 3 years.
    D. ₦2,000 or imprisonment for not more than 3 years.
    E. ₦50,000 or imprisonment for not more than 3 years.

48. Over-payment of tax is to be refunded to the taxpayer within ... days of the decision of the FIRS to make such refund.
    A. seven days
    B. twenty-one days
    C. Ninety days
    D. thirty days
    E. fourteen days

49. The FIRS may for the purpose of enforcing payment of the tax due, distrain the taxpayer by his goods or other chattels, bonds or other securities, etc. Things distrained may be kept for ... at the cost of the taxpayer.
    A. twenty-one days
    B. thirty days
    C. seven days
    D. fourteen days
    E. sixty days

50. The FIRS has power to administer the following enactments ...
    i. Taxes and Levies (Approved List for Collection) Act
    ii. Personal Income Tax Act
    iii. National Information Technology Development Agency Act
    iv. Stamp Duties Act

A. i, ii and iv only
B. ii and iv only
C. i, iii and iv only
D. iii and iv only
E. i, ii, iii and iv

Which of the options A to E is correct?

51. The Federal Inland Revenue Service Board consists of …
A. fifteen part-time members only.
B. fifteen full-time members only.
C. fifteen part-time members and five full-time members.
D. nine part-time members and one full-time member.
E. fourteen part-time members and one full-time member.

52. The FIRS (Establishment) Act, 2007 specifically requires … to keep proper accounting records in respect of revenues, expenditure, assets, liabilities and other financial transactions of the FIRS.
A. the Director of Finance of the FIRS
B. the Secretary to the FIRS Board
C. the Executive Chairman of the FIRS
D. the Legal Adviser of the FIRS
E. the Governor of the Central Bank of Nigeria

53. Who is required by the FIRS (Establishment) Act, 2007 to open a dedicated account into which is to be paid monies meant for settling tax refunds?
A. The Director of Finance of the FIRS
B. The Governor of the Central Bank of Nigeria
C. The Secretary to the FIRS Board
D. The Executive Chairman of the FIRS
E. The Accountant-General of the Federation

54. Who is charged with the responsibility of administering the dedicated account for tax refunds?
A. The Accountant-General of the Federation
B. The Director of Finance of the FIRS
C. The Governor of the Central Bank of Nigeria

D. The Federal Inland Revenue Service
E. The Secretary to the FIRS Board

55. The FIRS (Establishment) Act, 2007 specifically states that the dedicated account for tax refunds is be funded from the …as may be approved by the National Assembly.
A. treasury single account
B. federation account
C. non-oil and gas revenue
D. consolidated revenue account
E. miscellaneous revenue account

56. A taxpayer can ask for an extension of time within which to file the returns or further returns required by the FIRS. The FIRS Board may grant the extension of time provided:
i. the request is made in writing to the FIRS Board.
ii. the taxpayer has a tax clearance certificate.
iii. the application is made before the expiration of the time stipulated for making the returns.
iv. the taxpayer shows good cause for his inability to meet the dateline.
A. i, ii and iv only
B. ii and iv only
C. i, iii and iv only
D. iii and iv only
E. i, ii, iii and iv
Which of the options A to E is correct?

57. An officer of the FIRS may be authorized to enter into any premises through a warrant issued by …
A. the Commissioner of Police.
B. the Director of Legal Department of the FIRS.
C. the Secretary to the FIRS Board.
D. a judicial officer.
E. EFCC.

58. An officer of the FIRS may be authorized to enter into any premises to have access to documents, books, etc or carry out any other functions lawfully conferred on the FIRS. Such authorization should:

    i. be in the form prescribed in the Third Schedule to the FIRS (Establishment) Act.
    ii. be directed to a named officer of the FIRS.
    iii. state its period of validity or the date on which it expires.
    iv. be renewable by the Chairman of the FIRS on application.

    A. i, ii and iii only
    B. i and ii only
    C. i, iii and iv only
    D. iii and iv only
    E. i, ii, iii and iv

    Which of the options A to E is correct?

59. The FIRS (Establishment) Act, 2007 requires the occupier of a land, building or place that is entered or proposed to be entered by an authorized officer of the FIRS to:

    i. provide the officer with all reasonable facilities and assistance for the effective exercise of his powers under the Act.
    ii. provide accommodation and light refreshment for the authorized officer.
    iii. contact the Chairman of the FIRS to verify the identity of the authorized officer.
    iv. answer questions relating to the effective exercise of the officer's powers under the Act, orally, or if required by the officer, in writing, or by statutory declaration.

    A. i and iii only
    B. i and iv only
    C. i, iii and iv only
    D. iii and iv only
    E. i, ii, iii and iv

    Which of the options A to E is correct?

60. When a demand note is served on a company by the FIRS, the former has a period of grace of ... from the date of service of the demand note within which to make payment.
    A. twenty-one days
    B. one month
    C. two months
    D. three months
    E. fifteen days

61. The FIRS may for the purpose of enforcing payment of the tax due but not paid, distrain a taxpayer by his goods or other chattels, securities, etc if …
    i. he fails to produce for examination books, documents and other information as the FIRS may consider necessary.
    ii. an assessment has become final and conclusive.
    iii. a demand notice has been served upon the taxable person.
    iv. payment of the tax is not made within the time limited by the demand notice.
    A. i, ii, iii and iv
    B. i, iii and iv only
    C. i, ii and iii only
    D. iii and iv only
    E. ii, iii and iv only
    Which of the options A to E is correct?

62. Any officer duly authorized by the FIRS Board may execute any warrant of distraint and if necessary break open any building or place in the … for the purpose of levying such distraint.
    A. night time
    B. day time
    C. evening time
    D. morning time
    E. day or night time as agreed with the occupier of the building

63. Proceeds of sale of any property distrained are to be used in the following sequence:

i. to pay the amount of tax due.
ii. to pay the cost or charges of and incidental to the sale and keeping of the distraint and disposal.
iii. to pay the balance to the taxpayer.
A. i, ii and iii
B. i, iii and ii
C. ii, iii and i
D. iii,ii and i
E. ii, i and iii

64. The balance of proceeds of sale of any property distrained after paying expenses and tax liability is payable to the taxpayer on demand being made by him or on his behalf within...
A. one month of the date of sale
B. three months of the date of sale
C. six months of the date of sale
D. nine months of the date of sale
E. one year of the date of sale

65. According to section 48(1) of the FIRS (Establishment) Act, 2007, the FIRS may compound any offence under the Act. This implies that …
A. the FIRS has power to investigate to ascertain any violation of the Act.
B. the FIRS has powers to prosecute any offence under the Act.
C. the FIRS can pardon a taxpayer for any offence committed under the Act.
D. the FIRS can accept a sum of money not exceeding the maximum fine specified for the offence.
E. the FIRS can sue a taxpayer for several tax offences at once.

66. Who is to preside over the meeting of the Tax Appeal Tribunal in the absence of the Chairman?
A. The Secretary to the Tribunal
B. The Chairman of the Joint Tax Board
C. The Minister of Finance or his representative

D. The Vice Chairman of the Tribunal
E. Any of the Tax Appeal Commissioners appointed to be the Chairman by the other Commissioners.

67. What is the tenure of a Tax Appeal Commissioner in the first instance?
A. Three years
B. Two years
C. Four years
D. Five years
E. Six years

68. The tenure of a Tax Appeal Commissioner can be renewed ...
A. only once and no more.
B. two times.
C. three times.
D. four times.
E. five times.

69. Six members with relevant qualifications and expertise are appointed to the FIRS Board to represent each of the six geo-political zones in Nigeria. Who is responsible for the appointment of these six members?
A. The President of the Federal Republic of Nigeria
B. The Minister of Finance
C. The Senate
D. The Governors of the States within each geo-political zone
E. The Joint Tax Board

70. In the execution of any warrant of distraint and the levying of distraint, no person shall be bodily searched except ...
A. in the presence of other people.
B. in a private room or office.
C. by a person who is of the same gender as the person to be bodily searched.
D. by a law enforecemt agent.
E. he refuses to cooperate with the officer excuting the warrant.

71. Tax Appeal Tribunals have been created for the six geo-political zones of Nigeria. They usually sit in the following towns except …
    A. Bauchi
    B. Kaduna
    C. Lagos
    D. Port Harcourt
    E. Ibadan

72. The Tax Appeal Tribunals established for the six geo-political zones of Nigeria usually sit in the following towns except:

    A. Abuja
    B. Enugu
    C. Sokoto
    D. Benin
    E. Jos

73. What is the total number of Tax Appeal Commissioners appointed for the Tax Appeal Tribunals in Nigeria?
    A. Fifty
    B. Thirty
    C. Forty
    D. Sixty
    E. Forty-two

74. The Schedules to the FIRS (Establishment) Act include all the following except the ...
    A. Second Schedule – supplementary provisions relating to the Board.
    B. Third Schedule – form of authorisation to access lands, buildings, books and documents.
    C. Fourth Schedule – form of warrant of distraint.
    D. Fifth Schedule – establishment, jurisdiction, authority and procedure of the Tax Appeal Tribunal.
    E. Sixth Schedule – powers or duties which the Board may not delegate except to the Joint Tax Board with the consent of the Minister.

75. Which of the Schedules to the FIRS (Establishment) Act specifies the legislations to be administered by the FIRS?
    A. First Schedule
    B. Second Schedule
    C. Third Schedule
    D. Fourth Schedule
    E. Fifth Schedule

76. The Schedule to the Companies Income Tax Act which specifies the funds, bodies and institutions in Nigeria to which donations may be made is the ....
    A. First Schedule.
    B. Second Schedule.
    C. Third Schedule.
    D. Fourth Schedule.
    E. Fifth Schedule.

77. Which of the following Schedules to the Companies Income Tax Act deals with capital allowances?
    A. First Schedule
    B. Second Schedule
    C. Third Schedule
    D. Fourth Schedule
    E. Fifth Schedule

78. Which of the following is not a Schedule to the Companies Income Tax Act?
    A. First Schedule – powers or duties which the Board may not delegate except to the Joint Tax Board with the consent of the Minister
    B. Third Schedule – tax exemption on certain interests
    C. Fourth Schedule – warrant and authority to levy distress under the Companies Income Tax Act
    D. Sixth Schedule – warrant and authority to enter premises, offices, etc
    E. Seventh Schedule – double taxation agreements

Part II Short-Answer Questions

79. A document issued by the FIRS authorizing its officer(s) to enter a company's premises and related places to search, seize and remove any records, documents, etc is called …

80. Every bank is required to prepare upon demand by the FIRS, quarterly returns and deliver the returns to the FIRS specifying the names and addresses of all customers of the bank connected with transactions involving ₦ … million and above in the case of a body corporate.

81. Every bank is required to prepare upon demand by the FIRS, quarterly returns specifying the names and addresses of new customers of the bank and to deliver the returns to the FIRS not later than the …

82. For the purpose of obtaining information relative to taxation, a bank may be given a notice by the FIRS to provide information about its customer. As stipulated in the Federal Inland Revenue Service (Establishment) Act, the notice to the bank must be signed by …

83. All the members of the Federal Inland Revenue Service Board are part-time members except …

84. Non-public officers appointed to hear appeals made by taxpayers against income tax assessments are called

85. The FIRS can engage consultants to transact any business or do any act required to be transacted or done in the execution of its functions. However, the FIRS (Establishment) Act, 2007 specifically states that consultants cannot carry out duties of …

86. What is the penalty prescribed in the Federal Inland Revenue Service (Establishment) Act, 2007 for any tax official who demands more tax than the authorized tax assessment, misappropriates or embezzles a portion of the tax collected, renders false return of the

amount of tax collected by him, defrauds any person or uses his position to deal wrongfully with the FIRS?

87. What is the penalty prescribed in the FIRS (Establishment) Act, 2007 for any person who makes, signs and delivers any declaration, notice, certificate or other document or makes a statement for the purpose of tax which is untrue in any material particular?

88. What is the penalty prescribed in the FIRS (Establishment) Act, 2007 for failure to complete and deliver to the FIRS any return required or failure to produce books, documents, etc for examination at the place and time stated in the notice, or failure to appear personally before an officer of FIRS for examination or failure to give orally or in writing further information required?

89. What is the penalty prescribed in the FIRS (Establishment) Act, 2007 for failure of a bank to furnish the FIRS with quarterly returns on the names and addresses of all customers of the bank connected with the transactions involving ₦5 million and above in the case of an individual or ₦10 million and above in the case of a body corporate or failure to submit returns on the names and addresses of new customers of the bank or any other additional information about its customers required by the FIRS?

90. What is the penalty prescribed in the Federal Inland Revenue Service (Establishment) Act, 2007 for failure to deduct withholding tax or failure to pay withholding tax deducted to the FIRS within the stipulated period?

91. A judicial officer upon an application by an officer of the FIRS may authorize the officer by warrant to enter into any premises. What is the validity period of the warrant?

92. ... has responsibility for the overall supervision of the Federal Inland Revenue Service.

93. Unauthorized communication of confidential information by current or former member of the FIRS Board or current or former employee of the FIRS shall attract a fine not exceeding …

94. A devision of the Committee of the FIRS Board shal be of no effect until it is confirmed by the …

95. State two reasons under which the Appeal Commissioners may adjourn the hearing of an appeal against a tax assessment and order the appellant to make a deposit an account of tax charged before the day of the adjourned hearing?

96. The Tax Appeal Tribunal may adjourn the hearing of an appeal against a tax assessment and order the appellant to make a deposit with the FIRS before the day of the adjourned hearing. What is the amount of deposit that the appellant may be required to make? What will happen if the appellant fails to comply with the order?

97. The Tax Appeal Commissioners may dismiss an appeal against a tax assessment on the hearing of the appeal. State two grounds for dismissing an appeal.

98. Who may be appointed as a Tax Appeal Commissioner?

99. Give one reason why the Minister of Finance may remove a Tax Appeal Commissioner from office before the expiration of his tenure?

100. Federal Inland Revenue Service Board is subject to the authority, direction and control of the ...

101. Who are the members of the Technical Committee of the Federal Inland Revenue Service Board.

102. State any two functions of the Technical Committee of the Federal Inland Revenue Service Board.

103. The FIRS can exercise its power to seize and sell the taxpayer's goods, securities, land, premises, etc to recover the tax due but not paid. An immovable property cannot be sold without an order of a…

104. An officer of the FIRS exercising the power of entry into a private dwelling conferred by an authorization is to produce ... and … on first entering the private dwelling and whenever subsequently reasonably required to do so.

105. An authorized officer of the FIRS cannot enter into a private dwelling to have access to books, documents, etc except …

106. What action should be taken by a Tax Appeal Commissioner if he has a direct or indirect financial interest in an appeal pending before the Tax Appeal Tribunal?

6 Persons and Income Chargeable

Part I Multiple-Choice Questions

1. Personal Income Tax Act imposes tax on the income of all the following persons except ...
   A. companies.
   B. executors.
   C. trustees.
   D. communities.
   E. families.

2. Under the Personal Income Tax Act, which of the following is included in the definition of an individual?
   A. Trustee
   B. Partnership
   C. Executor
   D. Family
   E. Corporation sole

3. Income tax for a year of assessment may be collected from an individual only by the state in which ...
   A. he is a citizen.
   B. he is employed.
   C. he is resident.
   D. he is naturalised.
   E. he derives an income.

4. In which state is the income accruing to an executor of the estate of a deceased person assessable to personal income tax?
   A. The state in which the executor is deemed to be resident.
   B. The state in which the deceased was last deemed to be resident.
   C. The state in which the income of the estate arises.

D. Federal Capital Territory.
E. Any state in which the executor is found during the year.

5. Income chargeable to tax under the Personal Income Tax Act includes all the following except ...
A. annuity.
B. discount.
C. rent.
D. capital gains.
E. emoluments.

6. The income of the following is exempted from personal income tax provided such income is not derived from a trade or business carried on by such persons.
A. Trade union
B. Educational institution
C. Charitable organisation
D. Community
E. Statutory or registered friendly society
Which of the options A to E is not correct?

7. All the following incomes are exempted from personal income tax except ...
A. compensation for loss of employment.
B. income of a Local Government.
C. income earned by a church from its bookshop.
D. gratuity.
E. wound and disability pension granted to a member of the Armed Forces.

8. A Nigerian company is liable to income tax on ...
A. the profits attributable to Nigerian operations only.
B. the profits derived from Nigeria only.
C. the profits brought into Nigeria only.
D. the profits received in Nigeria only.
E. its global profits.

9. All the following incomes are chargeable to tax under the Companies Income Tax Act except ...
   A. gains arising from acquisition and disposal of short-term money instruments.
   B. interest.
   C. profits arising from petroleum operations.
   D. royalties.
   E. fees and allowances for services rendered.

10. Dividends received by a company from small companies in the manufacturing sector are exempted from income tax in the first ...
    A. three years of their operation.
    B. five years of their operation.
    C. four years of their operation.
    D. two years of their operation.
    E. six years of their operation.

11. According to the Companies Income Tax Act, which of the following can exempt any company or class of company or any profits of any company or class of company from any source from income tax?
    A. Joint Tax Board
    B. Federal Inland Revenue Service Board
    C. Federal Inland Revenue Service
    D. President of Nigeria
    E. Technical Committee of the FIRS Board

12. All the following dividends are not taxable under the Companies Income Tax Act except a …
    A. dividend distributed by a Nigerian company by way of bonus shares.
    B. dividend paid by a Nigerian company out of any profits exempted from tax under CITA.
    C. dividend paid out of profits chargeable to tax under Petroleum Profits Tax Act.

D. dividend paid by a Nigerian company out of any profits exempted from tax under the Industrial Development (Income Tax) Relief Act.

E. A dividend paid by a Nigerian company engaged in agricultural trade or business.

13. Interest payable on any foreign loan granted on or after 1st April, 1978 is exempted from tax in accordance with the Third Schedule to CITA. What is the rate of exemption for interest on a loan that has a repayment period of over 7 years with a grace period of not less than 2 years?

A. 0%
B. 40%
C. 70%
D. 50%
E. 100%

14. Interest on any loan granted by a bank on or after 1st January, 1997 to a company engaged in agricultural trade or business is exempted from tax provided the conditions stipulated in CITA are met. The bank is required to furnish the FIRS with the following information in respect of the loan except ...

A. the moratorium.
B. the amount of the loan.
C. the cash flows projection of the borrower.
D. the date repayment is due to commence and the amount of repayment showing capital and interest.
E. the full particulars of the recipient of the loan and its permanent address.

15. Interest on any loan granted by a bank on or after 1st January, 1997 to a company engaged in agricultural trade or business is exempted from tax provided ...

i. the moratorium is not less than eighteen months.
ii. the moratorium is not less than twenty-four months.
iii. the company is not engaged in other business activities besides agricultural business.

iv. the rate of interest on the loan is not more than the base lending rate at the time the loan was granted.

A. i and iv only
B. i and iii only
C. ii and iv only
D. ii, iii and iv only
E. i, iii and iv only

16. All the following are exempted from companies income tax except ..
A. interest earned by holders of short term Federal Government of Nigeria securities.
B. interest earned by holders of bonds issued by Federal, State and Local Governments and their Agencies.
C. interest earned by holders of bonds issued by corporate bodies including supranationals.
D. interest on any loan granted by a bank to a company engaged in non-agricultural trade or business.
E. dividend distributed by Unit Trust.

17. Who has power to amend the list of companies exempted from tax under the Companies Income Tax Act?
A. FIRS Board
B. Minister of Finance
C. Chairman of the FIRS
D. Joint Tax Board
E. President of Nigeria

18. An individual who is taxed in any state in which he is found during the year of assessment is .....
A. an itinerant worker.
B. an incapacitated individual.
C. an unemployed individual.
D. a non-resident individual.
E. a member of the Armed Forces of the Federation.

19. Profits of any company or institution engaged in ...... of a public character are exempt from income tax provided that such profits are

not derived from a trade or business carried on by the company or institution.

i. charitable activities
ii. ecclesiastical activities
iii. educational activities
iv. sporting activities

A. iv only
B. i, ii and iv only
C. i and iii only
D. i, ii, iii and iv
E. i, ii and iii only

Which of the options A to E is correct?

20. Profits of the following companies are exempted from companies income tax although they may be derived from a trade or business carried on by such companies.

A. The profits of any company being a body corporate established by or under any Local Government Law or Edict in force in any State in Nigeria.
B. The profits of any body corporate being a purchasing authority established by an enactment and empowered to acquire any commodity for export from Nigeria from the purchase and sale of that commodity.
C. The profits of any company formed for the purpose of promoting sporting activities where such profits are wholly expendable for such purpose.
D. The profits of any company or any corporation established by the law of a State for the purpose of fostering the economic development of that State.
E. The profits of a company established within an export processing zone or free trade zone provided that 100 per cent production of such company is for export.

21. Which of the following individuals are exempted from tax under the provisions of the Personal Income Tax Act?

A. Children
B. Incapacitated individuals

C. Married women
D. Aged men and women
E. None of the above

22. Which of the following emoluments are exempted from personal income tax as at 2018?
    A. Offical emoluments of the President of Nigeria
    B. Offical emoluments of the Vice President of Nigeria
    C. Offical emoluments of the State Governors in Nigeria
    D. Offical emoluments of the Deputy Governors of states
    E. None of the above

23. Which of the following individuals are exempted from tax under the Personal Income Tax Act irrespective of whether they have income derived from Nigeria?
    A. Members of the Armed Forces of the Federation
    B. Members of the Nigeria Police Force
    C. Officers of Nigerian Foreign Service
    D. Non-resident individuals
    E. None of the above

Part II Short-Answer Questions

24. A taxable person is defined in the Personal Income Tax Act as ...

25. In which state is the income of a community assessable to tax?

26. In which state is the income of a family assessable to personal income tax?

27. Income accruing to a trustee of a settlement or trust may be taxed by the state ...

28. Who is an itinerant worker?

29. Mention three types of income chargeable to tax under the PITA or CITA.

30. Under what condition can income earned from outside Nigeria by a temporary lecturer, teacher, nurse, doctor and other professionals and brought into Nigeria be granted 100% tax exemption?

31. Income earned from abroad by an author, sportsman, play writer, musician, artist and brought into Nigeria is exempted from tax. What is the condition to be fulfilled for this exemption to be granted?

32. Under what condition is dividend, interest, rent or royalty derived from a country outside Nigeria and brought into Nigeria is exempted from income tax?

33. Any company incorporated under the Companies and Allied Matters Act is referred to as ...

34. Any company established by or under any law in force in any territory or country outside Nigeria is referred to as ...

35. Mention two companies whose profits are exempted from tax in so far as such profits are not derived from a trade or business carried on by such companies.

36. Give three examples of dividend received by companies which are exempted from companies income tax.

37. What is the condition under which the profits of a Nigerian company in respect of goods exported from Nigeria are exempted from income tax?

38. State two situations that the profits of a non-Nigerian company are deemed to be derived from Nigeria.

39. In relation to PITA and CITA, when is a transaction deemed to be artificial or fictitious?

40. Documents, returns, assessments, etc relating to the profits of companies are to be treated as secret and confidential by the FIRS staff. State two circumstances that an employee of the FIRS having possession or control over such documents, etc can communicate the information contained therein to any person without being guilty of an offence.

41. A notice to be served on a company registered in Nigeria must be addressed to ...

42. A notice to be served on a company incorporated outside Nigeria must be addressed to ...

43. Under which tax law is the profit derived from a trade or business by an individual subject to tax?

44. Under which tax law is the profit derived from a trade or business by a company subject to tax?

7 Residence and Relevant Tax Authority

Part I Multiple-Choice Questions

1. Individual taxpayers whose relevant tax authority is the FIRS include all the following except ...
   A. members of the Nigerian Armed Forces.
   B. residents of the Federal Capital Territory.
   D. officers of the Nigerian Foreign Service.
   E. non-resident individuals who derive income from Nigeria.
   E. members of the Nigeria Police Force.

2. Principal place of residence means in the case of an individual who has a source of earned income other than a pension in Nigeria, ...
   A. that place of those places which is the Federal Capital Territory.
   B. that place which is his state of origin.
   C. that place of those places in which he usually resides.
   D. that place at which the head office or operational site of his employer is situated.
   E. that place of those places which on a relevant day is nearest to his usual place of work.

3. Principal place of residence means in the case of an individual who works in the branch office or operational site of a company, the place at which the branch office or operational site is situated provided that operational site shall include oil terminals, oil platforms, flow stations, factories, quarries and construction site with a minimum of ...
   A. one hundred workers.
   B. fifty workers.
   C. thirty workers.
   D. twenty workers.
   E. ten workers.

4. Mrs Giwa, an indigene of Cross River State, earns rent from her properties located in Abuja, Lagos, Port Harcourt and Kaduna but she had no residence on 1st January, 2018. For tax purposes, she would be deemed to be resident for that year of assessment ...
   A. in her state of origin, Cross River State.
   B. in the Federal Capital Territory.
   C. in the territory from which any part of the unearned income arose.
   D. in the territory that she has chosen to be her principal private residence.
   E. in the territory that accounted for the largest part of the income.

5. An individual resident in Nigeria is liable to tax on ...
   i. the aggregate amounts of his income from sources inside Nigeria only.
   ii. the gains or profits deemed to be derived from Nigeria only.
   iii. the aggregate amounts of his income from sources inside and outside Nigeria.
   iv. his total income in the territory he is deemed to reside irrespective of the territory from which each income is derived.
   A. iii only
   B. i, ii and iii only
   C. i, ii and iv only
   D. i and iv only
   E. iii and iv only
   Which of the options A to E is correct?

6. A non-resident individual is a person ....
   i. who is not a citizen of Nigeria.
   ii. who is not domiciled in Nigeria.
   iii. who is not subject to tax in Nigeria but derives income or profit from Nigeria.
   iv. who stays in Nigeria for less than 183 days in a 12-month period but derives income or profit from Nigeria

Which of the above statements is/are correct?

A. ii and iv only
B. i, ii and iv only
C. i and iv only
D. i, ii and iii only
E. i only

7. Which of the following statements is/are false?

i. A non-resident individual cannot claim certain allowances and reliefs.
ii. A non-resident individual is taxable only on the gains or profits deemed to be derived from Nigeria.
iii. A non-resident individual is liable to tax in Nigeria in the state from which his income is deemed to be derived.
iv. A non-resident individual is liable to tax in Nigeria on the aggregate amounts of his income from sources inside and outside Nigeria.

A. iv only
B. i, iv only
C. i and ii only
D. iii and iv only
E. i, iii and iv only

8. Which of the following persons is/are not deemed to be resident in the Federal Capital Territory?

A. Members of the Armed Forces of the Federation
B. Officers of the Nigerian Foreign Service
C. Itinerant worker
D. Persons resident outside Nigeria who derives income from Nigeria
E. Members of the Nigeria Police Force

9. An individual is deemed to be resident for a year of assessment in the Nigerian territory where his employer's principal office is situated on 1st January of that year. This rule for the determination of an individual's residence applies to a/an ...

A. foreign employment.
B. Nigerian employment.
C. Nigerian pension.
D. income from a trade or business.
E. unearned income.

10. Income derived from an employment, or a trade, business, profession or vocation is referred to as a/an ...
A. employment income.
B. earned income.
C. unearned income.
D. investment income.
E. foreign income.

11. Income derived form sources other than employment, trade, business, profession or vocation is referred to as a/an ...
A. foreign income.
B. Nigerian income.
C. unearned income.
D. earned income.
E. pension.

12. Which of the following is not an unearned income?
A. Wages
B. Royalty
C. Rent
D. Interest
E. Dividend

13. Earned income includes...
i. Pension
ii. Remuneration
iii. Royalty
iv. Business profit
A. i and ii only
B. ii and iv only
C. iii and iv only

D. i and iv only
E. i, ii and iv only

14. A dispute between two tax authorities over an individual's territory of residence is resolved by the ...
    A. State Board of Internal Revenue.
    B. Federal Inland Revenue Service Board.
    C. Joint State Revenue Committee.
    D. Joint Tax Board.
    E. Technical Committee of the FIRS Board.

Part II Short-Answer Questions

15. Territory refers to ...

16. A place available for an individual's domestic use in Nigeria on a relevant day is referred to as ...

17. Where an individual has more than one place of residence in different territories, he is deemed to be resident in the territory in which he has his ...

18. The principal place of residence of an individual who has no source of income other than a pension in Nigeria is…

19. The principal place of residence of an individual who has a source or sources of unearned income in Nigeria is ...

20. Where the duties of an employment are wholly performed outside Nigeria except during any temporary visit of the employee to Nigeria, the employment is said to be a ...

21. An employment where the duties are wholly or partly performed in Nigeria is referred to as a ...

22. Where is an individual holding a Nigerian employment deemed to be resident?

23. What is a Nigerian pension?

24. State the rules for the determination of the residence of an individual who has no place of residence but has a pension as his only source of earned income arising in Nigeria on 1st January of a year of assessment.

25. Where is an individual deemed to be resident if he has no place of residence but derives income from a trade, business, profession or vocation in Nigeria?

26. Where is an individual deemed to be resident if he has one or more sources of unearned income but has no place of residence?

27. Where is a corporation sole or body of individuals deemed to be resident for a year of assessment?

28. What is the relevant tax authority of an individual?

29. State the relevant tax authority of an executor of the estate of a deceased person.

30. State the relevant tax authority of a trustee of a trust or settlement.

31. What is the relevant tax authority of a partnership?

32. What is the relevant tax authority of a village or other indigenous community?

33. The relevant tax authority of a member of the Nigerian Army is ...

34. The relevant tax authority of a company is the ...

35. Mrs Boma lives both in Aba, Abia State and Uyo, Akwa Ibom State and lectures in the University of Uyo. Determine her residence for the purpose of income tax and give reason to support your answer.

36. Mr Etete graduated from the University of Lagos in June 2014 and was employed with effect from August 2014 to work in the branch office of BB Ltd in Ghana. The head office of the company is located in Kano. Determine Mr Etete's residence and give reason to support your answer.

37. Mr Agama is an employee of the Centra Bank of Nigeria, Lagos. He lives in Mowe, Ogun State and travels daily to work in Lagos. Determine his residence and give reason for your answer.

38. Dr James returned to Nigeria on 1st May 2014 having been recruited in London to work for MBA plc in Nigeria. He started work in the company's branch office in Lagos on 10th May 2014 and was transferred to the head office in Calabar on 1st June 2014. Determine his residence for the purpose of his income tax assessment for 2014 and give reason to support your answer.

39. Carter is a native of Port Harcourt and an employee of SPDC, Warri. He proceeded on annual vacation on 15th December 2014 and was in his home town till 10th January, 2015 when he returned back to Warri. Determine his residence and give reason to support your answer.

40. Given that Corporal Dogo is a member of the Nigeria Police Force and has been living in the Police Barrack, Owerri, Imo State since 2001, determine his residence for the purpose of income tax and give reason to support your answer.

41. Mr Edem is a retired civil servant now residing in London. His only source of income in Nigeria is a pension payable jointly by the Cross River State and Akwa Ibom State Governments. Determine Mr Edem's residence for income tax purpose and give reason to support your answer.

42. On 1st January 2014, Mr Dele lived in Ibadan and during the year he earned profit from his business in Lagos and rent from his

property in Abeokuta. Determine his residence and give reason to support your answer.

43. Mr Tobi lived in Paris in 2014 and during the year he derived income from Nigeria as follows:
    (a) Rent from his property in Kaduna.
    (b) Pension from Ogun State Government.
    (c) Profit from his business situated in Benin.
    (d) Dividend from a company based in Lagos.

    Determine his residence for income tax purpose and give reason to support your answer.

44. Given that Oku Iboku community, which is located in Akwa Ibom State, has a rubber plantation and during the year 2014 the community received ₦1 million from Delta Rubber Ltd, Sapele, Delta State for supplies made to the company, determine the community's residence for income tax purpose.

45. Mr Sani started to live in Kaduna on 1st April, 2014 when he was employed by NNPC. Prior to that date, he was unemployed and was living in Lagos. Determine his residence and give reason to support your answer.

46. When there is a dispute over an individual's territory of residence, the facts of the dispute may be referred to the Joint Tax Board. The JTB's determination of residence shall be binding on the affected parties. An appeal against the JTB's decision can be made to ...

8 Employment Income and Pay As You Earn

Part I Multiple-Choice Questions

1. An individual would normally be considered to be self-employed if
   A. he owns his own business.
   B. he provides the materials, equipment and machinery necessary for the job.
   C. he can provide the same services to more than one person or business at the same time.
   D. there is a master/servant or employer/employee relationship.
   E. he controls the hours of work in fulfilling the job obligation.
   Which of the options A to E is not correct?

2. An individual under a contract of service is referred to as
   A. an independent contractor.
   B. a partner.
   C. an itinerant worker.
   D. an employee.
   E. a self-employed individual.

3. An individual is said to be an employee if
   A. he is paid regular wage and salary.
   B. he has fixed hours of work.
   C. he provides his services exclusively to one employer.
   D. his employer has control over him.
   E. he owns the tools and equipment used for his employment.
   Which of the options A to E is not correct.

4. Employment income is assessable to tax on
   A. receipt basis.
   B. cash basis.
   C. current year basis.

D. preceding year basis.
E. prepayment basis.

5. Which of the following is/are true?
   i. Salaries taxable in a year of assessment are those actually received within the year.
   ii. Allowances payable at intervals exceeding one month are taxable in the year of assessment in which they are received.
   iii. Salaries taxable in a year of assessment are those earned within the year and not necessarily those received within the year.
   iv. Salaries and allowances are taxable in accordance with the accounting date of the employer.
   A. ii and iii only
   B. i and ii only
   C. iii and iv only
   D. i and iii only
   E. iii and iv only

6. All the following are non-taxable benefits in the hands of employees except ...
   A. reimbursement of employee's medical expenses.
   B. luncheon vouchers for employees.
   C. removal expenses arising from change of employee's residence.
   D. utility bills paid by an employer on behalf of employees.
   E. cost of passage to and from Nigeria incurred by employees.

7. Which of the following is/are completely exempted from income tax under PITA?
   i. Compensation for loss of employment
   ii. Gratuity
   iii. Retirement benefits from the contributory pension scheme
   iv. Meal subsidy
   A. i only
   B. ii only
   C. i, ii and iii only

D. iii and iv only
E. i and iv only

8. Which of the following benefits in kind provided by an employer to his employees is not taxable?
A. Living accommodation
B. Uniform or protective clothing
C. Company car
D. Domestic servants
E. Furniture in living accommodation

9. Consolidated relief allowance is deducted from the assessable employment income to arrived at ...
A. total income.
B. chargeable income.
C. adjusted income.
D. total free pay.
E. benefits in kind.

10. Which of the following is/are statutory deduction(s) from employees' emoluments?
i. Pension fund contribution
ii. PAYE
iii. National Housing Fund contribution
iv. Trade union dues
A. i, ii, and iii only
B. ii and iii only
C. ii only
D. iii only
E. ii and iv only

11. The current rate of minimum tax payable by employees is
A. 1% of total income.
B. 0.5% of basic salary.
C. 1.5% of total income.
D. 0.5% of total income.
E. 10% of total income.

12. A minimum tax is payable by an individual whose total income does not exceed ...
    A. ₦20,000 per annum.
    B. ₦50,000 per annum.
    C. ₦60,000 per annum.
    D. ₦10,000 per annum.
    E. ₦30,000 per annum.

13. An employee is required to contribute ... per cent of his monthly basic salary to the National Housing Fund.
    A. 2%
    B. 2.5%
    C. 5%
    D. 7.5%
    E. 10%

14. Employees usually pay their income tax through the .... system.
    A. self assessment
    B. direct assessment
    C. back duty
    D. PAYE
    E. VAT

15. A tax deduction card contains all the following particulars except
    A. the cumulative net emoluments.
    B. the cumulative free emoluments.
    C. the cumulative taxable emoluments.
    D. the tax receipt number.
    E. the cumulative tax.

16. Which of the following is usually issued to an employee at the end of the year as evidence of tax payment?
    A. Tax table
    B. Pay slip
    C. Notice of coding

D. Tax deduction card
E. Tax receipt

17. PAYE tax deductions are to be remitted to the relevant tax authority within
A. thirty days of the end of each month.
B. fifteen days of the end of each month.
C. seven days of the end of each month.
D. sixty days of the end of each month.
E. ten days of the end of each month.

18. The time limit for rendering annual returns in respect of PAYE to the relevant tax authority by an employer is
A. thirty days after the end of each year.
B. fourteen days after the end of each year.
C. seven days after the end of each year.
D. sixty days after the end of each year.
E. ninety days after the end of each year.

19. What is the income assessable to tax in 2014 based on the following information?

	₦
Salary for 2013	500,000
Salary for 2014	600,000
Bonus for 2013 paid in January 2014	41,666
Bonus for 2014 paid in November 2014	50,000
Bonus for 2012 paid in July 2013	35,000

A. ₦600,000
B. ₦650,000
C. ₦691,666
D. ₦1,221,000
E. ₦541,666

20. Mazi Okonkwo is an employee of Obi Limited with gross emoluments of ₦3,600,000 per annum. What is his consolidated relief allowance for 2014?

A. ₦725,000
B. ₦920,000
C. ₦200,000
D. ₦720,000
E. ₦756,000

21. Miss Ifeoma is an employee of Union Bank Limited with gross emoluments of ₦30,000,000 per annum. What is her consolidated relief allowance for 2014 year of assessment?
A. ₦6,200,000
B. ₦6,005,000
C. ₦300,000
D. ₦6,000,000
E. ₦6,300,000

22. The gross income of Mr Aki is ₦300,000. His consolidated relief allowance, NHF contribution and pension fund contribution are ₦260,000, ₦2,500 and ₦22,500 respectively. What is his income tax liability for 2014.
A. ₦1,050
B. ₦3,000
C. Nil
D. ₦1,500
E. ₦750

23. Which of the following tax authorities cannot collect PAYE?
i. Federal Capital Territory Internal Revenue Service
ii. Local Government Revenue Committee
iii. Federal Inland Revenue Service
iv. State Internal Revenue Service
A. ii and iii only
B. i, ii and iii only
C. i and iii only
D. iii only
E. ii only

24. Alhaji Doko is a Police Officer. He has his personal house in Aba, Abia State but lives in the Police Barrack, Owerri, Imo State. To which tax authority should his employer remit his PAYE tax deductions?
    A. Federal Capital Territory Internal Revenue Service
    B. Abia State Internal Revenue Service
    C. Imo State Internal Revenue Service
    D. Federal Inland Revenue Service
    E. Joint State Revenue Committee

25. Mallam Bello is a native of Kaduna. He lives at No. 2 Oku Iboku Street, Abuja and works in NECO office, Abuja. The head office of NECO is in Minna, Niger State. To which tax authority should NECO remit Mallam Bello's PAYE tax deductions?
    A. Federal Capital Territory Internal Revenue Service
    B. Kaduna State Internal Revenue Service
    C. Niger State Internal Revenue Service
    D. Federal Inland Revenue Service
    E. Joint State Revenue Committee

26. One of the following is not an employment income and that is ...
    A. transport allowance.
    B. housing allowance.
    C. meal allowance.
    D. basic salary.
    E. annuity.

27. When tax exempt deductions and consolidated relief allowance are granted in accordance with the Personal Income Tax Act, the balance of income above ₦3,200,000 is taxable at the rate of...
    A. 24%.
    B. 21%.
    C. 30%.
    D. 20%.
    E. 19%.

28. Ignoring minimum tax of 1% of gross income, what is the lowest rate of personal income tax in Nigeria?
    A. 7%
    B. 5%
    C. 0.5%
    D. 11%
    E. 15%

29. For the purpose of making contributions to the national pension scheme, the Pension Reform Act, 2014 defines employee's monthly emoluments to include his ...
    A. basic salary plus all the allowances payable in cash.
    B. basic salary plus all the allowances except meal subsidy.
    C. basic salary plus all the allowances except utility allowance.
    D. basic salary plus all the allowances except medical allowance.
    E. basic salary, housing allowance and transport allowance.

30. The Pension Reform Act, 2014 makes provisions for a uniform contributory pension scheme for both the public and private sectors in Nigeria. The minimum rates of contribution to be made by the employer and the employee as prescribed in the Pension Reform Act, 2014 are ...
    A. 20% and 8% of the employee's monthly emoluments to be contributed by the employer and the employee respectively.
    B. 7.5% and 7.5% of the employee's monthly emoluments to be contributed by the employer and the employee respectively.
    C. 15% and 8% of the employee's monthly emoluments to be contributed by the employer and the employee respectively.
    D. 8% and 8% of the employee's monthly emoluments to be contributed by the employer and the employee respectively.
    E. 10% and 8% of the employee's monthly emoluments to be contributed by the employer and the employee respectively.

31. If an employer takes full responsibility for making contribution to the uniform contributory pension scheme on behalf of its

employees, what is the minimum rate of contribution to be made by the employer as prescribed in the Pension Reform Act, 2014?

A. 10% of each employee's monthly emoluments
B. 18% of each employee's monthly emoluments
C. 15% of each employee's monthly emoluments
D. 7.5% of each employee's monthly emoluments
E. 20% of each employee's monthly emoluments

32. The following are taxable benefits in kind except …

A. living accommodation provided by an employer for an employee's use.
B assets rented by an employer for an employee's use.
C utility bills paid by an employer for the benefit of an employee.
D. employee's medical bills paid by an employer.
E. wages of domestic servants paid by an employer for the benefit of an employee.

33. What is the method of calculating taxable benefit in kind where an employer's asset is provided for an employee's use?

A. 10% of the cost of the asset is taxable in the employee's hands.
B. 15% of the cost of the asset is taxable in the employee's hands.
C. 5% of the cost of the asset is taxable in the employee's hands.
D. 1% of the cost of the asset is taxable in the employee's hands.
E. 2% of the cost of the asset is taxable in the employee's hands.

34. Minimum tax is payable by an individual if …

i his total income is not more than ₦30,000 per annum.
ii. the tax payable on the chargeable income is less than 1% of his total income.
iii. the individual has no chargeable income.
iv. his employment income is being owed by his employer.

A. i only.
B. i and ii only
C. i, ii and iv only

D. ii and iii only
E. i, ii and iii only

Which of the options A to E is correct?

35. An employee is not required to file a tax return if his employment income does not exceed …

A. ₦30,000 per annum.
B. ₦50,000 per annum.
C. ₦100,000 per annum.
D. ₦300,000 per annum.
E. ₦150,000 per annum.

36. The gain or profit from an employment is deemed to be derived from Nigeria if the duties of the employment are wholly or partly performed in Nigeria except …

i. the duties are performed on behalf of an employer who is in a country other than Nigeria.
ii. the employee is not in Nigeria for a period or periods amounting to 183 days or more in any twelve month period.
iii. the remuneration of the employee is liable to tax in that other country under the provisions of the avoidance of double taxation treaty with that other country.
iv. the employee is not a citizen of Nigeria.

A. i, ii and iii only.
B. i and ii only
C. i, ii and iv only
D. ii and iii only
E. all of the above

Which of the options A to E is correct?

37. The responsibilities of an employer in respect of PAYE include all the following except ...

A. to bring proceedings against any employee who refuses to join the PAYE scheme.
B. to register with the relevant tax authority for the operation of the PAYE scheme.
C. to remit to the relevant tax authority the tax deducted from his employees' emoluments.

D. to render annual returns in the prescribed form to the relevant tax authority.

E. to produce for inspection at his premises all the documents/records relating to employees' emoluments and PAYE deductions.

38. The time allowed for an employer to register for PAYE scheme with the relevant tax authority is …

A. within six years of commencing a business.
B. within three months of commencing a business.
C. within one month of commencing a business.
D. within sixty days of commencing a business.
E. within six months of commencing a business.

39. Under the Personal Income Tax Act, tax exempt deductions in the computation of an individual's income tax from employment income include all the following except …

A. contribution to National Housing Fund.
B. contribution to Industrial Training Fund.
C. contribution to National Pension Scheme.
D. contribution to National Health Insurance Scheme.
E. life assurance premium.

40. An individual taxpayer is entitled to consolidated relief allowance (CRA). What is the current rate of CRA?

A. The lower of ₦200,000 and 1% of gross income plus 20% of gross income.
B. Ther higher of ₦200,000 and 1% of gross income plus 20% of gross income.
C. ₦200,000 or 10% of gross income whichever is higher plus 20% of gross income.
D. ₦200,000 or 10% of gross income whichever is lower plus 20% of gross income.
E. The higher of ₦2,000,000 and 1% of gross income plus 20% of gross income.

41. What is the amount of contribution to be made by an employer to the Industrial Training Fund (ITF) in respect of each calendar year?

A. 1% of its/his total annual payroll
B. 10% of its/his total annual payroll
C. 5% of its/his total annual payroll
D. 7.5% of its/his total annual payroll
E. 2.5% of its/his total annual payroll

Use the information below to answer questions 42 to 44.

Mrs Yellow Sisi is an employee of Zobo Limited with the following salary structure:

(a)	Basic salary	-	₦10,000,000 per annum
(b)	Rent allowance	-	10% of annual basic salary
(c)	Transport allowance	-	₦200,000 per annum
(f)	Utility allowance	-	₦100,000 per annum

Mrs Yellow Sisi and her employer contribute 8% and 10% of her total emoluments (as defined in the Pension Reform Act, 2014) to an approved pension scheme respectively. She contributes 2.5% of her basic salary to the National Housing Fund and pays an annual premium of ₦200,000 on her life assurance policy.

42. What is Mrs Yellow Sisi's total contribution to pension fund in 2017 by herself and employer?
A. ₦2,034,000
B. ₦896,000
C. ₦2,460,000
D. ₦904,000
E. ₦2,016,000

43. The consolidated relief allowance and tax exempt deductions in 2017 amounted to ....
A. ₦4,926,000
B. ₦2,016,000
C. ₦2,460,000
D. ₦3,814,000
E. ₦3,806,000

44. What is Mrs Yellow Sisi's tax liability for 2017?
    A. ₦1,030,560
    B. ₦7,494,000
    C. ₦1,590,560
    D. ₦3,806,000
    E. ₦896,000

Part II Short-Answer Questions

45. Any appointment or office whether public or otherwise for which remuneration is payable is referred to as …

46. Give one difference between employment and self-employment

47. State the current rates of personal income tax.

48. Where an employee's emolument is given in a form other than cash, it is referred to as …

49. Give three examples of benefits in kind which are not taxable.

50. State the method of calculating taxable benefit in kind where a domestic servant is provided by ABC Ltd to its employee, Mr Soki.

51. State the method of calculating taxable benefits in kind where:
    (a) an asset is rented by an employer for an employee's use.
    (b) an employee's utility bills are paid by his employer.

52. A car is hired by a company for ₦300,000 per annum for its Chief Accountant. It would have cost the company ₦3,500,000 to buy the car. What is the assessable benefit in respect of the provision of the motor car?

53. Miss Susan is provided with a Toyota Carina by her company with effect from 1st January, 2014. The car cost ₦1,500,000 at acquisition some years ago but had a market value of ₦2,000,000 in 2014.

Required:

(a) Calculate the benefits, if any, assessable on Miss Susan in 2014.

(b) Assume that Miss Susan's company pays her ₦120,000 per annum as wages of her driver, what is the amount assessable in her hands in respect of the driver's wages.

54. XYZ Ltd rented a house for ₦300,000 which is occupied by its Personnel Manager, Mr Eso, who pays ₦60,000 rents per annum to the company. The annual rateable value of the house is ₦180,000. The company furnished the house at a cost of ₦480,000. What is Mr Eso's assessable benefits in respect of the provision of living accommodation and furniture?

55. A system of tax collection whereby employers are responsible for deducting income tax from the wages and salaries of their employees at the time of payment is referred to as …

56. The full meaning of the abbreviation PAYE is …

57. Where an employee leaves his employer to take up another employment, he will be issued with a transfer (or leaving) certificate. State three particulars that the certificate should contain.

58. What is the penalty stipulated in the Personal Income Tax Act for an employer who fails to make PAYE tax deduction or fails to account properly for the tax deducted?

59. Mr Okon's income is ₦734,200 per annum. If he is granted consolidated relief allowance of ₦346,840, compute his income tax liability. Ignore National Housing Fund and Pension Fund Contribution.

60. The allowance granted in the Personal Income Tax (Amendment) Act, 2011 to replace personal allowance, children allowance, dependent relative allowance, etc is known as …

9 Investment Income and Withholding Tax

Part I Multiple-Choice Questions

1. Which of the following is the relevant tax authority in Nigeria to which withholding tax should be remitted in respect of rent paid by a bank with head office in Abuja to Mr Koko who is resident in Ibadan in respect of his house situated in Lagos?
   - A. Federal Capital Territory Internal Revenue Service
   - B. Lagos State Internal Revenue Service
   - C. Oyo State Internal Revenue Service
   - D. Federal Inland Revenue Service
   - E. Joint Tax Board

2. XYZ Ltd situated in the Federal Capital Territory, Abuja made withholding tax deductions from payments made to the following:
   - i. BYC Plc located in Uyo, Akwa Ibom State
   - ii. Mate Ltd located in Abuja
   - iii. FOB Enterprises located in Abuja
   - iv. Eddie Bassey resident in the Republic of Ireland
   - v. Offiong Bassey & Co (Chartered Accountants), Abuja

   Which of the withholding tax deductions should be remitted to the Federal Inland Revenue Service?
   - A. All of the above stated withholding tax deductions
   - B. i, ii, iv and v only
   - C. i, ii, iii and v only
   - D. i and ii only
   - E. i, ii and iv only

3. King Guards Enterprises situated in the Federal Capital Territory, Abuja made withholding tax deductions from payments made to the following:

i. Kosoko Plc whose registered/head office is located in Abuja.
ii. Titi Enterprises located in Abuja of which the proprietor is resident in Abuja.
iii. Tete & Partners located in Abuja but the partners are resident in Ghana.
iv KYC Enterprises located in Abuja but the proprietor is resident in Lokoja.
v. KOB Consultants situated in Minna but the proprietors are resident in Abuja.

Which of the withholding tax deductions should be remitted to the Federal Capital Territory Internal Revenue Service?

A. i and ii only
B. i and v only
C. ii and v only
D. i, ii and v only
E. All of the above

4. The duty to deduct withholding tax from payments rests on those who make such payments (referred to as the payers). According to the Personal Income Tax Act, the payers include:
i. companies (corporate or unincorporated)
ii. government ministries and departments
iii. parastatals and statutory bodies
iv. other established organizations approved for the operation of PAYE system

A. iv only
B. i and iii only
C. ii and iii only
D. i, ii and iii only
E. All of the above

Which of the options A to E is correct?

5. The duty to deduct withholding tax from payments rests on those who make such payments (i.e. the payers). The other obligations of the payers include all the following except ...
A. assisting the persons who suffered the tax deductions to claim tax credit for the tax suffered at source.

B. remittance of the tax deducted to the relevant tax authorities or designated banks.

C. submission of withholding tax schedules to the relevant tax authorities.

D. collection of withholding tax credit notes or receipts from the relevant tax authorities in favour of each of the persons on the withholding tax schedules who suffered the tax deduction.

E. forwarding of the withholding tax credit notes or receipts collected from the relevant tax authorities to the persons who suffered the tax deduction.

6. Which of the following are not liable to withholding tax?

i. Insurance premium received by insurers

ii. Commission earned by insurance brokers

iii. Income earned by distributors or dealers from their trading activities

iv. Telephone bills

A. i and ii only

B. i and iv only

C. i, ii and iii only

D. i, ii and iv only

E. i, iii and iv only

7. Which of the following statement is not true?

A. Institutions exempted from payment of income tax are not authorised to deduct withholding tax at source from payments made by them.

B. The Revenue practice is that non-resident companies are not empowered to deduct any type of withholding tax.

C. Contracts and supplies of goods and services performed entirely outside Nigeria by non-resident persons are not liable to withholding tax.

D. Countries that have tax treaties with Nigeria are granted a reduced rate of withholding tax deduction.

E. The turnover/income earned by distributors or dealers from their trading activities (excluding commissions paid to them by their principals) are not liable to withholding tax.

8. Which of the following is not subject to tax on a preceding year basis?
   A. Rent
   B. Dividend
   C. Interest
   D. Royalty
   E. None of the above

9. Which of the following expenses is not allowed as a deduction in ascertaining the assessable rental income in connection with a building?
   A. Interest on loan used in acquiring the building.
   B. Remunerations of porters, cleaners and caretakers.
   C. Cost of advertising for new tenants.
   D. Extension of building.
   E. Cost of collecting rents.

10. All the following are disallowable expenses in ascertaining rental income for tax purposes except …
   A. capital expenditure.
   B. bad and doubtful debts.
   C. income tax.
   D. reserves.
   E. depreciation.

11. A landlord received rent in advance for a period of twenty years. For taxation purposes, the rent is deemed to accrue evenly over a period of … commencing from the date of payment.
   A. twenty years
   B. fifteen years
   C. ten years
   D. five years
   E. one year

12. Which of the following statements is not true of withholding tax?
    A. Withholding tax is an advance payment of income tax, but in some cases, it is a final tax.
    B. Withholding tax is not a separate type of tax.
    C. Agencies of government do not bear the burden of withholding tax.
    D. Withholding tax deduction is made by the recipient of the income.
    E. Withholding tax deduction is made when the affected income is paid or credited to the recipient.

13. Withholding taxes on individuals who are not deemed to be resident in the Federal Capital Territory are payable to the …
    A. Federal Inland Revenue Service.
    B. State Internal Revenue Service.
    C. Joint Tax Board.
    D. Local Government Revenue Committee.
    E. Joint State Revenue Committee.

14. Withholding taxes on companies are payable to the …
    A. Joint Tax Board.
    B. State Internal Revenue Service.
    C. Federal Inland Revenue Service.
    D. Joint State Revenue Committee.
    E. Local Government Revenue Committee.

15. Which of the following is not authorised to deduct withholding tax?
    A. Banks
    B. Government ministries
    C. Itinerant worker
    D. Universities
    E. Statutory bodies

16. Withholding taxes on the following individuals are payable to the Federal Inland Revenue Service except …
    A. residents of the Federal Capital Territory, Abuja.
    B. members of the Armed Forces.

C. members of the Nigeria Police Force.
D. officers of the Nigerian Foreign Affairs.
E. individuals resident outside Nigeria.

17. Withholding tax on … is a final tax.
A. professional fees
B. rent
C. director's fees
D. commission
E. dividend

18. Which of the following incomes is not subject to withholding tax?
A. Trading profit
B. Dividend
C. Interest
D. Royalty
E. Rent

19. Payments due in respect of all the following are subject to withholding tax except
A. contract of supplies through LPOs.
B. consultancy fees.
C. technical fees.
D. across-the-counter cash sales.
E. management fees.

20. Withholding tax is usually remitted to the tax office with a payment schedule containing all the following information except the …
A. gross amount of the payment subject to withholding tax.
B. names and addresses of those who suffered the tax deduction.
C. rate of any cash discount offered.
D. amount of withholding tax deducted.
E. nature of activities or services in respect of which payment/deduction was made.

21. According to the Personal Income Tax Act, withholding tax is to be remitted to the relevant tax authority within … from the date the tax was deducted or the date the duty to deduct arose.
    A. ten days
    B. sixty days
    C. thirty days
    D. seven days
    E. twenty-one days

22. According to the FIRS (Establishment) Act, withholding tax is to be remitted to the relevant tax authority within … from the date the tax was deducted or the date the duty to deduct arose.
    A. thirty days
    B. seven days
    C. ten days
    D. twenty-one days
    E. sixty days

23. Under the Companies Income Tax Act, withholding tax is to be remitted to the FIRS within … from the date the tax was deducted or the date the duty to deduct arose.
    A. ten days
    B. sixty days
    C. thirty days
    D. seven days
    E. twenty-one days

24. Based on the provisions of the Companies Income Tax Act, what is the deadline for the remittance of withholding tax deductions made by TYC Ltd from various payments made to other companies in September 2018?
    A. 30/9/18
    B. 31/10/18
    C. 30/10/18
    D. 31/12/18
    E. 21/10/18

25. The current rate of withholding tax on dividend is
    A. 5%.
    B. 15%.
    C. 10%.
    D. 12½ %.
    E. 20%.

26. The current rate of withholding tax on contract of supplies is
    A. 5%.
    B. 10%.
    C. 15%.
    D. 12½ %.
    E. 20%.

27. Which of the following is not an advantage of withholding tax to the government?
    A. It reduces the incidence of tax evasion.
    B. It reduces the cost of tax collection.
    C. It generates more revenue to the government.
    D. It helps to reduce the time and manpower required by the tax authorities for tax collection.
    E. It creates the incidence of double taxation.

28. Which of the following is not a problem militating against withholding tax system of tax collection?
    A. Failure of some organisations to deduct withholding tax at the time of payment.
    B. Failure of some organisations to remit the taxes withheld to the relevant tax authorities.
    C. Remittance of taxes withheld to the wrong tax authorities.
    D. Withholding tax receipts (credit notes) are sometimes not despatched to those who suffered the tax deduction.
    E. Adverse effect of double taxation.

29. Chief Makama owns a property located at Goodluck Street, Lagos. During the year ended 31st December 2014, he declared his net

rental income as ₦429,000 which was computed as follows:

		₦
Rent received (gross)		600,000
Less expenses:		
Water rates (including ₦1,000 for the landlord's flat)	6,000	
Tenement rates	25,000	
Depreciation	50,000	
Repairs	15,000	
Construction of fence	75,000	171,000
Net rent		429,000

What is the amount of rental income on which the landlord should be assessed to tax in 2015 year of assessment?

A. ₦480,000
B. ₦555,000
C. ₦554,000
D. ₦504,000
E. ₦430,000

30. OBJ Ltd proposes to pay a dividend of ₦2,000,000 to its shareholders for the year ended 31st December, 2014. The total profits for the same year amounted to ₦500,000. What is the company's income tax liability?

A. ₦150,000
B. ₦600,000
C. ₦450,000
D. ₦750,000
E. ₦200,000

31. Who is authorized to make regulations for the carrying out of the provisions of CITA relating to deduction of tax at source?

A. The Senate
B. The President
C. The FIRS Board
D. The President on the advice of the FIRS
E. The Minister of Finance on the advice of the FIRS

32. Under the Companies Income Tax Act, the current rate of withholding tax on all aspects of building, construction and related activities is …
    A. 15%.
    B. 12.5%.
    C. 10%.
    D. 5%.
    E. 2.5%.

33. The allowable expenses in computing net rental income of a building for tax purposes include all the following except …..
    A. installation of electric poles.
    B. repairs and maintenance of building.
    C. fire insurance premium.
    D. tenement rates.
    E. agent's commission.

34. The withholding tax deducted from payments made to a company is to be set off against the tax charged on such company by an assessment. If the withholding tax credit exceeds the tax assessment for a given year, the excess is to be refunded to the company by the FIRS within .... of the assessment if duly filed with the option to carry forward and set off against future taxes.
    A. sixty days
    B. thirty days
    C. seven days
    D. ninety days
    E. twenty-one days

35. According to the Companies Income Tax Act, the conditions under which interest on loans for agricultural trade or business may be exempted from companies income tax include ...
    i. At least 50% of the agricultural products must be exported.
    ii. The loan must have been granted on or after 1st January, 1997 to a company engaged in agricultural trade or business.
    iii. The moratorium must not be less than 18 months.

iv. The rate of interest on the loan must not be more than the base lending rate at the time the loan was granted.

A. i, iii and iv only
B. ii, iii and iv only
A. iii and iv only
D. i and iv only
E. All the above.

Which of the options A to E is correct?

36. The conditions under which interest on loans for manufacturing goods for export may be exempted from companies income tax are ..

i. The loan must have been granted on or after 1st April, 1980 for the purpose of manufacturing goods for export.
ii. At least 50% of the manufactured goods must be exported.
iii. Not less than 75% of the export proceeds are repatriated to Nigeria through government approved channels.
iv. At least 25% of the raw materials must be sourced from Nigeria.

B. i, ii and iii only
B. ii, iii and iv only
A. iii and iv only
D. i and iv only
E. All the above.

Which of the options A to E is correct?

37. The information to be stated in the directive given by the FIRS to a company that certain undistributed profits of the company should be treated as having been distributed include all the following except ..

A. the day to be taken for the purpose of the distribution.
B. the names of shareholders who should benefit from the undistributed profits.
C. the net amount of those profits so deemed to be distributed.
D. the rate of withholding tax deemed to be deducted.
E. the gross amount which after deducting withholding tax at the said rate leaves such net amount of those profits..

Part II Short-Answer Questions

38. A landlady received ₦3,000,000 as rent for fifteen years commencing from 1st July 2000. State his assessable income for the relevant years of assessment.

39. Nze Ego's building was rented by Rock Insurance Limited. The company paid rent of ₦594,000 net of withholding tax to its landlord for the year ended 31st December 2014. The landlord paid tenement rate of ₦25,000 in 2014. State Nze Ego's assessable rental income and the relevant year of assessment?

40. State the current rates of withholding tax on the following:
    (a) Interest
    (b) Director's fees
    (c) Consultancy services

41. What is the penalty under PITA for non-deduction or non-remittance of withholding tax to the relevant tax authority?

42. What is the penalty under CITA for non-deduction or non-remittance of withholding tax to the relevant tax authority?

43. Dividend, interest, rent or royalty derived from abroad are exempted from withholding tax provided they are brought into Nigeria through

44. When a taxpayer's liability is computed, credit is given for the withholding tax deducted at source on the presentation of the ...

45. Dividend received by a company after the deduction of withholding tax at source by the paying company is referred to as ...

46. What is the treatment of dividend which has suffered withholding tax deduction at source in the computation of the income tax liability of the company receiving the dividend?

47. Consolidated Breweries Plc paid dividends net of withholding tax to its shareholders on 31st March 2005 as follows:

	₦
B. Giwa	270,000
A. Adio	117,000
Emeka Esu	81,900

What is the income that each shareholder should show in his income tax returns?

48. Who is responsible for the administration of withholding tax?

49. Give three examples of non-investment income from which withholding tax is deductible at source and state their current rates of withholding tax.

50. How is rent defined in the Companies Income Tax Act?

51. In relation to CITA, when is interest deemed to be derived from Nigeria?

52. What is a foreign loan?

53. State the information that a bank is required to disclose to the FIRS in respect of an agricultural loan granted to a company.

54. What is the meaning of agricultural trade or business?

55. State any two conditions under which interest on foreign loans may be exempted from companies income tax.

56. What is dividend?

57. In relation to PITA, when is a dividend deemed to arise?

58. A Nigerian company under the control of not more than five persons may be referred to as a …

59. Under what circumstances can the FIRS direct that certain undistributed profits of a company be treated as having been distributed as dividend and taxed accordingly?

60. What is the time limit within which the FIRS can direct that certain undistributed profits of a company be treated as having been distributed?

61. Anas Limited received ₦2,280,000 during the year ended 31st December, 2009 for various supplies to companies and government through local purchase orders. The company also collected rents of ₦1,800,000 during the same year from properties let out to companies and government. All the payments were made to Anas Limited after the deduction of withholding tax. What is the total amount of withholding taxes suffered by Anas Limited during the year?

10 Ascertainment of Profits

Part I Multiple-Choice Questions

1. Receipts which are derived from the normal activities of a business, for example, receipts from sales of goods and services, rents, dividends, interests are referred to as …
   A. winfall.
   B. cash receipts.
   C. sales proceeds.
   D. capital receipts.
   E. revenue receipts.

2. Receipts which are not derived from the normal trading activities of a business, for example, receipts from the disposal of fixed assets are referred to as …
   A. winfall.
   B. cash receipts.
   C. sales proceeds.
   D. capital receipts.
   E. revenue receipts.

3. Which of the following is not included in the "badges of trade" which could be used to decide whether or not a given activity constitutes trading?
   A. Subject matter of the transaction
   B. Frequency or number of similar transactions by the same person
   C. Supplementary work on or in connection with the property realized
   D. Motive
   E. Cost/benefit analysis

4. The four conditions mentioned in PITA and CITA that an expense must fulfill before it can be treated as allowable deduction in computing assessable profit include all the following except ...
   A. exclusively.
   B. necessarily.
   C. reasonably.
   D. accountability.
   E. wholly.

5. Premium paid to an approved retirement benefit fund by a self-employed individual is an allowable deduction up to a maximum of
   A. 100% of his total income.
   B. 50% of his total income.
   C. 20% of his total income.
   D. 10% of his total income.
   E. 5% of his total income.

6. Which of the following expenses is allowable in computing the assessable profit of a company?
   A. Repair and maintenance costs
   B. Share issue expenses
   C. Fines and penalties
   D. Cost of tax appeals
   E. Preliminary expenses

7. All the following expenses are disallowable in computing the assessable profit of a business except
   A. income tax.
   B. depreciation.
   C. improvements to building.
   D. subscriptions to trade associations.
   E. proprietor's drawings.

8. All the following expenses are disallowable in computing the assessable profit of a business except
   A. loss on sale of fixed asset.
   B. profit transferred to reserves.

C. expenditure or losses recoverable under an insurance policy.
D. renewal of short lease.
E. defalcation perpetrated by a management staff (e.g. director).

9. Which of the following are allowable expenses in computing the assessable profit of a business?
   i. Trade debts written off
   ii. General provision for bad debts
   iii. Specific provision for bad debts
   iv. Staff debts written off
   A. i and iii only
   B. i and iv only
   C. i, iii and iv only
   D. i, ii and iv only
   E. iii and iv only

10. The FIRS may not allow deduction for bad or doubtful debts where
    A. the debts are of capital rather than revenue nature.
    B. the company has not made sufficient attempts to recover the debts.
    C. specific provision is made for each debt considered to be doubtful.
    D. it is not the customary practice to incur such debts in that kind of business.
    E. the debts were as a result of abuse of office.
    Which of the options A to E is not correct?

11. The FIRS may likely consider an irrecoverable debt to be an allowable deduction in computing the tax adjusted profit of a company where …
    A. the debt has become statute-barred
    B. the debtor has gone bankrupt or has been liquidated and the available assets cannot meet the debt.
    C. the debtor is dead and his estate is insolvent.

D. the debt was as a result of insider dealings.
E. the company has taken reasonable steps to recover the debt but without success.

12. Which one of the following bad debts is the FIRS likely to allow as a deduction in computing the adjusted profits of the affected companies?
    A. Some advances granted by TYC Ltd, a dealer in groundnuts, palm kernel, etc to produce buying agents.
    B. A loan granted by ABT Ltd (which is not a bank) to its subsidiary that latter went into liquidation.
    C. A loan granted by ABC Bank plc to its managing director's company, OBT Ltd, without collateral security.
    D. XYZ Ltd's provision for doubtful debts calaculated as a percentage of total debtors at the end of the accounting period.
    E. MON Ltd, a manufacturing company, sold one of its motor vehicles on credit. Part of the sales proceed could not not be recovered.

13. All the following expenses are allowable in computing the assessable profit of a business except …
    A. hire purchase interest.
    B. rent of business premises.
    C. renewal of a long lease.
    D. research expenses.
    E. contribution to approved pension fund.

14. Which of the following items of expenditure would be disallowed when computing the assessable profit of Zion Clinic owned by Dr Daniel?
    A. Course fees for training of the hospital personnel on the use of medical equipment.
    B. Legal expenses charged by the hospital's lawyer for defending a charge of negligence brought against the hospital by a patient.
    C. Salaries of Dr Daniel's wife who is a nurse in the hospital.

D. Hospital canteen expenses.
E. Cost of beds and television sets acquired for the hospital.

15. All the following expenses are allowable deductions in computing the assessable profits of Wellness Hospital plc except …
A. cost of medical journals.
B. repairs and maintenance of ambulance.
C. subscriptions to Nigerian Medical Association.
D. cost of installation of a new medical equipment.
E. medical bills of a patient written off as bad debts on the death of the patient.

16. Which one of the following items of expenditure will Barrister Opobo, a legal practitioner, be allowed to deduct in computing the adjusted profit of his firm for tax purposes?
A. Ransom paid to kidnappers to secure his release.
B. Payment to a Judge to fast track court judgment.
C. Travelling expenses incurred between his home and his chamber.
D. Political subscriptions.
E. Travelling expenses incurred between his chamber and court.

17. Which one of the following is an allowable expense in calculating the adjusted profit of a transport company for tax purposes?
A. Cost of putting a newly acquired second-hand vehicle into roadworthy condition.
B. VAT on motor vehicles acquired for the transport business.
C. Bribes to law enforcement officers on highways.
D. Fines for traffic offences committed by reckless drivers.
E. Cost of provision of uniforms to drivers.

18. One of the following is not an allowable expense in determining the assessable profit of a transport company and that is …
A. renewal of vehicles' particulars.
B. hire purchase interests on vehicles acquired on hire purchase.

C. cost of advertising an old car for sale.
D. motor park levies.
E. theft of cash by cashier selling bus tickets.

19. Which of the Schedules to CITA contains a list of funds, bodies and institutions in Nigeria to which donations may be made?
A. Fifth Schedule
B. Fourth Schedule
C. Third Schedule
D. Second Schedule
E. First Schedule

20. What is the maximum amount of donations allowable as deductions in ascertaining the profits of a company for any year of assessment?
A. 10% of the company's assessable profits for that year before charging the donations.
B. 10% of the company's total profits for that year before charging the donations.
C. 10% of the company's total profits for that year after charging the donations.
D. 15% of the company's total profits for that year before charging the donations.
E. 20% of the company's assessable profits for that year before charging the donations.

21. Donations are allowable as deductions in ascertaining the profits of a company if the following conditions are met:
A. Donations must be made out of the profits of the company.
B. Donations must not include payments made by a company for valuable considerations.
C. Donations are made to public funds, statutory bodies and institutions, ecclesiastical, charitable, benevolent, educational and scientific institutions established in Nigeria, which are specified in CITA.
D. Donations shall include any outgoings and expenses which are allowable as deductions in ascertaining the profits of a company.

E. Donations must not be expenditure of a capital nature except they are made to universities and other tertiary or research institutions.

22. Which of the following legal expenses is not allowable in computing the assessable profit of a company?
A. Legal expenses for recovery of trade debts.
B. Renewal of short lease.
C. Legal expenses for retention of the services of the company's lawyer.
D. Legal cost of a tax appeal.
E. Defending an action for breach of contracts and for damages arising from the normal business of the company.

23. Donations made to the following organisations and institutions by a company are allowed as deductions for tax purposes except…
A. the Nigeria Red Cross.
B. the Girls Guide of Nigeria.
C. the Nigeria Museum.
D. National Sports Commission.
E. the People's Club of Nigeria.

24. All the following are allowable donations in ascertaining a company's profits except donations made to …
A. ICAN Building Fund.
B. Nigeria Accounting Standard Board.
C. University Teaching Hospitals.
D. The Cocoa Research Institute of Nigeria.
E. private universities.

25. What is the maximum amount of rent for residential accommodation occupied by a company's employee which is allowable as deduction in computing the company's profits?
A. Maximum of ₦150,000 per annum.
B. 100% of the employee's basic salary.
C. The actual rent for the period or 100% of the employee's basic salary, whichever is higher.

D. The actual rent for the period or 150% of the employee's basic salary, whichever is lower.

E. The actual rent for the period or 100% of the employee's basic salary, whichever is lower.

26. Included in a company's profit and loss account for the year ended 31st December, 2005 is ₦1,000,000 for rent of five bungalows for residential accommodation of five managers of the company. Rent paid for each bungalow is ₦200,000 per annum. Each manager's remunerations include ₦100,000 basic salary plus ₦50,000 allowances per annum. What is the maximum rent allowable in computing the company's assessable profit under CITA?

A. ₦1,000,000
B. ₦200,000
C. ₦500,000
D. ₦750,000
E. ₦250,000

27. Pre-operational levy is a tax payable by a company which has not commenced business after a least …

A. 3 months since its incorporation.
B. 6 months since its incorporation.
C. 9 months since its incorporation.
D. 12 months since its incorporation.
E. 18 months since its incorporation.

28. The current rate of income tax levied on companies is …

A. 35% of total profits.
B. 40% of total profits.
C. 30% of total profits.
D. 30% of assessable profits.
E. 30% of adjusted profits.

29. What is the current rate of income tax payable by small companies earning annual turnover of less than ₦1 million and engaged in the types of business specified in CITA?

A. 30% of total profits
B. 0.5% of gross profits
C. 20% of total profits
D. 10% of assessable profits
E. 20% of assessable profits

30. Under which of the following circumstances is a company chargeable to a minimum tax in any year of assessment?
i. Where the ascertainment of total assessable profits from all sources of a company results in a loss.
ii. Where the ascertainment of total assessable profits from all sources of a company results in no tax payable.
iii. Where the ascertainment of total assessable profits from all sources of a company results in a tax payable which is less than the minimum tax.
iv. Where the true amount of the total assessable profits of a company cannot be readily ascertained.
A. i, ii and iv only
B. ii, iii and iv only
C. i, ii and iii only
D. i, iii and iv only
E. iii and iv only

31. All the following formulae are used in the computation of a company's minimum tax except …
A. 20 per cent of assessable profits.
B. 0.5 per cent of gross profits.
C. 0.5 per cent of net assets.
D. 0.25 per cent of paid-up capital.
E. 0.25 per cent of turnover of the company for the year.

32. The amount of reserve made out of profits by a company for research and development is allowed as a deduction in computing a company's assessable profit. What is the maximum amount of reserve for R & D allowable for any year of assessment?
A. 10% of the company's total profits for that year before any deduction is made for the reserve and donations.

B. 20% of the company's qualifying capital expenditure on research and development during the year.
C. 15% of the company's total profits for that year.
D. 25% of the tax payable in the year of assessment.
E. 10% of the company's total profits for that year before any deduction is made for donations.

33. Companies exempted from the payment of minimum tax include ...
i. a company carrying on agricultural trade or business.
ii. a company with at least 25% imported equity capital.
iii. any company that has incurred a loss in its trade or business in any year of assessment.
iv. any company in the first four calendar years of its commencement of business.
A. i and iii only
B. i, ii and iii only
C. ii, iii and iv only
D. i, ii and iv only
E. i, iii and iv only

34. Where a company has not commenced business after at least six months since its incorporation, it shall for each year it obtains a tax clearance certificate pay ...
A. a levy of 0.125% of turnover in excess of ₦500,000.
B. 20% of its total profits up to a maximum of five years of assessment.
C. a minimum tax at the rates specified in the Companies Income Tax Act.
D. a levy of ₦20,000 for the first year and ₦25,000 for every subsequent year.
E. a levy of ₦500 for the first year and ₦400 for every subsequent year.

35. Income tax may be assessed and charged on the turnover of a business if ....

i. the trade or business produces no assessable profits.
ii. the trade or business produces assessable profits which are less than what might be expected to arise from that trade or business.
iii. the true amount of the assessable profits of the business cannot be readily ascertained.
iv. the business exercises the option of being taxed on turnover instead of total profits at commencement of business.

A. i or ii only
B. i or iii only
C. ii or iii only
D. i or ii or iii only
E. ii or iii or iv only

36. A company can qualify for income tax assessment at a concessional tax rate of 20% of total profits instead of 30% if it is engaged in any of the following businesses except …

A. manufacturing.
B. agricultural production.
C. mining of solid minerals.
D. wholly export trade.
E. refining of crude oil.

37. A small company which engages in the business activities specified in the Companies Income Tax Act can pay small business rate of tax of 20% provided that its total gross sales (turnover) is …

A. more than ₦1,000,000 in each year.
B. less than ₦10,000,000 in each year.
C. less than ₦1,000,000 in each year.
D. more than ₦10,000,000 in each year.
E. less than ₦10,000,000 in each year.

38. An amount that can be set off against a taxpayer's tax liability is referred to as …

A. tax deferral.
B. tax debit.
C. tax adjudication.

D. tax credit.
E. tax concession.

39. Miss Shakara owns a boutique. The following deductions were included in her statement of profit or loss for the year ended 31/12/2017.
    i. ₦150,000 cost of acquisition of air-conditioner for her shop.
    ii. ₦40,000 cost of redecorating her shop.
    iii ₦500,000 cost of renovation of a newly acquired second-hand building which had to be refurbished before it could be put to use.
    iv. ₦20,000 subscriptions to Boutique Owners Association.
    v. ₦300,000 cost of generator.

    How much should be added back to the net profit when computing the adjusted profit for tax purposes?
    A. ₦1,010,000
    B. ₦990,000
    C. ₦970,000
    D. ₦950,000
    E. ₦450,000

40. Mrs Paloma has been in business for many years. During the year ended 31/12/2017 she withdrew goods costing ₦100,000 from the business for her own personal use. If she had sold the goods to a customer she would have sold at cost plus 10 per cent. What adjustment would you make to the net profit shown in the statement of profit or loss when computing her adjusted profit for tax purposes if she paid nothing for the goods?
    A. Add ₦100,000 to the net profit.
    B. Add ₦110,000 to the net profit.
    C. Add ₦10,000 to the net profit.
    D. No adjustment is required.
    E. Subtract ₦10,000 from the net profit.

41. Etim's income statement for the year ended 30/6/2017 included wages of ₦2,400,000 which comprised: Etim's drawings of ₦10,000 per week, his wife's wages of ₦40,000 per month (who

works full-time for the business) and his son's wages of ₦30,000 per quarter (a student who does not work for the business). What adjustment should be made to the net profit shown in the income statement when computing his adjusted profit for tax purposes?

A. Subtract ₦640,000 from the net profit
B. Add ₦1,000,000 to the net profit
C. Add ₦1,120,000 to the net profit
D. Add ₦600,000 to the net profit
E. Add ₦640,000 to the net profit

42. Okoro is a sole trader. Motor expenses included in his income statement for the year ended 31st March, 2018 are as follows:

		₦
i.	Fuel and oil	416,000
ii.	Vehicle license and insurance	15,000
iii.	Vehicle repairs	120,000
iv.	Loss on disposal of vehicle	50,000
v.	Fine for over-speeding by Okoro	25,000
vi.	Depreciation	100,000

It had been agreed with the tax authority that one-fifth of the motor vehicle expenses relate to private use.

How much must be added to the net profit figure when calculating the adjusted profit?

A. Add N285,200 to the net profit
B. Add N175,000 to the net profit
C. Add N110,200 to the net profit
D. Add N615,800 to the net profit
E. Add N440,800 to the net profit

43. Saleko has been in business for many years. His statement of profit or loss for the year ended included a deduction of 30th September, 2017 for repairs and renewals. These comprised:

	₦
Repainting of factory building	35,000
Extension of office building	115,000
Installation of new machine	108,000
Redecoration of retail shop	40,000

Construction of septic tank for office	230,000
Cleaning expenses	120,000

What are the repairs and renewals allowable for the year ended 30th September, 2017 in computing the adjusted profit for tax purposes?

A. ₦195,000
B. ₦453,000
C. ₦493,000
D. ₦155,000
E. ₦120,000

44. A company recorded a net profit of ₦650,000 on its statement of profit or loss for the year ended 31st December, 2017. The following expenses were taken into account before arriving at the net profit:

	₦
Registration of a sister company	125,000
Fees for investigation of a company to be considered for acquisition as a subsidiary	180,000
Share issue expenses	215,000
Land acquisition	30,000
Fine for late remittance of withholding tax	2,000

What is the company's adjusted profit for tax purposes for the year ended 31st December, 2017?

A. ₦552,000
B. ₦247,000
C. ₦897,000
D. ₦955,000
E. ₦1,202,000

45. XYZ Ltd made a net profit of N2,000,000 during the year ended 30th June, 2018 after charging donations of 1,700,000. Donations comprised:

	N
The Society for the Blind	300,000
University of Uyo	800,000
The Nigerian Museum	100,000
The Nigeria Red Cross	300,000

The Boys Scouts of Nigeria 200,000

Unrelieved losses brought forward and capital allowances for the year amounted to 70,000 and 130,000 respectively.

What is the maximum amount of allowable donations for 2018 year of assessment?

A. ₦350,000
B. ₦200,000
C. ₦170,000
D. ₦150,000
E ₦1,700,000

Use the information below to answer questions 46 and 47.

ABC Ltd is a small Nigerian company which commenced a manufacturing business on 1st January, 2014 and earns a total gross sales of below ₦1,000,000 annually.

46. What is the rate of income tax applicable to the company?
A. 30% of assessable profits
B. 20% of assessable profits
C. 20% of adjusted profits
D. 30% of total profits
E. 20% of total profits

47. The relevant years of assessment for the application of the small business rate of income tax to ABC Ltd are .....
A. 2014, 2015 and 2016 years of assessment.
B. 2015, 2016 and 2017 years of assessment.
C. 2014, 2015, 2016 and 2017 years of assessment.
D. 2014, 2015, 2016, 2017 and 2018 years of assessment.
E. 2015, 2016, 2017, 2018 and 2019 years of assessment.

48. Ima's income statement for the year ended 31st March, 2017 included ₦680,000 for bad and doubtful debts. The figure comprised trade debts and loan to former employee of ₦600,000 and ₦350,000 respectively written off during the year. Also included in the account were the increase in the general provision

for doubtful debts of ₦200,000 and a decrease in the specific provision for doubtful debts of ₦70,000. Bad debts of ₦400,000 previously written off but recovered during the year were also taken into account.

What adjustment must be made to the net profit figure when calculating the adjusted profit for tax purposes?

A. Deduct ₦550,000 from the net profit.
B. Deduct ₦130,000 from the net profit.
C. Add ₦550,000 to the net profit.
D. Add ₦470,000 to the net profit.
E. Add ₦600,000 to the net profit.

49. Which of the following will be taken into account in computing a company's profit for companies income tax?

A. Revaluation surplus.
B. Professional fees and valuation expenses relating to revaluation of property, plant and equipment.
C. Unrealised gains or loss arising from foreign currency translation.
D. Impairment losses.
E. Contribution paid to the pension fund by the company on behalf of its employees.

Part II Short-Answer Questions

50. Give one reason why the net profit shown in the profit and loss account may not agree with the assessable profit computed for income tax purposes.

51. What is the treatment of amount recovered in respect of bad debts previously written off?

52. Given that the general provision for bad debt is ₦605,000 at the beginning of the year and ₦350,000 at the end of the year, what adjustment should be made to the net profit as per profit and loss account for the purpose of taxation?

53. A company recorded a net profit of ₦1,500,000 after taking into account depreciation, general provision for bad debts and specific provision for bad debts of ₦350,000, ₦400,000 and ₦230,000 respectively. What is the adjusted profit for tax purposes?

54. Given that a company recorded a net loss of ₦250,000 after taking into account depreciation ₦113,000, donations to social clubs 150,000, profit on sale of fixed assets 2,000, what is the company's assessable profit or loss for income tax purpose.

55. Bad Debts Account

	₦		₦
Trade debts written off	842,000	Provision for bad debts b/f	
Ex-staff's loans written off	135,000	Specific provision	410,000
Provision for bad debts c/f		1% of other debts	550,000
Specific provision	330,000	Trade debts previously written off now recovered	680,000
1% of other debts	765,000	Profit and loss account	232,000
	1,872,000		1,872,000

What is the amount of bad debts allowable in computing the assessable profit?

56. Donations allowed as deductions for tax purposes are those made by companies to certain organisations and institutions specified in CITA. Mention any three of such organisations or institutions which are related to the disabled persons.

57. Donations made to the research institutes listed in the Fifth Schedule to CITA are allowable deductions. Mention three of the research institutes.

58. Donations made to the youth/philanthropic organisations listed in the Fifth Schedule to CITA are allowable deductions. Mention any three of such youth organisations.

59. Donations made to the educational institutions listed in the Fifth Schedule to CITA are allowable deductions. Mention any two of such institutions

60. Give two examples of legal expenses which are not allowable in computing assessable profit.

61. State the rate of minimum tax chargeable on a company where the company's turnover exceeds ₦500,000.

62. State the rate of minimum tax chargeable on a company where the company's turnover is ₦500,000 or below.

63. State one advantage and one disadvantage of charging minimum tax on a company.

64. Give one difference between the tax position of a shareholder and that of a sole trader.

65. Under what circumstance can income tax of 30% be imposed on a company's dividend in place of its total profits?

66. Mrs Ogene has been in business for many years. During the year ended 31st December, 2017 she withdrew goods costing ₦100,000 from the business for her own personal use. If she had sold the goods to a customer she would have sold at cost plus 10 per cent. What adjustment would you make to the net profit shown in the statement of profit or loss when computing her adjusted profit for tax purposes if she paid ₦100,000 from her pocket into the business for the goods?

11 Basis of Assessment

Part I Multiple-Choice Questions

1. The basis of assessment where the profits assessable to tax in a year of assessment are those of the accounting year ending in that year of assessment is referred to as …
   A. current year basis.
   B. accrual year basis.
   C. preceding year basis.
   D. penultimate year basis.
   E. cash basis.

2. The basis of assessment in which the profits assessable to tax in a year of assessment are those of the accounting year ended in the previous year of assessment is referred to as the …
   A. current year basis.
   B. actual year basis.
   C. preceding year basis.
   D. penultimate year basis.
   E. cash basis.

3. The normal basis of assessment of a taxpayer's profits from a trade or business is …
   A. current year basis.
   B. actual year basis.
   C. preceding year basis.
   D. penultimate year basis.
   E. cash basis.

4. The normal basis of assessment is not applicable in the following circumstances:
   i. commencement of a trade or business
   ii. cessation of a trade or business
   iii. change of accounting date of a trade or business

iv. change in the taxpayer's residence from one territory to another

A. i, ii and iv only
B. i, iii and iv only
C. i and ii only
D. ii, iii and iv only
E. i, ii and iii only

5. Mr Etim received income from the following sources during the year ended 31st December, 2014. All of them will be assessed to tax in 2015 year of assessment except …

A. interest on savings account
B. dividend.
C. salary as an executive director of a company.
D. rent.
E. royalties.

6. Which of the under-mentioned incomes is/are subject to preceding year basis of assessment.

i. Discount
ii. Annuity
iii. Pension
iv. Business profit

A. i, ii and iv only
B. iv only
C. iii and iv only
D. i and ii only
E. i, ii, iii and iv.

7. The first year's assessment of a new trade or business is based on the…

A. income of the first twelve months.
B. income of the preceding year.
C. income from the date of commencement to 31st December of the same year.

D. income from the date of commencement to 31st December of the following year.

E. income of the second year of business.

8. Where the profits assessable to tax are those of the first twelve months from the date of commencement of business, the assessment is for the

A. first year of assessment.

B. second year of assessment.

C. pre-penultimate year of assessment.

D. penultimate year of assessment.

E. ultimate year of assessment.

9. A taxpayer can exercise his right of election …

A. at the discretion of the tax authority.

B. within six years after the third year of assessment.

C. within twelve months after the third year of assessment.

D. within two years after the end of the second year of assessment.

E. within thirty days from the date of service of notice of assessment.

10. A taxpayer can revoke his earlier request for an election within …

A. two years after the end of the second year.

B. twelve months after the end of the third year of assessment.

C. 90 days from the commencement of the fourth year of assessment.

D. six years after the end of the third year of assessment.

E. thirty days from the date of service of the notice of election.

11. Penultimate year is associated with …

A. change of accounting date.

B. cessation of business.

C. commencement of business.

D. change of residence.

E. continuity of trade.

12. The assessment for the year of cessation is on the ...
    - A. income of the preceding year.
    - B. income of the ante-penultimate year.
    - C. income of the twelve months ended on the date of cessation.
    - D. income from 1st January of the year of cessation to the date of cessation.
    - E. income of the penultimate year to 31st December of the same year.

13. Which of the following circumstances may not necessitate a change of accounting date?
    - i. The need to synchronize the accounting date of a subsidiary with that of the holding company.
    - ii. The merger of two or more companies to form a new company.
    - iii. Government directive that certain companies should adopt a particular accounting date.
    - iv. Commencement or cessation of business.
    - A. i, ii and iii only
    - B. ii, iii and iv only
    - C. iii and iv only
    - D. i and ii only
    - E. iv only

14. Which of the following statements is/are not true?
    - i. The accounts of a business must be prepared yearly to 31st December.
    - ii. The closing down of a business for three months due to lack of raw materials is deemed to be cessation of business.
    - iii. The basis period for the second year of assessment of a new business is always the same as that for the third year of assessment.
    - iv The income assessable to tax in the year of assessment following that in which cessation occurs is the income of the year of cessation.
    - A. All of the above
    - B. i and iv only

C. iii and iv only
D. ii, iii and iv only
E. i only

15. Trading income will not be assessable to tax on preceding year basis under the following circumstances:
i. Cessation of a trade or business.
ii. Change of accounting date of a business.
iii. Temporary suspension of trading activities.
iv. Commencement of a trade or business.
A. i, ii and iii only
B. i, ii and iv only
C. ii, iii and iv only
D. i, ii, iii and iv
E. i, iii and iv only
Which of the options A to E is correct?

Use the information below to answer questions 16 to 19.

Isoko started trading on 1st September, 2016 and adopted 30th June as his annual accounting date. He prepared his first set of accounts to 30th June 2017.

16. What is the basis period for the first tax year?
A. 1 September 2016 to 30 June 2017
B. 1 September 2016 to 31 December 2016
C. 1 September 2016 to 31 August 2017
D. 1 January 2016 to 31 December 2016
E. 1 January 2017 to 30 June 2017

17. What is the basis period for the second tax year assuming that no right of election is exercised?
A. 1 September 2016 to 30 June 2017
B. 1 September 2016 to 31 December 2016
C. 1 September 2016 to 31 August 2017
D. 1 January 2016 to 31 December 2016
E. 1 January 2017 to 30 June 2017

18. What is the basis period for the third tax year assuming that no right of election is exercised?
    A. 1 September 2016 to 30 June 2017
    B. 1 September 2016 to 31 December 2016
    C. 1 September 2016 to 31 August 2017
    D. 1 January 2016 to 31 December 2016
    E. 1 January 2017 to 30 June 2017

19. Assuming that the right of election is exercised, the basis periods for the second and third tax years are ....
    i. 1 January 2018 to 31 December 2018
    ii. 1 September 2017 to 31 December 2018
    iii. 1 September 2016 to 31 August 2017
    iv. 1 January 2017 to 31 December 2017
    A. ii and i respectively.
    B. i and iv respectively.
    C. iii and ii respectively.
    D. iv and ii respectively.
    E. iv and i respectively.

Use the information below to answer questions 20 to 23.

Emeka started trading on 1st March, 2016 and prepares accounts to 31st August each year. His adjusted trading profits are as follows:

Period ended 31st August, 2016	₦60,000
Year ended 31st August, 2017	₦150,000

20. The assessable income for the year of commencement is ....
    A. ₦60,000.
    B. ₦120,000.
    C. ₦75,000.
    D. ₦135,000.
    E. ₦110,000.

21. Assuming that the right of election is not exercised, the assessable income for the second year of assessment is ....

A. ₦150,000.
B. ₦120,000.
C. ₦75,000.
D. ₦135,000.
E. ₦110,000.

22. Assuming that the right of election is not exercised, the assessable income for the third year of assessment is ....
A. ₦150,000.
B. ₦120,000.
C. ₦75,000.
D. ₦135,000.
E. ₦110,000.

23. The basis period for the second year of assessment overlaps with that of the first year. The overlap period and overlap profit are ... and ....
A. 1/3/16 to 31/8/16, ₦60,000.
B. 1/3/16 to 31/12/16, ₦110,000.
C. 1/3/16 to 28/2/17, ₦135,000.
D. 1/3/17 to 31/8/17, ₦75,000.
E. 1/9/16 to 31/12/16, ₦50,000.

Use the information below to answer questions 24 to 27.

Obaro commenced business on 1st March, 1999 and makes up his accounts annually to 30th September. The adjusted profits were as follows:

	₦
Period ended 30th September, 1999	240,000
Year ended 30th September, 2000	432,000
Year ended 30th September, 2001	300,000
Year ended 30th September, 2002	360,000

24. The total assessable income of Obaro for the first three years of assessment assuming that the right of election is not exercised is ...

A. ₦912,000
B. ₦1,062,000
C. ₦1,200,000
D. ₦972,000
E. ₦1,092,000

25. Assuming that the right of election is exercised, what is the total assessable income of Obaro for the first three years of assessment?
A. ₦1,062,000
B. ₦1,200,000
C. ₦912,000
D. ₦972,000
E. ₦1,092,000

26. Obaro can exercise his right of election on or before …
A. 31st December, 2000.
B. 31st December, 2001.
C. 31st December, 2002.
D. 31st December, 2003.
E. 30th September, 2001.

27. Obaro can revoke his notice of election on or before ..
A. 31st December, 2003.
B. 31st December, 2002.
C. 31st December, 2001.
D. 31st December, 2004.
E. 30th September, 2003.

28. Amaka started trading on 1st July, 2013 and ceased trading on 30th June, 2017. The basis period for the last year of assessment is….
A. 1/7/15 to 30/6/16
B. 1/1/17 to 30/6/17
C. 1/1/17 to 31/12/17
D. 1/7/17 to 31/12/17
E. 1/7/16 to 30/6/17

29. Okoro began trading on 1st October, 2012 and decided to prepare accounts to 30th September each year. He permanently ceased trading on 31st July, 2017. The basis period for the penultimate year of assessment is....
    A. 1/1/16 - 31/12/16
    B. 1/10/14 - 30/9/15
    C. 1/10/15 - 30/9/16
    D. Either 1/10/14 - 30/9/15 or 1/1/16 - 31/12/16, whichever produces the higher assessable income.
    E. Either 1/10/14 - 30/9/15 or 1/1/16 - 31/12/16, whichever produces the lower assessable income.

Use the information below to answer questions 30 to 32.

Titani Ltd, which has been in business for many years, permanently ceased trading on 30th June, 2005. Its adjusted profits were as follows:

	₦
Year ended 31st March, 2002	260,000
Year ended 31st March, 2003	306,000
Year ended 31st March, 2004	420,000
Year ended 31st March, 2005	360,000
Three months to 30th June, 2005	120,000

30. The total assessable profits of the company for the last three years of assessment amounted to ...
    A. ₦776,000.
    B. ₦755,000.
    C. ₦900,000.
    D. ₦1,086,000.
    E. ₦845,000.

31. The period whose profits escaped any charge to tax is ...
    A. 1st April, 2002 to 31st March, 2003.
    B. 1st April, 2004 to 31st December, 2004.
    C. 1st April, 2001 to 31st March, 2002.

D. 1st January, 2003 to 31st December, 2003.
E. 1st April, 2002 to 31st December, 2003.

32. The assessable profit which escaped any charge to tax as a result of the cessation is ...
A. ₦621,000.
B. ₦391,500.
C. ₦260,000.
D. ₦420,000.
E. ₦360,000.

Use the information below to answer questions 33 and 34.

Papa Ltd previously made up the accounts of its business to 31st August in each year before its adopted 28th February as the new accounting date. Its adjusted profits have been as follows:

	₦
Year ended 31st August 2000	600,000
Year ended 31st August 2001	396,000
Period ended 28th February 2002	196,000
Year ended 28th February 2003	288,000
Year ended 29th February 2004	420,000

33. Assuming that the old accounting date is adopted by the FIRS for the computation of assessment, what would be the total assessable profits for the three years of assessment affected by the change of accounting date?
A. ₦1,180,000
B. ₦880,000
C. ₦904,000
D. ₦1,090,000
E. ₦1,300,000

34. Assuming that the new accounting date is adopted by the FIRS for the computation of assessment, what would be the total assessable profits for the three years of assessment affected by the change of accounting date?

A. ₦1,090,000
B. ₦1,180,000
C. ₦1,300,000
D. ₦904,000
E. ₦880,000

Part II Short-Answer Questions

35. Year of assessment means a period of … months commencing from … and ending on …

36. State the year of assessment/basis period for the following under normal circumstance:
(a) Profits for the accounting year ended 31st March, 2010
(b) Profits for the accounting year ended 31st January, 2011
(c) Profits for the accounting year ended 31st December, 2014

37. State the basis of assessment of a new business for the first three years of assessment.

38. The right given to a taxpayer to choose to be assessed on the actual profits of the second and third years of assessment is referred to as ..

39. What is the option available to a taxpayer under the commencement rule to minimise his tax liability?

40. A taxpayer's request for the computation of his assessment for the second and third years of assessment based on the actual profits will not be effective except …
(a) ……………………………………
(b) ……………………………………
(c) ……………………………………

41. Oba Ltd commenced to trade on 1st May, 2013 and adopted 31st October as its permanent accounting date. State the assessment years and the basis periods for the first three years of assessment.

42. If Oba Ltd in question no. 31 exercises its right of election, what are the basis periods for the first three years of assessment?

43. The year of assessment preceding that in which cessation occurs is referred to as the...

44. What is the treatment of any sum received or paid after the cessation of a taxpayer's business?

45. The assessment for the penultimate year is based on...

Use the information below to answer questions 46 and 47.

Yawa had always made up the accounts of his business to 31st March. He permanently ceased business on 31st May 2006.

46. State the penultimate year of assessment and its basis period.

47. State the last year of assessment and its basis period.

48. When a taxpayer changes his accounting date, the assessable income for some years is computed on such basis as the tax authority in its discretion thinks fit. State the years of assessment concerned.

49. Summarise the procedure which may be followed by the tax authority in making assessment based on accounts where the date of the year-end has been changed.

50. Who has the right to decide on the basis of assessment of a business which has changed its accounting date?

51. Who exercises the right of election on:
    (a) commencement of a business?
    (b) cessation of a business?

52. When a company and another person are engaged in a partnership business, the company's share of the partnership's profits is

computed in accordance with the provisions of …, while any capital allowance due to the company is computed in accordance with the provisions of…

12 Capital Allowances

Part I Multiple-Choice Questions

1. An expenditure which results in the acquisition of fixed assets or advantage for the enduring benefit of a trade is referred to as ...
   A. accretion.
   B. capital allowance.
   C. capital expenditure.
   D. revenue expenditure.
   E. enhancement expenditure.

2. An expenditure which is incurred to maintain the operating capacity of fixed assets and for the day-to-day running of the business is referred to as ...
   A. amortization.
   B. capital allowance.
   C. capital expenditure.
   D. revenue expenditure.
   E. maintenance expenditure.

3. Which of the following allowances is granted in lieu of depreciation?
   A. Investment tax credit
   B. Capital allowance
   C. Balancing allowance
   D. Rural investment allowance
   E. Personal allowance

4. An allowance granted to a taxpayer for acquiring fixed assets and using them in his business is referred to as …
   A. personal allowance.
   B. capital allowance.
   C. depreciation.

D. investment allowance.
E. loss relief.

5. Capital expenditure on one of the following does not qualify for capital allowances and that is
   A. research and development.
   B. land.
   C. ranching and plantation.
   D. housing estate.
   E. mining.

6. Qualifying plant expenditure for capital allowances include ...
   A. repair of plant, machinery or fixtures.
   B. renewal, repair or alteration of implement or utensils.
   C. replacement of parts of a machine.
   D. purchase of loose tools.
   E. none of the above.

7. Which of the following will not be included in qualifying capital expenditure ?
   A. Cost of refurbishing a newly-acquired second-hand motor car before putting it to use.
   B. Cost of installation of a newly-acquired plant and machinery.
   C. Cost of extension of factory building.
   D. Customs duties and VAT on imported plant and machinery.
   E. Hire purchase interest on motor car bought on hire purchase.

8. All the following are not eligible for capital allowances except
   A. shares.
   B. stocks.
   C. non-industrial building.
   D. land.
   E. goodwill.

9. The following conditions must be fulfilled before a taxpayer can be granted capital allowances:

A. He must incur qualifying capital expenditure.
B. He must be the owner of the asset.
C. The asset must be in use.
D. He must make a claim for capital allowances.
E. He must be involved in research and development activities.

Which of the options A to E is not correct?

10. A certificate of acceptance is required to be obtained from the Inspectorate Division of the Federal Ministry of Industries for all qualifying capital expenditure incurred in a year in excess of …
    A. ₦1,000,000.
    B. ₦50,000.
    C. ₦5,000,000.
    D. ₦500,000.
    E. ₦1,500,000.

11. Which of the following is/are not true of initial allowance?
    i. It is granted once and for all to a particular taxpayer in respect of a particular asset.
    ii. It is granted in the basis period in which the asset is first put to use.
    iii. It is given in full irrespective of the length of the basis period.
    iv. It is not deducted from the cost of the asset when computing the tax written down value of the asset.

    A. iv only
    B. i, ii, and iii only
    C. iii and iv only
    D. i and ii only
    E. ii and iii only

12. For the purpose of initial allowance, when there is an interval between the basis periods for the penultimate year and the year of cessation, the interval is deemed to form part of the
    A. basis period for the pre-penultimate year of assessment.
    B. basis period for the penultimate year of assessment.
    C. basis period for the post-cessation year.

D. basis period for the year of cessation.
E. basis period for the year of commencement.

13. Which of the following allowances is calculated on a straight-line basis?
A. Investment allowance
B. Initial allowance
C. Annual allowance
D. Balancing allowance
E. Balancing charge

14. The straight line method used in calculating capital allowances in Nigeria was introduced in …
A. 1995.
B. 2005.
C. 1985.
D. 1980.
E. 1990.

15. Which of the following allowances is prorated if the basis period for a year of assessment is less than one year?
A. Initial allowance
B. Annual allowance
C. Investment allowance
D. Balancing allowance
E. EPZ allowance

16. What is the amount that must be retained in the books in respect of each asset until the asset is disposed of?
A. ₦100
B. ₦20
C. ₦10
D. ₦1,000
E. ₦50

17. Investment allowance is granted to a company which has incurred a qualifying expenditure on …

A. industrial building.
B. research and development.
C. plant and equipment.
D. housing estate.
E. plantation.

18. Investment allowance is granted at the rate of ...
A. 95% of the qualifying expenditure.
B. 10% of the qualifying expenditure.
C. 5% of the qualifying expenditure.
D. 50% of the qualifying expenditure.
E. 25% of the qualifying expenditure.

19. Investment allowance will be cancelled if any of the events stipulated in CITA occurred within a period of... starting from the date the expenditure was incurred.
A. five years
B. one year
C. three years
D. six years
E. four years

20. What is the rate of capital allowance granted to a company on qualifying expenditure on building and plant equipment in an approved manufacturing activity in an Export Processing Zone?
A. 100%
B. 95%
C. 50%
D. 90%
E. 75%

21. Rural investment allowance is granted to a company which has incurred capital expenditure on the provision of infrastructures for the purpose of a trade or business which is located at least ...... kilometres away from such facilities provided by the government.
A. 100
B. 50

C. 80
D. 20
E. 70

22. Which of the following statements is not true?
A. A company cannot claim both rural investment allowance and 10% investment allowance on the same assets.
B. A company granted EPZ allowance is not entitled to investment allowance.
C. Unrelieved rural investment allowance in a year of assessment cannot be carried forward to any subsequent year.
D. Expenditure on extension or improvement of an industrial building qualifies for capital allowance.
E. Investment allowance is pro-rated when the basis period for a year of assessment is less than twelve months.

23. Which of the following allowances is granted if the written down value of an asset disposed of exceeds the sales proceeds of the asset?
A. Annual allowance
B. Balancing allowance
C. Balancing change
D. Investment allowance
E. Investment tax credit

24. If the sales proceeds of an asset disposed of exceed the written down value of the asset at the date of disposal, the excess is regarded as a .
A. Annual allowance
B. Balancing allowance
C. Balancing change
D. Investment allowance
E. Investment tax credit

25. Who is entitled to claim capital allowances on an asset acquired/sold on hire purchase and what is the qualifying expenditure on which to claim capital allowances?

A. The hirer based on the full cash price irrespective of the dates of payment of instalments.
B. The hirer based on the amount of the instalments paid excluding hire purchase interest.
C. The hirer based on the amount of the instalments paid including hire purchase interest.
D. The seller based on the hire purchase price.
E. The seller based on the amount of the instalments received excluding hire purchase interest.

26. Which of the following is taxable?
A. Annual allowance
B. Balancing allowance
C. Investment allowance
D. Balancing charge
E. Investment tax credit.

27. The maximum amount of capital allowance claimable by a taxpayer in any year of assessment is …
A. $66^2/_3\%$ of chargeable profit.
B. $66^2/_3\%$ of total profit.
C. 75% of assessable profit.
D. 50% of assessable profit.
E. $66^2/_3\%$ of assessable profit.

28. What is the maximum number of years for carrying forward capital allowances?
A. Four years
B. Five years
C. Six years
D. Indefinitely
E. Ten years

29. Unrelieved capital allowances in the year of cessation of a business can be carried backward and set off against the profits of the preceding …
    A. four years.
    B. five years.
    C. six years.
    D. two years.
    E. three years.

30. The current rates of initial and annual allowances applicable to furniture are
    A. 15% and 10% respectively.
    B. 50% and 25% respectively.
    C. 25% and 20% respectively.
    D. 30% and 50% respectively.
    E. 95% and 0% respectively.

31. A new factory building was erected at a cost of ₦4,000,000 made up as follows:

	₦
Purchase price of land	200,000
Site preparation	150,000
Architect's fees	100,000
Construction materials	2,500,500
Labour costs	1,050,000

What is the qualifying expenditure on which capital allowances will be calculated?
    A. ₦4,000,000
    B. ₦3,800,000
    C. ₦2,750,000
    D. ₦2,850,000
    E. ₦2,700,000

32. Toro purchased a building on 1st November, 2002 and commenced business on 20th March, 2003, making up his accounts to 31st December each year. For 2002 year of assessment, Toro is entitled to claim

A. 15% initial allowance only.
B. 10% annual allowance only.
C. 15% initial allowance and 10% annual allowance.
D. neither initial allowance nor annual allowance.
E. 95% initial allowance only.

Use the information below to answer questions 33 to 37.

Thomas commenced business on 1st August, 1999 and makes up his accounts to 31st July each year. He incurred the following qualifying capital expenditure during the first few years:

Asset purchased	Date of purchase	Cost (₦)
Building	30/05/99	2,000,000
Plant and machinery	11/09/99	5,000,000
Fixtures and fittings	30/06/00	400,000
Motor vehicle (second-hand)	12/12/00	500,000
Building extension	10/01/01	300,000

33. The qualifying expenditure for claiming initial allowance in 1999 year of assessment is ...
A. ₦7,000,000.
B. ₦2,000,000.
C. ₦5,000,000.
D. ₦7,400,000.
E. Nil.

34. Assuming that no election is made, the qualifying expenditure for claiming initial allowance in 2000 year of assessment is ...
A. ₦7,000,000.
B. ₦900,000.
C. ₦500,000.
D. ₦400,000.
E. ₦7,900,000.

35. Assuming that no election is made, the qualifying expenditure for claiming initial allowance in 2001 year of assessment is ...

A. ₦7,900,000.
B. ₦900,000.
C. Nil.
D. ₦7,000,000.
E. ₦7,400,000.

36. Assuming that the right of election is exercised, the qualifying expenditure for claiming initial allowance in 2000 year of assessment is …
A. ₦400,000.
B. ₦900,000.
C. ₦500,000.
D. ₦7,900,000.
E. ₦7,000,000.

37. Assuming that the right of election is exercised, the qualifying expenditure for claiming initial allowance in 2001 year of assessment is …
A. ₦900,000.
B. ₦400,000.
C. ₦7,900,000.
D. ₦7,000,000.
E. ₦300,000.

Use the information below to answer questions 38 to 41.

Mr Kaki has been in business for many years preparing his accounts to 31st December each year. He purchased a motor vehicle for ₦600,000 on 1st March 1998 and later sold it for ₦400,000 on 25th December 2001. Assume that the initial and annual allowances were 50% and 25% respectively.

38. The total capital allowances granted before disposal amounted to …
A. ₦600,000.
B. ₦375,000.
C. ₦325,000.

D. ₦525,000.
E. ₦450,000.

39. The written down value of the asset before disposal was…
A. ₦75,000.
B. ₦325,000.
C. ₦150,000.
D. ₦375,000.
E. ₦125,000.

40. What is the balancing charge or allowance arising on the disposal of the motor vehicle?
A. Balancing allowance ₦75,000
B. Balancing allowance ₦325,000
C. Balancing charge ₦325,000
D. Balancing charge ₦150,000
E. Balancing charge ₦125,000

41. Assuming that the motor vehicle was sold for ₦650,000 instead of ₦400,000, what would have been the balancing charge?
A. ₦575,000
B. ₦525,000
C. ₦400,000
D. ₦75,000
E. ₦150,000

Use the information below to answer questions 42 to 44.

Lady Ego has been in business for many years and makes up her accounts to 31st December each year. She purchased a car costing ₦800,000 on 1st July 1998 and sold it for ₦350,000 on 30th June 2000. She has agreed with the tax authority that the vehicle was used 60% for business and 40% for private purposes. The initial and annual allowances were 50% and 25% respectively during the relevant years.

42. Lady Ego's capital allowances for 1999 assessment year amounted to …
    A. ₦500,000.
    B. ₦300,000.
    C. ₦400,000.
    D. ₦200,000.
    E. ₦450,000.

43. Lady Ego's capital allowances for 2000 assessment year amounted to …
    A. ₦100,000.
    B. ₦300,000.
    C. ₦60,000.
    D. ₦150,000.
    E. ₦40,000.

44. Lady Ego's balancing charge for 2001 assessment should be…
    A. ₦90,000.
    B. ₦60,000.
    C. ₦40,000.
    D. ₦200,000.
    E. ₦150,000.

Use the information below to answer questions 45 and 46.

BB Ltd completed the erection of its factory building on 1st December, 1995 at a cost of ₦3,500,000 and used it for its business in the same year. On 31st October, 2000, it sold the building to SS Ltd for ₦4,500,000. Each of the company has been in business for many years and makes up accounts to 31st December annually.

45. For 1996 year of assessment, BB Ltd is entitled to claim capital allowances of …
    A. ₦525,000.
    B. ₦822,500.
    C. ₦297,500.

D. ₦875,000.
E. ₦1,500,000.

46. For 2001 year of assessment, SS Ltd is entitled to claim capital allowances of …
A. ₦1,057,500.
B. ₦450,000.
C. ₦822,500.
D. ₦350,000.
E. ₦675,000

Use the information below to answer questions 47 to 50.

You have been given the following information about OB Ltd, which has been in business for many years:

	₦
Adjusted profit for the year ended 31/12/04	615,000
Capital allowances for 2005 assessment year	
Initial allowance	315,000
Annual allowance	44,000
Balancing allowance	56,000
Unrelieved capital allowances brought forward from 2004 year of assessment	180,000

47. What is the total profit for 2005 year of assessment if the company is not in agro-allied or manufacturing industry?
A. ₦205,000
B. ₦410,000
C. ₦20,000
D. ₦615,000
E. ₦200,000

48. What is the income tax payable for 2005 year of assessment if the company is not in agro-allied or manufacturing industry?
A. ₦60,000
B. ₦184,500
C. ₦6,000

D. ₦123,000
E. ₦61,500

49. What is the unrelieved capital allowances to be carried forward to 2006 year of assessment if the company is not in agro-allied or manufacturing industry?
A. ₦185,000
B. ₦595,000
C. ₦410,000
D. ₦875,500.
E. ₦180,000

50. Assuming that the company is in agro-allied or manufacturing industry, what is the total profit for 2005 year of assessment?
A. ₦20,000
B. ₦200,000
C. ₦205,000
D. ₦410,000
E. ₦615,000

51. Mbu, who has been in business for many years, ceased trading on 30th June 2005. His adjusted profits and the capital allowances due were as follows:

Assessment Year	Adjusted profits ₦	Capital Allowances ₦
1994	500,000	200,000
1995	660,000	400,000
1996	600,000	500,000
1997	576,000	360,000
1998	960,000	540,000
1999	480,000	2,280,000
2000	249,000	

Mbu will not be able to recoup the unabsorbed capital allowances of
A. ₦255,000.
B. ₦555,000.

C. ₦1,730,000.
D. ₦1,634,000.
E. ₦1,551,000.

Use the information below to answer questions 52 to 54.

Maxima Ltd has been in business since 1995 and usually prepares it accounts to 31st December annually. The written down values of its fixed assets at 1st January 2003 for capital allowances were:

	₦
Factory building (built in 1998)	1,500,000
Motor vehicles (purchased in 2002)	300,000
Additions during the year ended 31st December, 2003 were:	
Factory building	950,000
Motor vehicles	450,000

52. For 2004 year of assessment, Maxima Ltd is entitled to claim initial allowance of …
    A. ₦367,500.
    B. ₦742,500.
    C. ₦375,000.
    D. ₦567,500.
    E. ₦467,500.

53. For 2004 year of assessment, Maxima Ltd is entitled to claim annual allowance of …
    A. ₦137,000.
    B. ₦400,000.
    C. ₦156,250.
    D. ₦537,000.
    E. ₦380,750.

54. The tax written down values of buildings and motor vehicles after 2004 year of assessment are …
    A. ₦1,926,750 and ₦368,750 respectively.
    B. ₦726,750 and ₦168,750 respectively.

C. ₦1,200,000 and ₦200,000 respectively.
D. ₦1,826,750 and ₦368,750 respectively.
E. ₦1,726,750 and ₦268,750 respectively.

55. Given that the tax written down values of fixed assets after 2003 year of assessment were:

	₦
Factory building (residual years – 6)	900,000
Plant and machinery (residual years – 3)	1,200,000
Furniture (residual year – 1)	80,000

What is the annual allowance due for 2004 assessment year?
A. ₦550,000
B. ₦590,000
C. ₦400,000
D. ₦629,990
E. ₦529,990

56. The following conditions must be fulfilled before a balancing allowance or charge is given or made on disposal of an asset:
A. The affected taxpayer must have incurred qualifying capital expenditure in respect of the asset.
B. The affected taxpayer must have been the owner of the asset.
C. The asset disposed of must have been in use in the trade or business immediately before its disposal.
D. The asset must have been disposed of during the basis period for the relevant year of assessment.
E. The asset must have been bought and disposed of within the same basis period.

Which of the options A to E is not correct?

57. Which of the following is treated as an addition to assessable profit in the computation of a company's tax liability?
A. Balancing charge
B. Capital allowance
C. Balancing allowance
D. Investment allowance
E. Rural investment allowance

58. Which of the following is not deductible from the remainder of assessable profit to arrive at the total profit in the computation of a company's tax liability?
   A. Initial allowance
   B. Balancing charge
   C. Annual allowance
   D. Balancing allowance
   E. Investment allowance

59. What is the rate of capital allowance granted to a company for acquisition of plant and machinery to replace the old ones?
   A. 100% capital allowance in any year of assessment.
   B. Annual allowance of 90% with 10% retention for further investment.
   C. Once-and-for-all 95% capital allowance in the first year.
   D 20% annual allowance for five years.
   E. 50 capital allowance in the first year.

60. All the following are capital allowances except …
   A. initial allowance.
   B. annual allowance.
   C. balancing allowance.
   D. investment allowance.
   E. consolidated relief allowance.

61. Which of the allowances granted on qualifying capital expenditure are not to be deducted from the cost of the asset when computing the tax written down value of the asset?
   i.. initial allowance.
   ii. annual allowance.
   iii. investment allowance.
   iv. rural investment allowance
   A. i and ii only
   B. iii and iv only
   C. iii only
   D. i and iii only
   E. ii and iv only

62. Where a building has not been used by the original owner before sale, what is the qualifying expenditure on which the second-hand purchaser will claim capital allowances?
    A. The price paid by the second-hand purchaser for the building
    B. The original cost of construction of the building.
    C. The written down value of the building at the time of sale.
    D. The current market value of the building.
    E. The price paid by the second-hand purchaser for the building or the original cost of construction of the building, whichever is lower.

63. BC plc bought a brand new car in January 2015 for ₦3,000,000. After using the car for three years, the company sold it to OB Ltd in January 2018 for ₦1,600,000.
    Which of the following statements is/are true?
    i. BC plc is entitled to both initial and annual allowances on ₦3,000,000.
    ii. OB Ltd is entitled to both initial and annual allowances on ₦1,600,000.
    iii. OB Ltd is entitled to both initial and annual allowances on ₦3,000,000.
    iv. OB Ltd is only entitled to annual allowance on ₦1,600,000.
    A. i only
    B. ii only
    C. i and ii only
    D. i and iv only
    E. i and iii only

64. The rates of annual allowance for building, furniture and motor vehicle are 10%, 20% and 25% respectively. Therefore, annual allowance will be granted on building, furniture and motor vehicle for …
    A. 10, 5 and 4 years respectively.
    B. 4, 5 and 10 years respectively.
    C. 10, 4 and 5 years respectively.
    D. 5, 10 and 4 years respectively.
    E. 5, 4 and 10 years respectively.

65. XYZ Ltd has been in business for many years and usually makes up its accounts to 31st December. The company acquired a building in the Federal Capital Territory, Abuja on 1st January, 2017 for ₦30 million and used it for its business. The building was demolished on 31st October, 2017 on the order of the Minister of the Federal Capital Territory.

Which one of the following statements is correct?

A. XYZ Ltd is entitled to initial and annual allowances in 2018 year of assessment on ₦30 million.

B. XYZ Ltd is entitled to only annual allowance in 2018 year of assessment on ₦30 million for 10 months.

C. XYZ Ltd is entitled to initial and annual allowances in 2018 year of assessment on ₦30 million, but annual allowance will be prorated.

D. XYZ Ltd is entitled to both initial and annual allowances in 2018 year of assessment on ₦30 million, but both allowances will be prorated.

E. XYZ Ltd is not entitled to initial and annual allowances in 2018 year of assessment on ₦30 million.

Use the information below to answer questions 66 and 67.

BYC Ltd has been in business for many years and usually makes up its accounts to 31st December. The company acquired a motor vehicle on 1st July, 2009 for ₦10 million and used it in its business for 8 years before it was sold to Dada in 30th June, 2017. The rates of initial and annual allowances for motor vehicles are 50% and 25% respectively.

66. Which one of the following statements is correct?

A. BYC Ltd is entitled to annual allowance in 2010, 2011, 2012 and 2013 years of assessment.

B. BYC Ltd is entitled to annual allowance in 2009, 2010, 2011 and 2012 years of assessment.

C. BYC Ltd is entitled to annual allowance in 2010, 2011, 2012, 2013, 2014, 2015, 2016 and 2017 years of assessment.

D. Annual allowance would be prorated in 2010 year of assessment since the asset was in use for 6 months.

E. Dada is not entitled to initial allowance on the asset.

67. The year of assessment that BYC Ltd will start retaining ₦10 as the written down value of the asset is ....

A. 2013 year of assessment

B. 2017 year of assessment

C. 2012 year of assessment

D. 2018 year of assessment

E. 2016 year of assessment

68. ABC Ltd commenced business on 1st July, 2009 and makes up its accounts to 30th June annually. The company acquired a motor vehicle on 1st July, 2009 for ₦10 million and used it in its business. The rates of initial and annual allowances for motor vehicles are 50% and 25% respectively. Which of the following statements is/are correct?

i. The first year of assessment for granting initial and annual allowances is 2010.

ii. Initial allowance in the first year of assessment is 50% x 6/12 x ₦10,000,000.

iii. Initial allowance in the first year of assessment is 50% x ₦10,000,000.

iv. Annual allowance will be prorated in the first year of assessment.

A. i and ii only

B. ii and iv only

C. iv only

D. iii and iv only

E. iv only

69. Ngige Limited has been in business for many years making up its accounts to 31st December. The company purchased 6 motor vehicles on 1st March, 2017 at ₦5,000,000 each. What is the amount to be retained in the books of the company after 2021 year

of assessment? The rates of initial and annual allowances are 50% and 25% respectively.

A. ₦10
B. ₦30
C. ₦60
D. ₦600
E. ₦6,000

70. BB Ltd erected its industrial building at a cost of ₦4,000,000 and sold it to CY Ltd for ₦5,000,000. CY Ltd also sold the building to XY Ltd for ₦5,600,000. XY Ltd was in financial distress and had to sell the building to FC Ltd for ₦6,800,000. None of them actually put the building into use except FC Ltd.

A. FC Ltd is entitled to claim both initial and annual allowances on ₦4,000,000.
B. FC Ltd is entitled to claim only annual allowances based on ₦4,000,000.
C. FC Ltd is entitled to claim both initial and annual allowances on ₦6,800,000.
D. FC Ltd is entitled to claim only annual allowance based on ₦6,800,000.
E. FC Ltd is not entitled to claim both initial and annual allowances.

71. CB Plc has been in transport business for many years and prepares accounts to 30th September each year. On 31st December, 2014 the company purchased a motor van on hire purchase from Metropolitan Motors Ltd on the following terms:

	₦
Cash price	3,200,000
Hire purchase price	3,680,000
Deposit on purchase	800,000
Monthly instalments commencing from 31/1/15	120,000

Capital allowances were claimable at 50% initial allowance and 25% annual allowance.

What is the qualifying expenditure for 2016 year of assessment?

A. ₦1,700,000
B. ₦1,080,000
C. ₦3,200,000
D. ₦3,680,000
E. ₦1,880,000

72. The maximum amount of capital allowance claimable by a taxpayer in any year of assessment is $66^2/_3\%$ of assessable profit. This restriction is not applicable to individuals and companies engaged in
A. telecommunication industry.
B. manufacturing industry.
C. research and development activities.
D. independent power generation.
E. insurance companies.

73. The maximum amount of capital allowance claimable in any year of assessment by a taxpayer engaged in animal husbandry is limited to
A. $66^2/_3\%$ of the taxpayer's assessable profit.
B. $66^2/_3\%$ of the taxpayer's total profit.
C. $66^2/_3\%$ of the taxpayer's chargeable profit.
D. $66^2/_3\%$ of the remainder of assessable profit of the taxpayer.
E. the amount of the taxpayer's assessable profit which is available to absorb the capital allowance.

74. Which of the following statements is correct with regard to the computation of capital allowances?
A. Cost of employee benefits directly attributable to the construction or acquisition of property, plant and equipment shall be allowed for inclusion in the cost of the asset.
B. When an asset is revalued, capital allowances are computed on the revalued amount and not on the historical cost of the asset.
C. Computer software that forms integral part of a computer shall not be treated as qualifying plant expenditure.

D. Provision/estimate of cost of abandonment, dismantling, removing an item of property, plant and equipment and site restoration shall be allowed for inclusion in the cost of the asset.

E. Interest on loan incurred on any qualifying capital expenditure that is under construction shall not be capitalised with the cost of construction of the asset.

75. When two basis periods coincide …

A. the period common to both is deemed to belong to the second basis period only.

B. initial allowance in respect of qualifying capital expenditure incurred within the period will only be granted in the second year of assessment.

C. if the second year is a year of cessation, initial allowance in respect of qualifying capital expenditure incurred within the period will be granted in the year of cessation.

D. initial allowance will be computed and apportioned between the two basis periods.

E. initial allowance in respect of the qualifying capital expenditure incurred within the period will only be granted in the first year of assessment.

76. Which two of the following schedules deal with capital allowances?

A. 5th schedule to CITA and 2nd schedule to PITA

B. 5th schedule to CITA and 5th schedule to PITA

C. 2nd schedule to CITA and 4th schedule to PITA

D. 2nd schedule to CITA and 3rd schedule to PITA

E. 2nd schedule to CITA and 5th schedule to PITA

77. Which one of the following is not a qualifying capital expenditure?

A. Capital expenditure incurred on the acquisition of rights in or over mineral deposits.

B. Capital expenditure incurred on the purchase of information relating to the existence and extent of mineral deposits.

C. Capital expenditure incurred on the clearing of land for planting rubber.

D. Capital expenditure incurred on the planting of rubber (other than replanting).

E. None of the above.

78. According to PITA and CITA, the value of an asset at the date of its disposal is …

i. the total qualifying expenditure incurred by the owner on or before that date less the total of any initial or annual allowance made before that date.

ii. the net proceeds of the sale of the asset.

iii. the net proceeds of insurance or compensation monies if an asset is disposed of in such circumstances that insurance or compensation monies are received by the owner

iv. the amount the asset would have fetched if sold in the open market at that date less the amount of any expenses which the owner might reasonably be expected to incur if the asset were sold.

A. i

B. ii or iv

C. ii or iii

D. i or ii or iv

E. ii or iii or iv

79. When an asset is disposed of what is the highest amount that can be taken as a balancing charge?

A. Balancing charge is restricted to the tax written down value the asset before disposal.

B. Balancing charge is restricted to the cost of acquisition of the asset.

C. Balancing charge is restricted to the cost of replacement of the asset.

D. Balancing charge is restricted to the total of capital allowances granted on the asset before disposal.

E. Balancing charge is restricted to an amount determined by the relevant tax authority to be just and reasonable.

80. Any of the following events may lead to the cancellation of investment allowance earlier granted on plant and equipment except
    A. any appropriation of the asset to a purpose other than a chargeable purpose.
    B. any sale or transfer of the asset otherwise than to a person acquiring the asset for a chargeable purpose or for scrap.
    C. any temporary disuse of the asset at the end of the basis period during which it was acquired.
    D. any sale or transfer or other dealing with the asset where it appears that the purpose of obtaining tax allowances was the sole or main purpose for incurring or for so dealing with the asset.
    E. any sale or transfer or other dealing with the asset where it appears that the incurring of the expenditure and the asset being so dealt with were not bona fide business transactions.

81. Which one of the following assets may not be considered to be plant for the purpose of capital allowances?
    A. Mechanical workshop
    B Dock
    C. Jetty
    D. Wharf
    E. All of the above

Part II Short-Answer Questions

82. A loss in the value of an asset due to usage, obsolescence, passage of time and other factors is referred to as ...

83. List five categories of expenditure which qualify for capital allowances.

84. Capital expenditure incurred prior to the commencement of a business is deemed to have been incurred on …

85. State the general rule for determining in which year of assessment an initial allowance is to be granted on capital expenditure incurred in the basis period which is used for two years of assessment.

86. State the general rule for determining in which year of assessment an initial allowance is to be granted on capital expenditure incurred in the basis period which is not used for any year of assessment.

87. State the current rates of initial and annual allowances applicable to the following assets:
(a) Building
(b) Ranching and plantation
(c) Housing estate

88. When is a plant, machinery or fixture said to be disposed of?

89. When an asset is disposed of without change of ownership, what is the price at which the owner is deemed to have bought the asset immediately after the disposal?

90. What is the penalty for failure to disclose information to the FIRS regarding the occurrence of certain events which should result in the withdrawal of investment allowance earlier granted?

91. An allowance granted in respect of capital expenditure incurred for the provision of electricity, water or tarred road where such facilities are not provided by the government is referred to as ...

92. State the event which can give rise to a balancing allowance or charge.

93. The difference between the total qualifying expenditure on an asset on or before a certain date and the total capital allowances made before that date is referred to as …

94. What is the value of an asset at the date of its disposal, if it is disposed of without being sold?

95. State the rates of rural investment allowance granted to a company.

96. What is meant by the "relevant interest" in building?

97. On the purchase of a second-hand building which has been used by the original owner before sale, what is the qualifying expenditure on which the second-hand purchaser will claim capital allowances?

98. How is the capital allowance granted on an asset which is used for business and private purposes?

99. What is the maximum amount of capital allowances claimable by an individual or company in the agro-allied industry in any year of assessment?

13 Loss Reliefs

Part I Multiple-Choice Questions

1. ABC Plc can obtain relief for the loss incurred in its business by…
   A. setting off the loss against profits from other sources for that year of assessment in which the loss was incurred.
   B. setting off the loss against profits of the subsequent years from the same business in which the loss was incurred.
   C. a combination of methods A and B above.
   D. carrying back and setting off the loss against the remainder of assessable profits of the preceding five years.
   E. setting off the loss against capital allowances granted to the company.

2. A sole trader can obtain relief for the loss incurred in his trade by…
   A. setting off the loss against assessable income from other sources for that year of assessment in which the loss was incurred.
   B. setting off the loss against income of the subsequent years from the same trade in which the loss was incurred.
   C. a combination of methods A and B above.
   D. carrying back and setting off the loss against the remainder of assessable income of the preceding five years.
   E. setting off the loss against unrelieved capital allowances.

3. The profits of a company for each year of assessment from each source of its profits is referred to as the …
   A. total profits.
   B. total assessable profits.
   C. assessable profits.
   D. chargeable profits.
   E. remainder of assessable profits.

4. When the assessable profits of a company from various sources are added together but without taking into account balancing charge, loss relief and capital allowances, the result is referred to as the...
   A. total profits.
   B. total assessable profits.
   C. adjusted profits.
   D. chargeable profits.
   E. remainder of assessable profits.

5. The amount of a company's profits from all sources for a year of assessment after adding balancing charge and deducting loss relief and capital allowances is referred to as the ...
   A. total profits.
   B. total assessable profits.
   C. assessable profits.
   D. adjusted profits.
   E. remainder of assessable profits.

6. The amount of an individual's total income for a year of assessment after the exclusion of income exempted from tax and the deduction of reliefs is referred to as the ...
   A. adjusted income.
   B. total assessable income.
   C. assessable income.
   D. chargeable income.
   E. remainder of assessable income.

7. Current year loss relief is allowed against...
   A. income of the subsequent year from the ame trade or business in which the loss was incurred.
   B. income from other sources of the year in which the loss was incurred.
   C. income from other sources arising in the receding five years.
   D. income of the same trade or business aising in the preceding five years.
   E. other income of the following year.

8. What is the time limit for applying for a current year loss relief?
   A. Within twelve months after the end of the year of assessment for which the relief is claimed.
   B. It is granted automatically without an application being made.
   C. Within six years after the end of the year of assessment in which the loss was incurred.
   D. Within four years after the year of assessment in which the loss was incurred.
   E. Within twenty-four months after the year of assessment in which the loss was incurred.

9. A loss incurred in a non-agricultural trade or business carried on by an individual can be carried forward for a maximum of …
   A. one year.
   B. six years.
   C. four years.
   D. three years.
   E. two years.

10. What is the maximum number of years for carrying forward losses incurred by companies (excluding insurance companies)?
    A. Five years
    B. Six years
    C. Four years
    D. Three years
    E. Indefinitely

11. Which of the following statements is/are true?
    i. A terminal loss can be carried backward and set off against the previous five years' profits.
    ii. The aggregate deduction of a loss from assessable income cannot exceed the actual amount of loss.
    iii. Carry forward loss relief can be granted without a formal written claim being made by the taxpayer.
    iv. Current year loss relief is not allowable unless it is claimed in writing by the taxpayer.

A. ii, iii and iv only
B. ii and iii only
C. iii and iv only
D. i and ii only
E. i, ii and iii only

Use the information below to answer questions 12 to 14.

Mr Zobo has been in business as a distributor of fertilizer for many years, making up its accounts to 31st December each year. It made a loss of ₦350,000 in 2000 accounting year and profits of ₦90,000; ₦110,000; ₦50,000; ₦30,000 and ₦60,000 in 2001, 2002, 2003, 2004 and 2005 accounting years respectively.

12. What is the amount of loss available to be carried forward after 2005 year of assessment?
A. ₦350,000
B. ₦70,000
C. ₦280,000
D. ₦120,000
E. Nil

13. Assuming that Mr Zobo has been engaged in animal husbandry, what would have been the loss carried forward after 2005 year of assessment?
A. ₦350,000
B. ₦70,000
C. ₦280,000
D. ₦120,000
E. Nil

14. Assuming that Mr Zobo has been engaged in animal husbandry, what would have been the total profit for 2006 year of assessment?
A. ₦350,000
B. ₦70,000
C. ₦60,000

D. ₦10,000
E. Nil

Use the information below to answer questions 15 t) 17.

Bassey is a Chartered Accountant. He also has other sources of income. His adjusted profits/(loss) were as follows:

	Year ended 31st December		
	2000	2001	2002
	₦	₦	₦
Professional income	250,000	900,000	825,000
Trading profit/(loss)	350,000	(950,000)	560,000
Rental income	135,000	250,000	300,000

15. Assuming that Bassey has made a claim for current year loss relief, the total income for 2001 year of assessment is …
A. nil.
B. ₦735,000.
C. ₦215,000.
D. ₦385,000.
E. ₦950,000.

16. Assuming that Bassey has made a claim for current year loss relief, the total income for 2002 year of assessment is ..
A. Nil
B. ₦200,000.
C. ₦1,150,000.
D. ₦935,000.
E. ₦215,000.

17. Assuming that Bassey has made a claim for current year loss relief, the total income for 2003 year of assessment is ..
A. ₦1,470,000.
B. ₦1,685,000.
C. ₦735,000.
D. ₦1,125,000.
E. ₦860,000

18. Carter permanently ceased business on 31st March, 2006. His adjusted profits/(loss) were as follows:

	₦
Year ended 31st August, 2004	180,000
Year ended 31st August, 2005	480,000
Period ended 31st March, 2006	(140,000)

What is the assessable profit or loss for the penultimate year of assessment?

A. ₦180,000
B. ₦320,000
C. ₦240,000
D. ₦480,000
E. ₦140,000

Use the information below to answer questions 19 to 22.

FTC Ltd, which has various sources of income reported the following adjusted profits/(losses):

	Trade ₦	Transport ₦	Hotel ₦
Year ended 30th Sept. 2001	500,000	20,000	300,000
Year ended 30th Sept. 2002	650,000	140,000	(600,000)
Year ended 30th Sept. 2003	(200,000)	400,000	150,000

19. What is the company's total profit for 2002 year of assessment?
A. ₦220,000
B. ₦820,000
C. ₦520,000
D. ₦600,000
E. Nil

20. What is the company's total profit for 2003 year of assessment?
A. ₦1,090,000
B. ₦190,000
C. ₦790,000

D. ₦600,000
E. Nil

21. What is the company's total profit for 2004 year of assessment?
    A. ₦550,000
    B. ₦400,000
    C. ₦350,000
    D. ₦200,000
    E. Nil

22. What is the loss carried forward at the end of 2004 year of assessment?
    A. ₦200,000
    B. ₦600,000
    C. ₦450,000
    D. ₦650,000
    E. ₦300,000

23. When a loss is set off against other income of the year of assessment in which the loss was incurred, it is referred to as …
    A. terminal loss relief.
    B. early trade loss relief.
    C. current year loss relief.
    D. carry forward loss relief.
    E. concurrent year loss relief.

24. When a loss incurred in the previous years is set off against the subsequent years' income from the same trade or business in which the loss was incurred, it is referred to as …
    A. terminal loss relief.
    B. early trade loss relief.
    C. current year loss relief.
    D. carry forward loss relief.
    E. concurrent year loss relief.

25. A loss incurred in the letting of land and buildings by Alhaji Danbata can be relieved by …
    A. setting off against income from other sources for that year of assessment in which the loss was incurred.
    B. being set off against future rental income.
    C. a combination of methods A and B above.
    D. being set off against the remainder of assessable income of the preceding five years.
    E. being set off against unrelieved capital allowances.

26. What is the maximum number of years for carrying forward a loss incurred in an agricultural trade or business carried on by an individual?
    A. Five years
    B. Six years
    C. Four years
    D. Three years
    E. Indefinitely

27. Which two of the following are conditions for granting a current year loss relief to an individual?
    i. The individual must make a claim to the relevant tax authority within two years after the end of the year of assessment for which the relief is claimed.
    ii. The individual must make a written claim to the relevant tax authority.
    iii. The individual must make a claim to the relevant tax authority within 12 months after the end of the year of assessment for which the relief is claimed.
    iv. The individual would no longer be eligible for carry forward loss relief after claiming current year loss relief.
    A. ii and iii only
    B. i and ii only
    C. ii and iii only
    D. i, ii and iv only
    E. ii, iii and iv only

28. Chief Sabata has been in business for many years and usually makes up the accounts of his business to 30th September each year. For the year ended 30th September, 2010, the business made a loss of ₦200,000. Assuming that the business could not make sufficient profits to absorb the loss in the foreseeable future, in which year of assessment would the unrelieved loss lapse and could no longer be carried forward?
    A. 2013
    B. 2014
    C. 2015
    D. 2016
    E. 2017.

29. What is the maximum number of years for carrying forward losses incurred by African Insurance Plc which is engaged in non-life insurance business?
    A. Five years
    B. Six years
    C. Four years
    D. Three years
    E. Indefinitely

30. Current year loss relief can be claimed by …
    i. Champion Breweries Plc
    ii. Johnson Rock Ventures Limited
    iii. Taye and Kehinde Venture own by two brothers
    iv. Best Brain Bookshops own by Prof. Chukwu
    A. iv only
    B. ii and iii only
    C. i and ii only
    D. iii and iv only
    E. ii, iii and iv only

Part II Short-Answer Questions

31. State the method of loss relief available to a company.

32. State the methods of loss relief available to an individual.

33. State any one condition for granting a carry forward loss relief.

34. What is the relief available to a company which has unrelieved (terminal) losses in the year of cessation of its trade or business?

14 Partnership Assessment

Part I Multiple-Choice Questions

1. Which one of the following statements is true?
   - A. The profit or loss of a partnership is always allocated to the partners in equal proportion.
   - B. The partnership is responsible for the tax due on the profits allocated to each partner.
   - C. The profit or loss of a partnership is allocated between the partners according to the profit sharing ratio determined by the relevant tax authority.
   - D. Each partner is responsible for the tax due on the partnership profits allocated to him.
   - E. Commencement and cessation rules apply to all the partners whenever one partner joins or leaves the partnership.

2. All the following matters are usually dealt with in a partnership agreement except …
   - A. capital contribution by each partner.
   - B. sharing of profits and losses.
   - C. partners' residence.
   - D. interest on capital and interest on drawings.
   - E. partners' remunerations.

3. The time limit for registering changes to the particulars in the partnership agreement with the relevant tax authority is …
   - A. within 60 days of the agreement.
   - B. within 90 days of the agreement.
   - C. within 21 days of the agreement.
   - D. within 15 days of the agreement.
   - E. within 30 days of the agreement.

4. When there is no partnership agreement …
   A. the partnership's profits and losses are shared equally between the partners.
   B. partners contribute equal amount of capital.
   C. partner's capital attracts an interest of 5% per annum.
   D. partners are not entitled to remunerations.
   E. partner's advance attracts an interest of 5% per annum.
   Which of the options A to E is not true?

5. The income earned by a partner from a partnership business is assessable to tax on …
   A. current year basis.
   B. actual year basis.
   C. preceding year basis.
   D. ultimate year basis.
   E. cash basis.

6. Which of the following expenses are taken into account before arriving at the computed income of a partnership?
   i. Domestic expenditure
   ii. Remuneration of partners
   iii. Interest on capital
   iv. Cost of passages
   A. ii and iii only
   B. i, ii and iv only
   C. ii, iii and iv only
   D. iii and iv only
   E. i, ii and iii only

7. The assessable income of an individual from a partnership business includes all the following except …
   A. remuneration.
   B. interest on capital.
   C. interest on drawings.
   D. cost of leave or recreational passages.
   E. share of computed income.

8. Which of the following statements is/are true?
   - i. Capital allowances are not granted to individual partners in a partnership.
   - ii. The tax authority of an individual partners must be the same as that of the partnership.
   - iii. The certified copy of the partnership deed has to be registered with the tax authority of the partnership.
   - iv. Income tax assessment on the profits of a partnership is made on the firm and not on the individual partners.

   A. ii, iii and iv only
   B. ii and iii only
   C. iii and iv only
   D. iii only
   E. i, ii and iii only

Use the information below to answer questions 9 to 12.

Titi, Tata and Tete have been in partnership for many years, sharing profits in the ratio of 5:3:2. They receive a salary of ₦60,000, ₦72,000 and ₦84,000 respectively each year and interest on capital of 10% on their capital contributions of ₦1,000,000, ₦1,500,000 and ₦2,000,000 respectively. The adjusted profit for the year ended 31st December, 2005 before charging the partners' salaries and interest on capital was ₦266,000.

9. What is the partnership computed income or loss?
   A. ₦400,000 profit
   B. ₦666,000 loss
   C. ₦266,000 loss
   D. ₦666,000 profit
   E. ₦400,000 loss

10. What is Titi's assessable income or loss?
   A. ₦40,000 profit
   B. ₦40,000 loss
   C. ₦102,000 profit

D. ₦266,000 profit
E. ₦204,000 profit

11. What is Tata's assessable income or loss?
A. ₦102,000 profit
B. ₦266,000 profit
C. ₦204,000 profit
D. ₦40,000 loss
E. ₦40,000 profit

12. What is Tete's assessable income or loss?
A. ₦102,000 profit
B. ₦40,000 profit
C. ₦40,000 loss
D. ₦204,000 profit
E. ₦266,000 profit

13. Messrs Lion and Tiger have been in partnership for a number of years sharing profits and losses equally after charging salaries of ₦240,000 and ₦360,000 per annum respectively. With effect from 1st April, 2017 they agreed to share profits and losses in the proportions: Lion 60 per cent and Tiger 40 per cent. For the year ended 31st December, 2017, the adjusted profit before charging partners' salaries was ₦1,500,000. What is the assessable income of each partner for 2018 year of assessment?
A. Lion ₦742,500 and Tiger ₦757,500
B. Lion ₦172,500 and Tiger ₦202,500
C. Lion ₦585,000 and Tiger ₦540,000
D. Lion ₦757,500 and Tiger ₦742,500
E. Lion ₦900,000 and Tiger ₦600,000

Use the information below to answer questions 14 to 16.

Mbata, Dada and Oko have been in partnership for many years preparing accounts to 31 December each year and sharing profits and losses equally. Following the retirement of Mbata on 30th June, 2016 and the admission of Apa into the partnership on 1st July,

2016, the profit sharing ratio was changed to Dada 5, Oko 3, Apa 2. The partnership profit for the year ended 31st December, 2016 was ₦1,200,000 and for the year ended 31st December, 2017 was N1,500,000.

14. The partners assessable to tax in 2016 year of assessment and their assessable profits are…
    A. Mbata ₦200,000, Dada ₦500,000, Oko ₦380,000 and Apa ₦120,000.
    B. Mbata ₦200,000 and Apa ₦120,000.
    C. Dada ₦500,000, Oko ₦380,000.
    D. Dada ₦500,000, Oko ₦380,000 and Apa ₦120,000.
    E. Mbata ₦0, Dada ₦0, Oko ₦0 and Apa ₦0.

15. The partners assessable to tax in 2017 year of assessment and their assessable profits are ...
    A. Mbata ₦200,000, Dada ₦500,000, Oko ₦380,000 and Apa ₦120,000.
    B. Mbata ₦500,000, Oko ₦380 and Apa ₦120,000.
    C. Dada ₦500,000, Oko ₦380,000 and Apa N270,000.
    D. Dada ₦500,000, Oko ₦380,000 and Apa ₦300,000.
    E. Dada ₦500,000, Oko ₦380,000 and Apa ₦420,000.

16. The partners assessable to tax in 2018 year of assessment and their assessable profits are …
    A. Mbata ₦200,000, Dada ₦750,000, Oko ₦450,000 and Apa ₦300,000.
    B. Mbata ₦200,000 and Apa ₦300,000.
    C. Dada ₦500,000, Oko ₦380,000 and Apa N120,000.
    D. Dada ₦750,000, Oko ₦450,000 and Apa ₦420,000.
    E. Dada ₦750,000, Oko ₦450,000 and Apa ₦300,000.

Part II Short-Answer Questions

Use the information below to answer questions 17 to 20.

Adam, Eve, Cain and Abel are partners in a firm known as Adams & Co. The principal office or place of business of the partnership firm is situated in Abuja. Adam is resident in Abuja while Cain and Abel are resident in Lagos and Kano respectively. Abel is resident in Ghana.

17. What is the relevant tax authority of the partnership?

18. Which tax authority is responsible for the determination of each partner's profit or loss from the partnership?

19. Where is the income of each partner from the partnership firm deemed to be derived?

20. How is the income of the partnership firm assessed to tax?

21. Where a partner is aggrieved by his income tax assessment in respect of the partnership income he can appeal to …

22. When would you apply the commencement rules in assessing a partner's income from a partnership?

23. When would you apply the cessation provisions in assessing a partner's income from a partnership?

24. Where is a partner deemed to be resident if he has no place or principal place of resident in a year of assessment?

15 Estates, Trusts and Settlements

Part I Multiple-Choice Questions

1. The property of a deceased person is referred to as his …
   A. settlement.
   B. trust.
   C. legacy.
   D. annuity.
   E. estate.

2. A person appointed by a will to administer the estate of a deceased person is referred to as …
   A. an executor.
   B. an administrator.
   C. a settlor.
   D. an annuitant.
   E. a legatee.

3. Which of the following persons is appointed by the court to administer the estate of a deceased person who did not write his will or did not appoint an executor or the executor has failed to act?
   A. Settlor
   B. Legatee
   C. Administrator
   D. Trustee
   E. Annuitant

4. Which of the following persons is/are referred to as personal representative(s)?
   i. Administrator
   ii. Trustee
   iii. Settlor
   iv. Executor

A. ii and iii only
B. i only
C. iv only
D. i and iv only
E. i and ii only

5. An arrangement whereby a property is conveyed to one or more persons to hold and apply the benefits arising therefrom for the advantage of other persons is referred to as …
A. a legacy.
B. a trust.
C. an annuity.
D. a domicile.
E. a devise.

6. A person who holds property and apply the benefits arising out of the property for the advantage of other persons is referred to as a …
A. devisee.
B. legatee.
C. beneficiary.
D. trustee.
E. settllor.

7. A fixed annual amount payable to a person for a given number of years or until death is referred to as …
A. a legacy.
B. a settlement.
C. an annuity.
D. a devise.
E. a domicile.

8. Johnson owned two buildings in Abuja and Port Harcourt. He resided in Calabar on 1st January, 2014 and died in Owerri on 31st March, 2014 following a motor accident. He was buried in his hometown in Akwa Ibom State. His executor resides in Enugu. In which territory is the estate of Johnson liable to tax?

A. Federal Capital Territory
B. Rivers State
C. Cross River State
D. Akwa Ibom State
E. Enugu State

9. The remainder of the computed income of a year of assessment of a settlement, trust or estate after the deduction of all amounts apportioned to beneficiaries is assessable to tax in the name of the ...
   A. legatee.
   B. annuitant.
   C. devisee.
   D. trustee or executor.
   E. settlor.

10. The income from a settlement, trust or estate is assessable to tax in the hands of any trustee, executor, annuitant or beneficiary on …
    A. actual year basis.
    B. current year basis.
    C. preceding year basis.
    D. prepayment basis.
    E. cash basis.

11. Which of the following is/are taken into account in arriving at the computed income of a settlement, trust or estate?
    i. Trustee's or executor's expenses authorised by the deed or will.
    ii. Annuity paid out of income in accordance with the deed or will.
    iii. Interest on capital.
    iv. Capital allowances if the income includes profits from a trade or business.
    A. i, ii and iv only
    B. i and ii only
    C. iii and iv only
    D. i and ii only
    E. i and iv only

The following scenario relates to questions 12 to 16.

OBB made a will in favour of Imata and Amina. Barrister Ukwu was appointed as the executor. The records of the executor showed the following information in respect of OBB's estate for the year ended 31st December, 2013.

		₦
Receipts:		
Business profit		500,000
Rent of let property (gross)		381,000
Other income		268,000
Payments of expenses in respect of the let property:		
Repairs and maintenance of property		30,000
Tenement rate		15,000
Agent's commission		14,000
Construction of iron gate		42,000
Capital allowances in respect of the business		55,000
The will made provisions for:		
i.	Fixed annuity to Kanu Heart Foundation	38,000
ii.	Executor's remuneration per annum	40,000
iii.	Administrative expenses of the executor	24,000

iv. Ex-gratia payment to any of the beneficiary (in case of need) but should not exceed ₦40,000 per annum. During the year, the executor made ex-gratia payment of ₦33,000 to Imata.

v. The net distributable income of the estate is to be shared as follows: Imata one-half and Amina one-third.

12. What is the income assessable to tax in the hands of Imata?
    A. ₦483,000
    B. ₦450,000
    C. ₦300,000
    D. ₦150,000
    E. ₦350,000

13. What is the income assessable to tax in the hands of Amina?
    A. ₦450,000
    B. ₦150,000

C. ₦300,000
D. ₦483,000
E. ₦350,000

14. What is the income assessable to tax in the name of the executor?
A. ₦450,000
B. ₦300,000
C. ₦350,000
D. ₦150,000
E. ₦100,000

15. What is the total income of the estate?
A. ₦1,149,000
B. ₦1,094,000
C. ₦1,098,000
D. ₦993,000
E. ₦1,035,000

16. What is the computed income of the estate?
A. ₦1,047,000
B. ₦992,000
C. ₦933,000
D. ₦996,000
E. ₦891,000

17. The income from a settlement, trust or estate is assessable to tax in the hands of the trustee, executor, annuitant or beneficiary under the
A. Capital Gains Tax Act.
B. Capital Transfer Tax Act.
C. Personal Income Tax Act.
D. Companies Income Tax Act.
E. Settlement, Trust and Estate Tax Act.

Part II Short-Answer Questions

18. Apart from the normal deductions allowable in ascertaining the income of an individual, state two further deductions allowable in ascertaining the computed income of a settlement, trust or estate?

19. Who is responsible for the preparation of the accounts of a settlement, trust or estate?

20. State the accounting date or period that should be covered by the accounts of a settlement, trust or estate.

21. Personal reliefs are granted to a trustee when he is assessed in his official capacity as a trustee. True or false?

22. State any two conditions under which the income of a settlement or trust is deemed to be the income of the settlor or person creating the trust?

23. Under what condition is the income of a settlement paid to or for the benefit of the settlor's child treated as the income of the settlor?

24. Effiong created a trust on 1st January, 2008 in favour of his children. The trustee resides in Abeokuta, while the income of the trust arises in Ibadan. Which State should collect income tax on the income of the trust?

16 Tertiary Education Tax and National Information Technology Development Levy

Part I Multiple-Choice Questions

1. Tertiary education tax is chargeable at the rate of 2% of …
   A. total profit.
   B. chargeable profit.
   C. assessable profit.
   D. distributable profit.
   E. net profit.

2. Tertiary education tax is payable by ...
   A. non-resident companies.
   B. companies not registered in Nigeria.
   C. individuals engaged in trade or business.
   D. partnerships.
   E. companies registered in Nigeria.

3. Which of the following is responsible for the assessment and collection of tertiary education tax?
   A. Joint Tax Board
   B. Ministry of Finance
   C. State Internal Revenue Service
   D. Joint State Revenue Committee
   E. Federal Inland Revenue Service

4. The time limit for payment of tertiary education tax is within …
   A. thirty days after the service of notice of assessment.
   B. ninety days after the service of notice of assessment.
   C. ten days after the service of notice of assessment.
   D. seven days after the service of notice of assessment.
   E. sixty days after the service of notice of assessment.

5. Who is responsible for the management and disbursement of the tertiary education trust fund?
   A. Federal Inland Revenue Service.
   B. Minster of Finance
   C. Board of Trustees
   D. Minister of Education
   E. Joint Tax Board

6. The functions of the Board of Trustees of the Tertiary Education Trust Fund include all the following except ...
   A. updating the Federal Government on its activities and progress through annual and audited reports.
   B. investment of tertiary education tax in appropriate and safe securities.
   C. monitoring and evaluating execution of tertiary education projects.
   D. assessment and collection of education tax.
   E. receiving requests and approving admittable projects after due consideration.

7. Members of the Board of Trustees of the Tertiary Education Trust Fund are appointed by the ...
   A. Minister of Finance.
   B. Minister of Education.
   C. President on the recommendation of the Minister of Education.
   D. President on the recommendation of the Minister of Finance.
   E. President subject to the approval of the Senate.

8. Members of the Board of Trustees of the Tertiary Education Trust Fund include all the following except ...
   A. the Chairman of the Federal Inland Revenue Service.
   B. 6 persons, each representing a geo-political zone in the country.
   C. a representative each of the Federal Ministries of Finance and Education.

D. a representative each from the Universities, Polytechnics and Colleges of Education.
E. the Executive Secretary.

9. Each member (excluding ex-officio member) of the Board of Trustees of the Tertiary Education Trust Fund is to hold office for … years in the first instance and may be reappointed for another … years and no more.
A. 5
B. 3
C. 4
D. 6
E. 2

10. The Board of Trustees of the Tertiary Education Trust Fund shall meet for the conduct of its ordinary meetings …
A. eight times in a year.
B. twelve times in a year.
C. six times in a year.
D. five times in a year.
E. four times in a year.

11. The chief executive and accounting officer of the Tertiary Education Trust Fund is the…
A. Chairman of the Fund.
B. Minister of Education.
C. Minister of Finance.
D. Chairman of the FIRS.
E. Executive Secretary.

12. The Tertiary Education Trust Fund (Establishment, Etc.) Act, 2011 stipulates that a member of the Board of Trustees shall cease to hold office if…
A. he becomes of unsound mind.
B. he becomes bankrupt or makes a compromise with its creditors.

C. he is convicted of a felony or any offence involving dishonesty.
D. he holds a political appointment.
E. he is guilty of serious misconduct in relation to his duty.

Which of the options A to E is incorrect?

13. The distribution of the tertiary education trust fund among universities, polytechnics and colleges of education shall be in the ratio of ...
A. 5:3:2 respectively.
B. 2:1:1 respectively.
C. 3:2:1 respectively.
D. 4:2:1 respectively.
E. 1:3:2 respectively.

14. The FIRS is required to pay tertiary education tax collected into the Tertiary Education Trust Fund and render returns to the Board of Trustees. All the following information should be contained in the returns except ...
A. the name of the company making the payment.
B. the amount of teriary education tax collected.
C. the assessable profit of the company for the accounting period.
D. the precise grounds of objection against the assessment.
E. such other information as may be required by the Board of Trustees.

15. What is the penalty for failure to pay tertiary education tax on the due date?
A. 10% of the amount of tax unpaid
B. 20% of the amount of tax unpaid
C. 5% of the amount of tax unpaid
D. ₦5,000 and double the amount of tax unpaid
E. ₦1,000 and triple the amount of tax unpaid

16. Before the disbursement of the amount in the Tertiary Education Trust Fund ... per cent of the amount accruing to the Fund in the

preceding year is to be set aside to meet the cost of administration and management of the Fund.

A. 10
B. 20
C. 5
D. 15
E. 12

17. Which of the following is responsible for the assessment and collection of national information technology development levy?
A. Joint Tax Board
B. Ministry of Finance
C. National Information Technology Development Agency
D. Joint State Revenue Committee
E. Federal Inland Revenue Service

18. National information technology development levy is due and payable by companies within …
A. thirty days after the service of notice of assessment.
B. ninety days after the service of notice of assessment.
C. ten days after the service of notice of assessment.
D. seven days after the service of notice of assessment.
E. sixty days after the service of notice of assessment.

19. The penalty for failure to pay the national information technology development levy on the due date is …
A. 10% of the levy unpaid.
B. 2% of the levy unpaid.
C. 5% of the levy unpaid.
D. ₦5,000 and double the amount of levy unpaid.
E. ₦1,000 and triple the amount of levy unpaid.

The following scenario relates to questions 20 and 21.

The profit and loss account of XYZ Ltd, a manufacturing company, recorded a net profit of ₦1,600,000 for the year ended 31st December, 2012 after taking into account depreciation ₦200,000, donations to social clubs ₦100,000, profit on disposal of fixed assets ₦30,000 and general provision for bad debts ₦130,000. Capital allowances agreed with the FIRS amounted to ₦200,000.

20. What is the company's tertiary education tax liability?
    A. ₦90,000
    B. ₦40,000
    C. ₦6,000
    D. ₦40,400
    E. ₦32,800

21. What is the income tax liability of the company for 2013 year of assessment?
    A. ₦90,000
    B. ₦540,000
    C. ₦492,000
    D. ₦600,000
    E. ₦84,000

22. National information technology development levy is chargeable at the rate of …
    A. 1% of distributable profit.
    B. 2% of assessable profit.
    C. 2% of profit before tax.
    D. 1 % of profit before tax.
    E. 1% of gross profit.

23. All the following companies and enterprises are liable to pay national information technology development levy except …
    A. GSM service providers and all telecommunication companies.
    B. pension managers and pension related companies.
    C. banks, insurance companies and other financial institutions.
    D. cyber companies and internet providers.
    E. companies engaged in petroleum operations.

24. Each company listed in the National Information Technology Development Agency Act, 2007 is liable to pay the information technology development levy if it earns …
    A. an annual turnover of ₦100 million and above.
    B. an annual turnover of ₦200 million and above.
    C. an annual turnover of ₦300 million and above.
    D. an annual turnover of ₦400 million and above.
    E. an annual turnover of ₦500 million and above.

25. The assessment of a company for the national information technology development levy is to be done at the same time the company is assessed for …
    A. companies income tax.
    B. petroleum profits tax.
    C. capital gains tax.
    D. value added tax.
    E. stamp duties.

26. The Chairman and members of the Board of the National Information Technology Development Agency, other than the ex-officio members, are appointed by the ...
    A. National assembly.
    B. Minister of Science and Technology.
    C. President of the Federal Republic of Nigeria subject to the approval of the Senate.
    D. President of the Federal Republic of Nigeria on the recommendation of the Minister of Education.
    E. President of the Federal Republic of Nigeria on the recommendation of the Minister of Science and Technology.

27. The Board of the National Information Technology Development Agency consist of …
    A. 25 members.
    B. 20 members.
    C. 19 members.
    D. 15 members.
    E. 10 members.

28. The Chief Executive Officer of the National Information Technology Development Agency is designated as the …
    A. Registrar.
    B. Executive Secretary.
    C. Managing Director.
    D. Executive Chairman.
    E. Director General.

29. A member of the Board of Trustees of the Tertiary Education Trust Fund may be removed from office by the …
    A. National assembly.
    B. Minister of Finance.
    C. Chairman of the FIRS.
    D. Minister of Education.
    E. President of the Federal Republic of Nigeria.

30. When is the due date for filing NITDL returns and tertiary education tax returns after the end of the accounting year of an old company?
    A. Within nine months
    B. Within six months
    C. Within three months
    D. Within one months
    E. Within five months

Part II Short-Answer Questions

31. The Executive Secretary of the Tertiary Education Trust Fund is to hold office for … years.

32. Mention three purposes for which tertiary education tax is disbursed to Federal and State tertiary education institutions in Nigeria.

33. What is the penalty for any person guilty of an offence under the Tertiary Education Trust Fund (Establishment, Etc.) Act, 2011?

34. Which of the courts has jurisdiction to try offenders under the Tertiary Education Trust Fund (Establishment, Etc.) Act, 2011?

35. What is the penalty for any body corporate or person who commits an offence under the National Information Technology Development Agency Act, 2007 where no specific penalty is provided in the Act?

36. Given that the total profit of ABC Ltd for 2019 year of assessment is ₦500,000 after taking into account capital allowances and loss relief of ₦55,000 and ₦65,000 respectively, what is the tertiary education tax payable by the company for 2019 year of assessment ?

37. National information technology development levy is an allowable deduction in computing a company's profits for tax purposes. True or false?

38. Tertiary education tax is an allowable deduction in computing the assessable profit of a company engaged in petroleum operations. True or false?

39. Tertiary education tax is an allowable deduction in computing the assessable profit of a company not engaged in petroleum operations. True or false?

40. What should the FIRS do if a company liable to pay national information technology development levy fails to do so on the due date?

41. What is the deadline for filing NITDL returns by a newly incorporated company that is liable to pay the levy?

42. TYC Ltd is a Nigerian telecommunication company. The profit and loss account of the company for the year ended 31st December, 2018 recorded profit before tax of ₦3,720,000. What is the amount of national information technology development levy payable by the company?

17 Taxation of Specialized Companies

Part I Multiple-Choice Questions

1. What is the time limit within which a foreign shipping or airline company can make a claim for recomputation of its tax liability based on the ratios of profits and depreciation certified by the tax authority of its country instead of a fair percentage of its Nigerian turnover?
   A. Five years
   B. Six years
   C. Three years
   D. Two years
   E. Four years

2. The minimum tax payable in Nigeria by a foreign shipping company or airline in a year of assessment is
   A. 5% of Nigerian sales.
   B. 2% of Nigerian sales.
   C. 15% of Nigerian sales.
   D. 20% of Nigerian sales.
   E. 10% of Nigerian sales.

3. What is the time limit within which a life insurance company is required to furnish the FIRS with full particulars of an actuarial revaluation of unexpired risks carried out?
   A. Not later than six months after the revaluation.
   B. Not later than three months after the revaluation.
   C. Not later than nine months after the revaluation.
   D. Not later than two months after the revaluation.
   E. Not later than one month after the revaluation.

4. Which of the following is exempted from income tax?
   A. Dividend distributed by a unit trust.
   B. Dividend distributed by an insurance company.

C. Dividend distributed by a microfinance bank.
D. Dividend distributed by an airline company.
E. Dividend distributed by a shipping company.

5. In determining the profit of a non-Nigerian insurance company which carries on a non-life insurance business, CITA allows a deduction from the company's premium of an amount equal to ... for other reserves, claims and outgoings of the company.
   A. 25% of the total premium
   B. 15% of the total premium
   C. 10% of the total premium
   D. 5% of the total premium
   E. 2.5% of the total premium

6. CITA provides that not less than ... of a non-Nigerian insurance company which carries on a non-life insurance business in Nigeria shall be payable as income tax in a year of assessment.
   A. 35% of the total profit
   B. 25% of the total profit
   C. 20% of the total profit
   D. 15% of the total profit
   E. 10% of the total profit

7. For a non-Nigerian insurance company which carries on a life insurance business through a permanent establishment in Nigeria and whose profit arises wholly in Nigeria, CITA provides that after allowing for all the outgoing and capital allowances as may be restricted under the provision of the Act for any year of assessment, not less than an amount equal to ... shall be available as total profit of the company for tax purposes.
   A. 20% of the gross incomes
   B. 10% of the gross incomes
   C. 15 % of the gross incomes
   D. 10% of the gross incomes
   E. 30% of the gross incomes

8. Section 14(9) of CITA provides that an insurance company, in respect of its life insurance business, shall be allowed deduction from its investment incomes and other incomes, an amount which is equal to ... or 10% of profits (whichever is greater) to a special reserve fund and accumulated until it becomes the amount of the statutory minimum paid-up capital.
   A. 10% of gross premium
   B. 5% of gross premium
   C. 15% of gross premium
   D. 1% of gross premium
   E. 20% of gross premium

9. Section 14(10) of CITA provides that a reinsurance company shall be allowed deductions from its gross profit to be credited to a general reserve fund, an amount not more than ... if the fund is equal to or exceeds the initial statutory minimum authorized share capital.
   A. 25% of the reinsurer's gross profit for the year
   B. 15% of the reinsurer's gross profit for the year
   C. 5% of the reinsurer's gross profit for the year
   D. 20% of the reinsurer's gross profit for the year
   E. 2.5% of the reinsurer's gross profit for the year

10. Section 14(10) of CITA provides that a reinsurance company shall be allowed deductions from its gross profit to be credited to a general reserve fund, an amount not more than ... if the general reserve fund is less than the initial statutory minimum authorized share capital.
   A. 35% of the reinsurer's gross profit for the year
   B. 15% of the reinsurer's gross profit for the year
   C. 5% of the reinsurer's gross profit for the year
   D. 20% of the reinsurer's gross profit for the year
   E. 50% of the reinsurer's gross profit for the year

11. An insurance company that engages the services of an insurance agent, a loss adjuster and an insurance broker is required to include in its annual tax returns a schedule showing:

i. the name and address of that agent/loss adjuster/insurance broker.
ii. the date the services of that agent/loss adjuster/insurance broker were employed and terminated, as applicable.
iii. payments made to each such agent/loss adjuster/insurance broker for the period covered by the tax returns.
iv. the amount of the total profits of such agent/loss adjuster/insurance broker.

A. i, ii and iii only
B. i, ii and iv only
C. i, ii, iii and iv
D. i and ii only
E. i, iii and iv only.

12. CITA provides that where an insurance company carries on both life and non-life insurance businesses …
A. the funds and the books of accounts of one class of insurance are to be kept separate from the other.
B. the annual tax returns of the two classes of insurance business are to be made separately.
C. each class of business is to be assessed separately as "life assurance assessment" and "non-life (other) insurance assessment".
D. a loss incurred in one class of insurance business is available to be carried forward subject to a maximum of four years of assessment.
E. a loss incurred in one class of insurance business can be set off against profits from another class of insurance business.

The following scenario relates to questions 13 to 17.

The profit and loss account of Peacock Airline Limited, a non-Nigerian company, for the year ended 31st December, 2011 is as follows:

	₦
Income from cargo freight into Nigeria	18,000,000
Income from cargo freight out of Nigeria	6,000,000
Income from passenger freight into Nigeria	14,000,000

Income from passenger freight out of Nigeria		22,000,000
Income from passenger/cargo freight on other routes		20,000,000
		80,000,000
Less:		
Wages and salaries	17,000,000	
Depreciation	2,000,000	
Donation to political party	100,000	
Other expenses (including disallowable expenses of ₦900,000)	3,900,000	23,000,000
Net profit		57,000,000

13. What is the assessable profit of the company for Nigerian tax purposes?
    - A. ₦21,000,000
    - B. ₦60,000,000
    - C. ₦20,300,000
    - D. ₦59,300,000
    - E. ₦49,300,000

14. What is the global adjusted profit ratio of the company?
    - A. 35%
    - B. 47%
    - C. 75%
    - D. 65%
    - E. 55%

15. What is the global depreciation ratio of the company?
    - A. 3.3%
    - B. 2.5%
    - C. 7.1%
    - D. 3.5%
    - E. 1.5%

16. What is the total profit of Peacock Airline Ltd for Nigerian tax purposes?

A. ₦21,000,000
B. ₦60,000,000
C. ₦59,300,000
D. ₦20,300,000
E. ₦49,300,000

17. What is the income tax payable by the company?
A. ₦18,000,000
B. ₦14,790,000
C. ₦6,090,000
D. ₦6,300,000
E. ₦17,790,000

18. The financial statements of MBA Unit Trust Scheme for the year ended 31st December, 2014 recorded the following figures:

	₦	₦
Investment income		2,000,000
Wages and salaries	800,000	
Management expenses:		
- Manager's remunerations	400,000	
- Charitable donations	60,000	
- Depreciation	170,000	
- Loss on disposal of investment	75,000	
- Other expenses (all allowable)	115,000	1,620,000
Net profit		380,000

Capital allowances have been agreed at ₦140,000 with the tax authority

What is the income tax liability of the Unit Trust Scheme?
A. ₦205,500
B. ₦183,000
C. ₦163,500
D. ₦141,000
E. ₦143,500

Part II Short-Answer Questions

19. The profit or loss of a non-Nigerian company engaged in air transportation business which is deemed to be derived from Nigeria is …

20. State the ratios to be applied in determining the profits of a foreign shipping or air transport company subject to tax in Nigeria.

21. Under what condition may the FIRS compute the profits of a foreign shipping or air transport company on a fair percentage of the full sum receivable in respect of business done in Nigeria?

22. What is the allowance granted to a foreign shipping company or airline in lieu of capital allowance and how is it calculated?

23. In relation to an insurance company, what is a permanent establishment?

24. How would you determine the assessable profits of a non-Nigerian insurance company which carries on a life insurance business through a permanent establishment in Nigeria and whose profits arise wholly in Nigeria?

25. Amount distributed as dividend from the actuarial revaluation of unexpired risks is deemed to be part of the total profits of a life insurance company. True or false?

26. How is the assessable profit of an authorized unit trust computed?

27. What do you understand by "depreciation ratio" in relation to the taxation of shipping and airline companies?

28. What is "adjusted profit ratio" in relation to the taxation of shipping and airline companies?

29. Under the Companies Income Tax (Amendment) Act 2007, a non-Nigerian insurance company which carries on a non-life insurance business is allowed to deduct from its premium a reserve for unexpired risks in ascertaining the company's profits for tax purposes. State the reserve for unexpired risks allowable as deduction.

18 Pioneer Companies

The principal legislation on pioneer status is the Industrial Development (Income Tax Relief) Act, Cap. 17, LFN 2004. Nevertheless, the Nigerian Investment Promotion Commission which is charged with the administration of pioneer incentive (under the Nigerian Investment Promotion Commission Act) has issued the Pioneer Status Incentive Regulations, 2014. The Regulations came into force on 30th January, 2014. The Minister of Industry, Trade and Investment has also issued the Application Guidelines for Pioneer Status Incentive dated August 2017. Some of the provisions of the Regulations and Guidelines contradict that of the Industrial Development (Income Tax Relief) Act. Most of the qustions provided in this chapter are based on the provisions of the Industrial Development (Income Tax Relief) Act, Cap. 17, LFN 2004. However, questions 25 to 42 are based on the Pioneer Status Incentive Regulations and Application Guidelines for Pioneer Status Incentive.

Part I Multiple-Choice Questions

1. Under the Industrial Development (Income Tax Relief) Act, Cap. 17, LFN 2004, who may direct publication in the Gazette of a list of pioneer industries and pioneer products?
   A. FIRS Board
   B. Minister of Finance
   C. Chairman of the FIRS
   D. Joint Tax Board
   E. President of Nigeria

2. Which of the following Acts contains a list of pioneer industries and pioneer products?
   A. Value Added Tax Act
   B. Petroleum Profits Tax Act
   C. Companies Income Tax Act
   D. Industrial Development (Income Tax Relief) Act
   E. Taxes and Levies (Approved List for Collection) Act

3. Which of the following is not a condition necessary for an industry to qualify for inclusion in the list of pioneer industries?
   A. The industry has incurred capital expenditure to provide facilities such as electricity, water, tarred road, etc not provided by the government.
   B. The industry is not being carried on in Nigeria at all.
   C. The industry is being carried on in Nigeria on a scale, which is not suitable to the economic requirements of Nigeria.
   D. The industry has favourable prospects of further development in Nigeria.
   E. It is in the public interest to encourage the development or establishment of such industry in Nigeria.

4. In accordance with the Industrial Development (Income Tax Relief) Act, a company qualifying for a pioneer certificate must be ...
   A. a company other than a private company.
   B. limited by shares.
   C. incorporated and registered in Nigeria.
   D. resident in Nigeria.
   E. non-resident in Nigeria.

   Which of the options A to E is not true?

5. On what date is the trade of a company which operates a plantation deemed to commence if the company is granted a pioneer certificate?
   A. The date when certificate of incorporation was issued to the company by the Corporate Affairs Commission.
   B. The date when certificate to commence business was issued to the company.
   C. The date when planting first reaches maturity.
   D. The date when the company starts to sell its products to the public.
   E. The date when the company starts clearing land for planting.

6. The benefits or advantages which accrue to a company which has acquired a pioneer status include all the following except ...

A. rent-free land to be provided to the company by the government at construction stage.
B. corporate income tax relief of three to five years.
C. exemption of the company's shareholders from tax on the dividends paid out of exempted profits.
D. the net loss of the pioneer period is available for relief in computing the total profits of the company from new trade or business after the pioneer period.
E. the qualifying capital expenditure incurred during the pioneer period is eligible for capital allowances in the new trade or business after the pioneer period.

7. What is the minimum amount of qualifying capital expenditure to be incurred by an indigenous-controlled company on or before the production day before it can apply for a pioneer certificate?
A. ₦150,000
B. ₦50,000
C. ₦1,500,000
D. ₦500,000
E. ₦100,000

8. What is the minimum amount of qualifying capital expenditure to be incurred by a company which is not indigenous-controlled on or before the production day before it can apply for a pioneer certificate?
A. ₦150,000
B. ₦50,000
C. ₦1,500,000
D. ₦500,000
E. ₦100,000

9. An application for the issue of a pioneer certificate to a company will contain all the following information except …
A. whether the company is or shall be an indigenous-controlled company.
B. the particulars of assets on which capital expenditure will be incurred by the company.

C. the probable date of production day of the company.
D. the particulars of loans and share capital of the company.
E. conditions to be endorsed on the pioneer certificate when it is issued.

10. A company's application for a pioneer certificate must state the particulars of the assets on which qualifying capital expenditure will be incurred by the company during a period of ... years following production day.
A. five
B. six
C. seven
D. three
E. two

11. What is the amount of non-refundable fee that must accompany a company's application for a pioneer certificate as specified in the Industrial Development (Income Tax relief) Act?
A. ₦1,000,000
B. ₦100,000
C. ₦10,000
D. ₦1,000
E. ₦100

12. What is the penalty for any person who makes or presents any declaration or statement or invoice or undertaking which is false in any material particular for the purpose of obtaining a pioneer certificate?
A. A fine not exceeding ₦1,000 or 5 years' imprisonment or both.
B. A fine not exceeding ₦1,000 or 5 years' imprisonment.
C. A fine not exceeding ₦10,000 or 5 years' imprisonment or both.
D. A fine not exceeding ₦100,000 or 5 years' imprisonment.
E. A fine not exceeding ₦100,000 or 2 years' imprisonment or both.

13. What is the time limit within which a proposed company must be incorporated if an application for a pioneer certificate made on behalf of the company was approved before its incorporation?
    A. Not later than four months after the date of notification of the approval to the applicants.
    B. Not later than six months after the date of notification of the approval to the applicants.
    C. Not later than one month after the date of notification of the approval to the applicants.
    D. Not later than nine months after the date of notification of the approval to the applicants.
    E. Not later than three months after the date of notification of the approval to the applicants.

14. Within how many months after the production day is a pioneer company required to apply for the certification of its production day?
    A. Three months
    B. Two months
    C. Four months
    D. Six months
    E. One month

15. Who is responsible for proposing a date to be certified as the production day of a pioneer company?
    A. Federal Inland Revenue Service
    B. Industrial Inspectorate Division, Federal Ministry of Industries
    C. Pioneer company
    D. National Council of Ministers
    E. Joint Tax Board

16. Within how many months after the certification of the production day is a pioneer company required to apply for the certification of its qualifying capital expenditure incurred before the production day?
    A. One month
    B. Two months

C. Three months
D. Four months
E. Five months

17. Certificate of qualifying capital expenditure is issued to a pioneer company by the ...
A. Inspectorate Division of the Ministry of Industries.
B. Corporate Affairs Commission.
C. National Council of Ministers.
D. Federal Inland Revenue Service.
E. Joint Tax Board.

18. A pioneer company is usually granted a tax holiday of ...
A. four years.
B. three years.
C. two years.
D. six years.
E. seven years.

19. What is the maximum number of years that a pioneer company may be granted an extension of its tax relief period under the Industrial Development (Income Tax Relief) Act?
A. Four years
B. Three years
C. Two years
D. Six years
E. Seven years

20. What is the time limit within which a pioneer company can apply for an extension of its tax relief period?
A. One month after the end of the tax relief period.
B. Six months after the end of the tax relief period.
C. Three months after the end of the tax relief period.
D. Twelve months after the end of the tax relief period.
E. Eighteen months after the end of the tax relief period.

21. An extension of the tax relief period may be granted to a pioneer company by the President if he is satisfied as to the ...
    A. company's rate of expansion, standard of efficiency and level of development.
    B. relative importance of the industry in the economy of the country.
    C. level of losses incurred by the company.
    D. implementation of any scheme for the utilisation of local raw materials by the company.
    E. the need for the extension.

    Which of the options A to E is incorrect?

22. What is the period within which the FIRS or the relevant tax authority can raise an additional assessment upon a pioneer company or its shareholders following the cancellation of its pioneer certificate?
    A. Two years
    B. Three years
    C. Four years
    D. Five years
    E. Six years

23. A pioneer certificate to be issued to a proposed company shall be issued only after ...
    A. the incorporation of the company.
    B. the publication of the pioneer certificate.
    C. the certification of the production day.
    D. the certification of the qualifying capital expenditure.
    E. the tax relief period.

24. According to the Industrial Development (Income Tax Relief) Act, Cap. 17, LFN 2004, the list of pioneer industries and products may be amended by the ...
    A. Minister of Finance.
    B. Minister of Industries.
    C. Chairman of the FIRS.
    D. President of the Federal Republic of Nigeria.

E. President of the Federal Republic of Nigeria with the consent of the National assembly.

25. The Pioneer Status Incentive Regulations, 2014 was issued by the ..
A. FIRS Board.
B. Joint Tax Board.
C. Minister of Finance.
D. President of Nigeria.
E. Nigerian Investment Promotion Commission.

26. According to the Pioneer Status Incentive Regulations, 2014, one of the conditions to be fulfilled by a company applying for a pioneer status incentive before its application can be considered is that the company must have incurred a capital expenditure of not less than....
A. ₦1,000,000.
B. ₦50,000,000.
C. ₦10,000,000.
D. ₦100,000,000.
E. ₦50,000,000.

27. The Pioneer Status Incentive Regulations, 2014 specifies that an application for a pioneer status incentive must be made to the .....in the prescribed application form.
A. Joint Tax Board
B. Minister of Finance
C. Federal Inland Revenue Service
D. Nigerian Investment Promotion Commission (NIPC)
E. Industrial Inspectorate Department of the Federal Ministry of Industry

28. The Pioneer Status Incentive Regulations, 2014 provides that the certificate of a company that has been granted pioneer status incentive shall be revoked where ...
A. the company records negative pre-tax earnings.
B. the company has contravened any of the provisions of the Nigerian Investment Promotion Act.

C. the company has failed to fulfil any of the conditions of the certificate.

D. the information provided by the company for the processing of its application is falsified or misleading.

E. the company is engaged in any tax evasion under the cover of the pioneer status incentive.

Which of the options A to E is not correct?

29. Based on the Pioneer Status Incentive Regulations, 2014, which three of the following are reasons for the revocation of the certificate of a company that has been granted pioneer status incentive?

i. The company reneges on its commitment on the utilization of its tax savings accruing from the incentive without justifiable cause.

ii. The financial books of the company are compromised with the intent of short-changing the Commission of the 2 per cent service charge.

iii. There is an established case of abuse of the incentive.

iv. The company is unable to enjoy the incentive as a result of the host community hostility, natural disasters, strikes, insurgency or such other extenuating circumstance.

A. i, iii and iv

B. ii, iii and iv

C. i, ii and iv

D. iii and iv

E. i, ii and iii

30. The tenure of the pioneer status granted to a company can be suspended if the affected company is unable to enjoy the incentive due to suspension of its operations as a result of the host community hostility, natural disasters, strikes, insurgency or such other extenuating circumstance and the company has notified the Nigerian Investment Promotion Commission within ....of the continuous occurrence or persistence of the effect of the circumstance.

A. one month

B. three weeks

C. two months
D. two weeks
E. three months

31. The completed application form for pioneer status incentive should be submitted to the Nigerian Investment Promotion Commission together with the following
A. names and addresses of the company's auditors and tax representative.
B. a copy of the Commission registration certificate.
C. a copy of the applicant's Corporate Affairs Commission incorporation certificate.
D. a copy of the applicant's memorandum and articles of association.
E a copy each of the applicant's statement of share capital, form CAC 2 and particulars of persons who are first directors, form CAC 7.
Which of the options A to E is incorrect?

32. Which of the following is not required to be forwarded to the Nigerian Investment Promotion Commission together with the completed application form for pioneer status incentive?
A. The names and addresses of all the company's bankers.
B. A tax clearance certificate.
C. The relevant regulatory license to operate in the sector or business activity where required.
D. A copy of the business plan of the proposed or actual project which the pioneer status is sought.
E. Evidence of payment of a non-refundable processing fee as stated in the Regulations.

33. A company's application for a pioneer status incentive should be submitted to the Nigerian Investment Promotion Commission within
A. one month of the applicant's commencement of commercial production.
B. eighteen months of the applicant's commencement of commercial production.

C. three months of the applicant's commencement of commercial production.

D. six months of the applicant's commencement of commercial production.

E. one year of the applicant's commencement of commercial production.

34. A company applying for a pioneer status is required to pay to the Nigerian Investment Promotion Commission a ....service charge to be determined from its estimated savings.

A. 2 per cent

B. 5 per cent

C. 10 per cent

D. 15 per cent

E. 20 per cent

35. A company applying for a pioneer status is required to submit to the Nigerian Investment Promotion Commission its .... financial projections to assist the Commission in determining the service charge.

A. two years

B. three years

C. four years

D. five years

E. ten years

36. Where the financial projections submitted to the Nigerian Investment Promotion Commission by a company applying for a pioneer status incentive records negative pre-tax earnings, the service charge shall be determined as ...

A. 0.5 per cent of net assets.

B. 0.5 per cent of gross profits.

C. 0.25 per cent of paid-up capital.

D. 0.25 per cent of turnover of the company for the year.

E. the higher of 0.5% of its net assets or 0.25% of its turnover.

37. Which of the following is not a reason for the disqualification of an application for pioneer status under the Pioneer Status Incentive Regulations, 2014?
    A. The qualifying share capital of the company is less than ten million Naira.
    B. The information provided by the applicant company for the consideration of its application is discovered to be false or misleading.
    C. There is an established case of abuse of the incentive.
    D. The applicant for a pioneer status incentive is not a corporate body registered in Nigeria.
    E. The application is submitted after six months of the applicant's commencement of commercial production.

38. Which of the following industries is not included in the list of pioneer industries and products published in 2017?
    A. Photography
    B. Publishing of books
    C. Manufacture of pharmaceuticals and medical chemicals
    D. Tanning and dressing of leather
    E. Manufacture of soft drinks

39. All the following are included in the list of pioneer industries and products published in 2017 except ...
    A. production of bottle water.
    B. manufacture of tricycles and components.
    C. music production, publishing and distribution.
    D. manufacture of office machinery and equipment.
    E. manufacture of computer and peripheral equipment.

40. The list of pioneer industries and products, 2017 contains .... industries eligible to enjoy pioneer status incentives.
    A. 100
    B. 27
    C. 50
    D. 70
    E. 99

41. The Application Guidelines for Pioneer Status Incentive dated August 2017 was issued by
    A. FIRS Board.
    C. Minister of Finance.
    D. President of Nigeria.
    D Minister of Industry, Trade and Investment
    E. Nigerian Investment Promotion Commission.

42. According to the Application Guidelines for Pioneer Status Incentive, 2017, one of the considerations for the issuance of a pioneer status incentive to an applicant company is that the company must have a non-current tangible assets of over ....
    A. ₦1,000,000.
    B. ₦50,000,000.
    C. ₦10,000,000.
    D. ₦50,000,000.
    E. ₦100,000,000.

Part II Short-Answer Questions

43. Which of the Nigerian Tax Acts grants tax holidays to companies which are engaged in the production of pioneer products?

44. What is the relief available to a company under the Industrial Development (Income Tax Relief) Act?

45. State four industries which are included in the current approved list of pioneer industries and products.

46. What is a pioneer certificate?

47. State any two particulars that must be included in a company's application for a pioneer certificate as specified in the Industrial Development (Income Tax Relief) Act.

48. What is the name of the account to be credited with the non-refundable fee payable by a company when applying for a pioneer certificate?

49. What is the effective date of a pioneer certificate issued to a proposed company?

50. What is the effective date of cancellation of a pioneer certificate of a company?

51. State the effective date of cancellation of the pioneer certificate of a company which was granted a pioneer status on 1/6/03 but its pioneer certificate was cancelled on 31/3/06.

52. Give any two reasons that may cause the Minister of Industries to cancel a pioneer certificate earlier issued to a company?

53. Define an indigenous-controlled company.

54. What is meant by a production day certificate?

55. Production day certificate is issued to a pioneer company by ...

56. Why is the production day significant to a pioneer company?

57. What is meant by the certificate of qualifying capital expenditure?

58. In certifying the amount of capital expenditure incurred by a pioneer company before its production day, what is the treatment of the sales proceeds of an asset disposed of before the company's production day?

59. State one benefit which a pioneer company can enjoy after the expiration of its tax relief period.

60. What is an old trade or business in relation to a pioneer company?

61. The day on which the trade or business of a pioneer company commences is referred to as the …

62. When is a pioneer company deemed to commence a new trade or business?

63. State the accounting period of a pioneer company.

64. Under what circumstance is the profit earned by a pioneer company during its tax relief period subject to tax?

65. Under what circumstance is the dividend paid by a pioneer company subject to tax in the hands of the shareholders?

66. Qualifying capital expenditure incurred by a pioneer company during its tax relief period is deemed to have been incurred on …

67. When is a pioneer company entitled to claim capital allowances on assets acquired during its tax relief period?

68. How is a net loss incurred by a pioneer company to be treated at the end of the tax relief period?

69. Where a pioneer company carries on any trade or business other than its pioneer enterprise, the profits earned from such non-pioneer enterprise during the tax relief period are not liable to tax under CITA. True/false?

70. Any dividends paid out of the exempted profits of a pioneer company shall be subject to tax in the hands of the receipient shareholders. True/false?

19 Tax Returns, Assessments, Objections, Appeals and Collection

Part I Multiple-Choice Questions

1. The due date for the filing of self-assessment returns under the Personal Income Tax Act is ….
   A. on or before the 28th day of February of every year.
   B. on or before the 31st day of March of every year.
   C. on or before the 30th day of April of every year.
   D. on or before the 30th day of June of every year.
   E. on or before the 31st day of December of every year.

2. What is the time limit for a company to file its self-assessment return after the end of its accounting period?
   A. Within nine months
   B. Within six months
   C. Within three months
   D. Within one month
   E. Within five months

3. Which of the following documents/information may not be required for the registration of a company with the FIRS?
   A. A copy of the certificate of incorporation of the company.
   B. A copy of the memorandum and articles of association of the company.
   C. The date in each year to which accounts will be made up.
   D. The date on which the company will cease business if it is set up for a single adventure or undertaking.
   E. The registered address of the company.

4. Which of the following may not be contained in the tax return submitted to the FIRS by a company?

A. The audited accounts of the company
B. The capital allowances computation
C. The income tax computation
D. The list of the company's shareholders
E. A true and correct statement in writing containing the amount of the company's profit from each and every source

5. A system of assessment which requires a taxpayer to file a return of his or its income together with his or its own calculation of the amount of tax payable is referred to as …
A. revenue assessment.
B. best of judgement assessment.
C. back duty assessment.
D. jeopardy assessment.
E. self- assessment.

6. Where a taxpayer has failed to file his or its tax return with the relevant tax authority or where his or its tax return has been rejected, the tax authority may issue an estimated assessment referred to as …
A. protective assessment.
B. best of judgement assessment.
C. back duty assessment.
D. jeopardy assessment.
E. revised assessment.

7. Where an assessment has been made and later another assessment is raised to replace the original assessment, the new assessment is referred to as …
A. final and conclusive assessment.
B. best of judgement assessment.
C. back duty assessment.
D. jeopardy assessment.
E. revised/amended assessment.

8. An original assessment was issued for 2010 year of assessment. An additional assessment can no longer be raised after … except the taxpayer committed fraud, wilful default or neglect.

A. 2013
B. 2014
C. 2015
D. 2016
E. 2017

9. A company operating in the Nigerian Stock Exchange is required to file a return of its monthly transactions. The information to be included in the return if the transactions involve an offer in the primary market include all of the following except …
   A. the type of offer.
   B. the services rendered.
   C. the amount of tax deducted at source.
   D. the names and addresses of customers.
   E. the amount of value added tax payable.

10. A company operating in the Nigerian Stock Exchange is required to file a return of its monthly transactions. The information to be included in the return if the transactions involve operations in the secondary market include all of the following except …
   A. the number and value of transactions carried out during the relevant month.
   B. the names and addresses of the principal officers of the company.
   C. the commission received or paid.
   D. the amount of tax deducted at source.
   E. the amount of value added tax payable.

11. Which of the following is not an advantage of self-assessment system?
   A. It reduces the work load of the revenue staff.
   B. The taxpayer may need the services of tax consultants.
   C. With the approval of the tax authority the company can pay the tax due by instalments.
   D. It reduces the cost of tax collection to the government.
   E. It speeds up the process of tax collection and increases the revenue accruing to the government

12. A company has been in business for many years and makes up its accounts annually to 31st March. What is the deadline for the filing of the company's audited accounts and returns with the FIRS for the year ended 31st March, 2019?
    A. Not later than 30th June, 2019
    B. Not later than 31st May, 2019
    C. Not later than 31st July, 2019
    D. Not later than 31st December, 2019
    E. Not later than 30th September, 2019

13. The time limit for a company operating in the Nigerian Stock Exchange to file with the FIRS a return of its transactions during each calendar month is ...
    A. 30 days after the end of each calendar month.
    B. 21 days after the end of each calendar month.
    C. 7 days after the end of each calendar month.
    D. 15 days after the end of each calendar month.
    E. 10 days after the end of each calendar month.

14. The benefits of self-assessment system to the taxpayer include ...
    i. increasing the work load of the taxpayer.
    ii. exemption from payment of provisional tax.
    iii. instalmental payment of the tax due with the approval of the tax authority.
    iv. opportunity given to the taxpayer to understate his tax liability.
    A. ii, iii and iv only
    B. i, ii and iii only
    C. ii and iii only
    D. i and ii only
    E. iii and iv only

15. Where the relevant tax authority gives a notice to any taxable person calling for further returns, books, documents, information, etc, the period stipulated in the notice for compliance from the date of service of the notice must be at least ...

A. thirty days.
B. sixty days.
C. ninety days.
D. seven days.
E. fourteen days.

16. A notice of assessment contains all the following information except
    A. the amount of the total profits.
    B. the tax payable.
    C. the place at which payment should be made.
    D. a declaration by the company that the returns used for the assessment are true and complete.
    E. the rights of the company as contained in the relevant sections of CITA.

17. What is the time limit for raising an additional assessment on a taxpayer where the assessment is not as a result of fraud, wilful default or neglect on the part of the taxpayer?
    A. Six years
    B. Three years
    C. One year
    D. Six months
    E. Nine months

18. The FIRS is required to prepare a list of companies assessed to income tax. According to CITA, the assessment list should contain all the following information except …
    A. the names and addresses of the companies assessed to tax.
    B. the name and address of any person in whose name any such company is chargeable.
    C. evidence of payment of the whole or part of the tax due into a bank designated for the collection of tax.
    D. the amount of total profits of each company.
    E. the amount of tax payable by each company.

19. What is the time limit within which a notice of objection to an assessment must be given from the date of service of the notice of assessment?
    A. Thirty days
    B. Twenty one days
    C. Seven days
    D. Sixty days
    E. Fifteen days

20. If a company disagrees with its tax assessment, it may give a notice of objection to the …
    A. Joint Tax Board.
    B. Tax Appeal Tribunal.
    C. Federal Inland Revenue Service.
    D. Federal High Court.
    E. Court of Appeal.

21. An individual who is aggrieved by an income tax assessment made on him can send a notice of objection to the …
    A. Joint Tax Board.
    B. Tax Appeal Tribunal.
    C. Federal Inland Revenue Service Board.
    D. High Court.
    E. State Board of Internal Revenue.

22. Rearrange the following processes in sequential order:
    i. Appeal to the Court of Appeal
    ii. Objection to the FIRS
    iii. Appeal to the Federal High Court
    iv. Appeal to the Tax Appeal Tribunal
    A. iv, ii, iii and i
    B. ii, iv, i and iii
    C. iii, i, iv and i
    D. ii, iv, iii and i
    E. ii, i, iv and iii

23. What is the time limit within which an appeal can be made to the Tax Appeal Tribunal against an assessment from the date of service of the relevant tax authority's notice of refusal to amend the assessment?
    - A. Twenty-eight days
    - B. Thirty days
    - C. Sixty days
    - D. Ninety days
    - E. Seven days

24. A notice of appeal against an assessment should contain all the following except …
    - A. the amount of the tax charged by such assessment.
    - B. the amount of the total profits upon which such tax was charged as appearing in the notice of assessment.
    - C. the quantum of Pay As You Earn (PAYE) which the company deducted and remitted to the appropriate tax authority.
    - D. the date upon which the appellant was served with notice of refusal by the FIRS to amend the assessment as desired.
    - E. the precise grounds of appeal against the assessment.

25. What is the duration for payment of provisional tax by companies from the commencement of each year of assessment?
    - A. Within six months
    - B. Within nine months
    - C. Within three months
    - D. Within one month
    - E. Within five months

26. What are the conditions to be fulfilled by a company before it can be granted an extension of time for filing of returns and accounts?
    - i. The company must apply in writing to the FIRS for an extension of time for filing of returns.
    - ii. The application must be made before the expiration of the time allowed for filing of returns.

iii. The company must give satisfactory reasons for its inability to meet the dateline for submission of returns.

iv. The request for extension must be accompanied with evidence of payment of an amount equal to one-half of the tax paid in the preceding year.

A. i, ii, iii and iv
B. ii, iii and iv only
C. i, ii and iv only
D. i, ii and iii only
E. iii and iv only

27. If there is no objection or appeal against an income tax assessment, what is the time limit within which the tax must be paid after the date of service of the notice of assessment?
A. Ninety days
B. Two months
C. One month
D. Two weeks
E. Ten days

28. The time limit for payment of income tax where an objection or appeal has been determined is …
A. within one month of notification of the tax payable.
B. within two months of notification of the tax payable.
C. within ten days of notification of the tax payable.
D. within fifteen days of notification of the payable.
E. within sixty days of notification of the tax payable.

29. The time limit within which a company filing self-assessment return is required to pay the tax due in one lump sum from the date of filing the assessment is …
A. two months.
B. three months.
C. four months.
D. five months.
E. six months.

30. With the approval of the FIRS, a company filing self – assessment return may pay the tax due instalmentally, but the number of instalments must not exceed …
    A. five monthly instalments.
    B. three monthly instalments.
    C. four monthly instalments.
    D. nine monthly instalments.
    E. six monthly instalments.

31. Where a company filing self-assessment return is granted instalmental payment concession, the full payment must be made not later than … of the year of assessment for which the tax has been charged?
    A. 30th November
    B. 31st December
    C. 31st October
    D. 30th September
    E. 30th June

32. For a company filing self-assessment return to qualify for instalmental payment concession, the company's request for instalmental payment must be accompanied with …
    A. evidence of payment of the first instalment of its assessment.
    B. evidence of full payment of the previous year's tax assessment.
    C. a tax clearance certificate.
    D. evidence of payment of the last three year's tax assessment.
    E. evidence of remittance of withholding taxes.

33. XYZ Ltd was served a notice of assessment for ₦56,000 for 2018 year of assessment on 1st November, 2018. The tax charged must be paid not later than …
    A. 14th December, 2018.
    B. 31st December, 2018.
    C. 30th November, 2018.
    D. 31st March, 2019.
    E. 30th April, 2019.

34. For an objection to be valid, the notice of objection must:
    i. be given to the relevant tax authority in writing.
    ii. state the grounds of objection to the assessment.
    iii. be made within 30 days from the date of service of the notice of assessment.
    iv. be accompanied with evidence of payment of one half of the tax charged by the assessment.
    A. i, ii, iii and iv
    B. i, ii and iii only
    C. i, ii and iv only
    D. ii, iii and iv only
    E. ii and iii only
    Which of the options A to E is correct?

35. What is the time limit within which an individual or a company can apply for relief in respect of an error or mistake in a return submitted by him or it which has caused his or its assessment to be excessive?
    A. Within 3 years after the end of the year of assessment affected.
    B. Within 4 years after the end of the year of assessment affected.
    C. Within 5 years after the end of the year of assessment affected.
    D. Within 1 year after the end of the year of assessment affected.
    E. Within 6 years after the end of the year of assessment affected.

36. For how many days may things distrained be kept before disposal?
    A. Fifteen days
    B. Thirty days
    C. Twenty-one days
    D. Sixty days
    E. Fourteen days

37. An immovable property distrained cannot be sold by the tax authority without an order of …
    A. the Tax Appeal Tribunal.
    B. the Joint Tax Board.
    C. a High Court.
    D. a Magistrate Court.
    E. a Joint State Revenue Committee.

38. Measures adopted by the FIRS to enforce payment of tax due include all the following except …
    A. imposition of penalty for late payment.
    B. denial of clearance for any ship owned wholly or partly or chartered by the defaulting company.
    C. non-issuance of tax clearance certificate to the defaulting taxpayer.
    D. granting of tax holiday to the taxpayer.
    E. levying of distress on the property of the taxpayer.

39. The Nigeria Customs Service may be empowered to refuse clearance for any ship owned wholly or partly or chartered by a company which has defaulted in the payment of income tax due for more than …
    A. six months.
    B. nine months.
    C. four months.
    D. five months.
    E. three months.

40. A taxpayer can make a claim for repayment of income tax paid in excess of what he should have paid within … after the end of the year of assessment to which it relates.
    A. 6 years
    B. 5 years
    C. 4 years
    D. 3 years
    E. 2 years

41. Where there is no objection to or appeal against tax assessment, the tax charged is payable within two months after the date of service of the notice of assessment on the company but not later than ... of the year of assessment for which the tax has been charged even if the period of two months expires after that date.
    A. 1st December
    B. 31st December
    C. 15th December
    D. 21st December
    E. 14th December

42. The amount of provisional tax that a company is required to pay is an amount equal to ...
    A. $66\frac{2}{3}$% of the tax paid in the immediately preceding year of assessment.
    B. 50% of the tax paid in the immediately preceding year of assessment.
    C. 75% of the tax paid in the immediately preceding year of assessment.
    D. double the tax paid in the immediately preceding year of assessment.
    E. the tax paid in the immediately preceding year of assessment.

43. Which of the following statements is incorrect?
    A. Companies not filing self assessment are required to pay provisional tax.
    B. Provisional tax is not a separate tax on its own rather it is an advance payment of income tax.
    C. Provisional tax must be paid in one lump sum (except an approval is granted by the FIRS for the tax to be paid by instalments).
    D. Provisional tax is payable where the collection of tax is in abeyance because of an objection or an appeal against a tax assessment.
    E. Provisional tax is payable by a company when it does not

have sufficient funds to pay the full amount of tax stated in the notice of assessment.

44. A company has been in business for many years and makes up its accounts annually to 30th June. What is the deadline for the filing of the company's audited accounts and returns with the FIRS?
    A. not later than 30th September.
    B. not later than 31st October.
    C. not later than 30th November.
    D. not later than 31st December.
    E. not later than 31st August.

45. Which of the following information may not be required for the registration of a company with the FIRS?
    A. The date on which the company commenced or will commence business.
    B. The precise nature of the company's business.
    C. The names and addresses of the company's directors.
    D. The names and addresses of the company's debtors and creditors.
    E. The names and addresses of the company's bankers, auditors and tax representative.

46. What is the time limit for filing accounts and returns with the FIRS by a newly incorporated company?
    A. Within 18 months from the date of the company's incorporation.
    B. Within 18 months from the date of the company's incorporation or not later than 6 months after the end of its first accounting period, whichever is earlier.
    C. Not later than 6 months after the end of the company's first accounting period.
    D. Within 5 months after the end of the company's first accounting period.
    E. Not later than 30 days after the end of each year.

47. What is the time limit for filing of income tax return by an individual from the commencement of every year of assessment?
    A. Ninety days
    B. Sixty days
    C. Thirty days
    D. Fifteen days
    E. One hundred and twenty days

48. A company which has been in business for more than eighteen months is required to file with FIRS its audited accounts and returns not later than … after the end of the company's accounting year.
    A. nine months
    B. six months
    C. three months
    D. one month
    E. five months

49. A taxpayer may apply in writing to the Board of the relevant tax authority for an extension of time within which to file returns. Which of the following is not likely to be an acceptable reason for granting of extension of time for making returns?
    A. The death of the taxpayer within the period of filing of the returns in the case of an individual taxpayer.
    B. The death of any principal officer of the company (e.g. Chairman, Managing Director or Company Secretary) within the period of filing of the returns in the case of a company.
    C. Disagreement between partners in a partnership firm within the period of filing of the returns.
    D. The business experienced a natural disaster within the period of filing of the returns
    E. The death of a partner in a partnership firm within the period of filing of the returns.

50. The FIRS can raise an assessment on a company before the expiration of the time allowed for filing of tax returns if it considers

such assessment to be necessary for any reason of urgency. The FIRS refers to this assessment as ...

A. emergency assessment.

B. revised/amended assessment.

C. back duty assessment.

D. jeopardy/protective assessment.

E. administrative assessment.

51. The FIRS can raise an assessment on a taxpayer before the expiration of the time allowed for filing of tax returns if it considers such assessment to be necessary for any reason of urgency, which according to the FIRS, may include …

A. imminent sale or transfer of trade/business of the company to another.

B. intended remittances to foreign partners.

C. imminent liquidation of a company or an intention to dispose of its valuable assets.

D. where the true amount of the assessable profits of the taxpayer cannot be readily determined.

E. imminent escape by a taxpayer to foreign countries.

Which of the options A to E is not true?

52. XYZ Limited was given a notice of tax assessment of ₦800,000.00 on 1st July, 2019 for 2019 year of assessment. The assessment is expected to be paid …

A. between 1st July, 2019 and 30th September, 2019.

B. not later than 31st July, 2019.

C. by 14th December, 2019.

D. not later than 31st December, 2019.

E. between 1st July, 2019 and 31st August, 2019.

53. Where an agent has been engaged by a taxpayer for the purpose of filing of tax returns, the forms must be signed by ....

A. the agent alone.

B. the taxpayer in person in the case of filing of returns under the Personal Income Tax Act.

C. the Director or the Company Secretary in the case of filing returns under the Companies Income Tax Act.

D. the taxpayer or the Director or the Company Secretary as the case may together with the agent.

E. the taxpayer or the Director or the Company Secretary as the case may be together with the agent and a senior employee of the relevant tax authority.

54. A taxpayer must file tax returns under the self-assessment regime in person or engage the services of an accredited agent to file returns on his behalf. The agent must be ...

i. tax compliant.

ii. an employee of the relevant tax authority.

iii. fully certified by any one of the recognised professional bodies (CITN, ICAN or ANAN).

iv. have the accompanying seals of any of the recognised professional bodies.

A. iii and iv only

B. i and iii only

C. i, ii and iii only

D. i, iii and iv only

E. ii, iii and iv only.

55. Failure of a taxpayer to comply with the relevant tax laws can attract the following consequences except …

A. administrative tax (best of judgement) assessment.

B. sealing of the taxpayer's business premises.

C. search and seizure of records, documents, etc.

D. granting of tax amnesty to the taxpayer.

E. distrain.

56. Which one of the following is not a taxpayer's obligation?

A. To register with the relevant tax authority.

B. To assess himself or itself to tax.

C. To deduct or collect and remit VAT, WHT and PAYE.

D. To engage the services of a tax consultant or agent.

E. To make voluntary disclosure of all incomes and expenditures.

57. A taxpayer's obligations include all the following except ...

A. to keep proper records, documents and books of accounts.

B. to file tax returns on or before the due.

C. to declare and pay tax on or before the due date.

D. to furnish the tax authority with information about other taxpayers.

E. to cooperate with any authorised officer of the tax authority while on official duty.

58. A taxpayer has the right to ...

A. object to a tax assessment.

B. appeal against a notice of refusal to amend an assessment.

C. demand for a specific service from the government in return for the tax paid.

D. be issued a tax clearance certificate after discharge of his tax liabilities.

E. demand for proper identification from any person claiming to be a tax official.

Part II Short-Answer Questions

59. What condition must be fulfilled by the liquidator of a company being wound-up before distributing any of the company's assets to the shareholders?

60. State two consequences of failing to file a self-assessment return by a company.

61. State two reasons that may cause a tax authority to enter and search a taxpayer's premises.

62. ... is issued to authorize an officer of the FIRS to enter a taxpayer's premises to search, seize and remove any records, documents, etc.

63. Under what condition may the FIRS grant an extension of time for making an objection against an assessment?

64. When does the tax authority issue a notice of refusal to amend an assessment?

65. When is an assessment deemed to be final and conclusive?

66. The power which the tax authority has to sell a taxpayer's goods, bonds, securities, land, premises, etc, for the purpose of enforcing or recovering the tax overdue for payment is referred to as …

67. State the sequence for the utilization of the proceeds of sale of any property distrained by the FIRS or the State Internal Revenue Service.

68. What is the time limit for raising an assessment or additional assessment on a taxpayer where the assessment relates to fraud, wilful default or neglect on the part of the taxpayer?

69. Under which name can a company be chargeable to tax?

70. The due date for filing a company's returns in respect of CIT, CGT, education tax and NITDL are the same. True or false?

71. State any three documents or information that should be sent to the tax office to enable the office open a tax file for a company.

72. A company's returns are to be filed with the FIRS only on receipt of a demand notice. True or false

73. When a BOJ or administrative assessment is issued to a taxpayer, he is no longer required to file tax returns. True or false?

20 Tax Clearance Certificate

Part I Multiple-Choice Questions

1. A tax clearance certificate is usually issued to cover a period of … preceding the current year of assessment.
   A. one year
   B. two years
   C. three years
   D. six years
   E. five years

2. A tax clearance certificate contains all the following information except …
   A. the rights of the taxpayer.
   B. total profits or chargeable income.
   C. tax payable.
   D. tax paid.
   E. tax outstanding.

3. The following conditions must be fulfilled before a tax clearance certificate (TCC) is issued by the relevant tax authority:
   A. The taxpayer must apply in writing for the TCC.
   B. The taxpayer must have filed his tax returns up to date.
   C. The taxpayer must have paid the TCC fees.
   D. The taxpayer must have paid the tax assessed on him for the preceding three years.
   E. The taxpayer must have remitted all the taxes deducted by him to the relevant tax authority.

   Which of the options A to E is not true?

4. Within how many weeks is the tax authority required to issue a tax clearance certificate from the date of demand by the taxpayer?
   A. Four weeks
   B. Six weeks

C. Three weeks
D. Two weeks
E. Twelve weeks

5. All the following transactions require the production of a tax clearance certificate except …
A. application for approval of building plans.
B. application for firearms licence.
C. application for award of contracts by Government.
D. application for admission of a taxpayer's child into a University.
E. application for trade licence.

6. Which of the following transactions does not require the presentation of a tax clearance certificate?
A. Application for distributorship
B. Application for certificate of occupancy
C. Application for employment
D. Application for pools or gaming licence
E. Registration of motor vehicle

7. A person be it a government organization or corporate entity who fails to demand for a tax clearance certificate as required by section 85(2) of PITA is guilty of an offence and is liable on conviction to a fine of ...
A. ₦5,000,000 or 3 years' imprisonment or both.
B. ₦500,000 or 3 years' imprisonment or both.
C. ₦50,000 or 3 years' imprisonment or both.
D. ₦5,000,000 or 5 years' imprisonment or both.
E. ₦1,000,000 or to 4 years' imprisonment or both.

Part II Short-Answer Questions

8. What is a tax clearance certificate?

9. What is the penalty stipulated in PITA for obtaining a tax clearance certificate through misrepresentation, forgery, falsification or incorrect information?

21 Tax Evasion, Tax Avoidance, Tax Offences and Penalties

Part I Multiple-Choice Questions

1. Where a taxpayer arranges his affairs in such a manner that he reduces his tax liability without contravening the law, this is referred to as
   A. anti-avoidance.
   B. tax evasion.
   C. back duty.
   D. tax avoidance.
   E. fictitious transaction.

2. An illegal means adopted by a taxpayer to escape payment of tax or to reduce his tax liability is referred to as …
   A. tax planning.
   B. tax evasion.
   C. tax mitigation.
   D. tax avoidance.
   E. fictitious transaction.

3. Non-disclosure of some employees' allowances in the payroll in order to reduce their PAYE tax is an example of …
   A. anti-avoidance.
   B. tax evasion.
   C. tax mitigation.
   D. tax avoidance.
   E. artificial transaction.

4. All the following are examples of tax evasion except …
   A. financing a company with more loans than share capital.
   A. overstating expenses.
   B. failure to submit tax returns.

C. falsification of business records and books of accounts.
D. failure to pay tax.

5. All the following are examples of tax avoidance except ...
A. exercising right of election at commencement of business.
B. investing in preferred sectors to take advantage of incentives.
C. claiming roll-over relief on disposal of asset.
D. concealment of income.
E. taking advantage of the loopholes existing in the tax laws.

6. What is the penalty for collecting or attempting to collect personal income tax by an unauthorised person?
A. ₦5,000 or 5 years' imprisonment or both
B. ₦5,000 or 3 months' imprisonment or both
C. 10% per annum of the amount of tax
D. ₦5,000 or 10% of the amount of tax, whichever is higher
E. ₦1,000 or 3 years' imprisonment or both

Part II Short-Answer Questions

7. Under the Personal Income Tax Act, what is the penalty for a bank which fails to prepare and deliver a return at the end of each month stating the names and addresses of new customers of the bank?

8. Under CITA, what is the penalty for failure to file with the FIRS a company's audited accounts and returns within the stipulated time?

9. What are the penalties prescribed in PITA for making an incorrect return by omitting or understating any income liable to tax?

10. What is the penalty prescribed in PITA for a person on whom a warrant of search is served who refuses to co-operate with the officer(s) executing the warrant?

11. What is the penalty prescribed by CITA for any principal officer, agent, factor or representative of a company on whom a warrant of

search is served who refuses to co-operate with the officer(s) executing the warrant?

12. State the penalties for late payment of personal income tax.

13. What is the penalty prescribed in PITA for a tax official who demands more tax than the authorised tax assessment, misappropriates or embezzles the tax collected or renders false return of tax collected?

14. Under CITA, what is the penalty for a tax official who demands more tax than the authorised tax assessment, misappropriates or embezzles the tax collected or renders false return of tax collected?

15. Under CITA, what is the penalty for collecting or attempting to collect company's income tax by an unauthorised person?

16. An investigation into the affairs of a taxpayer by a tax authority with a view to recovering the tax lost or under-assessed or under-paid in the past years is known as …

22 Presumptive Taxation and Tax Amnesty

Part I Multiple-Choice Questions

1. Which one of the following statements is incorrect?
   - A. Nigeria has a very low tax compliance rate.
   - B. The tax to GDP of Nigeria is adjudged to be very high.
   - C. Nigeria has a large scale informal sector.
   - D. The formal sector accounts for most of Nigeria's tax revenue.
   - E. The Nigerian informal sector provides employment to more people in the country than the formal sector.

2. The characteristics of the informal sector as identified by the International Labour Organisation (1972) include all the following except ...
   - A. government ownership of enterprises.
   - B. skills acquired outside the formal school system.
   - C. unregulated markets.
   - D. reliance on indigenous resources.
   - E. ease of entry.

3. Which one of the following statements is not true of the Nigerian informal sector?
   - A. Most of the self-employed individuals and SMEs operate in the informal sector.
   - B. Most of the enterprises operating in the informal sector are not captured in the tax net.
   - C. Most of the enterprises operating in the informal sector are not registered with the relevant government authorities.
   - D. Most of the enterprises operating in the informal sector are taxed based on their financial statements.
   - E. Most of the enterprises operating in the informal sector have small scale of operations.

4. An indirect means of ascertaining tax liability by which the taxpayer is assessed to tax on the basis of his perceived income instead of the actual income is referred to as ......
   A. presumptive taxation.
   B. minimum taxation.
   C. tax mitigation.
   D. tax shifting.
   E. tax manipulation.

5. Majority of the enterprises operating in the informal sector are hard to tax because ...
   A. they do not have taxable income.
   B. their transactions are mostly cash-based and not documented.
   C. records are not kept in such a manner as would enable proper assessment of their income.
   D. they are not registered with the relevant government authorities.
   E. the tax authorities are overwhelmed by the large number of small businesses.

   Which of the options A to E is not correct?

6. Presumptive taxation was introduced into the Nigerian tax laws to ensure that ...
   A. tax incentives are granted to deserving taxpayers.
   B. many of the operators in the informal sector are captured in the tax net.
   C. best of judgement assessment is put in abeyance.
   D. cost of tax administration is maximized.
   E. non-governmental organizations (NGOs) are exempted from income tax.

7. The advantages of presumptive taxation include all the following except ...
   A. reducing cost of tax administration and enforcement by tax authorities.
   B. reducing taxpayers' compliance cost.

C. minimizing tax avoidance and tax evasion.
D. maximizing cost of tax administration and compliance.
E. broadening the tax base.

8. Presumptive income taxation is disadvantageous because …
A. it is a negation of the canons of a good tax system.
B. presumptive tax assessment can be arbitrary.
C. taxpayers may not be able to get relief for losses incurred in the past years.
D. presumptive tax assessment can be regressive.
E. it broadens the tax base.

9. Presumptive taxation methods used to estimate income of a taxpayer and assess tax liability include all of the following except …
A. a fixed percentage of the liabilities of the taxpayer's business.
B. a fixed percentage of the assets of the taxpayer's business.
C. a fixed percentage of the turnover of the taxpayer's business.
D. tax based on change in the taxpayer's net worth over the year.
E. tax based on deposits into the taxpayer's bank accounts.

10. Some of the presumptive taxation methods used to estimate income of a taxpayer and assess tax liability include all of the following except …
A. fixed amount of tax on taxpayers on the basis of trade, profession, industry, etc.
B. a fixed percentage of gross receipts of a business.
C. tax based on multiple factors or characteristics developed for particular industries.
D. tax based on change in the taxpayer's current liabilities over the year.
E. tax based on outward signs of lifestyle or conspicuous personal consumption of individuals.

11. A time-limited opportunity for tax defaulters to meet their tax obligations in respect of previous tax period(s) without having to

bear all or some of the punishment stipulated in the tax laws for their tax offences is referred to as …

A. presumptive taxation.
B. tax amnesty.
C. tax adjudication.
D. thin capitalization.
E. tax mitigation.

12. The advantages of tax amnesty program include all the following except that ….

A it allows the government to generate additional tax revenue especially in the short run.
B. it enlarges the tax base as more defaulting taxpayers come forward to register or file their tax returns.
C. it may weaken the tax morale of law-abiding taxpayers.
D. it reduces tax evasion and boast future tax compliance.
E. it enables the tax authority to save cost, time and other resources it would have expended in chasing, investigating and prosecuting defaulting taxpayers.

13. Which of the following is not a disadvantages of tax amnesty program?

A It can weaken the morale of law-abiding taxpayers.
B. The government may be perceived to be weak and unable to enforce tax laws.
C. Taxpayers may deliberately fail to discharge their tax obligations hoping that one day they will receive amnesty.
D. The government losses the penalties and interests that should have been realized from tax defaulters.
E. It is usually for an indeterminable period of time.

14. Which of the following Executive Orders granted tax defaulters immunity from prosecution and waiver of interest/penalties for truthfully and willingly declaring previously undisclosed assets and income and paying outstanding taxes?

A. Executive Order No. 001 of 2017
B. Executive Order No. 002 of 2017

C. Executive Order No. 003 of 2017
D. Executive Order No. 004 of 2017
E. Executive Order No. 005 of 2017

15. VAIDS is an abbreviation for …
A. Voluntary Assets and Income Declaration System.
B. Voluntary Assets and Investment Declaration Scheme.
C. Voluntary Assets and Income Distribution Scheme.
D. Voluntary Accounting for Income Declaration Scheme.
E. Voluntary Assets and Income Declaration Scheme.

16. VAIDS is targeted at all the following taxpayers except …
A. registered taxpayers who have not been filing returns.
B. taxpayers who have been underpaying or under-remitting taxes.
C. persons and entities that are under a process of tax audit or investigation.
D. taxpayers who are not prepared to settle their tax dispute out of court.
E. registered taxpayers who have additional disclosures to make.

17. VAIDS is targeted at …
A. persons and entities that are in default of their tax liabilities.
B. persons and entities that are yet to register with the relevant tax authorities.
C. persons and entities that have not been declaring their taxable income and assets.
D. taxpayers who are subject to multiplicity of taxes.
E. taxpayers who are engaged in a tax dispute with the relevant tax authority but are prepared to settle their tax dispute out of court.

Which of the options A to E is incorrect?

18. The Executive Order on the voluntary assets and income declaration scheme was made by the …

A. Minister of Finance.
B. FIRS Board.
C. Chairman of the FIRS.
D. National Assembly.
E. President.

19. All the following are covered under the voluntary assets and income declaration scheme except...
A. personal income tax.
B. tenement rate.
C. companies income tax.
D. petroleum profits tax.
E. capital gains tax.

20. Which of the following is not covered under the voluntary assets and income declaration scheme?
A. Individuals
B. Trusts
C. Executors
D. Registered companies
E. None of the above

21. The Voluntary Assets and Income Declaration Scheme was meant to encourage and provide an opportunity for eligible taxpayers to ...
A. ensure full tax compliance.
B. enjoy tax holiday.
C. regularize their tax status for all the relevant years.
D. pay all outstanding taxes.
E. prevent and stop tax evasion.
Which of the options A to E is incorrect?

22. The reliefs/benefits granted under the Voluntary Assets and Income Declaration Scheme were available in respect of...
A. all taxes administered by the FIRS only.
B. all taxes administered by the State Boards of Internal Revenue only.

C. all taxes administered by the FCT Internal Revenue Service only.

D. all taxes administered by the tax authorities of the three tiers of government in Nigeria.

E. all taxes administered by the FIRS as well as those administered by all States Boards of Internal Revenue.

23. Under the Voluntary Assets and Income Declaration Scheme, the benefits to be enjoyed by any taxpayer who truthfully and voluntarily declared his assets and income and paid all outstanding taxes include all the following except ...

A. invalidation of any court order or judgement already obtained for default in payment of tax.

B. immunity from prosecution for tax offences.

C. immunity from tax audit.

D. waiver of penalties.

E. waiver of interest.

Which of the options A to E is incorrect?

24. Under the Voluntary Assets and Income Declaration Scheme, any taxpayer who truthfully and voluntarily declared his assets and income and complied with the regulations and guidelines could be given the option of paying outstanding taxes by instalment over a maximum period of ….. as may be agreed with the relevant tax authority.

A. six years

B. five years

C. four years

D. three years

E. eighteen months

25. The consequences of the failure of any defaulting taxpayer to take advantage of the VAIDS are as follows …

A. extension of the period of relief which may have been granted to the taxpayer.

B. liability to undergo comprehensive tax audit.

C. liability to pay in full the principal sum due.

D. liability to be prosecuted in accordance with the relevant extant laws for tax offences.
E. liability to pay all interest and penalties arising therefrom.

26. The requirements for a valid declaration under the Voluntary Assets and Income Declaration Scheme include all the following except …
A. the disclosures by the taxpayer should be voluntary.
B. the disclosures must be full, frank, complete and verifiable in all material respects.
C. the assessment of tax payable must be carried out by the relevant tax authority.
D. the disclosures must be signed by a member of the Chartered Institute of Taxation of Nigeria or a recognized accountancy body in Nigeria.
E. the disclosures must be made using the VAIDS forms.

27. Under the Voluntary Assets and Income Declaration Scheme, taxpayers who were in default of their tax liabilities were to declare their assets and income relating to …
A. the preceding six years of assessment.
B. the preceding three years of assessment.
C. the preceding five years of assessment.
D. the preceding four years of assessment.
E. all the past years of assessment that taxes were under declared.

28. The period for voluntary assets and income declaration by defaulting taxpayers commenced from ……………and was to last for ….months. However, the period was extended by ….months.
A. 1/9/18, 9 months, 3 months
B. 1/7/18, 6 months, 3 months
C. 1/7/18, 9 months, 3 months
D. 1/7/18, 12 months, 3 months
E. 1/7/18, 9 months, 2 months

29. Which of the following Executive Orders granted immunity from prosecution and waiver of interest/penalties for truthfully and

willingly declaring previously undisclosed offshore assets and income from sources outside Nigeria?

A. Executive Order No. 001 of 2017
B. Executive Order No. 002 of 2017
C. Executive Order No. 003 of 2017
D. Executive Order No. 004 of 2017
E. Executive Order No. 008 of 2018

30. VOARS is an abbreviation for …

A. Voluntary Offshore Assets Redistribution Scheme.
B. Voluntary Assets Regularization Scheme.
C. Voluntary Offshore Accounting Regularization Scheme.
D. Voluntary Offshore Assets Regularization Scheme.
E. Voluntary Offshore Assets Regularization System.

31. VOARS is targeted at all the following taxpayers except …

A. taxpayers who are under investigation by law enforcement agencies in Nigeria or any other country and have been charged with any crimes including obtaining offshore assets through corrupt practices.
B. taxpayers who own offshore assets but are yet to declare them with the relevant authorities.
C. taxpayers who earn income on offshore assets but are yet to declare such income to the relevant tax authorities.
D. registered taxpayers who have additional disclosures to make or need to amend prior disclosures in respect of offshore assets and income on offshore assets.
E. taxpayers who have been under declaring their taxable income and offshore assets.

32. The Executive Order on voluntary offshore assets regularization scheme was made by the …

A. Minister of Finance.
B. FIRS Board.
C. Chairman of the FIRS.
D. National Assembly.
E. President.

33. The Executive Order No. 8 of 2018 mandated the ....to set up a Voluntary Offshore Assets Regularization Scheme for all categories of taxpayers who had defaulted in declaration of their offshore assets and payment of taxes due.
    A. Chairman, Federal Inland Revenue Service
    B. Attorney-General of the Federation and the Minister of Justice
    C. Minister of Finance
    D. Chairman, Joint Tax Board
    E. Governor, Central Bank of Nigeria

34. The Executive Order No. 8 of 2018 set up a Voluntary Offshore Assets Regularization Scheme in ....for all categories of taxpayers who had defaulted in declaration of their offshore assets and payment of taxes.
    A. New York
    B. Switzerland
    C. London
    D. Canada
    E. Abuja

35. The Voluntary Offshore Assets Regularization Scheme (VOARS) was meant to encourage and provide an opportunity for eligible taxpayers to regularize their offshore assets held anywhere in the world for the relevant years by voluntarily paying to the Federal Government of Nigeria (FGN) .....
    A. a one-time levy of 50% of their offshore assets in lieu of all outstanding taxes, penalties, and interests.
    B. a one-time levy of 25% of their offshore assets in lieu of all outstanding taxes, penalties, and interests.
    C. a one-time levy of 45% of their offshore assets in lieu of all outstanding taxes, penalties, and interests.
    D. a one-time levy of 35% of their offshore assets plus penaltie and interests.
    E. a one-time levy of 35% of their offshore assets in lieu of all outstanding taxes, penalties, and interests.

36. Under the Voluntary Offshore Assets Regularization Scheme, defaulting taxpayers are to declare their offshore assets and income from sources outside Nigeria relating to ....

    A. the preceding six years of assessment.
    B. the preceding five years of assessment.
    C. the preceding ten years of assessment.
    D. the preceding thirty years of assessment.
    E. all the past years of assessment that taxes were under declared.

37. The Voluntary Offshore Assets Regularization Scheme commenced from 8th October, 2018 and was to last for ....

    A. three months
    B. six months
    C. nine months
    D. twelve months
    E. twenty-four months

38. Under the Voluntary Offshore Assets Regularization Scheme, the benefits to be enjoyed by any taxpayer who truthfully and voluntarily declared his offshore assets and income include ...

    A. revocation of any court order or judgment already obtained in respect of any default in payment of tax for which interest and/or penalty had already accrued.
    B. waiver of interests and penalties on the declared and regularized offshore assets.
    C. permanent waiver of criminal prosecution for tax offenses and offenses related to the offshore assets.
    D. immunity from tax audit of the declared and regularized offshore assets.
    E. receipt from FGN an Offshore Assets Regularization Compliance Certificate on the declared and regularized offshore assets.

    Which of the options A to E is incorrect?

39. Failure of any defaulting taxpayer to take advantage of the Voluntary Offshore Assets Regularization Scheme will result in the following consequences at the expiration of the Scheme except …
    - A. investigations, charges and enforcement procedures concerning offshore assets.
    - B. loss of right to plea bargain.
    - C. liability to pay in full the principal sum due and interests and penalties arising therefrom.
    - D. withdrawal of any reliefs which may have been granted to the participant.
    - E. waiver of liability to undergo comprehensive tax audit.

23 Stamp Duties

Part I Multiple-Choice Questions

1. Which of the following is regarded as a tax on documents?
   A. Value added tax
   B. Capital gains tax
   C. Education tax
   D. Stamp duty
   E. Withholding tax

2. All the following instruments are subject to fixed duties except …
   A. cheque leaf.
   B. guarantor forms.
   C. bills of exchange payable at sight.
   D. promissory note.
   E. proxy forms.

3. Which of the following instruments is not subject to ad valorem duties?
   A. Property valuation
   B. Policy of life insurance
   C. Payment receipt
   D. Debenture
   E. Share capital

4. Which of the following can impose and collect stamp duties?
   i. Federal Government
   ii. State Government
   iii. Local Government
   iv. Village Council
   A. iii and iv only
   B. i only
   C. ii only

D. i, ii and iii only
E. i and ii only

5. Stamping of instruments can be done by ...
i. embossing with dies.
ii. affixing adhesive stamps.
iii. affixing postage stamps in place of adhesive stamps.
iv. printing on the instruments (as in the case of cheques).
A. I, II and III only
B. I and II only
C. III and IV only
D. I, II, III and IV
E. I, II and IV only

6. According to the Stamp Duties Act, the Commissioner of Stamp Duties is to be appointed by the ...
A. Federal Inland Revenue Service.
B. Civil Service Commission.
C. Joint Tax Board.
D. Tax Appeal Commissioners.
E. Ministry of Finance.

7. Which of the following duties is not performed by the Commissioner of Stamp Duties?
A. Custody of dies and adhesive stamps
B. Adjudication
C. Stamping instruments
D. Approving the use of a die of new design
E. Assessment of instrument

8. What is the penalty for failing to state on an instrument all the facts and circumstances affecting the liability of the instrument to stamp duty?
A. ₦100
B. ₦50
C. ₦20

D. ₦200
E. ₦40

9. What is the penalty for non-cancellation of adhesive stamp used to denote the stamp duty on an instrument?
A. ₦40
B. ₦20
C. ₦100
D. ₦50
E. ₦500

10. Which of the following statements is not true?
A. Two Commissioners can adjudicate on the same instrument.
B. An instrument relating to several distinct matters is to be separately and distinctly charged with duty in respect of each of such matters.
C. Any person may require the Commissioner to express his opinion on the amount of duty payable on any executed instrument.
D. Stamps of greater value than is required can be used upon any instrument.
E. The amount of the duty upon any instrument may be denoted by several stamps.

11. Where an instrument has been submitted to a Commissioner for his opinion before the expiration of the period for stamping, the instrument may be stamped in accordance with the Commissioner's assessment within …
A. 90 days after notice of the assessment.
B. 60 days after notice of the assessment.
C. 30 days after notice of the assessment.
D. 21 days after notice of the assessment.
E. 7 days after notice of the assessment.

12. Any person who is dissatisfied with the assessment of a Commissioner of Stamp Duties may appeal against the assessment to the …

A. Magistrate Court.
B. Joint Tax Board.
C. Federal Inland Revenue Service,
D. High Court of the State in which the assessment was made.
E. Court of Appeal.

13. Within how many days can an appeal be made against the assessment of a Commissioner of Stamp Duties after the date of the assessment?
A. 30 days
B. 60 days
C. 90 days
D. 21 days
E. 15 days

14. Within how many days after the execution of an unstamped or insufficiently stamped instrument can the instrument be stamped with an impressed stamp on payment of the unpaid duty without incurring a penalty?
A. 30 days
B. 21 days
C. 40 days
D. 60 days
E. 45 days

15. An unstamped or insufficiently stamped instrument which has been first executed outside Nigeria may be stamped within ... after it has been first received in Nigeria without incurring a penalty.
A. 30 days
B. 60 days
C. 90 days
D. 21 days
E. 45 days

16. The penalty for refusing any person authorized by the Commissioner of Stamp Duties access to rolls, books, documents, etc for inspection is a fine of ...

A. ₦100 for every such refusal.
B. ₦50 for every such refusal.
C. ₦20 for every such refusal.
D. ₦40 for every such refusal.
E. ₦1,000 for every such refusal.

17. The penalty for enrolling any instrument not duly stamped is a fine of …
    A. ₦20
    B. ₦40
    C. ₦50
    D. ₦100
    E. ₦200

18. What is the minimum period of notice to be given in the Gazette before the introduction of a die of new design of impressed stamp to replace an old die of another design?
    A. At least one month before the new die is used.
    B. At least three months before the new die is used.
    C. At least fifteen days before the new die is used.
    D. At least six months before the new die is used.
    E. At least ninety days before the new die is used.

19. What is the time limit within which a material stamped with a discontinued die and which has been rendered useless due to the introduction of a new die may be presented to the Accountant-General for a refund of the stamp duty paid?
    A. Within 6 months after the date of change to a new die.
    B. Within 3 months after the date of change to a new die.
    C. Within 1 months after the date of change to a new die.
    D. Within 4 months after the date of change to a new die.
    E. Within 5 months after the date of change to a new die.

20. Within how many years can proceedings for the recovery of any duty, fine and penalty imposed by the Stamp Duties Act be commenced or prosecuted after offence was committed?

A. 6 years
B. 3 years
C. 1 year
D. 5 years
E. 4 years

21. ... may by resolution increase, diminish or repeal the duty chargeable under any of the heads specified in the Stamp Duties Act in respect of documents regarding which the Government of the Federation is competent to make law.
A. The Federal Inland Revenue Service Board
B. The Commissioner of Stamp Duties
C. The Minister of Finance
D. The National Assembly
E. The Tax Appeal Tribunal

22. ... may by resolution increase, diminish or repeal the duty chargeable under any of the heads specified in the Schedule to the Stamp Duties Act in respect of documents regarding which the State Government is exclusively competent to make laws.
A. The State Board of Internal Revenue
B. The Commissioner of Stamp Duties
C. The State House of Assembly
D. The Commissioner of Finance
E. The Tax Appeal Tribunal

23. Stamp duties on instruments executed by individuals are collected by the...
i. FCT Internal Revenue Service.
ii. Federal Inland Revenue Service.
iii. Joint Tax Board.
iv. State Internal Revenue Service.
A. iv only
B. ii and iv only
C. i and iv only
D. i, iii and iv only
E. i, ii and iv only

24. Which one of the following assesses and collects stamp duties on instruments executed by companies?
    A. FCT Internal Revenue Service.
    B. Federal Inland Revenue Service
    C. Joint Tax Board
    D. State Internal Revenue Service
    E. Joint Revenue Committee

Part II Short-Answer Questions

25. Stamp duties which vary with the amount of the consideration for the document being stamped are referred to as …

26. Mention three instruments subject to fixed duties.

27. Mention any three instruments subject to ad valorem duties.

28. Which one of the tax authorities assesses and collects stamp duties on instruments executed by individuals residents in Abuja?

29. Stamp duty is managed by the …

30. The process of determining the appropriate amount of duty chargeable on an instrument by the Commissioner of Stamp Duties is referred to as …

31. What is the time limit within which any instrument left with or at the office of any Commissioner of Stamp Duties may by destroyed if not claimed by the owner?

32. An instrument denoted by an adhesive stamp shall not be deemed duly stamped unless the adhesive stamp is cancelled by the person required by law to do so. How is the adhesive stamp to be cancelled?

33. State the penalty for fraudulent removal of adhesive stamp from one instrument to another instrument or for postal purposes.

34. State the penalty for late stamping of instruments.

35. Where an instrument is chargeable with ad valorem duty in respect of any stock or marketable security, the duty is to be calculated on

36. Where an instrument is chargeable with ad valorem duty in respect of any money in any foreign currency, the duty is to be calculated on ...

37. A die of new design of impressed stamp cannot be procured to replace an old die of another design without the approval of ...

38. What is the relief available to an innocent person who suffers a fine, penalty or forfeiture by the production of an unstamped or insufficiently stamped instrument for which he was not the person originally responsible for having the document stamped?

39. State the circumstances under which the President (or Governor in the case of State) may make regulation for compounding any stamp duty?

40. With reference to the Stamp Duties Act, define the term charter party.

41. What are the terms upon which a charter party may be stamped after execution?

42. How are charter party first executed abroad perfected in Nigeria?

43. An instrument is defined in the Stamp Duties Act as ...

44. Stamp duties which remain the same irrespective of the consideration for the document being stamped are referred to as ...

24 Value Added Tax

Part I Multiple-Choice Questions

1. The administration of value added tax is vested in the …
   A. State Board of Internal Revenue.
   B. Nigeria Customs Service.
   C. Federal Inland Revenue Service.
   D. Joint Tax Board.
   E. Joint State Revenue Committee.

2. VAT was introduced in Nigeria to replace …
   A. capital transfer tax.
   B. education tax.
   C. property tax.
   D. inheritance tax.
   E. sales tax.

3. Which of the following statements is/are true?
   i. Government ministries, departments and agencies (MDAs) are not required to register for VAT.
   ii. Government ministries, departments and agencies (MDAs) are exempted from payment of VAT.
   iii. Where the taxable activity of an entity is carried on in branches or divisions or depots in different states of the Federation, each of the outlets must separately register for VAT.
   iv. Where goods or services are supplied to a person in Nigeria by a non-resident and the value of the transaction is expressed in foreign currency, the associated VAT must be remitted to the FIRS in Naira.
   A. ii and iv only
   B. iii only
   C. i, ii and iv

D. iii and iv only
E. None

4. The tax burden of VAT is borne by the ...
A. manufacturers.
B. wholesalers.
C. retailers.
D. consumers.
E. raw material suppliers.

5. The current rate of value added tax in Nigeria is ...
A. 5%.
B. 10%.
C. 15%.
D. 20%.
E. 25%.

6. Which of the following goods is currently exempted from VAT?
A. Newspapers and magazines
B. Soft drinks
C. Soaps and detergents
D. Furniture
E. Basic food items

7. Which of the following is not exempted from VAT?
A. Books and educational materials
B. Baby products
C. Plant and machinery imported for use in the EPZ
D. Sport equipment
E. Agricultural equipment

8. Which of the following services is exempted from VAT?
A. Accountancy services
B. Medical services
C. Restaurant services
D. Courier services
E. Legal Services

9. Which of the following statements is/are true of exempted supplies?
   i. VAT is charged on goods and services at zero rate.
   ii. VAT is not charged on goods and services.
   iii. VAT charged on inputs can be reclaimed.
   iv. VAT charged on inputs cannot be reclaimed.
   A. ii and iv only
   B. i and iii only
   C. i and iv only
   D. ii and iii only
   E. iii only

10. Which of the following statements are true of zero rated supplies?
    i. VAT is charged on goods and services supplied at the current rate.
    ii. VAT is charged on goods and services at zero rate.
    iii. VAT paid on inputs can be reclaimed.
    iv. VAT paid on inputs cannot be reclaimed.
    A. i and iv only
    B. ii and iv only
    C. i and iii only
    D. i and iv only
    E. ii and iii only

11. Members of the VAT Technical Committee include all the following except
    A. a Director from the National Planning Commission.
    B. all Directors in the FIRS.
    C. the Chairman of the FIRS.
    D. the Legal Adviser to the FIRS.
    E. a Director in the Nigeria Customs Service.

12. Which of the following is exempted from registration for VAT collection?
    A. Non-resident companies
    B. Agencies of government
    C. Clubs or associations

D. Professionals like lawyers, accountants, etc.
E. None of the above

13. Which of the following is not an obligation of a registered person under the VAT Act?
A. Keeping of adequate VAT records and accounts.
B. Rendering VAT returns to FIRS on the due date.
C. Accounting for VAT on all taxable supplies.
D. Issuing tax invoices for supply of taxable goods and services.
E. Deducting withholding tax at source.

14. Which of the following forms serves as a registration form for VAT?
A. Form VAT 001
B. Form VAT 002
C. Form VAT 003
D. Form VAT 004
E. Form VAT 005

15. Which of the following forms is used by a registered person to make monthly return to the FIRS in respect of VAT?
A. Form VAT 001
B. Form VAT 002
C. Form VAT 003
D. Form VAT 004
E. Form VAT 005

16. Which of the following forms is used to render returns of VAT collection made to the Federation account for each month?
A. Form VAT 005
B. Form VAT 004
C. Form VAT 003
D. Form VAT 002
E. Form VAT 001

17. Which of the following are shown on a VAT registration certificate?
    i. Registration number
    ii. Date of registration
    iii. Name of the registered or taxable person
    iv. Total amount of VAT payable
    A. i, ii and iii only
    B. All of the above
    C. ii and iii only
    D. i and iii only
    E. i, iii and iv only

18. A tax invoice contains all the following information except …
    A. the total VAT payable.
    B. a description of the goods and services supplied.
    C. customer's name and address.
    D. name, address and VAT registration number of the supplier.
    E. the amount of tax deducted at source.

19. Any unauthorised or unregistered person who issues an invoice which includes VAT is liable to a fine of…
    A. ₦5,000 per invoice.
    B. 50% of the cost of goods and services involved.
    C. 150% of the VAT involved.
    D. ₦50,000 or 5 years' imprisonment.
    E. ₦10,000 or 6 months' imprisonment.

20. A taxable person is required to make VAT returns to the FIRS. How often must the returns be made?
    A. Bi-monthly
    B. Semi-annually
    C. Annually
    D. Quarterly
    E. Monthly

21. What is the fine for failure to file the monthly VAT returns?
    A. ₦5,000 for every month of default
    B. ₦2,000 for every month of default

C. ₦10,000 or 6 months' imprisonment
D. ₦50,000 or 5 years' imprisonment
E. ₦150% of the month's VAT

22. Input tax is not allowed as a deduction from output tax if it is charged on …
    i. fixed assets which can be capitalized as part of the cost of the assets.
    ii. certain expenses which can be expended through the income statement.
    iii. goods purchased directly for resale.
    iv. raw materials used for the direct production of any new product on which the output tax is charged.
    A. i and ii only
    B. iii and iv only
    C. i and iv only
    D. ii and iii only
    E. i and iii only

23. Which of the following assists the Federal Inland Revenue Service in the collection of VAT on goods imported into Nigeria?
    A. Nigerian Ports Authority
    B. Nigeria Immigration Service
    C. Nigerian Airports Authority
    D. Nigeria Navy
    E. Nigeria Customs Service

24. Which of the following taxes is an example of indirect tax?
    A. Personal income tax
    B. Companies income tax
    C. Value added tax
    D. Petroleum profits tax
    E. Capital gains tax

25. A taxable person is required to register with the FIRS for VAT collection within …

A. 6 months of commencement of business.
B. 3 months of commencement of business.
C. 12 months of commencement of business.
D. 9 months of commencement of business.
E. 18 months of commencement of business.

26. A taxable person is required to render VAT returns and remittance to the FIRS on or before …
 A. the 30th day of the month following that in which the goods or services were purchased or supplied.
 B. the 15th day of the month following that in which the goods or services were purchased or supplied.
 C. the 10th day of the month following that in which the goods or services were purchased or supplied.
 D. the 7th day of the month following that in which the goods or services were purchased or supplied.
 E. the 21st day of the month following that in which the goods or services were purchased or supplied.

27. What is the penalty for failure to collect VAT by a taxable person?
 A. A penalty of 150% of the uncollected VAT plus 5% interest above the CBN rediscount rate.
 B. A penalty of ₦2,000 for every month in which the failure continues.
 C. A fine of ₦50,000 or imprisonment for a term of 5 years.
 D. A fine of ₦10,000 or imprisonment for a term of 6 months.
 E. A fine of twice the amount uncollected.

28. Any officer of FIRS or any other person who aids or abets the commission of any offence under the VAT Act is liable on conviction to a fine of…
 A. ₦5,000.
 B. ₦10,000 or 6 months' imprisonment or both.
 C. ₦30,000 or maximum of 3 years' imprisonment.
 D. ₦50,000 or 5 years' imprisonment.
 E. ₦2000.

29. CC Limited bought imported goods for ₦6.5 million paying VAT of 5% and later sold the goods to OP Limited for ₦6 million collecting VAT of 5%. Assuming that the prices quoted are before VAT, what is the net VAT payable by CC Ltd to or refundable by FIRS?
    - A. ₦25,000 payable to FIRS
    - B. ₦25,000 refundable by FIRS
    - C. ₦325,000 payable to FIRS
    - D. ₦300,000 refundable by FIRS
    - E. ₦50,000 refundable by FIRS

30. A distributor sold 15 crates of Hi-malt to a customer at ₦600 per crate subject to 2% trade discount. What is the amount of VAT payable to the FIRS by the distributor assuming that the price is VAT exclusive? VAT rate is 5%.
    - A. ₦450
    - B. ₦261
    - C. ₦429
    - D. ₦420
    - E. ₦441

The following scenario relates to questions 31 to 34.

A vatable product was sold by a retailer to the final consumers for ₦103,950. The raw materials used for the manufacture of the product were initially sold to the manufacturer by the raw materials supplier for ₦52,500. The finished product was sold by the manufacturer to the wholesaler for ₦78,750 and the wholesaler in turn sold the product to the retailer for ₦94,500. All the prices quoted are exclusive of VAT. VAT rate is 5%.

31. What is the amount of VAT payable by the raw material supplier?
    - A. ₦2,500.
    - B. ₦3,937.50.
    - C. ₦4,725.
    - D. ₦1,312.50.
    - E. ₦2,625.

32. What is the amount of VAT payable by the manufacturer?
    A. ₦3,937.50
    B. ₦1,312.50
    C. ₦3,750
    D. ₦2,437.50
    E. ₦1,250

33. What is the amount of VAT payable by the wholesaler?
    A. ₦4,725
    B. ₦4,500
    C. ₦787.50
    D. ₦562.50
    E. ₦1,312.50

34. What is the amount of VAT payable by the retailer?
    A. ₦4,950
    B. ₦225
    C. ₦472.50
    D. ₦5,197.50
    E. ₦4725

The following scenario relates to questions 35 to 37.

The following information have been extracted from the books of Kaikai Limited, a registered VAT agent of FIRS, for the year ended 31st December, 2005:

	₦
VAT paid on raw materials purchased	700,000
VAT paid on goods purchased for resale	325,000
VAT paid on plant purchased	150,000
VAT paid on consultancy services	13,000
VAT collected on goods sold	1,250,000
VAT collected on services provided	24,000

35. What is the total output tax?
    A. ₦1,025,000
    B. ₦1,188,000

C. ₦1,250,000
D. ₦1,274,000
E. ₦863,000

36. What is the total input tax?
A. ₦1,188,000
B. ₦1,025,000
C. ₦1,274,000
D. ₦1,250,000
E. ₦863,000

37. What is the net VAT payable to the FIRS?
A. ₦249,000
B. ₦86,000
C. ₦24,000
D. ₦411,000
E. ₦325,000

38. When a country imposes two or more rates of VAT so that different products and services are taxed at different VAT rates, the country is said to operate ...
A. double VAT rates.
B. single VAT rate.
C. complicated VAT rates.
D. multiple VAT rates.
E. compounded VAT rates.

39. According to the Value Added Tax Act 2004, ... can amend the rate of VAT chargeable by order published in the Gazette.
A. the Minister of Finance
B. the President of Nigeria
C. the Chairman of the FIRS
D. the Minister of National Planning
E. the Senate

40. Under the current tax laws, an appeal against the decision of the FIRS in connection with VAT should be referred to the ...

A. VAT Tribunal
B. Tax Appeal Committee
C. Tax Appeal Tribunal
D. VAT Technical Committee
E. Joint Tax Board

41. Based on the Minister of Finance's Value Added Tax Order 2014 which is to be in force for a period of five years from 25/7/14, the following commissions are to be exempted from VAT:
A. commissions earned on traded value of shares.
B. commissions payable to Securities and Exchange Commission.
C. commissions payable to the Nigerian Stock Exchange.
D. commissions payable to agents.
E. commissions payable to the Central Securities Clearing System.
Which of the options A to E is incorrect?

42. VAT refund can be made by …
A. credit method only.
B. direct cash refund method only.
C. both credit and direct cash refund methods.
D. both addition and subtraction methods.
E. invoice credit method only.

43. Which of the following is not true of VAT in Nigeria?
A. It is a multi-stage tax.
B. The burden of VAT is ultimately borne by the final consumers.
C. Government agencies are exempted from VAT.
D. Nigerian VAT system is invoice-based.
E. Nigeria operates a single rate VAT system as at 2018.

44. Which of the following taxes is a tax on consumption or expenditure?
A. Withholding tax
B. Capital gain tax

C. PAYE
D. Stamp duties
E. VAT

45. All the following will not attract VAT except …
A. interest on loans/advances and overdraft facilities.
B. interest on savings accounts.
C. commission on turnover (COT).
D. interest on bank deposits.
E. interbank placements.

46. All the following will be liable to VAT except …
A. commissions paid to brokers, reinsurers, underwriters and other insurance agents by an insurer.
B. commissions on sale of bankdrafts/certified cheques.
C. premium on insurance policies.
D. legal and other fees chargeable on lease arrangements.
E. fees charged for advisory services.

47. Which of the following is/are not liable to VAT?
i. Commisssions/fees charged on forex trading
ii. Dividends
iii. Fees chargeable on stock brokerage
iv. Profit/gain on disposal of government securities
A. i and iii only
B. ii and iv only
C. ii only
D. iv only
E. i, iii and iv only

48. Zero-rated goods and services include …
i. Non-oil exports.
ii. Goods and services purchased by diplomats.
iii. Services rendered by mortgage institutions.
iv. Goods purchased for use in humanitarian donor funded projects.

A. i and ii only
B. iii and iv only
C. i, ii and iv only
D. i, iii and iv only
E. i, ii, iii and iv.

49. Which of the following statements is not true?
A. A non-resident company that carries on business in Nigeria is not required to include VAT in its invoice.
B. Companies operating in the oil and gas sector are required to withhold and remit to FIRS the VAT due on contracts awarded by them.
C. Where a company in Nigeria has awarded a contract to a non-resident company, the Nigerian company has to remit the VAT due on the contract to FIRS even if the foreign company has not charged VAT in its invoice.
D. Non-governmental organisations (NGOs) that are exempted from income tax are required to pay VAT on vatable goods and services consumed by them.
E. Every government ministry, department or agency is required at the time of making payment to a contractor to hold back VAT due on the contract and remit same to the FIRS.

The following scenario relates to questions 50 and 51.

ABC Ltd supplied taxable goods to Mr Bola on 15th June for ₦500,000 (excluding VAT). Cash discount of 10% is offered to the customer if payment is made within 30 days.

50. What is the VAT payable on the supply if Mr Bola pays on 10th July, 2018?
A. ₦25,000
B. ₦50,000
C. ₦52,500
D. ₦83,333
E. ₦22,500

51. What is the VAT payable on the supply if Mr Bola pays on 20th July, 2018?
    A. ₦25,000
    B. ₦50,000
    C. ₦52,500
    D. ₦83,333
    E. ₦22,500

The following scenario relates to questions 52 to 54.

OBT Ltd supplied raw materials to XYZ Ltd for ₦1,600,000 (excluding VAT) and XYZ Ltd used the raw material for production and sold the finished goods to a consumer for ₦1,800,000 (excluding VAT).

52. Assuming that the raw materials are liable to VAT, what is the VAT refundable to or payable by XYZ Ltd if the finished goods are exempted from VAT?
    A. No output VAT is payable by XYZ Ltd but input VAT of ₦80,000 is refundable by FIRS.
    B. Net VAT of ₦10,000 is payable to FIRS by XYZ Ltd.
    C. ₦90,000 output VAT is payable by XYZ Ltd and no input VAT is refundable.
    D. No output VAT is payable by XYZ Ltd but the input VAT of ₦80,000 payable by XYZ Ltd is non-refundable by FIRS.
    E. ₦80,000 output VAT is payable to FIRS by XYZ Ltd.

53. Assuming that the raw materials are liable to VAT, what is the VAT refundable to or payable by XYZ Ltd if the finished goods are zero-rated?
    A. No output VAT is payable by XYZ Ltd but input VAT of ₦80,000 is refundable by FIRS to XYZ Ltd.
    B. Net VAT of ₦10,000 is payable to FIRS by XYZ Ltd.
    C. ₦90,000 output VAT is payable by XYZ Ltd and no input VAT is refundable.

D. No output VAT is payable by XYZ Ltd and no input VAT is refundable by FIRS.

E. ₦80,000 input VAT is payable to FIRS by XYZ Ltd.

54. Assuming that the raw materials are liable to VAT, what is the VAT refundable to or payable by XYZ Ltd if the finished goods are neither exempted nor zero-rated?

A. No output VAT is payable by XYZ Ltd but input VAT of ₦80,000 is refundable by FIRS to XYZ Ltd.

B. Net VAT of ₦10,000 is payable to FIRS by XYZ Ltd.

C. ₦90,000 output VAT is payable by XYZ Ltd and no input VAT is refundable.

D. No output VAT is payable by XYZ Ltd and no input VAT is refundable by FIRS.

E. ₦80,000 input VAT is payable to FIRS by XYZ Ltd.

Part II Short-Answer Questions

55. What you understand by the term value added tax?

56. Give one difference between value added tax and withholding tax.

57. Tax period is defined in the Value Added Tax Act as …

58. Who is a taxable person under the VAT Act?

59. What is meant by taxable goods and services in connection with VAT?

60. How is the value of taxable goods and services determined for the purpose of VAT?

61. What is the value of imported taxable goods for the purposes of VAT?

62. State three categories of goods exempted from Value Added Tax.

63. Mention three services exempted from Value Added Tax.

64. Give the difference between zero rated supplies and exempted supplies.

65. State two functions of the VAT Technical Committee.

66. State the provision of the Value Added Tax Act with regard to the registration of Government Ministries.

67. State the provision of the Value Added Tax Act with regard to the registration of non-resident companies.

68. What is the penalty for failure to register for VAT?

69. List three particulars that should be stated on a VAT invoice.

70. VAT paid on purchases of goods and services is referred to as … while VAT charged on sales of goods and services is referred to as...

71. State two circumstances in which input VAT is non-deductible from output VAT.

72. The net VAT payable to the VAT office is the excess of … over …

73. The FIRS has to make a refund to the taxable person if … exceeds...

74. VAT return/remittance in respect of all taxable goods and services supplied during the month of January 2015 is due on or before …

75. Who is charged with the responsibility of remitting to the FIRS the VAT included in an invoice issued by a non-resident company?

76. What kind of assessment will the FIRS give to a taxable person if he fails to render VAT returns or renders an incomplete or inaccurate return?

77. State two offences which may be committed by a taxable person under the VAT Act and the penalties for each offence

78. The penalty for non-remittance of VAT within the stipulated time is

79. State one advantage of VAT to the Government.

80. State one disadvantage of VAT to the taxpayer.

81. State one problem of VAT assessment and collection in Nigeria.

82. If the rate of VAT is 5% and the price of an article is ₦240,000 inclusive of VAT, what is the amount of VAT charged on the article?

83. Which Act governs the administration of VAT?

25 Capital Gains Tax

Part I Multiple-Choice Questions

1. Which of the following is not a chargeable assets?
   - A. Foreign currency
   - B. Options, debts and incorporeal property
   - C. Stocks and shares
   - D. Plant and machinery
   - E. Furniture

2. An asset is deemed to be acquired or disposed of ...
   - i. on the date of the contract to acquire or dispose of the asset.
   - ii. on the date when the contract to acquire or dispose of the asset is enforceable.
   - iii. where the contract is subject to any condition, the date on which the condition is satisfied.
   - iv. where an option is conferred by any contract, the date when the option is exercised.
   - A. i and ii only
   - B. iii and iv only
   - C. ii, iii and iv only
   - D. i, ii and iii only
   - E. All of the above.

3. The imposition of capital gains tax on individuals resident in Abuja is the responsibility of the ...
   - A. Federal Inland Revenue Service.
   - B. State Board of Internal Revenue.
   - C. Joint Tax Board.
   - D. FCT Internal Revenue Service.
   - E. Joint State Revenue Committee.

4. Which of the tax Acts governs the taxation of chargeable gains accruing to any person on disposal of assets?

A. Petroleum Profits Tax Act
B. Companies Income Tax Act
C. Industrial Development (Income Tax Relief) Act
D. Capital Gains Tax Act
E. Personal Income Tax Act

5. Capital gains accruing to companies and non-resident individuals are taxable by the ...
A. Federal Inland Revenue Service.
B. State Board of Internal Revenue.
C. FCT Internal Revenue Service.
D. Local Government Revenue Committee.
E. Joint State Revenue Committee.

6. The imposition of capital gains tax on individuals resident in any State in Nigeria is the responsibility of the ...
A. Federal Inland Revenue Service.
B. State Board of Internal Revenue.
C. Joint Tax Board.
D. FCT Internal Revenue Service.
E. Joint State Revenue Committee.

7. Which of the following is not an allowable expenditure in computing the capital gains accruing to a taxpayer on the disposal of an asset?
A. Cost of acquisition of the asset
B. Depreciation
C. Incidental costs of acquisition
D. Enhancement or improvement expenditure
E. Incidental costs of disposal of the asset

8. Capital gains are assessable to tax on...
A. preceding year basis.
B. current year basis.
C. prepayment basis.
D. accrual basis.
E. cash basis.

9. The current rate of capital gains tax in Nigeria is…
   A. 30% of chargeable gains.
   B. 25% of chargeable gains.
   C. 15% of chargeable gains.
   D. 20% of chargeable gains.
   E. 10% of chargeable gains.

10. Which of the following persons are not connected?
   A. Husband and wife
   B. A partner with his other partners
   C. A trustee of a settlement and the settlor
   D. A tenant and his landlord
   E. A subsidiary company and its parent company

11. Under the Capital Gains Tax Act, disposal of asset does not include
   A. where any capital sum is derived by way of compensation for any loss of office or employment.
   B. where any capital sum is received under a policy of insurance for damage or injury to or the loss of assets.
   C. where any capital sum is received in return for forfeiture or surrender of rights, or for refraining from exercising rights.
   D. where any revenue is received for the sale of stock in trade or provision of services.
   E. where any capital sum is received as consideration for use or exploitation of any asset.

12. Gains accruing on the disposal of the following assets are exempted from capital gains tax except…
   A. main residence.
   B. private motor car.
   C. decoration awarded for valour other than for a consideration in money.
   D. chattel where the consideration exceeds ₦1,000 in a year of assessment.
   E. compensation for any wrong or injury suffered by an individual.

13. Capital gains tax is not chargeable on the gains accruing from the disposal of all the following except...
    A. Nigerian currency.
    B. gifts.
    C. investment held as part of approved retirement benefits schemes.
    D. land and buildings.
    E. Nigerian Government securities.

14. All the following classes of assets are eligible for rollover relief in connection with the replacement of business assets except
    A. motor vehicle.
    B. land and buildings.
    C. ship.
    D. aircraft.
    E. goodwill

15. The time limit within which compensation received for an asset lost or destroyed must be used to acquire a replacement asset for the purpose of rollover relief is ...
    A. one year of receipt.
    B. two years of receipt.
    C. six years of receipt.
    D. three years of receipt.
    E. five years of receipt.

16. Within how many years can a claim for relief for delayed remittance of chargeable gains be made after the end of the year of assessment in which that gains accrued?
    A. Six years
    B. Three years
    C. Five years
    D. Four years
    E. One year

Use the information below to answer questions 17 to 19.

Mimiko Limited purchased a building on 1st July, 2005 and sold it on 31st December, 2014 to Sabina Ltd. The following details are given:

	₦
Purchase price of the building	805,000
Legal expenses incurred on acquisition	40,250
Cost of renovation prior to sale	150,000
Cost of advertising the building for sale	35,000
Fire insurance premiums on the building sold	59,000
Depreciation of the building in 2014	16,100
Wages to security guards in 2014	60,000
Sale proceeds on disposal of the building	1,750,000
Sales agent's commission	87,500

17. The capital gain arising from the disposal of the building is …
    A. ₦632,285.
    B. ₦632,250.
    C. ₦632,115.
    D. ₦782,250.
    E. ₦945,000.

18. The capital gains tax payable by Mimiko Limited is …
    A. ₦126,450.
    B. ₦63,229.
    C. ₦63,212.
    D. ₦63,225.
    E. ₦78,225.

19. The year of assessment of the capital gains is
    A. 2005.
    B. 2003.
    C. 2006.
    D. 2002.
    E. 2014.

20. Zambawa acquired a building costing ₦750,000 in June 2002 and spent ₦240,000 on improving it in December 2002. He sold the building to his sister for ₦1,200,000 in November 2013 after ascertaining from his professional valuers that the building could be sold for ₦1,500,000 as at that date. What is the capital gains tax payable by Zambawa?
    A. ₦510,000
    B. ₦51,000
    C. ₦102,500
    D. ₦210,000
    E. ₦21,000

21. Under the Capital Gains Tax Act, when an asset is partly disposed of, the cost attributable to the part disposed of is calculated as:

$$\frac{A}{A + B} \times C$$

    What does "B" stand for?
    A. The amount of the consideration for the part disposed of
    B. The market value of the part not disposed of
    C. The cost attributable to the part disposed of
    D. The cost attributable to the part not disposed of
    E. The total cost of the asset

Use the information below to answer questions 22 to 25.

Baba Limited acquired an oil palm plantation in Oku Iboku, Akwa Ibom State in 1998 at a cost of ₦2,600,000 plus professional fees of ₦150,000. On 1st March, 2014 the company sold part of the plantation for ₦2,000,000, incurring costs relating to the disposal of ₦100,000. The market value of the undisposed part of the plantation on that date was put at ₦3,500,000.

22. What is the cost attributable to that part of the plantation sold?
    A. ₦1,000,000
    B. ₦945,455
    C. ₦1,571,429

D. ₦900,000
E. ₦600,000

23. What is the chargeable gain arising from the disposal?
A. ₦650,000
B. ₦900,000
C. ₦954,545
D. ₦328,571
E. ₦1,000,000

24. What is the cost attributable to the undisposed portion of the plantation?
A. ₦1,850,000
B. ₦1,178,571
C. ₦3,500,000
D. ₦942,705
E. ₦1,750,000

25. What is the capital gains tax payable by Baba Limited?
A. ₦130,000
B. ₦90,000
C. ₦65,000
D. ₦100,000
E. ₦95,455

26. Given that Mamora purchased a house on 4th January, 2005 for ₦1,000,000 and resided in it until 30th June, 2013 when he sold the house for ₦5,000,000, what is the capital gains tax payable as a result of the transaction.
A. ₦400,000
B. ₦4,000,000
C. ₦800,000
D. ₦200,000
E. Nil

27. IBB Ltd acquired a building for ₦1,000,000 in January 1998 and extended it at a cost of ₦100,000 in June 2000. In April 2014 the

company sold the building for ₦1,800,000 incurring expenses relating to the disposal of ₦180,000. Another building which the company purchased for ₦1,200,000 in September 1999 was sold for ₦1,250,000 in July 2014, the expenses of sale being ₦125,000. What is the capital gains tax payable on the disposal of the building?

A. ₦520,000
B. ₦104,000
C. ₦89,000
D. ₦52,000
E. ₦44,500

28. Which of the following statements is/are correct?

i. Insurance premium is an allowable deduction in computing capital gains on the disposal of an asset.
ii. A loss made on the disposal of one asset can be set off against chargeable gains arising on the disposal of another asset.
iii. Capital gains accruing to any Local Government Council on the disposal of an asset is exempted from capital gains tax.
iv. Gains arising from merger, takeover or absorption are exempted from capital gains tax if only shares are exchanged for shares.

A. ii and iv only
B. i and iv only
C. iii and iv only
D. iv only
E. iv only.

29. Which of the following is not a condition to be fulfilled before roll-over relief can be granted?

A. The consideration for the disposal of an old asset must be reinvested wholly or partly in the acquisition of a new asset.
B. The acquisition of a new asset must be made for the purpose of its use in the trade not wholly or partly for the purpose of realizing a gain from the disposal of the new asset.
C. The sales proceeds of an old asset must be reinvested in the

acquisition of a new asset of the same class within 12 months before and 12 months after the disposal of the old asset.

D. The person carrying on the trade must make a claim for the roll-over relief.

E. Cash does not form part of the consideration offered for the asset disposed of.

30. Capital gains accruing to residents of the Federal Capital Territory, Abuja are taxable by the …

A. Joint Tax Board.

B. Joint State Revenue Committee.

C. Federal Inland Revenue Service.

D. State Board of Internal Revenue.

E. Federal Capital Territory Internal Revenue Service.

31. Seewell Motors Ltd usually buys and sells motor vehicles. The profits made by the company from the sale of motor vehicles are taxable under the …

A. Stamp Duties Act

B. Capital Gains Tax Act

C. Personal Income Tax Act

D. Companies Income Tax Act

E. Tertiary Education Trust Fund (Establishment, Etc) Act

32. ABC Transport plc is in business as a transporter. If the company disposes of its office building at a profit, it will be subject to ..

A. NITD levy.

B. capital gains tax.

C. personal income tax

D. tertiary education tax.

E. companies income tax

33. A chargeable person under the Capital Gains Tax Act includes any person to whom any chargeable gains accrue but does not include …

A. a family.

B. a trustee.

C. a company.
D. an individual.
E. a government agency.

34. All the following are examples of incorporeal properties except ...
A. patents.
B. goodwill.
C. copyrights.
D. trademarks.
E. stocks and shares.

35. The incidental costs of acquisition or disposal of a landed property does not include...
A. costs of transfer or conveyance (including stamp duties).
B. fees or commission paid for the professional services of an estate agent or legal adviser.
C. any premium paid under a policy of insurance against the risk of any kind of damage to the property.
D. cost of advertising to find a seller in the case of an acquisition or a buyer in the case of a disposal.
E. costs reasonably incurred in making any valuation or apportionment required for the purposes of computing the capital gains.

36. The period within which a new asset must be acquired to replace an old asset for a roll-over relief to be granted is the period beginning
A. 24 months before and ending 24 months after the date of disposal of the old asset.
B. 6 months before and ending 6 months after the date of disposal of the old asset.
C. 3 months before and ending 3 months after the date of disposal of the old asset.
D. 18 months before and ending 18 months after the date of disposal of the old asset.
E. 12 months before and ending 12 months after the date of disposal of the old asset.

37. Capital gains on the disposal of a chattel is exempted from capital gains tax if the total proceeds in a year of assessment is...
    A. ₦2,000 or less.
    B. ₦10,000 or less.
    C. ₦1,000 or less.
    D. ₦100,000 or less.
    E. ₦20,000 or less.

38. When the disposal proceeds is payable instalmentally over a period exceeding ... from the date of disposal, the chargeable gain is deemed to accrue in proportionate parts over the instalmental payment period.

    A. 36 months
    B. 30 months
    C. 24 months
    D. 12 months
    E. 18 months

39. An asset valued ₦800,000 is used as a security for a debt of ₦600,000. What is the consideration for acquisition if the asset is sold for ₦400,000 and the purchaser assumed liability for the debt?
    A. ₦1,000,000
    B. ₦1,400,000
    C. ₦1,200,000
    D. ₦400,000
    E. ₦800,000

40. X Ltd took an asset with a market value of ₦500,000 in full satisfaction of a debt of ₦580,000 owed by Y Ltd and later disposed of the asset for ₦660,000. The chargeable gain is .....
    A. ₦160,000.
    B. ₦580,000.
    C. ₦660,000.
    D. ₦1,240,000.
    E. ₦80,000.

41. A building which was acquired by XYZ Ltd on 18th January, 2012 at a cost of ₦10,000,000 plus professional charges of ₦1,000,000 was disposed of on 1st November, 2017 for ₦9,650,000 and disposal expenses of ₦965,000 were incurred. What is the capital gains tax or loss relief arising on the disposal of the building?
    A. No capital gains tax is payable but XYZ can claim loss relief of ₦2,315,000.
    B. No capital gains tax is payable and no loss relief is available.
    C. No capital gains tax is payable but XYZ can claim current year loss relief of ₦2,315,000.
    D. No capital gains tax is payable but XYZ can claim carry forward loss relief of ₦2,315,000.
    E. Capital gains tax of ₦868,500.

42. Zico bought a piece of furniture for ₦350 on 12th August, 2014 and sold it for ₦1,300 on 13th July, 2017. What is the capital gains tax payable assuming that the rate of CGT is 20%?
    A. ₦190
    B. ₦150
    C. ₦260
    D. ₦95
    E. ₦35

43. How is capital gains tax chargeable on the disposal of a chattel restricted if the consideration for the sale is more than ₦1,000?
    A. CGT is limited to $66^{2}/_{3}$% x (Consideration – ₦1,000)
    B. CGT is limited to $66^{2}/_{3}$% of the taxpayer's assessable profits
    C. CGT is limited to a maximum of $^{5}/_{3}$ x (Consideration – ₦6,000)
    D. Either 10% of capital gains or ½ x (Consideration – ₦1,000), whichever is lower
    E. Either 10% of capital gains or ½ x (Consideration – ₦1,000), whichever is higher

Use the information below to answer questions 44 and 45.

Bayo acquired a chargeable asset for ₦8,000,000 in September 2011. He incurred enhancement expenditure of ₦1,000,000 in 2011 and ₦2,000,000 in 2015. He disposed of the asset in March 2018 for ₦14,000,000.

44. What is the capital gains tax payable if the asset was sold by way of a bargain made at arm's length?
   A. ₦600,000
   B. ₦800,000
   C. ₦1,400,000
   D. ₦300,000
   E. ₦500,000

45. What is the capital gains tax payable if the asset was sold to a connected person and had a market value of ₦16,000,000 as at the date of sale?
   A. ₦300,000
   B. ₦800,000
   C. ₦1,400,000
   D. ₦1,600,000
   E. ₦500,000

46. Tom and Dick have been in partnership business for many years. Their profit-sharing agreement provides that Tom and Dick should share profits or losses in the ratio 3:2. The partnership bought a chargeable asset in March 2010 for ₦7,000,000 and incurred enhancement expenditure of ₦500,000 in 2012 and a further ₦800,000 in 2013. In March 2018 the asset was sold for ₦10,000,000 and the sales agent collected a fee of 5% of the gross proceeds. What is the capital gains tax payable and by whom?
   A. ₦120,000 payable by the partnership firm.
   B. ₦72,000 by Tom and ₦48,000 by Dick.
   C. ₦120,000 assessable in the name of Tom on behalf of the firm.

D. ₦120,000 assessable in the name of Dick on behalf of the firm.

E. Partnership firm is exempted from CGT.

47. Amaka purchased a landed property situated along Awka Road in 2004 for ₦1,640,000. As a result of Onitsha/Awka Road construction, the landed property was compulsorily acquired by the Federal Government on 21st June, 2017 and she was paid a compensation of ₦1,900,000. Fearing that the road construction might be extended to Awka/Enugu Road in the near future, Amaka quickly advertised and disposed of her land at No. 40 Enugu Road on 21st November, 2017 for ₦10,000,000, incurring cost relating to disposal of ₦2,000,000. She acquired the land five years ago at a cost of ₦5,000,000. What is the capital gains tax payable by Amaka?

A. ₦26,000
B. ₦326,000
C. Nil
D. ₦274,000
E. ₦300,000

48. Usman owns a building having five flats which originally cost him ₦1,000,000 on 1st January, 2005. He used four of the flats for his business and one flat for his private residence. He sold the building on 31st December, 2017 for ₦1,800,000. What is the capital gains tax payable?

A. ₦64,000
B. ₦640,000
C. ₦800,000
D. ₦80,000
E. ₦900,000

Use the information below to answer questions 49 and 50.

Baba bought a five-acre plot of land for ₦3,000,000 on 14th March, 2010. On 1st June, 2015, he sold two of the acres for ₦1,500,000. The market value of the remaining three acres of land on that date was put at ₦2,500,000. On 31st March, 2018, Baba sold the remaining three acres for ₦3,500,000.

49. What is Baba's capital gains tax for 2015 tax year?
 A. ₦50,000
 B. ₦30,000
 C. ₦200,000
 D. ₦37,500
 E. ₦16,250

50. What is the Baba's capital gains tax for 2018 tax year?
 A. ₦500,000
 B. ₦300,000
 C. ₦200,000
 D. ₦37,500
 E. ₦162,500

Use the information below to answer questions 51 and 52.

XYZ Limited sold its factory building on 31st December, 2017 and made a gain of ₦2,000,000. The company wishes to purchase another building for its business using all the proceeds from the sale of the building and to make a claim for relief for replacement of business asset.

51. What is the period within which the company must purchase the new building in order to be able to claim the relief?
 A. Between 1/1/2017 and 31/12/2018
 B. Between 1/1/2017 and 31/12/2017
 C. Between 1/1/2018 and 31/12/2018
 D. Between 1/7/2017 and 30/6/2018
 E. Between 1/1/2018 and 30/6/2018

52. Assuming that the company purchased another factory building on 1/1/2018 using all the proceeds from the sale of the old building, when will the deferred gain of ₦2,000,000 be subject to capital gains tax if the new building is to be sold on 31/12/2025?

A. 2024 year of assessment
B. 2018 year of assessment
C. 2025 year of assessment
D. 2026 year of assessment
E. 2017 year of assessment

53. Feedwell Ltd completed the erection of its office building in June 2003 at a cost of ₦1,000,000. On 14th April, 2018, the company sold the building for ₦1,800,000. What is the capital gains tax chargeable and rollover relief available to the company assuming that it acquired another building five months later for ₦2,8000,000 and made a claim for the relief in 2018?
A. CGT ₦800,000, rollover relief ₦80,000.
B. CGT ₦0.00, rollover relief ₦800,000.
C. CGT ₦80,000, rollover relief ₦0.00.
D. CGT ₦0.00, rollover relief ₦0.00.
E. CGT ₦100,000, rollover relief ₦0.00.

54. Bebobsco bought plant and machinery for ₦2,400,000 in 2013. He sold the asset for ₦3,000,000 in May 2018 and immediately bought a new plant and machinery for ₦1,700,000 to replace the one sold. What is the capital gains tax chargeable and rollover relief available to him if he makes a claim for the relief in 2018?
A. CGT ₦60,000, rollover relief ₦70,000.
B. CGT ₦0.00, rollover relief ₦60,000.
C. CGT ₦30,000, rollover relief ₦0.00
D. CGT ₦0.00, rollover relief ₦0.00
E. CGT ₦60,000, rollover relief ₦0.00

Use the information below to answer questions 55 and 56.

Tata Ltd bought a warehouse for ₦1,600,000 in 2014. The company sold the asset for ₦2,600,000 in 2018 and immediately bought a new warehouse for ₦2,200,000 to replace the one sold.

55. What is the capital gains tax chargeable and rollover relief available to the company if it makes a claim for the relief in 2018?

A. CGT ₦40,000, rollover relief ₦600,000.
B. CGT ₦40,000, rollover relief ₦0.00.
C. CGT N0.00, rollover relief ₦600,000
D. CGT N0.00, rollover relief ₦0.00
E. CGT ₦40,000, rollover relief ₦40,000

56 What is the deemed or carrying cost of the new asset for the purpose of future computation of capital gains tax on the new asset when it is eventually disposed of?
A. ₦1,600,000
B. ₦2,600,000
C. ₦2,200,000
D. ₦600,000
E. ₦400,000

57. Stone Ltd sold an asset on 30th June, 2018 for ₦2,000,000 which cost ₦1,500,000 to acquire on 1st January, 2017. The sale agreement provided for payment by five equal instalments of ₦400,000, the first instalment being paid on the day of sale and the remaining instalments payable every six months. What is the capital gains tax payable in 2018?
A. ₦500,000
B. ₦400,000
C. ₦200,000
D. ₦100,000
E. ₦50,000

58. On 1st July, 2012, Okoro Limited purchased a generating plant on hire purchase and paid a deposit of ₦1,200,000 on that date. The balance of the hire purchase price was paid over a period of 2 years at the rate of ₦200,000 per month commencing on 1st August, 2012. The interest element in each instalment was ₦20,000. On 31st January, 2017, the company sold the plant for ₦6,400,000 incurring costs relating to the disposal of ₦70,000.
What is the capital gains tax payable by Okoro Limited and the year of assessment?

A. CGT ₦473,000, YOA 2017
B. CGT ₦81,000, YOA 2018
C. CGT ₦33,000, YOA 2018
D. CGT ₦33,000, YOA 2017
E. CGT ₦81,000, YOA 2017

Part II Short-Answer Questions

59. A year of assessment for capital gains tax begins from …and ends on …

60. Under the Capital Gains Tax Act, when does a part disposal of asset occur?

61. State the formula for calculating cost attributable to a part disposal of an asset?

62. A tangible movable asset is referred to as a …

63. What is the maximum capital gains tax chargeable on the disposal of a chattel if the total proceeds is more than ₦1,000 in a year of assessment?

64. State the time limit within which an individual may decide to the tax authority which of his two or more residences is his main residence.

65. Where the relevant tax authority determines an individual's main residence because of his failure to do so, he may appeal to the Tax Appeal Tribunal against that determination within … days of service of the notice of determination.

66. State the conditions under which the capital gains accruing to a person on compulsory acquisition of his land by the government will not be subject to CGT.

67. At what consideration is an asset deemed to be disposed of by the owner on the date of his death and acquired by his personal

representative? Is the gain arising therefrom chargeable to capital gains tax?

68. What is the formula for calculating the chargeable gains deemed to accrue in each year of assessment when the consideration for an asset disposed of is payable instalmentally?

69. When is a transaction between connected persons deemed to be artificial or fictitious?

70. What is the consideration for capital gains tax purposes where the disposal or acquisition of an asset takes place between connected persons?

71. What is the market value of an asset for the purpose of capital gains tax?

72. How is chargeable gains accruing on the disposal of a partnership asset assessable to capital gains tax?

73. Gains accruing to some institutions or societies are exempted from capital gains tax provided the gains are not derived from the disposal of assets acquired in connection with any trade or business carried on by the institutions or societies. Mention any four of such institutions or societies.

74. Under the Capital Gains Tax Act, when an asset is partly disposed of, the cost attributable to the part disposed of is calculated as:

$$\frac{A}{A + B} \times C$$

What does “C” represent?

75. What is the relief granted to a taxpayer who disposes of an asset and reinvests the whole sales proceeds in the acquisition of another asset?

76. In relation to capital gains tax, what is rollover relief?

77. State one advantage or benefit of claiming roll-over relief.

78. State the conditions under which a person may be granted relief for delayed remittance of chargeable gains accruing from the disposal of assets outside Nigeria.

79. State the provision of section 25 of CGTA with regards to the situation of a registered shares or securities.

80. Under the Capital Gains Tax Act, there is no loss relief for a loss made on the disposal of a chargeable asset. True or false?

81. What is capital gain in relation to capital gains tax?

82. What do you understand by capital gains tax?

83. The cost attributable to the part disposed of is calculated as:

$$\frac{A}{A + B} \times C$$

What does "A" represent in the formula?

26 Petroleum Profits Tax

Part I Multiple-Choice Questions

1. Activities in the oil and gas sectors are guided by various regulations enacted at various times. Which one of the following legislations has nothing to do with the regulation of petroleum industry in Nigeria?
   A. Petroleum Act
   B. Petroleum Profit Tax Act
   C. Industrial Development Income Tax Relief Act
   D. Petroleum (Drilling and Production) Regulations
   E. Deep Offshore and Inland Basin Production Sharing Contract Act

2. Which one of the following is not concerned with the regulation of petroleum operations in Nigeria?
   A. Ministry of Petroleum Resources
   B. Nigerian National Petroleum Corporation (NNPC)
   C. Department of Petroleum Resources (DPR)
   D. Securities and Exchange Commission
   E. Organization of the Petroleum Exporting Countries (OPEC)

3. Petroleum Profits Tax Act imposes tax on the profits of companies engaged in…
   A. oil prospecting, exploration and production.
   B. refining of crude oil.
   C. transportation of chargeable oil from Nigeria to other countries.
   D. marketing and distribution of petroleum products.
   E. providing technical services to oil companies.

4. Which of the following activities carried out by companies in the Nigerian oil industry is subject to tax under the Petroleum Profits Tax Act?
   - A. Refining of crude oil
   - B. Marketing of refined petroleum products
   - C. Transportation of crude oil by ocean going tankers
   - D. Provision of technical support services
   - E. None of the above

5. Profits earned from refining of crude oil are assessable to tax under the …
   - A. Petroleum Profits Tax Act.
   - B. Companies Income Tax Act.
   - C. Capital gains Tax Act.
   - D. Industrial Development (Income Tax Relief) Act.
   - E. Value Added Tax Act.

6. Which of the following is responsible for the assessment, collection and accounting for petroleum profits tax?
   - A. Nigerian National Petroleum Company (NNPC)
   - B. Central Bank of Nigeria
   - C. Department of Petroleum Resources
   - D. Joint Tax Board
   - E. Federal Inland Revenue Service

7. The basis of assessment of companies engaged in petroleum operations is
   - A. preceding year basis.
   - B. cash basis.
   - C. accrual basis.
   - D. incremental basis.
   - E. current year basis.

8. What is the accounting period of a company engaged in petroleum operations where the company has been in that business for many years?

A. A period of one year ending in the preceding year of assessment.

B. A period of one year from the date the company first makes a sale or bulk disposal of chargeable oil.

C. A period of one year beginning from 1st January and ending on 31st December of the same year.

D. A period of one year ending on 31st December of the year preceding the year of assessment.

E. A period of one year commencing on 1st April and ending on 31st March of the following year.

9. The profit of an accounting period is the aggregate of all the following except …

A. income from refining of crude oil.

B. proceeds of sales of all chargeable oil sold.

C. value of all chargeable oil disposed of.

D. value of all chargeable natural gas.

E. incidental income from petroleum operations.

10. In relation to petroleum profits tax, the adjusted profit less loss relief is referred to as the …

A. assessable profit.

B. remainder of assessable profit.

C. chargeable profit.

D. profit of the accounting period.

E. total profit.

11. In relation to petroleum profits tax, the assessable profit less capital allowances is referred to as the …

A. adjusted profit.

B. remainder of assessable profit.

C. chargeable profit.

D. profit of the accounting period.

E. total profit.

12. All the following expenses are allowable deductions in computing the adjusted profit from petroleum operations except …

A. rents.
B. royalties.
C. any loss recoverable from insurance.
D. customs and excise duties.
E. stamp duties.

13. All the following expenses are disallowable in computing the adjusted profit from petroleum operations except …
A. cost of purchasing information on the existence/extent of petroleum deposits.
B. capital expenditure.
C. first two appraisal wells expenditure.
D. income tax.
E. depreciation.

14. Which of the following expenses is disallowable in computing the adjusted profit from petroleum operations?
A. Loan interest
B. Repairs of fixed assets
C. Bad debts
D. General provision for bad debts
E. Contribution to approved pension fund

15. Over how many years can losses incurred in petroleum operations be recouped?
A. Four years
B. Five years
C. Six years
D. Two years
E. Indefinitely

16. What is the time limit within which a request can be made for the deferment of loss deduction from one accounting period to another after the end of the accounting period in which the loss deduction should have been made?
A. Five months
B. Six years

C. Two years
D. Six months
E. One year

17. Which of the following capital expenditure is not to be treated as a qualifying expenditure for capital allowances under the Petroleum Profits Tax Act?
A. Capital expenditure on plant, machinery and fixtures
B. Capital expenditure on ocean going oil tanker plying between Nigeria and other country
C. Capital expenditure on buildings, structures and works of permanent nature
D. Capital expenditure on pipelines and storage tanks
E. Qualifying drilling expenditure

18. Which of the following allowances under CITA is similar to petroleum investment allowance under PPTA?
A. Annual allowance
B. Balancing allowance
C. Export Processing Zone allowance
D. Initial allowance
E. Rural investment allowance

19. What is the rate of petroleum investment allowance on qualifying expenditure in respect of operations in territorial waters and continental shelf area between 100 and 200 metres depth?
A. 5%
B. 10%
C. 15%
D. 20%
E. 25%

20. In respect of Petroleum Profits Tax, annual allowance is granted on qualifying capital expenditure for …
A. ten years.
B. four years.
C. fifteen years.

D. five years.
E. six years.

21. Petroleum investment allowance is usually deducted from the …
A. chargeable tax.
B. assessable tax.
C. assessable profit.
D. chargeable profit.
E. adjusted profit.

22. Investment tax credit is usually deducted from the
A. chargeable tax.
B. assessable tax.
C. assessable profit.
D. chargeable profit.
E. adjusted profit.

23. What is the percentage of the initial cost of an asset used in petroleum operations that is to be retained in the books until the asset is disposed of?
A. 10%
B. 5%
C. 20%
D. 15%
E. 1%

24. When the written down value of an asset is less than the net sales proceeds, the difference is referred to as …
A. balancing charge.
B. petroleum investment allowance.
C. annual allowance.
D. balancing allowance.
E. initial allowance.

25. The excess of the written down value of an asset over the net sales proceeds of the asset is referred to as …

A. balancing charge.
B. petroleum investment allowance.
C. annual allowance.
D. balancing allowance.
E. initial allowance.

26. Which of the following is treated as an incidental income of a company engaged in petroleum operations for the purpose of PPT?
A. Balancing allowance
B. Balancing charge
C. Petroleum investment allowance
D. Profit on sale of asset
E. Annual allowance

27. Within how many months after the end of an accounting period is a company engaged in petroleum operations required to file its accounts and necessary particulars for that period with the FIRS?
A. Nine months
B. Six months
C. Twelve months
D. Three Months
E. Five months

28. Section 28 of PPTA requires a company engaged in petroleum operations to file its accounts and all the following particulars with the FIRS except …
A. a computation of estimated tax for the period.
B. a computation of its estimated chargeable profits of that period.
C. a computation of capital allowances due to it for that period.
D. a computation of its estimated adjusted profit or loss.
E. a description of the crude oil supplied.

29. The minimum period of notice that the FIRS is required to give a company engaged in petroleum operations within which to complete and deliver to the FIRS fuller or further information, returns, books, etc is …

A. thirty days.
B. twenty-one days.
C. fifteen days.
D. seven days.
E. sixty days.

30. The time limit within which a company engaged in petroleum operations is required to file a return of its estimated tax after the commencement of each accounting period is ...
A. six months.
B. nine months.
C. one month.
D. two months.
E. twelve months.

31. Within how many days must a notice of objection be made against petroleum profits tax assessment from the date of service of the notice of assessment?
A. Thirty days
B. Fifteen days
C. Seven days
D. Sixty days
E. Twenty-one days

32. What is the number of days allowed for making an appeal against petroleum profits tax assessment?
A. Thirty days
B. Sixty days
C. Twenty-one days
D. Fifteen days
E. Forty-five days

33. After the expiration of the period allowed for making an appeal against petroleum profits tax assessment, a period of extension may be granted if the company gives satisfactory reasons for its inability to meet the dateline. What is the maximum extension that may be granted?

A. Thirty days
B. Sixty days
C. Twenty-one days
D. Fifteen days
E. Forty-five days

34. The assessable tax of a company engaged in petroleum operations is computed at the rate of …
A. 85% of the assessable profit of an accounting period.
B. 85% of the adjusted profit of an accounting period.
C. 30% of the assessable profit of an accounting period.
D. 85% of the chargeable profit of an accounting period.
E. 50% of the assessable profit of an accounting period.

35. Companies engaged in petroleum operations which have production sharing contract with NNPC are taxable at the rate of … during the duration of the contract as stipulated in the Deep Offshore and Inland Basin Production Sharing Contracts Act 1999.
A. 50% of chargeable profit
B. 65.75% of the chargeable profit
C. 30% of chargeable profit
D. 85% of the chargeable profit
E. 50% of assessable profit

36. The estimated petroleum profits tax.for each year is payable in equal monthly instalments. Where the accounting period is a year, the first monthly instalment is due and payable not later than …
A. 31st January of the accounting period.
B. 28th February of the accounting period.
C. 31st March of the accounting period.
D. 30th April of the accounting period.
E. 31st May of the accounting period.

37. Petroleum profits tax is payable over …
A. six instalments.
B. three instalments.
C. twelve instalments.

D. nine instalments.
E. fifteen instalments.

38. When is the first monthly instalment of petroleum profits tax due and payable if the accounting period is a year (i.e. 12 months)?
A. Not later than 31st March of the accounting period.
B. Not later than 31st January of the accounting period.
C. Not later than 28th February of the accounting period.
D. Not later than 30th June of the accounting period.
E. Not later than 31st December of the accounting period.

39. Within how many days is the final instalment of petroleum profits tax due and payable after the service of the notice of assessment for the accounting period on the company by the FIRS?
A. Thirty days
B. Sixty days
C. Ninety days
D. Twenty-one days
E. Fifteen days

40. What is the time limit within which to make a claim for the repayment of any petroleum profits tax overpaid after the end of the accounting period to which it relates?
A. Five years
B. Four years
C. Three years
D. Six years
E. One year

41. In relation to petroleum profits tax, within how many years can a claim for double taxation relief be made after the end of the accounting period to which it relates?
A. Six years
B. Five years
C. Four years
D. Three years
E. Two years

42. What is the penalty for collecting or attempting to collect petroleum profits tax by an unauthorised person?
    A. ₦600 or 3 years' imprisonment or both
    B. ₦1,000 or 3 years' imprisonment or both
    C. ₦1,000 and triple the amount of tax
    D. ₦1,000 and double the amount of tax
    E. ₦5,000 or 5 years' imprisonment or both

43. What is the penalty for a tax official who demands more petroleum profits tax than the authorised tax assessment, misappropriates or embezzles the tax collected or renders false returns of tax collected?
    A. 200% of the tax plus interest at the prevailing commercial rate
    B. ₦600 or 3 years' imprisonment or both
    C. ₦1,000 and double the amount of tax
    D. ₦1,000 and triple the amount of tax
    E. ₦10,000 plus ₦2,000 for each day

44. Memorandum of understanding credit is deductible from the …
    A. assessable tax.
    B. assessable profit.
    C. chargeable profit.
    D. adjusted profit.
    E. accounting profit.

Use the following information relating to Bonga Petroleum Company Ltd to answer questions 45 and 46.

	₦
Adjusted profit for the year ended 31/12/13	2,000,000
Unrelieved losses brought forward	300,000
Capital allowances agreed with the FIRS	600,000
Tax rate – 85%	

Note that the company is engaged in petroleum operations.

45. What is the assessable tax assuming that the company has applied for the deferment of loss deduction?

A. ₦835,000
B. ₦935,000
C. ₦1,090,000
D. ₦1,190,000
E. ₦1,700,000

46. What is the assessable tax assuming that the company has not applied for the deferrment of loss deduction?
A. ₦935,000
B. ₦1,700,000
C. ₦1,190,000
D. ₦835,000
E. ₦1,090,000

Use the information below to answer questions 47 to 49.

Oguta Petroleum Ltd is engaged in petroleum operations. Between 1st January, 2010 and 31st December, 2010, the company incurred qualifying capital expenditure on plant, machinery and fixtures amounting to ₦20,000,000 in respect of:

	₦
Onshore operations	9,000,000
Offshore (up to and including 100 metres of water depth)	6,000,000
Offshore (between 100 and 200 metres of water depth)	5,000,000

47. The petroleum investment allowance for 2010 year of assessment is
A. ₦2,050,000.
B. ₦4,000,000.
C. ₦5,000,000.
D. ₦1,800,000.
E. ₦8,000,000.

48. The annual allowance for 2012 year of assessment is
A. ₦1,800,000
B. ₦4,000,000
C. ₦2,050,000

D. ₦5,000,000
E. ₦8,000,000

49. The annual allowance for 2014 year of assessment is …
A. ₦3,800,000
B. ₦4,000,000
C. ₦1,800,000
D. ₦2,000,000
E. ₦5,000,000

50. Given that a company engaged in petroleum operations acquired a plant for ₦1,500,000 and later sold it for ₦1,650,000 after claiming capital allowances amounting to ₦900,000, what is the balancing charge or allowance arising on the disposal of the asset?
A. ₦1,050,000 balancing charge
B. ₦600,000 balancing charge
C. ₦750,000 balancing charge
D. ₦150,000 balancing charge
E. ₦900,000 balancing charge

51. Given that an old established company engaged in petroleum operations acquired and disposed of three plants as stated hereunder, what is the balancing charge or allowance arising on the disposal?

Date of acquisition	01/05/2000
Date of disposal	30/12/2003
Cost of acquisition	₦10,000,000
Proceeds of disposal	₦3,500,000

A. ₦500,000 balancing charge
B. ₦4,000,000 balancing allowance
C. ₦2,000,000 balancing charge
D. ₦2,500,000 balancing allowance
E. ₦500,000 balancing allowance

Use the information below to answer questions 52 to 54.

The following figures have been extracted from the books of Ogoni Petroleum Plc for the accounting period ended 31st December, 2009:

	₦
Adjusted profit	50,000,000
Losses brought forward	4,000,000
Petroleum investment allowance	5,000,000
Capital allowances:	
Brought forward	31,000,000
Annual allowance	9,000,000
Balancing allowance	600,000

52. What is the assessable profit of the company for the accounting period ended 31st December, 2009?
A. ₦15,400,000
B. ₦46,000,000
C. ₦400,000
D. ₦36,000,000
E. ₦56,000,000

53. The amount of capital allowances deductible from the assessable profit for the accounting period ended 31st December, 2009 is restricted to …
A. ₦45,600,000.
B. ₦39,100,000.
C. ₦30,600,000.
D. ₦15,000,000.
E. ₦15,400,000.

54. What is the chargeable profit of the company for the accounting period ended 31st December, 2009?
A. ₦46,000,000
B. ₦400,000
C. ₦6,900,000
D. ₦15,400,000
E. ₦15,000,000

Use the information below to answer questions 55 to 57.

JJ Oil Ltd is a Nigerian company engaged in petroleum operations. The following information was obtained from the books of the company for the year ended 31st December, 2010.

Crude oil exported	350,000 barrels
Crude oil locally disposed of at ₦35 per barrel	50,000 barrels
Posted price for crude oil exported	₦800 per barrel
Incidental income from petroleum operations	₦1,500,000
Production and administrative expenses	₦42,275,000

55. What is the education tax payable by JJ Oil Ltd for the relevant year of assessment?
    A. ₦4,819,500
    B. ₦5,665,000
    C. ₦4,725,000
    D. ₦4,225,000
    E. ₦5,725,000

56. What is the assessable profit of JJ Oil Ltd for the relevant year of assessment?
    A. ₦240,975,000
    B. ₦4,725,000
    C. ₦283,250,000
    D. ₦216,250,000
    E. ₦236,250,000

57. What is the relevant year of assessment based on the information given?
    A. 2010
    B. 2011
    C. 2012
    D. 2009
    E. 2013

58. During the accounting period ended 31st December, 2011, Niger Delta Petroleum Limited exported 1,000 barrels of crude oil. The posted price of crude oil was US$30 per barrel at the standard API gravity 30^0. For every degree increase or decrease in API gravity above or below the standard API gravity, the price is increased or decreased by US$0.05. US$1 is equivalent to ₦105. What was the value of crude oil exported assuming that the API gravity of crude oil exported was 35^0?
    A. ₦3,176,250
    B. ₦3,123,750
    C. ₦3,150,000
    D. ₦3,165,750
    E. ₦3,156,250

Use the information below to answer questions 59 and 60.

The estimated liability of Aziza Petroleum Ltd was stated as ₦36 million in its return of estimated tax for the year ended 31st December, 2011. In September 2011, the company submitted another return to the FIRS showing its revised estimated tax for the year to be ₦45.6 million.

59. What is the amount of each monthly instalment payable between March and August 2011?
    A. ₦6,000,000
    B. ₦4,600,000
    C. ₦3,000,000
    D. ₦3,165,750
    E. ₦3,156,250

60. What is the amount of each monthly instalment payable between September 2011 and February 2012?
    A. ₦6,000,000
    B. ₦4,600,000
    C. ₦3,000,000
    D. ₦3,165,750
    E. ₦3,156,250

61. Which of the following is designed to guarantee the oil companies a certain profit margin irrespective of market conditions.
    A. Sole risk
    B. G-factor allowance
    C. Joint venture contract
    D. Production sharing contract
    E. Memorandum of understanding

62. A company engaged in petroleum operations commenced a sale of chargeable oil under a programme of continuous production and sales on 1st September, 2013. What is the basis period for the second year of assessment?
    A. 1/9/13 – 31/8/14
    B. 1/9/13 – 31/12/13
    C. 1/1/13 – 31/12/13
    D. 1/1/14 – 31/12/14
    E. 1/9/13 – 31/12/14

63. A company engaged in petroleum operations commenced a sale of chargeable oil under a programme of continuous production and sales on 1st August, 2013. What is the basis period for the first year of assessment?
    A. 1/8/13 – 31/7/14
    B. 1/8/13 – 31/12/13
    C. 1/1/13 – 31/12/13
    D. 1/1/14 – 31/12/14
    E. 1/8/13 – 31/12/14

64. A company engaged in petroleum operations ceased business on 31st March, 2013. What is the basis period for the year of cessation?
    A. 1/1/12 – 31/3/13
    B. 1/1/13 – 31/3/13
    C. 1/3/13 – 31/12/13
    D. 1/1/13 – 31/12/13
    E. 1/1/14 – 31/12/14

65. The ownership and control of all minerals, mineral oils and natural gas in Nigeria are vested in the ....
    A. Ministry of Petroleum Resources.
    B. Nigerian National Petroleum Corporation (NNPC).
    C. Central Bank of Nigeria.
    D. Federal Inland Revenue Service.
    E. Federal Government of Nigeria.

66. Activities in the downstream sector of the oil industry include all the following except ...
    A. oil well development.
    B. transportation of crude oil.
    C. oil distribution and marketing.
    D. conversion of crude oil into usable petroleum products.
    E. provision of various services to oil producing companies.

67. The operating or financing arrangements in the Nigerian upstream oil industry include all the following except ...
    A. sole risk.
    B. trade by barter.
    C. service contract.
    D. joint venture (JV).
    E. production sharing contract (PSC).

68. ... is a contractual arrangement between the NNPC and the oil company whereby the oil company (contractor) carries out petroleum operations in NNPC's acreages by providing the funds necessary for the operations and bearing all the risks alone and when oil is discovered in commercial quantity, the company recovers its costs, pays royalty and tax, while the balance of the oil is shared between the NNPC and the oil company in accordance with the terms of the contract.
    A. Sole risk
    B. Joint venture
    C. Service contract
    D. Marginal field operation
    E. Production sharing contract

69. ... is a contractual arrangement whereby the NNPC and the oil company jointly contribute to the cost and share the benefits of petroleum operations in accordance with their equity interest in the venture.
    A. Sole risk
    B. Joint venture
    C. Service contract
    D. Marginal field operation
    E. Production sharing contract

70. According to the Deep Offshore and Inland Basin Production Sharing Contracts Act, royalties payable in respect of deep offshore production sharing contracts are as follows:

A.	In areas from 201 to 500 metres water depth	12%
B.	In areas from 501 to 800 metres water depth	8%
C.	In arears from 800 to 1000 metres water depth	4%
D.	In areas in excess of 1000 metres depth	5%
E.	Inland basin	10%

Which of the options A to E is not correct?

71. In relation to petroleum profits tax, the profit of an accounting period less allowable expenses is referred to as the …
    A. total profit.
    B. adjusted profit.
    C. assessable profit.
    D. chargeable profit.
    E. remainder of assessable profit.

72. If there is no loss relief, the assessable profit of a company engaged in petroleum operations will be the same as …
    A. total profit.
    B. adjusted profit.
    C. chargeable profit.
    D. remainder of assessable profit.
    E. profit of an accounting period.

73. What is the rate of annual allowance on qualifying capital expenditure on an asset used in petroleum operations?
    A. 20% for five years.
    B. 25% for five years.
    C. 20% for the first four years and 1% in the fifth year.
    D. 25% for the first four years and 1% in the fifth year.
    E. 20% for the first four years and 19% in the fifth year.

74. Which of the following taxes is not payable by a company engaged in petroleum operations?
    A. Value added tax
    B. Capital Gains tax
    C. Petroleum profits tax
    D. Tertiary education tax
    E. Information technology development levy.

75. The schedules to the Petroleum Profits Tax Act are .....
    A. four.
    B. five.
    C. six.
    D. three.
    E. two.

76. The schedules to the Petroleum Profits Tax Act include all the following except ...
    A. first schedule – powers or duties to be performed or exercised by the Board alone.
    B. second schedule – capital allowances.
    C. third schedule – time for payments.
    D. fourth schedule.
    E. fifth schedule – G-factor allowance.

77. The activities in the Nigerian oil industry are often grouped under upstream and downstream sectors. Which one of the following activities does not belong to the upstream sector?
    A. Mineral rights acquisition
    B. Exploration and drilling

C. Oil distribution
D. Oil well development
E. Production

78. Examples of revenue accruable to the Federal Government from the petroleum industry include all the following except ...
A. petroleum profits tax.
B. signage.
C. signature bonuses.
D. tertiary education tax.
E. royalties.

79. Blends of crude oil produced in Nigeria include all the following except ...
A. Bonny light.
B. Qua Iboe.
C. Oloibiri.
D. Escravos.
E. Focardos.

80. The types of mineral rights licences granted in the oil industry include ...
i. Oil Exploration Licence (OEL).
ii. Oil Mining Lease (OML).
iii. Oil Development Licence (ODL).
iv. Oil Prospecting Licence (OPL).
A. i, ii and iii only
B. i, iii and iv only
C. i, ii and iv only
D. iii and iv only
E. ii, iii and iv only

81. Profits attributable to the transportation of chargeable oil from Nigeria to other countries by ocean going tankers operated by a petroleum company are taxable under the ...
A. Petroleum Profits Tax Act.
B. Companies Income Tax Act.

C. Capital gains Tax Act.
D. Industrial Development (Income Tax relief) Act.
E. Value Added Tax Act.

82. Examples of income accruable to the Federal Government from the Nigerian petroleum industry include all the following except ...
A. license fees.
B. gas flaring penalties.
C. sales proceeds of crude oil.
D. concession rentals.
E. national information technology development levy.

83. When there is any dispute over the date of commencement or cessation of petroleum operations, the date will be determined by the ...
A. Joint Tax Board.
B. Tax Appeal Tribunal.
C. Minister of Petroleum Resources.
D. Federal Inland Revenue Service.
E. Nigerian National Petroleum Corporation.

84. Which of the following statements is not correct?
A. Initial allowance is granted under CITA while petroleum investment allowance is granted under PPTA.
B. Under PPTA, annual allowance is granted over 5 years while under CITA different years are applicable to different classes of assets.
C. Where the basis period for a year of assessment is less than 12 months, annual allowance is prorated under CITA but is not prorated under PPTA.
D. Under PPTA, 1% of the initial cost of an asset is retained in the books until the asset is disposed of, while ₦10 is retained in respect of each asset under CITA.
E. Under CITA and PPTA, capital allowances granted in a year of assessment are restricted to $66\frac{2}{3}$% and 85% of the company's assessable profits respectively.

85. Which one of the following African countries is not a member of OPEC as at 2018?
    A. Equatorial Guinea
    B. Gabon
    C. Egypt
    D. Algeria
    E. Angola

86. The founding members of OPEC include all the following except …
    A. Iran
    B. Iraq
    C. Libya
    D. Kuwait
    E. Venezuela

Part II Short-Answer Questions

87. In relation to petroleum profits tax, define the term chargeable oil.

88. In relation to PPT, define the terms natural gas and liquefied natural gas.

89. In relation to PPT, define the term chargeable natural gas.

90. What is posted price?

91. Define the term petroleum.

92. What is petroleum operation?

93. What is casing head petroleum spirit?

94. With reference to PPTA, define the term "non-productive rent".

95. In relation to PPTA, define "intangible drilling expenditure".

96. What constitutes the value of chargeable oil?

97. What constitutes the value of chargeable natural gas?

98. G-Factor means ....

99. For an expenditure to be treated as allowable deduction in computing the adjusted profit of a company engaged in petroleum operations, it must satisfy three fundamental conditions. State these conditions.

100. Capital expenditure incurred prior to the first accounting period of a company is deemed to have been incurred on ...

101. What is the treatment of (i) loss and (ii) profit on disposal of an asset before the beginning of the first accounting period of a company engaged in petroleum operations?

102. State three conditions that must be satisfied by a company engaged in petroleum operations before being granted capital allowances.

103. State the rates of petroleum investment allowance on qualifying expenditure in respect of onshore and offshore operations.

104. How is capital allowance computed for an asset which is used partly for petroleum operations and partly for other purposes?

105. What is the maximum amount of capital allowances to be allowed as a deduction from the assessable profits of an accounting period of a company engaged in petroleum operations?

106. Which of the companies engaged in petroleum operations can claim an investment tax credit?

107. State the investment tax credit available to an oil producing company which executed a production sharing contract with the NNPC in 1993.

108. In relation to the memorandum of understanding between the Federal Government and oil companies, what is the minimum guaranteed notional margin granted to the oil companies?

109. In relation to PPT, when a company is resident in Nigeria it means ..

110. State the three ways in which the amount of credit admissible to a company engaged in petroleum operations under a double taxation arrangement may be granted.

111. If a company engaged in petroleum operations or the FIRS is dissatisfied with the decision of the Tax Appeal Commissioners, it may appeal to the … within … days after the date on which the decision was given. Further appeal shall lie to the …

112. Assessable tax less tax offsets is referred to as …

113. The currency for assessment and payment of petroleum profits tax is

114. State the due dates for payment of petroleum profits tax.

115. What is the penalty for failing to pay petroleum profits tax on the due date?

116. What is the penalty for non-deduction or non-remittance of withholding tax under the Petroleum Profits Tax Act?

117. What is the penalty for aiding, abetting, counselling, inciting or inducing any other person to make or deliver a false return or statement or keep or prepare a false account or particulars affecting petroleum profits tax or unlawfully refuse or neglect to pay petroleum profits tax?

118. What is the penalty for making incorrect accounts, schedules and statements by omitting or understating petroleum profits or overstating losses and expenditure?

119. Akwa Ibom Oil Company Limited is in production sharing contract with NNPC. Given the following production data in respect of the company's operations for 2007, compute the royalty payable by the company for 2007:

Water Depth	Production Barrels	Royalty Rate
Between 201 and 500 metres	18,000	12%
Inland basin	28,600	10%

Realizable price (RP) as advised by NNPC is $79.1423.

120. Under the production sharing contract between the NNPC and the oil company, the quatity of crude oil that remains after the royalty oil, cost oil and tax oil have been lifted is referred to as …

121. Which of the tax Acts governs the taxation of companies engaged in petroleum operations?

122. ... is charged with the administration of the Petroleum Profits Tax Act.

123. The profits of companies engaged in the marketing of refined petroleum products (diesel, petrol, kerosene, etc) are assessable to tax under … Act.

124. The profits of companies engaged in the upstream sector of the Nigerian oil industry are subject to tax under the …

125. The profits of companies engaged in the downstream sector of the Nigerian oil industry is subject to tax under the …

126. Companies operating in the Nigerian oil industry which are engaged in oil prospecting, exploration and production belong to the … sector of the petroleum industry.

127. Companies operating in the Nigerian oil industry which are engaged in the conversion of crude oil into diesel, petrol, kerosene, etc belong to the … sector of the petroleum industry,

128. Mention three activities carried out by companies in the Nigerian oil industry which are included in the downstream sector.

129. State the accounting period of a company engaged in petroleum operations in the year which the company first makes a sale or bulk disposal of chargeable oil.

130. State the accounting period of a company engaged in petroleum operations in the year in which the company ceases to be engaged in petroleum operations.

131. Any liquid hydrocarbons obtained in Nigeria from natural gas by separation or by any chemical or physical process but before the same has been refined or otherwise treated is referred to as …

132. In relation to petroleum profits tax, define the term crude oil.

27 Double Taxation Relief and Taxation of Non-residents

Part I Multiple-Choice Questions

1. An individual is deemed to be resident in Nigeria throughout an assessment year if he…
   i. is domiciled in Nigeria.
   ii. stays in Nigeria for a period or periods amounting to 183 days or more in any 12- month period.
   iii. serves as a diplomatic agent of Nigeria in a country other than Nigeria.
   iv. carries on a trade, business, profession or vocation in Nigeria.
   A. iii and iv only
   B. i, ii and iii only
   C. ii and iii only
   D. i and iii only
   E. ii and iv only

2. A company is deemed to be resident in Nigeria if …
   A. it has its place of management in Nigeria.
   B. its directors are resident in Nigeria.
   C. it is registered or incorporated in Nigeria.
   D. it has a permanent establishment in Nigeria.
   E. it is liable to tax in Nigeria.

3. A resident company is subject to tax in Nigeria on its
   A. profits brought into Nigeria only.
   B. profits derived from Nigeria only.
   C. profits attributable to Nigerian operations only.
   D. profits received in Nigeria only.
   E. worldwide profits.

4. A non-resident company is subject to tax in Nigeria on its …
   A. profits brought into Nigeria only.
   B. profits derived from Nigeria only.
   C. profits attributable to foreign operations only.
   D. profits received in Nigeria only.
   E. global profits.

5. The profits of a non-resident company from a trade or business is deemed to be derived from Nigeria if the company …
   A. has a fixed base in Nigeria from which it carries on its business or trade in Nigeria.
   B. habitually operates a trade or business through a dependent agent in Nigeria authorized to conclude contracts or deliver goods or merchandise on its behalf.
   C. executes a turnkey project in Nigeria.
   D. does not have a permanent establishment in Nigeria.
   E. carries on transactions or operations with its Nigerian subsidiary.

   Which of the options A to E is not correct?

6. A situation that two different taxpayers are assessed to tax on the same income by more than one country is referred to as …
   A. juridical double taxation.
   B. multiple taxation.
   C. tax sparing.
   D. domestic double taxation.
   E. economic double taxation.

7. A situation where similar taxes are imposed by two or more countries on the same taxpayer in respect of the same profit or income is referred to as …
   A. juridical double taxation.
   B. treaty shopping.
   C. tax sparing.
   D. tax mitigation.
   E. economic double taxation.

8. A tax treaty which is between two countries is said to be …
   A. unilateral.
   B. multilateral.
   C. bilateral.
   D. treaty shopping.
   E. domestic.

9. There is a double taxation treaty between country A and country B. Philip Ltd which is resident in country C (which does not have a tax treaty with country A or B) establishes a legal entity in country B through which it invests in country A in order to take advantage of country A/country B tax treaty to minimise its tax liability. This situation where a non-resident of either of the treaty countries establishes an entity in one of the treaty countries in order to take advantage of the benefits of the double taxation treaty is referred to as …
   A. tax heaven.
   B. tax sparing.
   C. treaty shopping.
   D. tax mitigation.
   E. mutual agreement procedure.

10. Which of the following is granted to a taxpayer to mitigate the adverse effect of paying tax on the same income or profit in two or more countries?
    A. Personal relief
    B. Loss relief
    C. Investment tax credit
    D. Memorandum of understanding credit
    E. Double taxation relief

11. Within how many years can a claim for Commonwealth income tax relief be made after the end of the year of assessment to which it relates?
    A. 6 years
    B. 5 years
    C. 1 year

D. 2 years
E. 3 years

12. At what rate will Commonwealth income tax relief be granted to a Nigerian company or an individual resident in Nigeria if the Commonwealth rate of tax exceeds one-half of the Nigerian rate of tax?
A. Commonwealth rate of tax
B. One-half of the Nigerian rate of tax
C. One-half of the Commonwealth rate of tax
D. Difference between Nigerian rate of tax and one-half of the Commonwealth rate of tax
E. Nigerian rate of tax

13. At what rate will Commonwealth income tax relief be granted to a non-Nigerian company or a non-resident taxpayer if the Commonwealth rate of tax does not exceed the Nigerian rate of tax?
A. Commonwealth rate of tax
B. One-half of the Commonwealth rate of tax
C. One-half of the Nigerian rate of tax
D. Nigerian rate of tax
E. Difference between Nigerian rate of tax and one-half of the Commonwealth rate of tax

14. Within how many years can a claim for relief under double taxation agreement be made after the end of the year of assessment to which it relates?
A. 6 years
B. 5 years
C. 1 year
D. 2 years
E. 3 years

15. Permanent establishment includes …
i. the operations of an independent agent.
ii. the operations of a dependent agent.
iii. a fixed base.

iv. a sales outlet.

A. ii, iii and iv only

B. iii and iv only

C. i and ii only

D. iii only

E. i, iii and iv only

16. According to Article 5 of the double taxation agreement between Nigeria and the United Kingdom, a permanent establishment includes:

A. the use of facilities solely for the purpose of storage, display or delivery of goods or merchandise belonging to an enterprise.

B. the maintenance of a stock of goods or merchandise belonging to an enterprise solely for the purpose of processing by another enterprise.

C. the maintenance of a fixed place of business solely for the purpose of collecting information for an enterprise.

D. the maintenance of a fixed place of business solely for the purpose of carrying on for an enterprise any activity of a preparatory or auxiliary character.

E. a place of management.

17. According to Article 5 of the double taxation agreement between Nigeria and the United Kingdom, a permanent establishment includes all the following except …

A. Facilities used solely for storage or display of goods or merchandise.

B. A mine, an oil or gas well, a quarry or any other place of extraction of natural resources.

C. A building site or construction or assembly project which exists for more than three months.

D. The provision of supervisory activities for more than three months on a building site or construction or assembly project.

E. A workshop.

18. The remuneration of a United Kingdom professor who is in Nigeria for the purpose of teaching or research is exempted from Nigerian tax for a period of not exceeding …
    A. 6 years from the date of his arrival in Nigeria.
    B. 2 years from the date of his arrival in Nigeria.
    C. 1 year from the date of his arrival in Nigeria.
    D. 3 years from the date of his arrival in Nigeria.
    E. 4 years from the date of his arrival in Nigeria.

19. Where there is a double taxation agreement between Nigeria and another country, and a resident of that country derives profit from the operation of ships or aircrafts in international traffic to and from Nigeria, but such profit is not derived by a resident of Nigeria from similar operation to and from the other country, tax is chargeable on the earnings from Nigeria by that non-resident at the rate of …
    A. 2 ½%.
    B. 5%.
    C. 10%.
    D. 2%.
    E. 1%.

Use the information below to answer questions 20 to 24.

ABB Ltd is a Nigerian company, which has its head office in Lagos and a branch office in Gambia. A summary of the company's profit and loss account for the year ended 31st December, 2012 is as follows:

	Nigeria	Gambia
	₦	₦
Turnover	7,000,000	4,000,000
Less cost of sales	3,400,000	1,600,000
Gross profit	4,600,000	2,400,000
Less:		
Administration expenses	1,350,000	830,000
Marketing expenses	700,000	500,000
Donations to social clubs	100,000	
Depreciation	50,000	30,000

Gambian income tax paid		350,000
Net profit	2,200,000	690,000
	4,600,000	2,400,000
Capital allowances agreed for the assessment year	89,000	70,000

Note that Gambia is a Commonwealth country and does not have a separate double taxation agreement with Nigeria.

20. What is the assessable profit for 2013 year of assessment?
    - A. ₦2,890,000
    - B. ₦2,731,000
    - C. ₦3,261,000
    - D. ₦3,420,000
    - E. ₦11,000,000

21. What is the total profit for 2013 year of assessment?
    - A. ₦10,841,000
    - B. ₦2,731,000
    - C. ₦3,261,000
    - D. ₦3,420,000
    - E. ₦1,261,000

22. ABB Ltd is entitled to a Commonwealth income tax relief of
    - A. ₦350,000.
    - B. ₦150,000.
    - C. ₦300,000.
    - D. ₦100,000.
    - E. ₦250,000.

23. The final income tax liability of ABB Ltd to the Nigerian Government for 2013 year of assessment is
    - A. ₦828,300.
    - B. ₦978,300.
    - C. ₦1,328,300.
    - D. ₦1,806,600.
    - E. ₦1,000,000.

24. The education tax payable for 2013 year of assessment is
A. ₦171,000.
B. ₦65,220.
C. ₦54,620.
D. ₦57,800.
E. ₦68,400.

Use the information below to answer questions 25 to 28.

Bobo Ltd is a Nigerian company. Its profits for 2013 year of assessment are as follows:

	₦
Nigerian profit before taxation	700,000
Foreign profit before taxation	500,000
Nigerian tax	30%
Foreign tax	40%

25. What is the credit to be given to Bobo Ltd in respect of the tax paid on its foreign profit?
A. ₦150,000
B. ₦125,000
C. ₦200,000
D. ₦175,000
E. ₦225,000

26. What is the total profit of Bobo Ltd?
A. ₦690,000
B. ₦1,200,000
C. ₦3,583,000
D. ₦1,000,000
E. ₦600,000

27. What is the total income tax liability of Bobo Ltd to the Nigerian Government?
A. ₦360,000
B. ₦210,000
C. ₦150,000

D. ₦125,000
E. ₦200,000

28. What is the final tax liability of Bobo Ltd to the Nigerian Government?
    A. ₦125,000
    B. ₦150,000
    C. ₦210,000
    D. ₦175,000
    E. ₦235,000

29. Which of the following is not an objective of entering into a double taxation agreement?
    A. To avoid double taxation or to afford relief from double taxation.
    B. To prevent or reduce tax evasion and tax avoidance at the international level.
    C. To ensure co-operation between the countries entering into the agreement on tax matters.
    D. To ensure that there is no mutual agreement procedure on tax matters between the countries entering into the agreement.
    E. To ensure that the nationals of one country are not unfairly treated in another country in respect of tax matters.

30. Which of the following is not a feature of a country or territory perceived to be a tax haven?
    A. There is effective exchange of information with foreign tax authorities.
    B. The country imposes zero or low tax rates on certain kinds of income.
    C. A tax haven may supply foreign governments or tax authorities with little or no information on financial transactions which take place in that jurisdiction.
    D. There is lack of transparency in the operation of legislative, legal or administrative provisions.

E. There is absence of a requirement for a substantive local presence.

31. Paragraph 3 of Article 23 of the Double Taxation Agreement between Nigeria and Pakistan states, "For the purpose of allowance as credit against the tax payable in Nigeria or Pakistan, as the context requires, the tax payable in a Contracting State shall be deemed to include the tax which is otherwise payable in that State but has been reduced or exempted by the State in pursuance of its tax incentive programme". This provision is referred to as …
A. treaty shopping provision.
B. mutual agreement provision.
C. tax heaven provision.
D. tax sparing provision.
E. force of attraction provision.

32. In the double taxation agreement between the Government of the Federal Republic of Nigeria and the Government of the Kingdom of Belgium, the two countries are referred to as ...
A. contractual parties.
B. compentent authorities.
C. contacting states.
D. independent nations.
E. associated parties.

33. In a double taxation agreement between two countries, the individual, ministry, board, etc appointed by each country to be its representative is referred to as ...
A. contractual party.
B. compentent authority.
C. contacting party.
D. independent agent.
E. associated party

34. It is possible for a person to be deemed to be resident in two countries at the same time. The double taxation agreement provides

the rules for resolving the problem of dual residence. These are referred to as the ..

A. tax sparing rules.
B. tie breaker rules.
C. treaty shopping rules.
D. force of attraction rules.
E. force of attribution rules.

35. A Nigerian branch of a foreign company is treated as a corporate entity and any income or profits derived by it from Nigeria is taxable in Nigeria. However, a branch of a foreign company may not be so treated if …

i. the branch is used solely for storage or display of goods or merchandise.
ii. the branch operates in Nigeria through a dependent agent authorized to conclude contracts or deliver goods or merchandise on its behalf.
iii the branch executes a turkey project in Nigeria.
iv. the branch is used solely for the collection of information.

A. ii, iii and iv only
B. i and iv only
C. ii only
D. i only
E. ii and iii only

36. Which of the following is not applicable to a Nigerian subsidiary of a foreign company?

A. The Nigerian subsidiary is expected to incorporate in Nigeria.
B. The Nigerian subsidiary is expected to operate as a separate legal entity from the parent company.
C. The Nigerian subsidiary is deemed to be a resident of Nigeria since it is incorporated in Nigeria.
D. The Nigerian subsidiary is liable to tax in Nigeria.
E. Only expenses incurred in Nigeria are allowable deductions in computing the taxable profits of the Nigerian subsidiary.

37. In determining the profit deemed to be derived from Nigeria by a non-resident corporation, the FIRS states that the relevant questions to ask are:
    - A. does the corporation have a "fixed base" in Nigeria?
    - B. does the corporation operate in Nigeria through a dependent agent authorized to conclude contracts or deliver goods or merchandise on its behalf?
    - C. is the corporation executing a turkey project in Nigeria?
    - D. is the operation between the corporation and its Nigerian subsidiary at arm's length?
    - E. is the corporation resident in two or more countries?

    Which of the options A to E is not correct?

38. A fixed base does not include:
    - i. facilities used solely for storage or display of goods or merchandise.
    - ii. facilities used solely for the collection of information.
    - iii facilities such as a factory, an office, a branch, a mine, gas or oil well, etc.
    - iv. activities such as building, construction, assembly or installation.
    - A. iii and iv only
    - B. i, ii and iv only
    - C. ii and iii only
    - D. i and ii only
    - E. ii and iv only

39. Article 4 of the Double Taxation Agreement between Nigeria and the United Kingdom provides the rules for resolving the problem of dual residence (referred to as the "tie breaker rules"). The first rule to be applied in resolving a case where an individual is a resident of Nigeria and the United Kingdom is based on …
    - A. nationality.
    - B. habitual abode.
    - C. permanent home.
    - D. mutual agreement.
    - E. center of vital interest.

40. Which of the following countries does not have a Double Taxation Agreement with Nigeria?
    A. South Africa
    B. China
    C. France
    D. Bahamas
    E. Belgium

41. Income tax may be imposed on the turnover of a non-resident individual or company in respect of the trade or business carried on in Nigeria if …
    i. the trade/business has no fixed base in Nigeria.
    ii. the trade/business has produced no assessable profits.
    iii. the assessable profits produced appear less than might be expected to arise from such a trade or business.
    iv. the true amount of the assessable profits of the company cannot be readily ascertained.
    A. ii or iii or iv is applicable
    B. i or ii or iv is applicable
    C. I or ii or iii or iv is applicable
    D. i or ii is applicable
    E. iii or iv is applicable

42. With reference to the Double Taxation Agreement between Nigeria and the United Kingdom, the competent authority in the case of Nigeria is …
    A. the Nigerian Ambassador to the Uk or his authorized representative.
    B. Minister of Foreign Affairs or his authorized representative.
    C. Minister of Finance or his authorized representative.
    D. the FIRS or its authorized representative.
    E. Prsident or his authorized representative.

43. With reference to the Double Taxation Agreement between Nigeria and other countries, international traffic is used in connection with
    A. ships only.
    B. trains only.

C. aircrafts only.
D. heavy trucks only.
E. ships and aircrafts.

44. Under the source rule, an income is subject to tax in the ...
A. country where the income is utilised.
B. country where the income is derived.
C. country where the company is incorporated.
D. country where the owner of the income is resident.
E. country where the owner of the income is domicled.

45. The different names by which a tax treaty is called include all the following except …
A. tax sparing.
B. tax agreement.
C. tax convention.
D. bilateral tax agreement.
E. avoidance of double taxation agreement.

46. Which one of the following statements is not true? The profits of a non-resident company from a trade or business are subject to tax in Nigeria ...
A. where the company has a fixed base of business in Nigeria and the profits are attributable to that fixed base.
B. where the company executes a single contract for survey, deliveries, installation or construction in Nigeria and the profits are attributable to that contract.
C. where the profits derived from Nigeria are not taxed in the country in which the company is deemed to be resident.
D. where the company habitually conducts a trade or business through an agent in Nigeria who is authorized to conclude contracts on its behalf and the profits are attributable to the business or trade carried on through that agent.
E. where the company habitually maintains a stock of goods or merchandise in Nigeria from which deliveries are regularly made by an agent on behalf of the company and the profits are attributable to the business carried on through that agent.

47. Where the transactions between a non-resident company and its Nigerian subsidiary are in the opinion of the FIRS deemed to be artificial, the profits deemed to be derived from Nigeria shall be so much of the profits adjusted by the FIRS to reflect arm's length transactions. The FIRS can make appropriate adjustment to the profits of the Nigerian company where the following circumstances prevail.
    - A. Where there is a controlling interest in the Nigerian company.
    - B. The presence of a control of a Nigerian company may be exercised directly or indirectly by a parent company.
    - C. The conditions imposed must be similar to what would obtain between independent parties or in an open market situation.
    - D. Such relationship and conditions lead to the transfer of goods and services at prices not at arm's length.
    - E. Where the profits declared for the Nigerian tax are understated.

Part II Short-Answer Questions

48. How would you determine the Commonwealth rate of tax?

49. The rate at which Commonwealth income tax relief will be given to a Nigerian company or resident individual if the Commonwealth rate of tax does not exceed one-half of the Nigerian rate of tax is ...

50. At what rate will Commonwealth income tax relief be given to a non-Nigerian company or non-resident individual if the Commonwealth rate of tax exceeds the Nigerian rate of tax?

51. What is double taxation agreement?

52. State two purposes of double taxation agreement.

53. Mention any three countries which have double taxation agreements with Nigeria.

54. State the relief available to a non-resident taxpayer whose income is subject to Nigerian tax and foreign tax.

55. What is the maximum credit allowable in any year of assessment under a double taxation arrangement?

56. Under a double taxation arrangement, relief for foreign tax is granted as a credit against tax payable. How is relief granted for Commonwealth income tax?

57. A fixed place of business through which the business of an enterprise is wholly or partly carried on is referred to as …

58. Give three examples of a permanent establishment.

59. A Nigerian company carries on business in United Kingdom through a permanent establishment. Is the profits of the company taxable in United Kingdom?

60. In relation to double taxation agreement, define the term international traffic?

61. In relation to double taxation agreement, when is an enterprise said to be associated with another enterprise?

62. An individual who stays in Nigeria for less than 183 days in a 12-month period but derives income or profit from Nigeria is referred to as …

63. A company that is not registered or incorporated in Nigeria but which derives income or profit from Nigeria is referred to as …

64. According to section 105 of CITA 2004, "any company incorporated under the Companies and Allied Matters Act or any enactment replaced by that Act" is referred to as a …

65. According to section 105 of CITA 2004, "any company or corporation (other than a corporation sole) established by or under any law in force in any territory or country outside Nigeria" is referred to as a ..

66. The profits of a Nigerian branch of a foreign company is taxable in Nigeria. Give two circumstances under which the branch may not be taxed in Nigeria.

67. State two circumstances under which a non-resident individual or company is assessable to tax on the turnover of his or its trade or business.

68. A single contract involving survey, deliveries, installation or construction is referred to as a …

69. A country or territory where no taxes or very low rates of taxes are imposed is referred to as a ...

70. Under what circumstance is Commonwealth income tax relief granted to a company?

71. How is the Nigerian rate of tax determined?

72. The profits derived from another country by a company resident in Nigeria are only subject to tax in Nigeria if the profits are not taxed in the foreign country in which they are derived. True or false?

73. State two ways adopted by a typical tax treaty to eliminate double taxation.

28 Transfer Pricing, Thin Capitalization and Electronic Commerce

Part I Multiple-Choice Questions

1. The price charged for goods or services supplied or transferred by one subunit of an organization to another subunit or one member of a group to another is referred to as...
   - A. a premium price.
   - B. an economy price.
   - C. a price skimming.
   - D. a bundle price.
   - E. a transfer price.

2. Which of the following companies is not a multinational company?
   - A. Cadbury
   - B. Guinness
   - C. MTN
   - D. Unilever
   - E. None of the above.

3. The objectives of the Income Tax (Transfer Pricing) Regulations, 2018 issued by the Board of the FIRS include all the following except to …
   - A. reduce the consumption of certain goods and services considered to be harmful or non-essential.
   - B. provide the Nigerian authorities with the tools to fight tax evasion through over or under-pricing of controlled transactions between associated enterprises.
   - C. reduce the risk of economic double taxation.
   - D. provide a level playing field between multinational enterprises and independent enterprises doing business within Nigeria.

E. provide taxable persons with certainty of transfer pricing treatment in Nigeria.

4. Which of the following is not a transfer pricing method to be applied in determining whether transactions between associated enterprises are consistent with the arm's length principle?
   A. Comparable uncontrolled price method
   B. Resale price method
   C. Cost plus method
   D. Adjusted profit method
   E. Transactional net margin method

5. In determining the most appropriate transfer pricing method to use in evaluating each transaction between connected taxable persons, the following factors should be considered:
   A. possibility of double taxation.
   B. the respective strengths and weaknesses of the transfer pricing method in the circumstances of the case.
   C. the appropriateness of a transfer pricing method having regard to the nature of the controlled transaction.
   D. the availability of reliable information needed to apply the transfer pricing method.
   E. the degree of comparability between controlled and uncontrolled transactions.

   Which of the options A to E is not correct?

6. According to the Income Tax (Transfer Pricing) Regulations, 2018, a request by a connected taxable person to the FIRS to enter into an Advance Pricing Agreement (APA) shall be accompanied by …
   A. a description of the activities of the taxable person to be addressed by the Advance Pricing Agreement.
   B. a proposal by the taxable person for the determination of the transfer prices for the transactions to be covered by the Advance Pricing Agreement.
   C. the identification of any other country or countries that the person wishes to participate in the Advanced Pricing Agreement.

D. evidence of payment of a non-refundable fee of ₦100,000 which shall be credited to the Consolidated Revenue Fund of the Federation.

E. any other relevant information that the FIRS may require to complete its analysis of the Advance Pricing Agreement request.

Which of the options A to E is not true?

7. The FIRS may cancel an Advance Pricing Agreement (APA) entered into with a connected taxable person if:

A. the connected taxable person has failed to materially comply with fundamental terms of the Advance Pricing Agreement.

B. the Advance Pricing Agreement was entered into based on a misrepresentation, mistake or omission by the connected taxable person.

C. the connected taxable person has neglected or refused to comply with a notice delivered to him/it by the FIRS, without showing any reasonable cause.

D. there has been a material breach of one or more of the critical assumptions underlying the Advance Pricing Agreement.

E. there is a change in the tax law that is materially relevant to the Advance Pricing Agreement.

Which of the options A to E is not correct?

8. An Advance Pricing Agreement entered into under the Income Tax (Transfer Pricing) Regulations, 2018 shall apply to the affected controlled transactions for a period not exceeding …

A. three years.

B. five years.

C. ten years.

D. two years.

E. twenty years.

9. In determining whether two or more transactions are comparable, the Income Tax (Transfer Pricing) Regulations, 2018 stipulates that the following factors should be considered to the extent that they are

economically relevant to the facts and circumstances of the transactions:

A. the characteristics of the goods, property or services transferred or supplied.

B. the functions undertaken by the person entering into the transaction taking into account the assets used and risks assumed.

C. the contractual terms of the transactions.

D. the economic circumstances under which the transactions were undertaken.

E. whether the connected taxable person is a resident or non-resident individual or company.

Which of the options A to E is not true?

10. A connected person is required to make and submit to the FIRS a Transfer Pricing Declaration not later than .....

A. eighteen months after the date of incorporation or within six months after the end of the accounting year, whichever is later.

B. twelve months after the date of incorporation or within six months after the end of the accounting year, whichever is earlier.

C. eighteen months after the date of incorporation or within twelve months after the end of the accounting year, whichever is earlier.

D. eighteen months after the date of incorporation or within six months after the end of the accounting year, whichever is earlier.

E. twelve months after the date of incorporation or within three months after the end of the accounting year, whichever is earlier.

11. A connected person shall make an updated Transfer Pricing Declaration and submit to the FIRS upon the occurrence of any of the following events ...

A. compulsory liquidation of the connected person's business.
B. merger of the person's parent with another company outside the group.
C. acquisition of up to 20% of the person's parent by persons not connected to the group.
D. merger or acquisition of the person by another company outside the group.
E. sale or acquisition of a subsidiary by the person.

Which of the options A to E is not correct?

12. The Income Tax (Transfer Pricing) Regulations, 2018 stipulates that a connected person shall make an updated Transfer Pricing Declaration and submit to the FIRS upon the …
A. acquisition of up to 5% of the person by persons not connected to the group.
B. acquisition of up to 20% of the person by persons not connected to the group.
C. acquisition of up to 10% of the person by persons not connected to the group.
D. acquisition of up to 15% of the person by persons not connected to the group.
E. acquisition of up to 50% of the person by persons not connected to the group.

13. A connected person is required to make an updated Transfer Pricing Declaration and submit to the FIRS upon the occurrence of any of the events stated in the Income Tax (Transfer Pricing) Regulations, 2018. The updated declaration is to be submitted to the FIRS ….
A. within three months of the end of the accounting year in which the event occurred.
B. within eighteen months of the end of the accounting year in which the event occurred.
C. within six months of the end of the accounting year in which the event occurred.
D. within two months of the end of the accounting year in which the event occurred.

E. within five months of the end of the accounting year in which the event occurred.

14. A connected person who fails to submit a declaration or notification, as the case may be, to the FIRS in respect of merger, acquisition, any other change in the structure, arrangement or circumstances of the person as specified in the Income Tax (Transfer Pricing) Regulations, 2018 shall be liable to an administrative penalty of …
    A. twenty-five thousand naira for each day in which the failure continues.
    B. ten thousand naira for every day in which the failure continues.
    C. five thousand naira for each day in which the failure continues.
    D. ten million naira in addition to one thousand naira for every day in which the failure continues.
    E. ten million naira in addition to ten thousand naira for every day in which the failure continues.

15. A connected person who fails to make or submit a declaration of its relationship with all connected persons in the prescribed form within the time specified in the Income Tax (Transfer Pricing) Regulations, 2018 shall be liable to an administrative penalty of …
    A. ten million naira or one per cent of the value of transactions with connected persons, whichever is higher.
    B. ten million naira plus one per cent of the value of transactions with connected persons.
    C. ten million naira in addition to ten thousand naira for every day in which the failure continues.
    D. ten million naira in addition to one thousand naira for every day in which the failure continues.
    E. one hundred million naira in addition to ten thousand naira for every day in which the failure continues.

16. For each year of assessment, a connected person is required to make a disclosure of transactions that are subject to Income Tax (Transfer

Pricing) Regulations. The disclosure is to be made and submitted to the FIRS not later than …

A. six months after the end of each accounting year or eighteen months after the date of incorporation, whichever is earlier.

B. six months after the end of each accounting year or eighteen months after the date of incorporation, whichever is later.

C. twelve months after the date of incorporation or within six months after the end of the accounting year, whichever is earlier.

D. eighteen months after the date of incorporation or within twelve months after the end of the accounting year, whichever is earlier.

E. eighteen months after the date of incorporation or within nine months after the end of the accounting year, whichever is earlier.

17. A connected person who fails to make disclosures of transactions which are subject to Income Tax (Transfer Pricing) Regulations within the period specified in the Regulations shall pay an administrative penalty of ….

A. ten million naira or one per cent of the value of transactions with connected persons, whichever is higher.

B. ten million naira or one per cent of the value of controlled transaction not disclosed, whichever is higher.

C. ten million naira or one per cent of the value of controlled transaction not disclosed, whichever is lower, plus ten thousand naira for every day in which the failure continues.

D. ten million naira plus ten thousand naira for every day in which the failure continues.

E. ten million naira or one per cent of the value of controlled transaction not disclosed, whichever is higher, plus ten thousand naira for every day in which the failure continues.

18. A connected person who makes an incorrect disclosure of transactions which are subject to Income Tax (Transfer Pricing) Regulations shall be liable to an administrative penalty of' …

A. ten million naira or one per cent of the value of controlled transactions incorrectly disclosed, whichever is lower.
B. ten million naira or one per cent of the value of transactions with connected persons, whichever is higher.
C. ten million naira or one per cent of the value of controlled transaction not disclosed, whichever is lower.
D. ten million naira or one per cent of the value of controlled transactions incorrectly disclosed, whichever is higher.
E. ten million naira or one per cent of the value of controlled transactions incorrectly disclosed, whichever is higher, plus ten thousand naira for every day in which the misdemeanour continues.

19. For each year of assessment, a connected person is required to make a disclosure of transactions that are subject to Income Tax (Transfer Pricing) Regulations. Presently, the transfer pricing disclosure form makes provision for the following information .....
A. Particulars of the reporting company or entity.
B. Income from controlled transactions.
C. Costs of controlled transactions.
D. Transfer pricing method and documentation.
E. Details of transfer pricing penalties paid during the year of assessment.

Which of the options A to E is not correct?

20. A connected person is required to make and submit to the FIRS a Transfer Pricing Declaration. The declaration shall be in the form as may be prescribed by the FIRS from time to time. Presently, the transfer pricing declaration form makes provision for the following information except ...
A. Particulars of the connected person's bankers.
B. Particulars of external auditors of reporting company.
C. Particulars of tax consultants of reporting company.
D. Particulars of company secretary of reporting company.
E. Particulars of the person making the declaration.

21. The transfer pricing declaration to be made by a connected person to the FIRS shall be in the form prescribed by the FIRS. Presently, the transfer pricing declaration form makes provision for the following information except …
    A. Particulars of immediate parent company.
    B. Debtors and creditors of the reporting company.
    C. Major shareholders of reporting company.
    D. Ownership structure of reporting company.
    E. Subsidiaries and other connected persons.

22. The Decision Review Panel set up in accordance with the Income Tax (Transfer Pricing) Regulations, 2018 comprises ...
    i. the Head of the Transfer Pricing Department of the FIRS.
    ii. a representative of the Legal Department of the FIRS, not below the rank of Deputy Director.
    iii. three other employees of the FIRS, not below the rank of Deputy Director.
    iv. a representative of the Attorney-General of the Federation.
    v. a representative of the Tax Appeal Tribunal.
    A. i, ii and iii only
    B. i, ii, iv and v only
    C. i and iii only
    D. i, ii and v only
    E. i, ii, iii and v only

23. The Decision Review Panel set up in accordance with the Income Tax (Transfer Pricing) Regulations, 2018 consists of …
    A. four members
    B. seven members
    C. five members
    D. six members
    E. eight members

24. How many members are needed to form a quorum at any meeting of the Decision Review Panel set up in accordance with the Income Tax (Transfer Pricing) Regulations, 2018?

A. The Head of the Transfer Pricing Function and any other three members.
B. The Head of the Transfer Pricing Function and any other four members.
C. The Head of the Transfer Pricing Function and any other five members.
D. The Head of the Transfer Pricing Function and any other two members.
E. Any three members.

25. Who should be the Chairman of the Decision Review Panel set up in accordance with the Income Tax (Transfer Pricing) Regulations, 2018?
A. The most senior officer among members of the Panel.
B. The Head of the Transfer Pricing Department of the FIRS.
C. A representative of the Legal Department of the FIRS.
D. A representative of the Attorney-General of the Federation.
E. A representative of the Tax Appeal Tribunal.

26. If a taxable person is not satisfied with the assessment arising from an adjustment to its controlled transactions, it may object to the assessment within ....
A. sixty days of the receipt of the assessment.
B. twenty-one days of the receipt of the assessment
C. fourteen days of the receipt of the assessment.
D. seven days of the receipt of the assessment.
E. thirty days of the receipt of the assessment.

27. If a taxable person is not satisfied with the assessment arising from an adjustment to its controlled transactions, it may object to the assessment to the Decision Review Panel set up in accordance with the Income Tax (Transfer Pricing) Regulations, 2018. In rendering a decision on a matter presented before it, the Panel is to take into consideration .....
A. double taxation agreement.
B. the adjustment or assessment issued.
C. the basis on which the adjustment or assessment was issued.

D. the taxable person's objection.
E. the evidence presented to it by the parties.
Which of the options A to E is not correct?

28. All records and books of account, as well as data relating to any trade carried out by the taxpayer, inclusive of recorded details from which the taxpayer's returns were prepared for assessment of taxes, are to be retained for a period of ....from the date on which the return relevant to the last entry was made.
A. six years
B. five years
C. four years
D. seven years
E. three years

29. What is the penalty to be imposed on a taxable person who contravenes any of the provisions of the Income Tax (Transfer Pricing) Regulations for which no specific administrative penalty is stipulated in the Regulations?
A. One per cent of the total value of controlled transactions in addition to ten thousand naira for each day in which the failure continues.
B. Ten million naira or one per cent of the value of controlled transactions, whichever is lower.
C. Twenty-five thousand naira for each day in which the failure continues.
D. Ten million naira in addition to ten thousand naira for every day in which the failure continues.
E. As prescribed in the relevant tax law.

30. A connected taxable person is to record sufficient information or data with an analysis of such information and data to verify that the pricing of controlled transactions is consistent with the arm's length principle. The documentation shall be submitted to the FIRS within..
A. 21 days of receiving a request from the FIRS.
B. 7 days of receiving a request from the FIRS.
C. 14 days of receiving a request from the FIRS.

D. 30 days of receiving a request from the FIRS.
E. 60 days of receiving a request from the FIRS.

31. A connected taxable person is to record sufficient information or data with an analysis of such information and data to verify that the pricing of controlled transactions is consistent with the arm's length principle. If the reporting entity fails to submit the documents to the FIRS on request within the specified time, it shall be liable to an administrative penalty of a sum equal to ……
A. ten million naira or 1% of the total value of all controlled transactions, whichever is higher and ten thousand naira for every day in which the failure continues.
B. one per cent of the total value of controlled transactions in addition to ten thousand naira for each day in which the failure continues.
C. ten million naira or one per cent of the value of controlled transactions, whichever is lower.
D. twenty-five thousand naira for each day in which the failure continues.
E. ten million naira in addition to ten thousand naira for every day in which the failure continues.

32. A connected person whose total value of controlled transactions is less than ………… may choose not to maintain contemporaneous documentation. Nevertheless, where the FIRS deems it necessary, it may demand that relevant documentation shall be prepared and submitted to the FIRS not later than ………… from the date of receipt of a notice from the FIRS.
A. three hundred million naira; 90 days
B. one hundred million naira; 60 days
C. two hundred million naira; 30 days
D. three hundred million naira; 60 days
E. two hundred million naira; 90 days

33. The Income Tax (Country by Country Reporting) Regulations, 2018 was issued by the ...
A. Minister of Finance.

B. President of Nigeria.
C. FIRS.
D. FIRS Board with the approval of the Minister of Finance.
E. National Assembly.

34. The objectives of the Income Tax (Country by Country Reporting) Regulations, 2018 include all the following except to …
A. provide tax authorities with information about multinational enterprises' global activities, profits and taxes.
B. provide tax authorities with information to better assess international tax avoidance risks.
C. improve transparency of MNEs in their tax practices.
D. encourage repatriation of foreign earnings to Nigeria.
E. prevent tax evasion or avoidance through base erosion and profit shifting.

35. The deadline for the filing of Country-by-Country Report (CbCR) with the FIRS is not later than ….after the last day of the reporting accounting year of the MNE group.
A. 12 months
B. 6 months
C. 4 months
D. 3 months
E. 2 months

36. Any constituent entity of an MNE group that is resident for tax purposes in Nigeria is required to notify the FIRS whether it is the ultimate parent entity or surrogate parent entity …
A. not later than 30th June of the MNE group's accounting year
B. not later than 31st December of the MNE group's accounting year
C. not later than the first day of the MNE group's reporting accounting year
D. not later than the last day of the MNE group's reporting accounting year.
B. not later than 31st March of the MNE group's accounting year

37. What information is the constituent entity of an MNE group that is resident for tax purposes in Nigeria required to furnish the FIRS if it is neither the ultimate parent entity nor the surrogate parent entity and what is the deadline for the provision of the information?
    A. The identity and tax residence of the reporting entity not later than the last day of the MNE group's reporting accounting year.
    B. The official language for filing the country-by-country report not later than the last day of the MNE group's reporting accounting year.
    C. The identity and tax residence of the reporting entity not later than 31st December of the MNE group's accounting year.
    D. The official language for filing the country-by-country report not later than the first day of the MNE group's reporting accounting year.
    E. Transactions with related companies not later than the last day of the MNE group's reporting accounting year.

38. The filing of the country-by-country report (CbCR) with the FIRS is mandatory for MNE group with total consolidated group revenue of
    A. ₦100 billion in the immediately preceding accounting year.
    B. ₦150 billion in the immediately preceding accounting year.
    C. ₦120 billion in the immediately preceding accounting year.
    D. ₦200 billion in the immediately preceding accounting year.
    E. ₦160 billion in the immediately preceding accounting year.

39. The FIRS shall use the country-by-country report for purposes of
    A. assessing high level transfer pricing risks.
    B. assessing the risk of non-compliance by members of the MNE Group with applicable transfer pricing rules.
    C. economic and statistical analysis, where appropriate.
    D. transfer pricing adjustments.
    E. assessing base erosion and profit shifting related risks in Nigeria.

40. The penalty for non or late filing of country-by-country report by a reporting entity is …
   A. ₦10 million in the first instance and ₦1million for every month in which the default continues.
   B. ₦1million in the first instance and ₦100,000 for every month in which the default continues.
   C. ₦100,000 in the first instance and ₦10,000 million for every month in which the default continues.
   D. ₦10,000 in the first instance and ₦1,000 for every month in which the default continues.
   E. ₦100 million in the first instance and ₦10 million for every month in which the default continues.

41. The penalty for filing an incorrect or false country-by-country report by a reporting entity is …
   A. ₦100 million.
   B. ₦50 million.
   C. ₦30 million.
   D. ₦20 million.
   E. ₦10 million.

42. Any constituent entity of an MNE group that is resident for tax purposes in Nigeria is required to notify the FIRS whether it is the ultimate parent entity or surrogate parent entity and if it is neither the ultimate parent entity nor the surrogate parent entity, it is to notify the FIRS of the identity and tax residence of the reporting entity. The penalty for failure to provide the information is …
   A. ₦5 million in the first instance and ₦10,000 for every month in which the default continues.
   B. ₦10 million in the first instance and ₦100,000 for every month in which the default continues.
   C. ₦100,000 in the first instance and ₦10,000 million for every month in which the default continues.
   D. ₦10,000 in the first instance and ₦1,000 for every month in which the default continues.
   E. ₦5 million in the first instance and ₦10,000 for every day in which the default continues.

43. The Income Tax (Country by Country Reporting) Regulations, 2018 requires that a country-by-country report with respect to an MNE group should contain aggregate information relating to ……. with regard to each jurisdiction in whuch the MNE group operates.
    A. the amount of revenue, profit or loss before income tax
    B. income tax paid and income tax accrued
    C. capital and accumulated earnings
    D. number of employees
    E. intangible assets
    Which of the options A to E is not correct?

44. The effective date of the Income Tax (Country by Country Reporting) Regulations, 2018 is …
    A. 1/1/18
    B. 1/4/18
    C. 1/5/18
    D. 1/10/18
    E. 1/7/18

Part II Short-Answer Questions

45. The buying and selling of goods and services over the internet is referred to as …

46. State one challenge or problem of e-commerce transactions to the Nigerian tax authorities.

47. What is thin capitalization?

48. Suggest any one measure which could be instituted by your country to counter the negative effects of thin capitalization.

49. ....is required to file a country-by-country report (CbCR) for a MNE with the FIRS annually.

50. The official language for filing a country-by-country report is ….

51. The abbreviation BEPS represents …

52. The principle that the conditions of a controlled transaction should not differ from the conditions that would have applied between independent persons in comparable transactions carried out under comparable circumstances is referred to as …

53. In the Income Tax (Transfer Pricing) Regulations, 2018, where one person has the ability to control or influence the other person in making financial, commercial or operational decisions, the persons are deemed to be …

54. A commercial or financial transaction between connected persons or related parties are referred to as … in the Income Tax (Transfer Pricing) Regulations, 2018.

55. Enterprises or persons that are not related to one another are referred to as … in the Income Tax (Transfer Pricing) Regulations, 2018.

56. Based on the Income Tax (Transfer Pricing) Regulations, 2018, the decision of the Decision Review Panel on any adjustment or assessment in relation to controlled transactions shall represent the final position of the FIRS. True or false?

57. The decision of the Decision Review Panel on any adjustment or assessment in relation to controlled transactions shall not be subject to futher appeal. True or false?

58. Subject to the extension of time, any person who fails to furnish the FIRS with any information or document concerning controlled transaction within the time specified in a notice shall be liable to an administrative penalty of a sum equal to …

29 Merger, Acquisition, Tax Incentives and Tax Planning

Part I Multiple-Choice Questions

1. After the merger of three companies (A Ltd, B Ltd and C Ltd), one of the merging companies (A Ltd) survives with its old name to inherit the assets, liabilities and operations of the merging parties. Which of the following statements is not true?
   A. The commencement provisions will apply to the surviving company.
   B. The surviving company will not be allowed to claim investment allowance and initial allowance on the assets transferred to it.
   C. The surviving company may claim annual allowance on the tax written down values of the assets transferred to it.
   D. The surviving company may not inherit the unabsorbed losses and capital allowances of the merging companies.
   E. The surviving company must file its tax returns as an existing (old) company.

2. Where a merger or consolidation results in the cessation of business of all or any of the merging companies …
   A. the cessation provisions will apply to those companies which have ceased business permanently.
   B. any unrelieved capital allowances at cessation can be carried backward and set off against the remainder of assessable profits of the relevant companies for the five years preceding the year of cessation.
   C. any unrelieved losses at cessation cannot be carried backward to be set off against the assessable profits of the preceding years of assessment.
   D. any sum received by the company, its receivers or liquidators after the date of cessation which would have

been taken into account in the computation of assessable profits if it had been received before that date, shall be deemed to have been received by the company on the last day before such cessation occurred.

E. any company that has ceased business must file its tax returns within 18 months of cessation.

3. CITA provides that where a business carried on by a company is sold or transferred to a Nigerian company for the purposes of better organisation of the trade or business or the transfer of its management to Nigeria and any asset employed in such trade or business is sold or transferred, if the FIRS is satisfied that one company has control over the other or that both are controlled by some other person or are members of a recognised group of companies, the FIRS may in its discretion direct that ...

A. the commencement and cessation provisions shall not apply to such trade or business.

B. assets shall be deemed to have been sold at their tax written down values on the day following such sale or transfer.

C. the company acquiring each such asset shall not be entitled to any initial allowance with respect to that asset.

D. the company acquiring each such asset shall not be entitled to any allowance deemed to have been received by the vendor company.

E. assets shall be deemed to have been sold to the new company at their agreed values and not written down values.

Which of the options A to E is not true?

4. Which of the following is not a reason for offering tax incentives to investors by the Government?

A. To attract foreign investment into Nigeria.

B. To encourage investors to invest in certain preferred sectors of the economy.

C. To avoid budget deficit.

D. To promote exports.

E. To encourage repatriation of foreign earnings to Nigeria.

5. Which of the following is not a disadvantage of tax incentive schemes?
   A. Loss of revenue to the government since most tax incentives result in the taxpayers paying less tax or no tax at all.
   B. The government has to incur additional costs to monitor the schemes to forestall abuses.
   C. They are inducements for foreign direct investment (FDI).
   D. Tax incentives granted by Nigeria to a foreign investor are offset or reduced by taxes imposed by the investor's country of residence.
   E. Tax incentive schemes are prone to abuses by some taxpayers.

6. Companies engaged in agricultural trade or business are ..
   A. exempted from the payment of minimum tax.
   B. allowed to carried forward losses for more than four years.
   C. allowed to claim 100% capital allowances in a year of assessment provided the assessable profit is sufficient to absorb the allowances.
   D. are granted 95% initial allowance on the cost of an agricultural plant and equipment and plantation equipment in the first year.
   E. exempted from tax indefinitely.

   Which of the options A to E is not true?

7. Under what condition is a company engaged in agricultural production assessable to income tax at the rate of 20% for the first five years of assessment?
   A. If its annual turnover is less than ₦1 million.
   B. If its annual turnover is less than ₦10 million.
   C. If its net assets amount to ₦1 million or below.
   D. If its net assets amount to less than ₦10 million.
   E. If its annual turnover is less than ₦100 million

8. A manufacturing company and a company engaged in wholly export trade with an annual turnover of less than ₦1 million is assessable to income tax at the rate of ..

A. 20% for the first five years of assessment.
B. 20% for the first three years of assessment.
C. 10% for the first five years of assessment.
D. 30% for the first five years of assessment.
E. 25% for the first five years of assessment.

9. A new company engaged in the mining of solid minerals is exempted from tax for the …
A. first ten years of its operation.
B. first five years of its operation.
C. first four years of its operation.
D. first three years of its operation.
E. first two years of its operation.

10. As an alternative to the granting of an initial tax free period of three years to a company engaged in gas utilization (downstream operations), the company may be granted an additional investment allowance of …
A. 35%.
B. 5%.
C. 25%.
D. 45%.
E. 50%.

11. The profits of an export oriented undertaking within and outside Export Free Zone is exempted from tax for the first three years if:
A. the undertaking is wholly export oriented.
B. the undertaking is not formed by splitting or reconstructing an existing business or undertaking.
C. during the relevant year, the undertaking manufactures and exports articles and the export proceeds make up 75% of its turnover.
D. the company incurred an expenditure on electricity, water or tarred road for the purpose of its trade or business where such facilities are not provided by the government.

E. at least 75% of the undertaking's export earnings are repatriated to Nigeria and deposited in a domiciliary account in a recognized bank in Nigeria.

Which of the options A to E is not true?

12. The investment tax credit granted to a company engaged in research and development activities for commercialisation is …
    A. 20% of its qualifying capital expenditure.
    B. 20% of its total profits.
    C. 25% of its qualifying capital expenditure.
    D. 15% of its qualifying capital expenditure.
    E. 10% of its qualifying capital expenditure.

13. Investment tax relief available to a company located in the rural areas cannot be claimed for more than …
    A. five years.
    B. three years.
    C. seven years.
    D. ten years.
    E. four years.

14. Investment tax relief is granted to a company that has incurred an expenditure on the provision of electricity, water, tarred road or telephone for the purpose of the company's trade or business which is located at least …… away from such facilities provided by the government.
    A. 100 kilometres
    B. 50 kilometres
    C. 80 kilometres
    D. 20 kilometres
    E. 70 kilometres

15. Where a company has incurred an expenditure on the provision of electricity for the purpose of the company's trade or business in an area which is far away from such facility provided by the government, the company shall be allowed investment tax relief for each year expenditure is incurred on such facility at the rate of …

A. 100% of the expenditure
B. 50% of the expenditure
C. 30%% of the expenditure
D. 15% of the expenditure
E. 5% of the expenditure

16. A company can minimize its potential tax liability without contravening the law through …
A. tax evasion.
B. window dressing of financial statements.
C. tax planning.
D. litigation.
E. adjudication.

17. Which of the following is not a tax planning or tax avoidance option that may be adopted by a company to reduce its tax burden?
A. Manipulation of financial statements.
B. Financing operations with more loans than share capital.
C. Taking advantage of the tax incentives offered by the government.
D. Claiming roll-over relief on disposal of asset.
E. Investing in tax heavens.

18. The Companies Income Tax Act provides that a company which is engaged in mining of solid minerals and earns an annual turnover of less than ₦1 million is assessable to income tax at the rate of … for the first five years of assessment.
A. 20%.
B. 5%
C. 10%
D. 30%
E. 25%

19. After granting an initial allowance on qualifying mining expenditure … is retained in the books until disposal.
A. 20%.
B. 5%

C. 10%
D. 30%
E. 25%

20. Initial allowance is granted on qualifying mining expenditure at the rate of …..
A. 15%.
B. 50%
C. 30%
D. 95%
E. 25%

21. Which of the following incentives is not granted to companies or enterprises engaged in mining operations under the Nigeria Minerals and Mining Act?
A. 20% investment tax credit on their qualifying expenditure.
B. Exemption from payment of customs and import duties in respect of plant, machinery, equipment and accessories imported specifically and exclusively for mining operations.
C. Personal remittance quota for expatriate personnel free from any tax imposed by any enactment for the transfer of external currency out of Nigeria.
D. Free transferability of funds through the CBN in convertible currency in respect of the remittance of foreign capital in the event of sale or liquidation of the mining operations or any interest therein attributable to foreign investment.
E. The Minister may defer payment of royalty on any minerals for a specific period, on the approval of the Federal Executive Council.

22. Under the Nigeria Export Processing Zone Act, approved enterprises operating within export processing zones in Nigeria are granted all the following incentives except …
A. exemption from all federal, state and local government taxes, levies and rates.
B. exemption from the requirement for import or export licences.

C. rent-free land at construction stage.
D. repatriation of foreign capital investment in the Zones at any time with capital appreciation of the investment.
E. interest-free loans.

23. Which of the following incentives is not granted to approved enterprises operating within export processing zones in Nigeria under the Nigeria Export Processing Zone Act?
A. Exemption from legislative provisions pertaining to taxes, levies, duties and foreign exchange regulations.
B. Up to 100% foreign ownership of business in the Zones is allowable.
C. Remittance of profits and dividends earned by foreign investors in the Zones.
D. Up to 75% of production may be sold in the customs territory against a valid permit and on payment of appropriate duties.
E. Foreign managers and qualified personnel may be employed by companies operating in the Zones.

24. Companies and other organizations engaged in research and development activities for commercialization are allowed initial allowance of .... on qualifying research and development expenditure.
A. 15%.
B. 50%
C. 30%
D. 95%
E. 25%

25. The Companies Income Tax (Road Infrastructure Development and Refurbishment Investment Tax Credit Scheme) Order, 2019 was signed by the President of the Federal Republic of Nigeria on 25th January, 2019. The scheme is to be in force for a period of ....from the date of commencement of the Executive Order.
A. four years
B. five years

C. three years
D. six years
E. ten years

26. The Companies Income Tax (Road Infrastructure Development and Refurbishment Investment Tax Credit Scheme) Order, 2019 is …
A. Executive Order No. 001 of 2019.
B. Executive Order No. 004 of 2019.
C. Executive Order No. 005 of 2019.
D. Executive Order No. 006 of 2019.
E. Executive Order No. 007 of 2019.

27. Members of the Road Infrastructure Development and Refurbishment Investment Tax Credit Scheme Management Committee include all the following except …
A. Minister of Works.
B. Minister of Finance.
C. representative from Federal Inland Revenue Service (FIRS).
D. Director-General of the Manufacturers Association of Nigeria (MAN).
E. representatives from relevant government ministries and agencies.

28. The Chairman and Deputy Chairman of the Road Infrastructure Development and Refurbishment Investment Tax Credit Scheme Management Committee are ….
A. Minister of Works and Minister of Finance respectively.
B. Minister of Finance and Minister of of Works respectively.
C. Minister of Finance and Chairman of FIRS respectively.
D. Minister of Finance and Permanent Secretary of the Federal Ministry of Finance respectively.
E. Minister of Finance and Minister of Industries respectively.

29. Who is the Secretary to the Road Infrastructure Development and Refurbishment Investment Tax Credit Scheme Management Committee?

A. Permanent Secretary of the Federal Ministry of Works
B. Legal Adviser to the FIRS
C. Chairman of the FIRS
D. Permanent Secretary of the Federal Ministry of Finance
E. Permanent Secretary of the Federal Ministry of Industries

30. Which one of the following is not allowed to participate in the Road Infrastructure Development and Refurbishment Investment Tax Credit Scheme?
A. Nigerian company
B. Pension fund administrator
C. Insurance company
D. Investment bank
E. Corporation sole

31. Road Infrastructure Development and Refurbishment Investment Tax Credit Scheme allows companies to finance the construction or refurbishment of eligible road projects in Nigeria. Who gives final approval for a company to participate in the scheme?
A. Minister of Works
B. Minister of Finance
C. Chairman of FIRS
D. President of Nigeria
E. Road Infrastructure Development and Refurbishment Investment Tax Credit Scheme Management Committee

32. An applicant may become eligible to participate in the Road Infrastructure Development and Refurbishment Investment Tax Credit Scheme upon provision of the following documents to the management committee of the scheme:
i. a written notification of expression of interest in the construction or refurbishment of an identified road project.
ii. a valid and current tax clearance certificate.
iii. bank guarantee to sponsor the project.
iv. project cost and timeline bids.
A. i, iii and iv only
B. i, ii and iv only

C. i and iv only
D. ii, iii and iv
E. i, ii and iii only

33. The Road Infrastructure Development and Refurbishment Investment Tax Credit Scheme Management Committee shall recommend the eligibility of an applicant to participate in the Scheme where it determines that the applicant's proposed road project is economically viable, cost efficient and can be completed within …
    A. twelve to twenty-four months.
    B. twelve to eighteen months.
    C. six to forty-eight months.
    D. eighteen to twenty-four months.
    E. twelve to forty-eight months.

34. The responsibility for issuing a Road Infrastructure Tax Credit Certificate to a participant in the Road Infrastructure Development and Refurbishment Investment Tax Credit Scheme on an annual basis is vested in the …
    A. Minister of Works.
    B. Federal Inland Revenue Service.
    C. Minister of Finance.
    D. Permanent Secretary of the Ministry of Works.
    E. Road Infrastructure Development and Refurbishment Investment Tax Credit Scheme Management Committee.

35. … is responsible for approving a participant's application for road infrastructure tax credit.
    A. Minister of Works
    B. Federal Inland Revenue Service
    C. Minister of Finance
    D. Permanent Secretary of the Ministry of Works
    E. Road Infrastructure Development and Refurbishment Investment Tax Credit Scheme Management Committee

36. The Road Infrastructure Tax Credit Certificate shall only be issued upon presentation of the following except…
    A. a confirmation of authorization to participate in the Scheme issued by the Management Committee of the Scheme.
    B. approval of the project cost and completion timeline bid by the Management Committee of the Scheme.
    C. contract award letter.
    D. the participant's five years' financial statements.
    E. certification of work done issued by the Management Committee of the Scheme.

37. With the exception of Road Infrastructure Tax Credit issued with respect to an eligible road in an economically dsadvantaged area, the tax credit that may be utilised by a participant in the Road Infrastructure Development and Refurbishment Investment Tax Credit Scheme in any year of assessment is limited to …
    A. 50% of the participant's assessable profit in that year.
    A. 50% of the participant's companies income tax payable in that year.
    C. $66^2/_3$% of the participant's companies income tax payable in that year.
    D. $66^2/_3$% of the participant's assessable profit in that year.
    E. 75% of the participant's companies income tax payable in that year.

38. Which of the following is not true of Road Infrastructure Tax Credit?
    A. It can be set off against the participant's companies income tax from the relevant fiscal year in which the project cost is incurred.
    B. Unutilised tax credit in any year of assessment can be carried forward to subsequent tax years until fully utilised.
    C. The tax credit cannot be set off against companies income tax unless claimed by a participant or beneficiary in its tax returns for that year of assessment.

D. No other tax credit, capital allowance, relief or incentive on the project cost incurred in respect of eligible road can be claimed in addition to the road infrastructure tax credit.
E. A participant cannot dispose of the whole or part of its road infrastructure tax credit certificate to a willing buyer.

39. Participants in the Road Infrastructure Development and Refurbishment Investment Tax Credit Scheme may be unable to recoup the full/actual project cost incurred as the aggregate professional service fees admissible on road project with a refurbishment or construction cost of ₦10 billion and above is restricted to …
A. 10% of the project cost.
B. 5% of the project cost.
C. 25% of the project cost.
D. 1.50% of the project cost.
E. 1.25% of the project cost.

40. Participants in the Road Infrastructure Development and Refurbishment Investment Tax Credit Scheme are entitled to …
i. utilise the project cost as a tax credit against companies income tax payable.
ii. claim capital allowances as well as road infrastructure tax credit on the capital expenditure incurred on the eligible road project.
iii. a non-taxable single uplift (similar to interest) equivalent to the prevailing monetary policy rate of the Central Bank of Nigeria plus 2% of the project cost.
iv. utilize the uplift as a tax credit against companies income tax payable.
A. i, ii and iii only
B. i, iii and iv only
C. i and ii only
D. ii, iii and iv only
E. i, ii and iv only

Part II Short-Answer Questions

41. Is it necessary to obtain the Federal Inland Revenue Service's consent or direction before a merger, take-over, transfer or restructuring of the trade or business carried on by a company can be consummated?

42. State the condition for exemption of 25% of a hotel's income from income tax.

43. State the investment tax relief granted to a company for being located in areas without government infrastructure such as electricity, water and tarred road.

44. State any two tax incentives offered by the Federal Government to enhance the development of the manufacturing sector of the economy.

45. State any two tax incentives offered by the Federal Government to enhance the development of the agricultural sector of the economy.

46. Under what condition is interest on loan granted by a bank on or after 1st January, 1997 to a company engaged in agricultural trade or business exempted from tax?

47. Interest on loan granted by a bank on or after 1st April, 1980 for the purpose of manufacturing goods for export is exempted from tax as stipulated in the Third Schedule to CITA. Present the Third Schedule to CITA.

48. Gas utilization is defined in the Companies Income Tax Act as...

49. Mention one tax incentive granted to a company engaged in gas utilization (downstream operations).

50. On which day does the tax free period of a company engaged in gas utilization (downstream operations) start?

51. A company engaged in gas utilization (downstream operations) shall be granted accelerated capital allowances after the tax free period. State the rates of the accelerated capital allowances.

52. Which of the Executive Orders allows companies to finance the construction or refurbishment of eligible road infrastructure projects in Nigeria in return for a tax credit based on the project cost?

53. State the tax incentive granted to a 100% export-oriented undertaking?

54. A Road Infrastructure Tax Credit may qualify as an asset in a participant or beneficiary's financial records. True or False?

55. A pioneer company can claim investment tax relief. True or false?

56. What is tax planning?

57. Any gains arising on the disposal of a road infrastructure tax credit shall be subjected to tax in the manner prescribed by the applicable tax legislation. True or False?

30 Tax Implications of Leasing

Part I Multiple-Choice Questions

1. An agreement whereby the owner of an asset conveys to another party the right to use the asset for an agreed period of time in return for a payment or series of payments is referred to as ...
   A. deferred payment plan.
   B. hire purchase.
   C. charter party.
   D. credit sale.
   E. leasing.

2. Which of the following is not a feature of a finance lease?
   A, The risks and rewards of ownership are substantially transferred from the lessor to the lessee.
   B. The lessee is responsible for insurance, maintenance and similar charges on the leased asset.
   C. The lease is for a short period usually significantly less than the economic life of the asset.
   D. The lease term covers a substantial part of the economic life of the asset.
   E. The lease is non-cancellable.

3. Which of the following is not a feature of an operating lease?
   A. The lessor pays for insurance, maintenance and similar charges on the leased asset.
   B. The lease is cancellable, that is, the lessee can terminate the lease with proper notice.
   C. The lease is for a short period usually significantly less than the economic life of the asset.
   D. The lessee has an option to purchase the asset for a nominal amount when the lease expires.
   E. The lease agreement does not transfer the risks and rewards of ownership of the asset to the lessee.

4. XYZ Ltd acquires an asset and leases it out to ABC Ltd under a finance lease contract for use in ABC Ltd's business. Which one of the companies is eligible to claim capital allowances and what is the qualifying capital expenditure (QCE) on which to claim capital allowances?
   A. XYZ Ltd and the QCE is the cost of the asset.
   B. ABC Ltd and the QCE is the cost of the asset.
   C. Neither XYZ Ltd nor ABC Ltd is eligible to claim capital allowances.
   D. XYZ Ltd and the QCE is limited to the amount of the total lease payments due from the lessee during the basis period but excluding any interest charges payable.
   E. ABC Ltd and the QCE is limited to the amount of the total lease payments due from the company during the basis period but excluding any interest charges payable.

5. AB Ltd acquires an asset and leases it out to YZ Ltd under an operating lease contract for use in ZY Ltd's business. Which of the companies is eligible to claim capital allowances and what is the qualifying capital expenditure (QCE) on which to claim capital allowances?
   A. AB Ltd and the QCE is the cost of the asset.
   B. ZY Ltd and the QCE is the cost of the asset.
   C. Neither AB Ltd nor ZY Ltd is eligible to claim capital allowances.
   D. ZY Ltd and the QCE is limited to the amount of the total lease payments due from the lessee during the basis period but excluding any interest charges payable.
   E. AB Ltd and the QCE is limited to the amount of the total lease payments due from the lessee during the basis period but excluding any interest charges payable.

6. A Ltd (the lessor) acquires an asset and leases it to B Ltd (the Lessee) under an operating lease contract. Which of the following statements is not correct?
   A. The total lease rental received or receivable by A Ltd is income and it is wholly taxable.

B. B Ltd is to deduct withholding tax at the rate of 10% from the rental payment to the lessor and remit same to the FIRS.

C. A Ltd is to include a 5% VAT charge on the lease rental income on its invoice to the lessee.

D. The VAT charged on the lease rental is an input tax to the B Ltd and should not be charged to its profit and loss account.

E. The rental charges and other associated expenses are allowable deductions in computing B Ltd's profits for tax purposes.

7. XYZ Ltd (the lessor) acquires an asset and leases it to BYC Ltd (the lessee) under a finance lease contract. Which of the following statements is not correct?

A. Withholding tax at the rate of 10% is computed only on the interest portion of the total lease payment due from the BYC Ltd.

B. Capital portion of the lease rental receivable by XYZ Ltd is subject to companies income tax.

C. If the asset is disposed of at the expiration of the lease period, any capital gain realised by XYZ Ltd would be subject to capital gains tax.

D. The interest portion of the periodic lease rent and other related expenses such as insurance and maintenance cost are deductible expenses for income tax purposes.

E. The interest portion of the rent earned by XYZ Ltd constitutes taxable income in the hand of the company.

Part II Short-Answer Questions

8. FFF Limited leased manufacturing equipment from GGG Leasing Limited. The total lease sum is ₦15 million but the fair market value is ₦10 million. The equipment has an economic life of 5 years. The lease term is 4 years with an option to buy the equipment for ₦100,000 by the lessee. The lease is not cancellable and the lessee is responsible for maintenance, insurance and upkeep of the equipment. *(Source: FIRS Information Circular No. 2010/1 of 12/4/2010)*

Is the above stated transaction a finance lease or an operating lease?

9. MAN Haulage Company Limited leased a truck from Auto Motors Limited. The cost of the truck is ₦15 million and monthly lease payment is ₦300,000 payable at the beginning of each month. The lessor is responsible for repairs, maintenance and registration of the vehicle while the lessee takes care of fuelling, lubrication, tyre replacements. The expected useful life of the truck is 10 years. The lease term is 2 years in the first instance and it is renewable subject to agreement by the two parties; either party can also opt out of the arrangement after 3 months' notice. *(Source: FIRS Information Circular No. 2010/1 of 12/4/2010).*
   Is the above stated transaction a finance lease or an operating lease?

10. XYZ Limited sells it building to ABC Finance Company Limited and simultaneously leases (rents) the building back from the finance company. This transaction is referred to as ...

31 Taxation of Non-Governmental Organizations (NGOs)

Part I Multiple-Choice Questions

1. Which of the following is not a feature of non-governmental organizations (NGOs)?
   - A. NGOs are mostly established and financed by the government.
   - B. NGOs are voluntary organizations.
   - C. NGOs operate independently of the government.
   - D. NGOs are not-for-profit organizations.
   - E. NGOs may be financed by voluntary contributions or donations.

2. NGOs include organizations, institutions and companies engaged in
   - A. ecclesiastical activities.
   - B. charitable activities.
   - C. benevolent activities.
   - D. educational activities of a public character.
   - E. research and development activities for commercialization.

   Which of the options A to E is incorrect?

3. A non-governmental organization (NGO) is exempted from payment of income tax. Nevertheless, the NGO is required to ...
   - A. devote the whole of its profits to ecclesiastical, charitable, benevolent or educational activities.
   - B. pay tax on profits derived from business or trading activities.
   - C. obtain a tax clearance certificate.
   - D. file tax returns every year.
   - E. register with the FIRS.

   Which of the options A to E is incorrect?

4. A non-governmental organization (NGO) is expected to register with the relevant tax office. Which of the following may not be required for the registration?
   A. A copy of registration certificate issued by the Corporate Affairs Commission.
   B. Certified copy of memorandum or constitution, rules and regulations governing the NGO.
   C. List and profiles of the trustees/board members nominated.
   D. Particulars of the prospective shareholders stating names, addresses and amount of shareholding.
   E. A copy of the current tax clearance certificate of each of the trustees.

5. In line with section 55 of CITA, it is mandatory for every NGO to file a self-assessment return at least once a year and such return shall contain ...
   A. the audited accounts.
   B. tax and capital allowance computations.
   C. a true and correct statement in writing containing the amounts of its profits from each and every source .
   D. the amount of VAT payable during the year.
   E. a declaration to be signed by a director or secretary of the organization that the information contained in the return is true and correct.

   Which of the options A to E is incorrect?

6. Besides the obligation to file tax returns, NGOs are required to ...
   A. maintain proper books of accounts.
   B. file a return in the prescribed form of their transactions in the capital market.
   C. maintain accurate record of employees.
   D. pay tax as and when due on non-exempt activities.
   E. deduct PAYE and withholding tax and remit same to the appropriate tax authorities.

   Which of the options A to E is incorrect?

7. Which of the following statements is true?
   A. NGOs are exempted from payment of VAT.
   B. NGOs are exempted from the filing of annual tax returns if they are not engaged in any trade or business.
   C. Goods purchased by NGOs for use in humanitarian donor funded projects are zero rated under the Value Added Tax Act.
   D. Any donation made by a company to an NGO is to be treated as an allowable deduction in computing the assessable profit or loss of that company.
   E. Capital gain which accrues to an NGO is exempted from tax although it may be derived from the disposal of an asset acquired in connection with any trade or business carried on by the NGO.

32 Tax Audit and Investigation

Part I Multiple-Choice Questions

1. The routine (or normal) examination of the accounts, books, records, documents, etc of a taxable person by the relevant tax authority in order to ascertain the level of compliance with the relevant tax laws is referred to as ...
   A. value for money audit.
   B. management audit.
   C. tax investigation.
   D. statutory audit.
   E. tax audit.

2. An enquiry to ascertain the level of fraud or wilful default or neglect perpetrated by a taxpayer and to obtain evidence for possible prosecution of the culprit is referred to as ...
   A. value for money audit.
   B. procedural audit.
   C. tax investigation.
   D. statutory audit.
   E. tax audit.

3. Which of the following is not an objective of tax audit?
   A. To form an opinion as to whether the taxpayer's balance sheet and profit and loss account are in agreement with the accounting records and returns.
   B. To ensure that the taxpayer has maintained all the relevant documents, records and accounts to facilitate tax assessment.
   C. To discourage taxpayers from engaging in tax evasion.
   D. To ensure that the correct amount of income has been declared and the tax has been correctly computed and paid in accordance with the tax laws and regulations
   E. To update the database of existing taxpayers and to bring more eligible taxpayers into the tax net.

4. Some of the circumstances that may trigger off a tax audit of a company include:
   A. A claim for tax refund by the company.
   B. Failure of the company to respond to tax queries arising from desk examination.
   C. Information from the intelligence unit or other departments of the tax authority, newspaper publications, third parties, tip-off, etc.
   D. Where the company has not received adequate returns from branches
   E. Referrals from other regulatory agencies or directive from higher government authority.

   Which of the options A to E is not correct?

5. Some of the circumstances that may cause a company to be selected for tax audit or investigation by the FIRS include:
   A. The balance sheet and profit and loss account of the company not being in agreement with the accounting records.
   B. Suspicion of inter-group transactions not being made at arm's length.
   C. Non-filing of tax returns or filing of returns which show poor performance repeatedly.
   D. The company making unusual request or taking extra-ordinary decisions (e.g. mergers, acquisitions, re-organizations, etc)
   E. Suspicion of the existence of tax fraud or evasion.

   Which of the options A to E is not correct?

6. Where the tax authority has evidence or strong suspicion of the existence of tax fraud or tax evasion, it may carry out a …
   A. value for money audit.
   B. procedural audit.
   C. tax investigation.
   D. statutory audit.
   E. tax audit.

7. Tax investigation covers the following stages except ...
   A. surveillance or pre-investigation activities.
   B. evidential audit or investigation.
   C. case preparation.
   D. arraignment.
   E. adjudication.

8. An investigation of tax fraud or evasion may be terminated if ...
   A. there is insufficient evidence to proceed further with the case.
   B. it is discovered that criminality is not involved.
   C. the suspect dies or becomes insane.
   D. the suspect makes a claim for tax refund.
   E. the case becomes statute barred.

   Which of the options A to E is not correct?

9. All the following activities can be carried out by a tax auditor before embarking on a tax audit exercise except ...
   A. selection of the taxpayer to be audited.
   B. preparation of interim audit report.
   C. preliminary review of taxpayer's file in the tax office.
   D. preparation of audit plan.
   E. notification of the taxpayer about the proposed audit.

10. All the following activities can take place after a field audit exercise except ...
    A. reconciliation meeting.
    B. preparation and submission of the interim audit report.
    C. preparation and submission of the final audit report.
    D. preparation of audit checklist.
    E. issuance of notice of additional assessment

11. In carrying out a tax audit, the tax auditors from Lagos State Internal Revenue Service may not be interested in the documents/ information pertaining to ...
    A. PAYE.
    B. stamp duties.

C. capital gains tax.
D. tertiary education tax.
E. withholding tax.

12. In carrying out a tax audit, the tax auditors from the Federal Inland Revenue Service may not be interested in the documents/information pertaining to ...
A. national information technology development levy.
B. tertiary education tax.
C. withholding tax.
D. tenement rate.
E. stamp duties.

13. Which of the following is the end product of a tax audit?
A. Tax audit plan
B. Tax audit checklist
C. Tax audit evidence
D. Tax audit working papers
E. Tax audit report

14. .... contains a list of the work to be done during the tax audit to ensure that the audit exercise is carried out systematically and no work is duplicated or overlooked.
A. Preliminary review
B. Tax audit checklist
C. Tax audit evidence
D. Tax audit working papers
E. Tax audit report

15. Which of the following is prepared at the planning stage of a tax audit exercise?
A. Preliminary review
B. Tax audit checklist
C. Tax audit evidence
D. Tax audit working papers
E. Tax audit report

16. Where an audit is carried out in the tax office by way of examining the returns rendered by the taxpayer and raising queries on matters that need further clarifications or making demands for additional information, it is referred to as …
    A. evidential audit or examination
    B. analytical review.
    C. adjudication.
    D. desk audit.
    E. field audit.

17. Where the audit of the taxpayer's records, accounts, returns, documents, etc takes place in the taxpayer's premises, it is referred to as …
    A. evidential audit or examination.
    B. analytical review.
    C. adjudication.
    D. desk audit.
    E. field audit.

18. Techniques of obtaining tax audit evidence include all the following except
    A. analytical reviews.
    B. observation.
    C. subrogation.
    D. inspection.
    E. enquiry.

19. A good tax audit report must be ...
    A. clear.
    B. accurate.
    C. subjective.
    D. timely prepared.
    E. presented in a logical and concise manner.

    Which of the options A to E is not correct?

20. Which one of the following statements is not true in relation to a limited liability company?
    - A. Both statutory audit and tax audit of a company must be carried out every year.
    - B. Statutory audit and tax audit of a company are governed mainly by the provisions of the Companies and Allied Matters Act and tax Acts respectively.
    - C. Statutory audit report and tax audit report of a company are addressed to the shareholders of the company and the management of the relevant tax authority respectively.
    - D. Statutory audit of a company is carried out by a Chartered Accountant whereas a tax auditor may not be a Chartered Accountant or Chartered Tax Practitioner.
    - E. Statutory auditors of a company are appointed at each annual general meeting of a company while tax auditors are members of staff of the tax authority or tax consultants engaged by the tax authority or the government.

21. The FIRS wishes to carry out a tax audit of ABC Limited. Who among the following may not be engaged to carry out the assignment on behalf of the FIRS?
    - A. The members of staff of the FIRS.
    - B. A tax consultant engaged by the FIRS.
    - C. The External auditors of the company.
    - D. A combined staff of the tax authority and the tax consultant.
    - E. A committee established for that purpose.

22 Your audit team has been assigned to carry out a tax investigation of XYZ Company Plc. Which of the following is not likely to be an objective of the exercise?
    - A. To ascertain the level of tax fraud or wilful default perpetrated by the company.
    - B. To recover the tax lost or undercharge in the previous years of assessment.
    - C. To enable the tax authority to impose penalties for breach of the tax laws by the company.

D. To form an opinion as to whether proper accounting records have been kept by the company.

E. To obtain evidence for possible prosecution of the company for tax evasion.

23. The Lagos State Internal Revenue Service (LIRS) has recently informed the Group Managing Director of Dagogo Plc of its intention to carry out a tax audit of the company. Which of the following documents might not be of much interest to the tax auditors from the LIRS conducting the tax audit?

A. Evidence of remittance of VAT.

B. Withholding tax deduction/remittance schedules and receipts

C. Evidence of payment of development levy, business premises registration/renewal fees.

D. Evidence of remittance of PAYE tax.

E. Evidence of remittance of contributions to Pension Fund, National Housing Fund and National Health Insurance.

24. A team of tax auditors from the Lagos State Internal Revenue Service is carrying out a tax audit on Chop-I-Chop Limited. Which of the following documents might not be of much interest to the Tax auditors from the LIRS conducting the tax audit?

A. List of staff and their designations

B. Names and addresses of directors of the company

C. Certificate of capital importation

D. List of company houses and occupiers

E. Staff salary structure

25. A team of tax auditors from the Lagos State Internal Revenue Service is carrying out a tax audit on Wazobia Limited. Which of the following documents would not be of interest to the tax auditors?

A. Schedule of company vehicles and users

B. Rent agreement/schedule, names and addresses of landlords

C. Staff payroll for the audit period

D. Particulars of the shareholders

E. List of suppliers/contractors

26. The problems or challenges confronting tax authorities in carrying out tax audit of small enterprises in Nigeria include ...
    A. difficulty in locating or tracking down small scale enterprises/owners for tax audit.
    B. difficulty in ascertaining the correct income in the absence complete records/accounts of business transactions.
    C. indiscriminate imposition of taxes on small enterprises by different tiers of government.
    D. inadequate resources to audit numerous small scale businesses scattered all over the country.
    E. the cost of conducting the audit of small scale businesses might be excessive compared to the revenue to be generated from the exercise.

27. The following are the benefits to be derived from the tax audit programme except that ...
    A. it provides details of the work to be carried out during the tax audit exercise.
    B. it enables the auditor to obtain background information about the taxpayer to be audited.
    C. it facilitates the allocation of jobs/responsibilities among the team members.
    D. it facilitates supervision and control of the audit.
    E. it facilitates the performance of the audit assignment in an orderly and systematic manner.

28. Ways of ensuring effective quality control of a tax audit engagement include all the following except that ...
    A. an audit plan should be drawn up after the commencement of the actual audit.
    B. contentious matters must be brought to the attention of the team leader.
    C. all work done during the audit and conclusions reached must be carefully and completely recorded in the working papers.
    D. all audit work done and the working papers must be fully reviewed by superiors.

E. proper briefing of staff on the audit objective, audit plan, timing requirements, audit test/procedures to be carried out, etc.

29. You are an Inspector of Taxes in the Federal Inland Revenue Service, Lagos and has been mandated to lead a team of tax auditors to carry out a tax audit of XYZ Limited. The areas/matters that you will discuss with the company's management or representative(s) during the initial meeting before the commencement of the actual field audit include all the following except...
A. introduction of the audit team members.
B. briefing the company's management on the purpose of the audit.
C. obtaining background information about the company or confirming background information earlier obtained.
D. soliciting for the co-operation of the company's management in terms of providing necessary information, books, records, etc promptly.
E. determining whether the company agrees with the result of the audit work.

30. In assessing the reliability of tax audit evidence, which of the following statements is not true?
A. Documentary evidence is more reliable than oral evidence.
B. Evidence obtained from independent sources outside the organization is more reliable than that obtained from internal sources (within the organization).
C. Evidence originated by the auditor is more reliable than that obtained from other sources.
D. The reliability of the audit evidence obtainable from different sources is enhanced where the audit evidence obtained from one source is inconsistent with that obtained from another source.
E. Original documents are more reliable than their photocopies.

31. The first set of audited accounts of TB Limited was made up to 31st December, 2017 and it was filed with the FIRS together with the tax

computations. Assuming that on examination of the tax returns you have queried the expenses on purchases of raw materials, which of the following documents might not be relevant in verifying the expenses on purchases of raw materials?

A. Insurance policies
B. Purchase invoices
C. Goods delivery notes or waybills
D. Goods received notes
E. Stock cards

32. BYC Limited has submitted its audited accounts for the year ended 30th June, 2017 to FIRS together with the tax computations. Assuming that you are the Inspector of Taxes and upon examination of the tax returns, you have raised query on the expenses on rent. Which of the following documents might not be relevant in verifying the expenses on rent?

A. Receipt issued by the landlord
B. Bank statement
C. Architect's certificate
D. Withholding tax receipt or credit note
E. Rent agreement

33. The statute of limitation for a tax audit or investigation where the tax authority has no evidence or suspicion of the existence of tax evasion is limited to …

A. five years.
B. four years.
C. seven years.
D. six years.
E. any number of years necessary to uncover tax evasion.

34. Where a case of tax fraud or evasion is established against a taxpayer, a tax investigation into the taxpayer's affairs is limited to

A. five years. C. seven years.
B. four years. D. six years.
E. any number of years necessary to uncover the tax evasion.

Solutions to Multple-Choice and Short-Answer Questions

1 Introduction to Taxation

Part I Multiple Choice Questions

1.	A	2.	D	3.	B
4.	B	5.	B	6.	A
7.	E	8.	C	9.	C
10.	A	11.	B	12.	E
13.	C	14.	B	15.	E
16.	C	17.	E	18.	C
19.	D	20.	A	21.	E
22.	B	23.	A	24.	C

Part II Short-Answer Questions

25. A tax is a compulsory payment made by individuals and organisations to the government in accordance with predetermined criteria for which no direct or specific benefit is received by the taxpayer.

26. Indirect taxes are taxes which are levied on goods and services or expenditure.

27. Direct taxes take into account the taxpayer's ability to pay tax, therefore, it is progressive in nature.

28. Direct taxes are very unpopular and the degree of voluntary compliance is low. The rate of tax evasion is high. It may cost the tax authority a lot of time, energy and money to track down tax evaders.

29. False

30. True

31. Specific tax is levied on each unit of a commodity produced or sold, for example, a tax of ₦20 on every crate of beer sold by a brewery, while ad varolem tax is levied on the value (price) of the product being taxed, for example, VAT of 5% on the price of a crate of beer sold.

32. Ability to Pay or Faculty Theory – This theory dictates that every taxpayer should be taxed according to his ability to pay, that is, wealthy persons should be taxed more heavily than those who are poor.

2 Nigerian Tax System and National Tax Policy

Part I Multiple Choice Questions

1.	E	2.	A	3.	E
4.	A	5.	C	6.	B
7.	A	8.	C	9.	D
10.	C	11.	A	12.	A
13.	A	14.	E	15.	A
16.	E	17.	A	18.	C
19.	A	20.	C	21.	C
22.	E	23.	C	24.	B
25.	D	26.	E	27.	D
28.	D	29.	A	30.	A
31.	B	32.	E	33.	A
34.	C	35.	D	36.	A
37.	E	38.	E		

Part II Short-Answer Questions

39. Federal Government only

40. (a) Federal Government
    (b) State Government
    (c) Local Government

41. Local Government

42. (a) Petroleum profits tax
    (b) Capital gains tax on bodies corporate
    (c) Stamp duties on bodies corporate

43. (a) Business premises registration fees
    (b) Road taxes
    (b) Stamp duties on instruments executed by individuals

44. (a) Religious places establishment permit fees
    (b) Customary burial ground permit fees
    (c) Wrong parking charges

45. Problem of ascertaining the correct income or profits of the taxpayer due to the unwillingness or inability of many businesses to document or keep complete records or accounts of their business transactions.

3 Administration of Personal Income Tax

Part I Multiple-Choice Questions

1.	C	2.	C	3.	B
4.	C	5.	E	6.	E
7.	B	8.	A	9.	A
10.	A	11.	C	12.	A

13.	A	14.	E	15.	D
16.	A	17.	E	18.	B
19.	E	20.	B	21.	E
22.	E	23.	A	24.	A
25.	C	26.	D	27.	D
28.	A	29.	D	30.	E
31.	C	32.	E	33.	E

Part II Short-Answer Questions

34. The State Board of Internal Revenue

35. (a) To advise the State Board of Internal Revenue on all its powers and duties specifically mentioned in the Personal Income Tax Act.
(b) To consider all matters that require professional and technical expertise and make recommendations to the State Board of Internal Revenue.

36. (a) He receives and examines the taxpayer's completed tax returns and issues tax assessments based on the returns. In the absence of a completed tax return or if the return is rejected, he issues a best of judgement (BOJ) assessment.
(b) He deals with the taxpayer's objections against assessments and attempts to reach an agreement with the taxpayer, if possible.

37. Local Government Revenue Committee.

38. (a) The Supervisor for Finance as Chairman.
(b) Three Local Government Councillors as members.
(c) Two other members experienced in revenue matters nominated by the Local Government Chairman on their personal merits.

39. The notice must be addressed to the last known business or private address of such individual or body of persons.

40. It is deemed to have been served on the day succeeding the day on which the addressee of the registered letter containing the notice would have been informed in the ordinary course of events that such registered letter is awaiting him at a post office. If the addressee proves that no notification was left at the address given on such registered letter, the notice shall not be deemed to have been served.

4 Federal Capital Territory Internal Revenue Service Act, 2015

Part I Multiple-Choice Questions

1.	E	2.	C	3.	E
4.	D	5.	A	6.	C
7.	B	8.	D	9.	E
10.	A	11.	D	12.	B
13.	A	14.	C	15.	E
16.	E	17.	E	18.	D
19.	D	20.	D	21.	D
22.	B	23.	C	24.	B
25.	D	26.	A	27.	A
28.	A	29.	C	30.	D
31.	D	32.	B	33.	C
34.	D	35.	D	36.	A
37.	C	38.	A	39.	E
40.	B	41.	E	42.	A
43.	B	44.	D	45.	C
46.	C	47.	A	48.	A
49.	D	50.	D	51.	E
52.	A	53.	A	54.	A
55.	A	56.	E	57.	A
58.	B	59.	C	60.	E
61.	D	62.	B	63.	D
64.	C	65.	D	66.	E

67.	E	68.	B	69.	A
70.	B	71.	C	72.	A
73.	E	74.	A	75.	E

Part II Short-Answer Questions

76. According to section 50(2) of the FCT IRS Act, 2015, the Tax Appeal Commitee shall consist of a Chairman and 5 other members. On the other hand, paragraph 2(1) of the Fourth Schedule to the Act states that the committee shall consist of 5 members.

77. The Area Council Revenue Committee shall be responsible for the assessment and collection of all taxes, fines, rates, charges or other revenue under its jurisdiction and shall account for all amounts so collected in a manner to be prescribed by the Chairman of the Area Council, subject to the financial memorandum and guidelines on Area Council Administration.

78 Federal Capital Territory Internal Revenue Service

79. Section 12(3) of the FCT Internal Revenue Service Act, 2015 stipulates that any five members of the Board, one of whom shall be the Chairman or a Director, shall constitute a quorum. However, paragraph 3 of the Second Schedule to the Act states that a quorum at a meeting of the Board shall be not less than one-third of the total number of members of the Board at the date of the meeting.

80. The FCT Internal Revenue Service Board from the list and in accordance with the guidelines supplied by the Auditor-General for the Federation.

81. Section 50(7)(b) of the FCT IRS Act, 2015 provides that a Tax Appeal Commissioner may hold office for a period of 3 years from the date of appointment. On the other hand, paragraph 4 of the Fourth Schedule to the Act states that a Tax Appeal Commissioner shal hold office for a term of 3 years, renewable for another term of

3 years only and no more, from the date on which he assumes his office or until he attains the age of 70 years whichever is earlier.

82. A fine equivalent to 200 per cent of the amount in question or to imprisonment for a term of 3 years or both.

83. A fine of ₦200,000 and twice the amount of tax undercharged or would have been undercharged as a result of the incorrect return or information.

84. A fine of ₦50,000 or to a term of imprisonment not exceeding 3 months or to both such fine and imprisonment.

85. The person is liable to pay the tax withheld or not remitted in addition to a penalty of 10% of the tax withheld or not remitted per annum and interest at the prevailing commercial rate.

86. The FCT Internal Revenue Service Board

87. The Minister of the Federal Capital Territory

88. If the representative of the FCT IRS proves to the satisfaction of the Tax Appeal Committee that:
    (a) the appellant has for the year of assessment concerned, failed to prepare his tax returns and deliver to the Service;
    (b) the appeal is frivolous or vexation or is an abuse of the appeal process;
    (c) it is expedient to require the appellant to pay an amount as security for prosecuting the appeal.

89. An amount equal to the tax charged upon the appellant for the preceding year of assessment or one half of the tax charged by the assessment under appeal, whichever is the lesser, plus a sum equal to ten per cent of the said deposit.

90. The assessment against which he has appealed shall be confirmed and the appellant shall have no further right of appeal with respect to that assessment.

911. Where upon the hearing of an appeal:
   (a) no accounts, books or records relating to profits were produced by or on behalf of the appellant;
   (b) such accounts, books or records were so produced but rejected by the Committee on the ground that it had been shown to its satisfaction that they were incomplete or unsatisfactory.

92. If the Minister is satisfied that it is not in the interest of the FCT IRS or of the public for the person to continue in office.

93. The Court of Appeal and thereafter to the Supreme Court.

94. The Minister of the Federal Capital Territory

95. (i) The Chairman of the FCT IRS Board
   (ii) Two Directors appointed to the Board from within the FCT IRS
   (iii) The Director of Legal Services of the FCT IRS or his representative not below the rank of the Director

96. (i) To consider all tax matters that require professional and technical expertise and make recommendations to the FCT IRS Board.
   (ii) To advise the FCT IRS Board on all its powers and duties specifically mentioned in the FCT IRS Act and on any aspect of the functions and powers of the FCT IRS under the Act.
   (iii) To attend to such other matters as may, from time to time, be referred to it by the FCT IRS Board.

97. A Judge of the Federal High Court

98. Power to distrain

99. Proceeds of sale of any property distrained are to be used in the following sequence:
   (a) to pay the cost or charges of and incidental to the sale and keeping of the distress and disposal;
   (b) to pay the amount of tax due.

   The balance after the payment of (a) and (b) shall be payable to the taxpayer on demand being made by him or on his behalf within one year of the date of sale or shall be forfeited.

100. The assessment can be raised at any time and as often as may be necessary to recover the tax lost or underpaid.

5 Federal Inland Revenue Service (Establishment) Act, 2007

Part I Multiple-Choice Questions

1.	A	2.	E	3.	B
4.	E	5.	D	6.	A
7.	D	8.	B	9.	C
10.	C	11.	D	12.	C
13.	C	14.	D	15.	D
16.	E	17.	D	18.	C
19.	C	20.	C	21.	C
22.	D	23.	C	24.	A
25.	A	26.	A	27.	C
28.	A	29.	A	30.	C
31.	D	32.	D	33.	A
34.	A	35.	C	36.	A
37.	E	38.	A	39.	C
40.	A	41.	A	42.	D
43.	B	44.	E	45.	C

46.	A	47.	B	48.	C
49.	D	50.	E	51.	E
52.	C	53.	E	54.	D
55.	B	56.	C	57.	D
58.	A	59.	B	60.	B
61.	E	62.	B	63.	E
64.	E	65.	D	66.	E
67.	A	68.	A	69.	A
70.	C	71.	D	72.	C
73.	C	74.	E	75.	A
76.	E	77.	B	78.	E

Part II Short-Answer Questions

79. Warrant

80. ₦10 million

81. Seventh day of the following month.

82. The Executive Chairman of the FIRS on the advice of the Technical Committee of the Board.

83. The Executive Chairman of the FIRS

84. Tax Appeal Commissioners

85. Assessing and collecting tax or routine responsibilities of tax officials.

86. A fine equivalent to 200% of the sum in question or to imprisonment for a term not exceeding three years or to both fine and imprisonment.

87. A fine not exceeding ₦200,000 in addition to payment of the amount of tax unpaid or overpayment made in respect of any

repayment or to imprisonment for a term not exceeding three years or to both fine and imprisonment.

88. Liable on conviction in respect of each offence to a f ne of 100% of the amount of the tax liability.

89. A fine not exceeding ₦500,000 on corporate customers and not exceeding ₦50,000 in the case of an individual customer.

90. Liable on conviction to pay the tax withheld or not remitted in addition to a penalty of 10% per annum of the tax withheld or not remitted and interest at the prevailing CBN minimum re-discount rate and imprisonment for a period of not more than three years.

91. A period of 3 months from the date of its issue or such lesser period as the judicial officer considers appropriate.

92. Federal Inland Revenue Service Board.

93 ₦200,000 or imprisonment for a term not exceeding three years or to both such fine and imprisonment.

94. FIRS. Board

95. If the representative of the relevant tax authority proves to the satisfaction of the Appeal Commissioners that
   (a) the appellant has failed to prepare and deliver to the tax authority the tax returns for the year of assessment concerned; or
   (b) it is expedient to require the appellant to pay an amount as security for prosecuting the appeal.

96. The deposit is an amount equal to the tax charge on the appellant for the preceding year of assessment, or one half of the tax charged by the assessment under the appeal whichever is lower, plus 10% of the said deposit.

Where the appellant fails to comply with the order, the assessment against which it has appealed shall be confirmed and the appellant shall have no further right of appeal with respect to the assessment.

97. Where, upon the hearing of an appeal;
    (a) no accounts, books or records relating to the profits were produced by or on behalf of the appellant; or
    (b) the appellant or his representative at the hearing of the appeal has neglected or refused to comply with a precept delivered or sent to him by the secretary to the Appeal Commissioners without showing any reasonable excuse.

98. A person who is knowledgeable in the laws, regulations, norms, practices and operations of taxation in Nigeria as well as a person that have shown capacity in the management of trade or business or a retired public servant in tax administration.

99. Gross misconduct

100. Minister of Finance.

101. (a) The Executive Chairman of the FIRS.
    (b) All the Directors and Heads of Department of the FIRS.
    (c) The Legal Adviser in the FIRS.

102. (a) To consider all tax matters that require professional and technical expertise and make recommendations to the FIRS Board.
    (b) To advise the FIRS Board on all its powers and duties specifically stated in CITA.

103. High court.

104. The written authorization
    The evidence of identity

105. With the consent of the occupier of the private dwelling or pursuant to an authorization issued by a judicial officer.

106. The Tax Appeal Commissioner concerned is to declare such interest to the other Tax Appeal Commissioners and must not sit at any meeting for the hearing of that appeal.

6 Persons and Income Chargeable

Part I Multiple-Choice Questions

1.	A	2.	E	3.	C
4.	B	5.	D	6.	D
7.	C	8.	E	9.	C
10.	B	11.	D	12.	E
13.	E	14.	C	15.	A
16.	D	17.	E	18.	A
19.	E	20.	D	21.	E
22.	E	23.	E		

Part II Short-Answer Questions

24. An individual or body of individuals having any income which is chargeable with tax under the provisions of the Personal Income Tax Act.

25. In the state in which the community is situated.

26. In the state in which the member of the family who customarily receives the family income usually resides.

27. Income accruing to a trustee of a settlement or trust may be taxed by the state in which all the income of the settlement or trust arises but where the income arises in more than one state, it is under the jurisdiction of the Federal Inland Revenue Service.

28. An itinerant worker includes an individual irrespective of his status who works at any time in any state during a year of assessment (other than as a member of the armed forces) for wages, salaries or livelihood by working more than one state and work for a minimum of twenty (20) days in at least three (3) months of every assessment year (PITA 2004, section 108).

29. (a) Profits from any trade or business.
    (b) Rent or any premium arising from a right granted to any other person for the use or occupation of any property.
    (c) Dividend, interest, royalties, etc.

30. On the condition that such income is deposited in a domiciliary account in an authorised bank in Nigeria.

31. Such income must be brought into Nigeria in foreign currencies and paid into a domiciliary account in an authorised bank in Nigeria.

32. Such income must be deposited in a domiciliary account in an authorised bank in Nigeria.

33. A Nigerian company

34. A foreign company

35. (a) Any company being a statutory registered friendly society.
    (b) Any company being a registered co-operative society.

36. (a) Dividend distributed by Unit Trust.
    (b) Dividend received from small companies in the manufacturing sector in the first 5 years of their operation.
    (c) Dividend received from investment in wholly export-oriented businesses.

37. On the condition that the proceeds from such export are repatriated to Nigeria and are used exclusively for the purchase of raw materials, plants, equipment and spare parts.

38. (a) If the non-Nigerian company has a fixed base of business in Nigeria, to the extent that the profit is attributable to that fixed base.
    (b) If the trade or business or activity involves a single contract for surveys, deliveries, installation or construction, the profit from that contract.

39. A transaction is deemed to be artificial or fictitious if the transaction is made between connected persons (e.g. a holding company and its subsidiary, a husband and wife) and the tax authority is of the opinion that such transaction has not been made on terms which might fairly have been expected to have been made by independent persons engaged in the same or similar activities dealing with one another at arm's length.

40. (a) Where the FIRS has authorised him to communicate the information to such person.
    (b) Where such communication is for the purpose of the FIRS (Establishment) Act or of any other enactment in Nigeria imposing tax on income of persons.

41. The registered office or any known address of the company.

42. The individual authorised to accept such a notice under Companies and Allied Matters Act (CAMA) at the address filed with the Registrar-General of companies or to the registered office of the company wherever it may be situated.

43. Personal Income Tax Act

44. Companies Income Tax Act

7 Residence and Relevant Tax Authority

Part I Multiple-Choice Questions

1.	B	2.	E	3.	B
4.	C	5.	E	6.	A
7.	D	8.	C	9.	A
10.	B	11.	C	12.	A
13.	E	14.	D		

Part II Short-Answer Questions

15. Territory refers to a State of the Federation and includes the Federal Capital Territory, Abuja.

16. Residence

17. Principal place of residence

18. That place of those places in which he usually resides.

19. That place of those places in which he usually resides.

20. Foreign employment

21. Nigerian employment

22. An individual holding a Nigerian employment is deemed to be resident in the Nigerian territory in which he has a place or principal place of residence on 1st January of the year of assessment. Where the individual was on leave from a Nigerian employment on 1st January, he is deemed to be resident in the territory where he had a place or principal place of residence before proceding on leave. Where an individual enters a Nigerian employment during the year and becomes liable to Nigerian income tax for the first time, he is deemed to be resident for that year in the territory in which he has a

place or principal place of residence on the day on which he takes up the full duties of that employment in Nigeria.

23. PITA defines a Nigerian pension as a pension in respect of past service under, and payable by, a Government or Governments in Nigeria.

24. If the pension is a Nigerian pension only payable by the Government of one territory, he is deemed to be resident in that territory. If it is payable by more than one Government or if there are two or more pensions arising in different territories, he is deemed to he resident in the Federal Capital Tèrritory. If the pension is not a Nigerian pension, he is deemed to be resident in the territory where the principal office of the pension fund or other person authorizing payment of the pension is situated in Nigeria.

25. If the whole of his income arising in Nigeria is derived from one territory, he is deemed to reside in that territory. If any part or the whole of the income is derived from more than one territory, he is deemed to reside in any of the territories.

26. If all the unearned income arises in one territory, he is deemed to reside in that territory, but where the income arises in more than one territory, he is deemed to reside in the territory from which any part of the unearned income arises.

27. It is deemed to be resident in the territory in which its principal office is situated in Nigeria on 1st January of the year of assessment. If it has no office in Nigeria on that day, it is deemed to reside in the territory in which any part or the whole of its income liable to tax in Nigeria arises for that year.

28. The tax authority of the territory in which the individual is deemed to be resident.

29. It is the relevant tax authority of the territory in which the deceased individual was last deemed to be resident or would have been

deemed to be resident if PITA had been in force before the date of his death.

30. The tax authority of the territory in which the whole income of the settlement or trust arises, but where the income arises in more than one territory, the Federal Inland Revenue Service is the relevant tax authority.

31. The tax authority of the territory in which the principal office or place of business of the partnership is situated in Nigeria on the first day of the year of assessment, or is first established during that year.

32. The tax authority of the territory in which that community is to be found.

33. Federal Inland Revenue Service

34. Federal Inland Revenue Service

35. Mrs Boma has two places of residence which are not within the same State, therefore, his principal place of residence is in Akwa Ibom State which is nearest to his usual place of work.

36. Mr Etete is engaged on foreign employment, therefore, he is deemed to reside in Kano State where his employer's principal office is situated in Nigeria on the day his employment commenced.

37. Mr Agama has a place of residence in Ogun State although his place of work is in Lagos State. The mere fact that he works in Lagos State is not a determinant of his residence or tax authority.

38. Where an individual first becomes liable to income tax in Nigeria for a year of assessment because of entering a Nigerian employment during that year, he is deemed to be resident for that year in the State in which he has a place or principal place of residence on the day on which he enters upon the full duties of that employment in Nigeria. Therefore, Dr James is deemed to be resident in Lagos State.

39. Since Mr Carter was on leave from a Nigerian employment on 1st January, 2015, he is deemed to be resident for that year in Delta State where he had a place of residence immediately before he proceeded on leave.

40. As an employee of the Nigeria Police Force, Corporal Dogo is deemed to be resident in the Federal Capital Territory in accordance with section 2(i) of PITA.

41. Mr Edem has no residence in Nigeria and is in receipt of a Nigerian pension payable by more than one Government, therefore, he is deemed to be resident in the Federal Capital Territory.

42. Mr Dele is deemed to be resident in Oyo State. Although his business is located in Lagos and his property in Ogun State, he does not have a place of residence in any of the two States.

43. Mr Tobi has many sources of income, namely: rent, pension, profit and dividend, therefore, his place of residence is determined according to the first numbered paragraph of the First Schedule to Personal Income Tax Act which is applicable to his circumstances. The first numbered paragraph applicable to his circumstances is pension, hence, his residence is Ogun State.

44. Oku Iboku community is situated in Akwa Ibom State, therefore, it is deemed to be resident in Akwa Ibom State for the year of assessment.

45. For 2014 year of assessment, Mr Sani is deemed to be resident in Kaduna State, being the territory in which he had a place of residence on the day on which he entered upon the full duties of a Nigerian employment.

46. The High Court of the territory of the tax authority which made the relevant assessment. An appeal from a decision of a High Court in respect of the individual's territory of residence shall lie to the Court of Appeal.

8 Employment Income and Pay As You Earn

Part I Multiple-Choice Questions

1.	D	2.	D	3.	E
4.	C	5.	A	6.	D
7.	C	8.	B	9.	B
10.	A	11.	A	12.	E
13.	B	14.	D	15.	D
16.	E	17.	E	18.	A
19.	C	20.	B	21.	E
22.	B	23.	E	24.	D
25.	A	26.	E	27.	A
28.	A	29.	E	30.	E
31.	E	32.	D	33.	C
34.	E	35.	A	36.	A
37.	A	38.	E	39.	B
40.	B	41.	A	42.	E
43.	E	44.	C		

Workings

Question 19

	₦
Salary for 2014	600,000
Bonus for 2013 paid in Jan. 2014	41,666
Bonus for 2014 paid in Nov. 2014	50,000
	691,666

Salary is taxable in the year it is earned, while bonus payable at intervals exceeding one month is taxable in the year it is paid.

Question 20

Mazi Okonkwo - Consolidated Relief Allowance

= ₦200,000 or 1% of gross income whichever is higher plus 20% of gross income

= ₦200,000 or 1% x ₦3,600,000 whichever is higher + 20% x ₦3,600,000

= ₦200,000 + ₦720,000

= ₦920,000

Question 21

Miss Ifeoma - - Consolidated Relief Allowance for 2014

=	₦200,000 or 1% of gross income whichever is higher + 20% of gross income
=	₦200,000 or 1% x ₦30,000,000 whichever is higher + 20% x ₦30,000,000
=	₦300,000 + ₦6,000,000
=	₦6,300,000

Question 22

Mr Aki – Computation of Income Tax liabilityfor 2014

	₦	₦
Gross income		300,000
Less:		
Consolidated relief allowance	260,000	
NHF contribution	2,500	
Pension fund contribution	22,500	285,000
Chargeable income		15,000
Tax liability		
Based on chargeable income (7% x 15,000)		1,050
Minimum tax - 1% of gross income (1% x 300,000)		3,000

Note: Since the tax payable on the chargeable income is less than 1% of the taxpayer's gross income, the minimum tax payable

Questions 42 - 44

Mrs Yellow Sisi

Computation of Income Tax Liability for 2017 Year of Assessment

	₦	₦
Basic salary		10,000,000
Rent allowance		1,000,000
Transport allowance		200,000
Utility allowance		100,000
Gross income		11,300,000
Less CRA and tax exempt deductions:		
CRA (Higher of 200,000 and 1% x 11,300,000 + 20% x 11,300,000 = 200,000 + 2,260,000)	2,460,000	

Life assurance premium		200,000	
NHF contribution		250,000	
Pension fund contribution		896,000	3,806,000
Chargeable income			7,494,000
Tax liability:			
First	₦300,000 @ 7%		21,000
Next	₦300,000 @ 11%		33,000
Next	₦500,000 @ 15%		75,000
Next	₦500,000 @ 19%		95,000
Next	₦1,600,000 @21%		336,000
Balance	₦4,294,000 @24%		1,030,560
Income tax liability			1,590,560

Part II Short-Answer Questions

45. Employment

46. Under a contract of employment, the employee earns remuneration from his employer. The remuneration is assessable to tax on a current year basis with the tax being deducted at source under the Pay-As-You-Earn (PAYE) system.

In the case of self-employment, the person carries on his own trade, business, profession or vocation. He is his own employer. He is assessable to tax on his profits on a preceding year basis. Withholding tax may also be deducted at source for certain payments made to him.

47. Current rates of personal income tax.
1. First ₦300,000 @ 7%
2. Next ₦300,000 @ 11%
3. Next ₦500,000 @ 15%
4. Next ₦500,000 @19%
5. Next ₦1,600,000 @ 21%
6. Above ₦3,200,000 @ 24%

Minimum tax = 1% of gross income

48. Benefits in kind.

49. Three examples of non-taxable benefits in kind:
    (a) Uniforms, overall or other protective clothing provided by an employer to employees.
    (b) Provision of meals to employees in any canteen in which meals are provided to staff generally or of luncheon vouchers for employees so far as those vouchers are not assignable by the employees to whom they are issued.
    (c) Free medical services provided to employees by an employer.

50. The actual wages of the domestic servant are deemed to be additional income to Mr Soki and the amount will be taxable in Mr Soki's hands.

51. Methods of calculating taxable benefits in kind:
    (a) An asset rented by an employer for an employee's use:
        (i) Living accommodation – rateable value of the premises.
        (ii) Other assets – actual cost of rent.
    (b) An employee's utility bills paid by his employer – actual amount of the utility bills paid by the employer.

    Any amount refunded by the employee to the employer is used to reduce the value of the benefits taxable.

52. The assessable benefits is ₦300,000, that is, the cost of hire.

53. (a) Benefits assessable on Miss Susan is 5% of the cost of the car. 5/100 x ₦1,500,000 = ₦75,000.
    (b) Driver's wages of ₦120,000 are assessable in the hands of Miss Susan.

54.

Mr Eso's assessable benefits in kind:	**₦**
Accommodation (rateable value)	180,000
Furniture (5% x ₦480,000)	24,000
	204,000
Less rent paid by Mr Eso	60,000
Assessable benefits in kind	144,000

55. Pay-As-You-Earn (PAYE).

56. PAYE means Pay-As-You-Earn.

57. (a) Name, address and identification number of the employee.
    (b) Date of commencement and cessation of the employment.
    (c) Cumulative emoluments and corresponding cumulative tax at the date of leaving.

58. A penalty of 10% per annum of the amount of tax plus interest at the prevailing commercial rate.

59. Mr Okon – Computation of Income Tax Liability

	₦
Gross income	734,200
Less consolidated relief allowance	346,840
Chargeable income	387,360
First ₦300,000 @ 7%	21,000
Balance 87,360 @ 11%	9,610
Income tax liability	30,610

60. Consolidated relief allowance

9 Investment Income and Withholding Tax

Part I Multiple-Choice Questions

1.	C	2.	E	3.	C
4.	E	5.	A	6.	E
7.	A	8.	E	9.	D
10.	B	11.	D	12.	D
13.	B	14.	C	15.	C
16.	A	17.	E	18.	A
19.	D	20.	C	21.	C
22.	A	23.	E	24.	E
25.	C	26.	A	27.	E
28.	E	29.	B	30.	B
31.	E	32.	D	33.	A

34.	D	35.	B	36.	B
37.	B				

Workings

Question 29

Chief Makama - Assessable rental income

	₦	₦
Net rent as per accounts		429,000
Add disallowable expenses:		
Water rate for landlord's flat	1,000	
Depreciation	50,000	
Construction of fence	75,000	126,000
Assessable rental income		555,000

Question 30

Since the dividend paid is higher than the total profits, the dividend will be charged to tax as if it were the total profits of the company for the year of assessment. Therefore, the company's income tax liability is 30% of ₦2,000,000 = ₦600,000.

Part II Short-Answer Questions

38. **Computation of Assessable Rental Income**

Year of Assessment	Basis Period	Computation	Assessable Income (₦)
2001	1/7/00 - 31/12/00	(6 months x 3,000,000) / 60 months	300,000
2002	1/1/01 - 31/12/01	(12 months x 3,000,000) / 60 months	600,000
2003	1/1/02 - 31/12/02	(12 months x 3,000,000) / 60 months	600,000
2004	1/1/03 - 31/12/03	(12 months x 3,000,000) / 60 months	600,000
2005	1/1/04 - 31/12/04	(12months x 3,000,000) / 60 months	600,000
2006	1/1/05 - 30/06/05	(6 months x 3,000,000) / 60 months	300,000

Notes

Where rent is received in advance for a period exceeding five years, the whole of the rent is treated as accruing evenly from day to day over the five years commencing on the first day of that said period.

39. **Nze Ego's Assessable Rental Income for 2015 Year of Assessment**

	₦
Gross rent (100/90 x 594,000)	660,000
Less tenement rate	25,000
Assessable rental income	635,000

40. Withholding tax rates

	Individuals	Companies
Interest	10%	10%
Director's fees	10%	10%
Consultancy services	5%	10%

41. A fine of ₦5,000 or 10% of the amount of tax due, whichever is higher in addition to interest at the prevailing commercial rate.

42. A fine of 200% of the tax not withheld or not remitted as the case may be plus interest at the prevailing commercial rate.

43. Government approved channels.

44. Original withholding tax receipts (credit notes).

45. Franked investment income.

46. The dividend has to be excluded from the total profits of the company receiving the dividend before the computation of the company's income tax liability since the dividend is not subject to further tax in the hands of the recipient company.
Where the dividend is redistributed, the withholding tax suffered on the dividend received by the company can be used to offset the withholding tax due on the dividend redistributed.

47. Gross dividend should be shown in the income tax returns of each shareholder as follows:

	₦
B. Giwa (100/90 x ₦270,000)	300,000
A. Adio (100/90 x ₦117,000)	130,000
Emeka Esu (100/90 x ₦81,900)	91,000

48. (a) Withholding tax on individuals resident in each State is administered by the State Internal Revenue Service.
(b) Withholding tax on individuals resident in the Federal Capital Territory, Abuja is administered by the Federal Capital Territory Internal Revenue Service.
(c) Withholding tax on companies, non-resident individuals and members of the Nigeria Police Force and Armed Forces of the Federation is administered by the Federal Inland Revenue Service.

49. Non-investment incomes subject to withholding tax

Income	WHT Rate	
	Individuals	Companies
Contract of supplies	5%	5%
Commissions	5%	10%
Consultancy, technical and management services	5%	10%

50. Rent is defined in CITA as payments for the use of or hire of any equipment, payments for charter vessels, ship or aircraft and all such other payments for the use or hire of movable and immovable property.

51. CITA provides that interest shall be deemed to be derived from Nigeria if:
(a) there is liability to payment of the interest by a Nigerian company or a company in Nigeria regardless of where or in what form the payment is made; or

(b) the interest accrues to a foreign company or person from a Nigerian company or a company in Nigeria regardless of whichever way the interest may have accrued.

52. Foreign loan means any loan granted by a foreign company with moneys brought into Nigeria from any territory or country outside Nigeria, or any loan granted by that company in any territory or country outside Nigeria, in a currency other than Nigerian currency.

53. (a) The amount of the loan;
(b) The moratorium;
(c) The date repayment is due to commence;
(d) The amount of repayment showing capital and interest; and
(e) The full particulars of the recipient of the loan and its permanent address.

54. Agricultural trade or business means any trade or business connected with –
(a) the establishment or management of plantations for the production of rubber, oil palm, cocoa, tea and similar crops;
(b) the cultivation or production of cereal crops, tubers, fruits of all kinds, cotton, beans, groundnut, sheanuts, beniseed, vegetables, pineapples, bananas and plantains;
(c) animal husbandry, that is to say, poultry, piggery, cattle rearing, fish farming and deep-sea fish trawling.

55. (a) The amount (or aggregate amount) of the loan granted in any calendar year must not be less than ₦5,000,000.
(b) The loan must be used for the purposes of the trade, business, profession or vocation carried on in Nigeria by the borrower and the interest must be derived or deemed to be derived from Nigeria.

56. Dividend means:
(a) in relation to a company not being in the process of being wound up or liquidated, any profits distributed whether such profits are of a capital nature or not, including an amount

equal to the nominal value of bonus shares, debentures or securities awarded to the shareholders; and

(b) in relation to a company that is being wound up or liquidated, any profits distributed whether in money or money's worth or otherwise, other than those of a capital nature earned before or during the winding up or liquidation.

57. Dividend is deemed to arise on the day that payment of the dividend becomes due.

58. Close company

59. (a) Where it appears that the non-distribution of profits in the accounting period was with a view to reducing the aggregate of the tax chargeable in Nigeria on the profits or income of the company and its shareholders;

(b) Where it appears that the profits could have been distributed without detriment to the company's business, as it existed at the end of the accounting period.

60. The directive with respect to the profits of any accounting period of a company shall be made not later than two years after the receipt by the FIRS of the duly audited accounts of the company for that period.

61. Withholding tax suffered by Anas Limited

		₦
(a)	Contract of supplies (5/95 x 2,280,000)	120,000
(b)	Rent (10/90 x 1,800,000)	200,000
		320,000

10 Ascertainment of Profits

Part I Multiple-Choice Questions

1.	E	2.	D	3.	E
4.	D	5.	D	6.	A
7.	D	8.	D	9.	A
10.	C	11.	D	12.	A
13.	C	14.	E	15.	D
16.	E	17.	E	18.	C
19.	A	20.	B	21.	D
22.	D	23.	E	24.	E
25.	E	26.	C	27.	B
28.	C	29.	C	30.	C
31.	A	32.	A	33.	D
34.	D	35.	D	36.	E
37.	C	38.	D	39.	D
40.	B	41.	E	42.	A
43.	A	44.	E	45.	A
46.	E	47.	D	48.	D
49.	E				

Workings & Comments

26. Maximum rent allowable = actual rent of each bungalow for the period or 100% of each employee's basic salary, whichever is lower.
5 managers = ₦100,000 x 5 = ₦500,000

39. Miss Shakara
The cost of redecorating her shop and subscriptions to Boutique Owners Association are allowable expenses in calculating the adjusted profit. The other items of expenditure are disallowed because they are capital expenditure and must be added back to the net profit.

40. Mrs Paloma

Cost	₦100,000
10% mark-up (10% x N100,000)	₦10,000

Since she paid nothing for the goods, N110,000 should be added to the net profit.

41. Etim

Wages of ₦480,000 (i.e. ₦40,000 x 12 months) paid to Etim's wife as an employee of the business are allowable expenses. Etim's drawings of ₦520,000 per annum (i.e. ₦10,000 x 52 weeks) are considered to be appropriations of profit and are not allowable. His son's wages of ₦120,000 per annum (i.e. ₦30,000 x 4 quarters) are not allowable as he is not an employee of the business.

42. Okoro

Loss on disposal of vehicle, fine for proprietor's over-speeding and depreciation are completely disallowed and must be added back. Fuel and oil, vehicle repairs, license and insurance are allowable expenses but the private element (1/5) is disallowed and must be added back to the net profit.

43. Saleko

Extension of office building, installation of new machine and construction of septic tank for office are capital expenditure and are not allowable in computing adjusted profit. Repainting of factory building, redecoration of retail shop and cleaning expenses are allowable expenses in computing adjusted profit for tax purposes.

44. All the expenses are disallowable and must be added back to the net profit when calculating the adjusted profit.

45. XYZ Ltd

All the donations were made to approved bodies. However, CITA stipulates that donations allowable for any year of assessment must not exceed 10% of the company's total profits for that year before charging the donations.

	₦
Net profit	2,000,000
Add donations	1,700,000
Adjusted/assessable profit before donations	3,700,000
Less unrelieved losses brought forward	70,000
	3,630,000
Less capital allowances	130,000
Total profit before donations	3,500,000

Allowable donations = 10% of total profit before charging donations (10% x 3,500,000) = ₦ 350,000

48. Ima

General provision for bad debts is not an allowable deduction. Bad debts arising from loans to employee occurred outside the normal business of the company. The computation of bad and doubtful debts allowable is as follows:

		₦
Trade debts written off		600,000
Decrease in specific provision	70,000	
Bad debts recovered	400,000	(470,000)
Allowable bad debts		130,000
Bad debts per P&L A/C		680,000
Bad debts disallowed		550,000

Another method of calculation is as follows:

	₦
Loans to employee written off	350,000
Increase in general provision	200,000
Bad debts disallowed	550,000

Part II Short-Answer Questions

50. Some expenses charged in the profit and loss account in accordance with generally acceptable accounting principles, accounting standards or Companies and Allied Matters Act are disallowed by PITA or CITA in the computation of assessable profit for taxation purposes. Furthermore, some incomes credited in the profit and loss account and forming part of the net profit are exempted from tax or are not taxable under PITA or CITA.

51. Amount recovered in respect of bad debts previously written off is treated as an income of the year in which the recovery is made. For example, ₦500,000 bad debts recovered in 2014 is treated as income in 2014 and taxed in 2015 on preceding year basis.

52. The sum of ₦255,000 should be subtracted from the net profit as per profit and loss account for the purpose of taxation.

53. **Computation of Adjusted profit**

	₦
Net profit per accounts	1,500,000
Add disallowable expenses:	
Depreciation	350,000
General provision for bad debts	400,000
Adjusted profit	2,250,000

54. **Computation of Assessable Profit**

	₦	₦
Net loss per accounts		250,000
Add profit on sale of fixed assets		2,000
		252,000
Less:		
Depreciation	113,000	
Donations	150,000	263,000
Assessable profit		11,000

55. **Computation of Allowable Bad Debts**

	₦	₦
Trade debts written off		842,000
Less decrease in specific provision for bad debts		
Balance brought forward	410,000	
Balance carried forward	330,000	
	80,000	
Bad debts recovered	680,000	760,000
Allowable bad debts		82,000

56. (a) The Nigeria Society for Deaf and Dumb.
(b) The Society for the Blind.
(c) Training centres and residential schools for the blind.

57. (a) The Cocoa Research Institute of Nigeria
(b) The Nigeria Institute of Oil Palm Research
(c) The Nigeria Institute for Trypanosomiasis Research

58. (a) The Boys Brigade of Nigeria
(b) The Girls Guide of Nigeria
(c) The National Youth Council of Nigeria

59. (a) The Institute of Medical Laboratory Technology.
(b) Any educational institute affiliated under any law with any University in Nigeria, or established under any law in Nigeria and any other educational institution recognised by any Government in Nigeria.

60 Disallowable legal expenses
(a) Court fines/penalties for breach of the law.
(b) Acquisition of a new lease.

61. The minimum tax is calculated as 0.125% of turnover in excess of ₦500,000 plus the highest of:
(a) 0.5% of gross profits; or
(b) 0.5% of net assets; or

(c) 0.25% of paid-up capital; or
(d) 0.25% of turnover of the company for the year.

62. The minimum tax shall be:
(a) 0.5% of gross profits; or
(b) 0.5% of net assets; or
(c) 0.25% of paid-up capital; or
(d) 0.25% of turnover of the company for the year, whichever is the highest

63. Advantage of minimum tax
The government is able to raise more revenue since a company has to pay income tax whether it makes a profit or loss.

Disadvantages
The company may be paying tax out of its capital since it has not made any profit.

64. A shareholder earns dividend which is subject to withholding tax at source. The withholding tax is the final tax on the dividend. On the other hand, a sole trader earns profits from his trade or business. These profits are subject to tax in the hands of the sole trader.

65. Income tax of 30% can be imposed on dividend in place of total profits in a situation that any dividend is paid out of profits on which no tax is payable due to no total profits or total profits which are less than the amount of dividend which is paid. The dividend is, therefore, treated as if it were the total profits of the company for the year of assessment which relates to accounts out of which the dividend is declared.

66. Mrs Ogene

Cost	₦100,000
10% mark-up (10% x ₦100,000)	₦10,000

Since she had already paid ₦100,000 for the goods, ₦10,000 should be added to the net profit.

11 Basis of Assessment

Part I Multiple-Choice Questions

1.	A	2.	C	3.	C
4.	E	5.	C	6.	A
7.	C	8.	B	9.	D
10.	B	11.	B	12.	D
13.	E	14.	A	15.	B
16.	B	17.	C	18.	C
19.	E	20.	E	21.	D
22.	A	23.	B	24.	C
25.	A	26.	C	27.	B
28.	B	29.	D	30.	E
31.	E	32.	A	33.	D
34.	B				

Workings

Questions 20 & 23

Emeka – Computation of Assessable Income

Year of Assessment	Basis Period	Assessable Income ₦
2016 (1st Year)	1/3/16 - 31/12/16 ₦60,000 + (4/12 x 150,000)	110,000
2017 (2nd Year)	1/3/16 - 28/2/17 ₦60,000 + (6/12 x 150,000)	135,000
2018 (3rd Year)	1/9/16 - 31/8/17	150,000

Questions 24 - 27

Obaro – Computation of Assessable Income

1st Three Years of Assessment (without election)

Year of Assessment	Basis period	Assessable Income ₦
1999	01/03/99 – 31/12/2000	
	(240,000 + 9/12 x 432,000)	348,000
2000	01/03/99 – 29/02/2000	
	(240,000 + 5/12 x 432,000)	420,000
2001	01/10/99 – 30/09/2000	432,000
		1,200,000

1st Three Years of Assessment (on Election)

		₦
1999	01/03/2000 – 31/12/2000	
	(240,000 + 3/12 x 432,000)	348,500
2000	01/01/2000 – 31/12/2000	
	(9/12 x 432,000 + 3/12 x 300,000)	399,000
2001	01/01/2001 – 31/12/2001	
	(9/12 x 300,000 + 3/12 x 360,000)	315,000
		1,062,000

Questions 30 - 32

Titani Ltd – Computation of Assessable Profit

Year of Assessment	Basis Period	Assessable Profit ₦	₦
2003	1/4/01 – 31/3/02		260,000
2004	(Penultimate Year)		
	Either Preceding Year Basis:		
	1/4/02 – 31/12/04	306,000	
	Or Actual Basis:1/1/04 – 31/12/04		
	(3/12 x 420,000 + 9/12 x 360,000)	375,000	375,000
	whichever is higher		
2005	1/1/05 – 30/6/05 (3/12 x 360,000 + 120,000)		210,000
			845,000

The period whose profits escaped any charge to tax is 1/4/02 – 31/12/03 and the assessable profit of that period is:

1/4/02 – 31/3/03		306,000
1/4/03 – 31/12/03	(9/12 x 420,000)	315,000
		621,000

Questions 33 & 34

Papa Ltd – Computation of Assessable Profits

Based on Old Accounting Date

Year of Assessment	Basis Period	Assessable Profits
		₦
2002	1/9/00 – 31/8/01	396,000
2003	1/9/01 – 31/8/02 (196,000 + 6/12 x 288,000)	340,000
2004	1/9/02 – 31/8/03 (6/12 x 288,000 + 6/12 x 420,000)	354,000
		1,090,000

Based on New Accounting Date

2002	1//00 – 28/2/01 (6/12 x 600,000 + 6/12 x 396,000)	498,000
2003	1/3/01 – 28/2/02 (6/12 x 396,000 + 196,000)	394,000
2004	1/3/02 – 28/2/03	288,000
		1,180,000

Part II Short-Answer Questions

35. Year of assessment means a period of twelve months commencing from 1st January and ending on 31st December of the same year.

36.

	Year of Assessment	Basis Period
(a)	2011	1/4/09 - 31/3/10
(b)	2012	1/2/10 - 31/1/11

(c) 2015 1/1/14 - 31/12/14

37. Basic of assessment of a new business:

(i) 1st year of assessment –	Actual profits from the date of commencement to 31st December of the same year.
(ii) 2nd year of assessment –	Profits of the first 12 months from the date of commencement.
(iii) 3rd year of assessment –	Preceding year basis, that is, profits of the year immediately preceding the year of assessment.

38. The right of election.

39. He can request that the assessment for the second and third years of assessment be computed based on the actual profits of those years.

40. (a) The request is given in writing to the relevant tax authority.
(b) The request is given to the tax authority within two years after the end of the second year of assessment.
(c) The request is for both the second and third years of assessment.

41.

Assessment year	Basis period
2013	01/05/13 – 31/12/13
2014	01/05/13 – 30/04/14
2015	01/11/13 – 31/10/14

42.

2013	01/05/13 – 31/12/13
2014	01/01/14 – 31/12/14
2015	01/01/15 – 31/12/15

43. Penultimate year

44. Any sum received or paid which would have been accounted for if it had been received or paid before the date of cessation is treated as

having been received or paid by the taxpayer on the last day before such cessation occurred.

45. The assessment for the penultimate year is based on either:
   (i) the profits of the year immediately preceding the penultimate year (i.e. preceding year basis), or
   (ii) the actual profits from 1st January of the penultimate year to 31st December of the same year (i.e. actual or current year basis) whichever is greater.

46. Penultimate year of assessment: 2005
   Basis period: Either 01/04/2003 – 31/03/2004 (preceding year)
   Or 01/01/2005 – 31/12/2005 (actual year)
   whichever is higher.
   The tax authority will choose the one that produces a higher assessable income.

47. Last year of assessment: 2006
   Basis period: 01/01/2006 – 31/05/2006

48. The year of assessment in which the change of accounting date occurred and the following two years of assessment.

49. The tax authority will determine the year of assessment in which the change of accounting date occurred and the following two years and compute the assessable profits for the three years based on the old and new accounting dates. It will choose the basis (accounting date) resulting in higher assessable profits.

50. The relevant tax authority (e.g. FIRS for companies, State Internal Revenue Service for individuals resident in the State).

51. The right of election is exercised by:
   (i) the taxpayer on commencement of a business;
   (ii) the relevant tax authority on cessation of a business.

52. Company's share of partnership's profits is computed in accordance with the Personal Income Tax Act (PITA), while capital allowance due to the company is computed in accordance with the Companies Income Tax Act (CITA).

12 Capital Allowances

Part I Multiple-Choice Questions

1.	C	2.	D	3.	B
4.	B	5.	B	6.	E
7.	E	8.	C	9.	E
10.	D	11.	A	12.	B
13.	C	14.	C	15.	B
16.	C	17.	C	18.	B
19.	A	20.	A	21.	D
22.	E	23.	B	24.	C
25.	B	26.	D	27.	E
28.	D	29.	B	30.	C
31.	B	32.	D	33.	A
34.	D	35.	C	36.	B
37.	E	38.	D	39.	A
40.	C	41.	B	42.	B
43.	C	44.	A	45.	B
46.	D	47.	A	48.	E
49.	A	50.	A	51.	B
52.	A	53.	D	54.	A
55.	D	56.	E	57.	A
58.	B	59.	C	60.	E
61.	B	62.	B	63.	C
64.	A	65.	E	66.	A
67.	A	68.	D	69.	C
70.	A	71.	A	72.	B
73.	E	74.	A	75.	E

76.	E	77.	E	78.	E
79.	D	80.	C	81.	E

Workings

Question 31

Capital allowances are not granted on the cost of land. Therefore, qualifying capital expenditure is ₦4,000,000 – ₦200,000 = ₦3,800,000.

Questions 33 – 37

Without Election

YOA	Basis Period for Assessable Profits	Basis Period for Initial Allowance	Qualifying expenditure
1999	1/8/99 – 31/12/99	1/8/99 – 31/12/99	2,000,000 + 5,000,000 = 7,000,000
2000	1/8/99 – 31/7/00	1/1/00 – 31/7/00	400,000
2001	1/8/99 – 31/7/00	-	0

On Election

YOA	Basis Period for Assessable Profits	Basis Period for Initial Allowance	Qualifying expenditure
1999	1/8/99 – 31/12/99	1/8/99 – 31/12/99	2,000,000 + 5,000,000 = 7,000,000
2000	1/1/00 – 31/12/00	1/1/00 – 31/12/00	400,000 + 500,000 = 900,000
2001	1/1/01 – 31/12/01	1/1/01 – 31/12/01	300,000

Questions 38 - 41

Kaki – Computation of Capital Allowances on Motor vehicle

Rates: 1A 50%
AA 25%

	₦
1999 Assessment Year (1/1/98 – 31/12/98)	600,000
Cost	
Initial allowances (50% x 600,000)	300,000
Balance after initial allowance	300,000
Annual allowance (25% x 300,000)	75,000
WDV c/f	225,000
2000 Assessment Year (1/1/99 – 31/12/99)	
Annual allowance	75,000
WDV c/f	150,000

2001 Assessment Year (1/100 – 31/12/00)	
Annual allowance	75,000
WDV c/f	75,000
2002 Assessment Year (1/1/01 – 31/12/01)	
Sales proceeds	400,000
Balancing charge	325,000

If the motor vehicle was sold for ₦650,000, the balancing charge would have been computed as follows:

2002 Assessment Year (1/1/01 – 31/12/01)	
Sale proceeds	650,000
WDV brought forward	75,000
Balancing charge	575,000

Since a balancing charge cannot exceed the total of capital allowances granted in respect of the asset before disposal, the balancing charge is ₦525,000 and not ₦575,000.

Questions 42 - 44

Lady Ego

Computation of Capital Allowances & Balancing Charge

Rates: 1A 50%

AA 25%

			₦
1999	Assessment Year (1/1/98 – 31/12/98)		
	Cost		800,000
	Initial allowance (50% x 800,000)	400,000	
	AA (25% x {800,000 – 400,000})	100,000	500,000
	WDV c/f		300,000
2000	Assessment Year (1/1/99 – 31/12/99)		
	Annual allowance		100,000
	WDV c/f		200,000
2001	Assessment Year (1/1/00 – 31/12/00)		
	Sale proceeds		350,000
	Balancing charge		150,000

Capital allowances granted to the business are limited to:

Assessment Year		Allowance
		₦
1999	60% x 500,000	300,000
2000	60% x 100,000	60,000
Balancing charge is limited:		
2001	60% x 150,000	90,000

Questions 45 & 46

BB Ltd (Original Owner) – Computation of Capital Allowances

1999	Assessment Year (1/1/95 – 31/12/95)	₦	₦
	Cost		3,500,000
	Initial allowance (15% x 3,500,000)	525,000	
	Annual allowance		
	(10% x {3,500,000 – 525,000})	297,500	822,500
	WDV c/f		2,677,500

SS Ltd (Second-hand Purchaser)

2001	Assessment Year (1/1/00 – 31/12/00)		
	Either:		
	Purchase price of second hand building	4,500,000	
	Or		
	Original cost of second hand building	3,500,000	3,500,000
	whichever is lower		
	Annual allowance (10% x 3,500,000)		350,000
	WDV c/f		3,150,000

Questions 47 - 50

OB Ltd – Computation of Total Profits and Tax Liability for 2005 Year of Assessment

	₦	₦
Assessable profits		615,000
Less:		
Capital allowances brought forward	180,000	
Capital allowances for the year		
Initial allowance	315,000	
Annual allowance	44,000	
Balancing allowance	56,000	
Total capital allowances	595,000	
Capital allowances granted (restricted to $66^2/_3\%$ of assessable profits,)	410,000	410,000
Unrelieved capital allowances c/f	185,000	
Total profits		205,000
Income tax payable (30% x 205,000)		61,500
If the company is in agro-allied, total profits will be:		
Assessable profits		615,000
Less total capital allowances (no restriction)		595,000
Total profits		20,000

Question 51

Any unrelieved capital allowance in the year of cessation (i.e. 2005) can be carried backward and set off against the remainder of assessable profits for the preceding five years (i.e. 2004, 2003, 2002, 2001 and 2000). Adjusted profit from 2000 to 2005 assessment years amounted to ₦3,525,000, while capital allowances amounted to ₦4,080,000. Therefore, Mr. Abu will not be able to recoup capital allowances of ₦555,000.

Questions 52 – 54

Maxima Ltd – Computation of Capital Allowances

	Building	MV
Rates: 1A	15%	50%
AA	10%	25%
	₦	₦
2004 YOA (1/1/03 – 31/12/03)		
WDV b/f	1,500,000	300,000
Additions	950,000	450,000
	2,450,000	750,000
1A	142,500	225,000
AA on assets b/f (WDV / Residual years)	300,000	100,000
AA on 2004's additions	80,750	56,250
WDV c/f	1,926,750	368,750

Question 55

	Building	P & M	Furniture
Residual years	6	3	1
	₦	₦	₦
WDV brought forward	900,000	1,200,000	80,000
Annual allowance (WDV / Residual years)	150,000	400,000	79,990
WDV carried forward	750,000	800,000	10

Question 71

CB Plc

(1) No. of instalments

			₦
Hire purchase price			3,680,000
Less deposit paid			800,000
Balance			2,880,000
No. of monthly instalments	$\frac{2,880,000}{120,000}$	=	24

(2) Interest element of the hire purchase price

		₦
Hire purchase price		3,680,000
Less cash price		3,200,000
Total interest		480,000
Interest element of each instalment	$\frac{480,000}{24}$ =	20,000

(3) Capital (or cash price) element of each instalment

Amount of each instalment	120,000
Less interest element of each instalment	20,000
Capital element of each instalment	100,000

2016 YOA (1/10/14 – 30/9/15)

Deposit	800,000
Instalments (9 months x ₦100,000)	900,000
Qualifying capital expenditure	1,700,000

Part II Short-Answer Questions

82. Depreciation

83. (a) Qualifying plant expenditure
(b) Qualifying building expenditure
(c) Qualifying mining expenditure
(d) Qualifying plantation expenditure
(e) Qualifying public transportation motor vehicle expenditure

84. The first day on which the individual or company carries on that trade or business.

85. Where two basis periods coincide or overlap, the period common to both is deemed to belong to the first basis period only. Therefore, initial allowance in respect of the capital expenditure will only be granted in the first year of assessment.

86. Where there is an interval or gap between the basis periods for two successive years of assessment, the interval is deemed to be part of the second basis period except the second year of assessment is the year of cessation of the trade or business. Therefore, initial allowance will only be granted in the second year of assessment, but if the second year is a year of cessation, it will be granted in the penultimate year of assessment.

87.

	Initial allowance	Annual Allowance
(a) Building	15%	10%
(b) Ranching and plantation	30%	50%
(c) Housing estate	50%	25%

88. When it is sold, discarded or ceased altogether to be used for the purposes of a trade or business carried on by the owner thereof.

89. The price is equal to the residue of the qualifying expenditure (i.e. tax written down value of the asset) at the date of the disposal plus the amount of any balancing charge or minus the amount of any balancing allowance arising from the disposal.

90. A penalty of not more than ₦100 plus the amount of tax lost by granting the investment allowance.

91. Rural investment allowance.

92. Balancing allowance or charge arises on the disposal of an asset. Where the written down value of the asset disposed of is more or less than the sale proceeds, there will be balancing allowance or balancing charge.

93. Residue of qualifying expenditure (tax written down value)

94. It is the amount which, in the opinion of the relevant tax authority, such asset or the relevant interest therein, as the case may be, would have fetched if sold in the open market at that date, less the amount

of any expenses which the owner might reasonably be expected to incur if the asset were sold.

95. Rates of rural investment allowances:

(i)	No facilities at all	– 100%
(ii)	No electricity	– 50%
(iii)	No water	– 30%
(iv)	No tarred road	– 15%

96. Relevant interest means, in relation to any expenditure incurred on the construction of a building, structure or works, the interest in such building, structure or works to which the person who incurred such expenditure was entitled when he incurred it.

97. The price paid by the second-hand purchaser for the building or the original cost of construction of the building, whichever is lower.

98. Capital allowances are calculated on the full cost of the asset as if the assert was used wholly and exclusively for the business, but only the proportion of the allowances attributable to the business (as the tax authority considers to be just and reasonable) will be granted as relief.

99. There is no restriction on the amount of capital allowances claimable by an individual or company in the agro-allied industry in any year of assessment as far as there is assessable profit to absorb the capital allowances.

13 Loss Reliefs

Part I Multiple-Choice Questions

1	B	2.	C	3.	C
4.	B	5.	A	6.	D
7.	B	8.	A	9.	C

10.	E	11.	A	12.	E
13.	B	14.	E	15.	B
16.	C	17.	D	18.	D
19.	B	20.	C	21.	B
22.	D	23.	C	24.	D
25.	B	26.	E	27.	A
28.	C	29.	C	30.	D

Workings

Questions 12 - 14

Mr Zobo - Computation of Losses Available for Carry - Forward

2001	Assessment Year	
	Loss for the year c/f	350,000
2002	Assessment Year	
	Assessable profit	90,000
	Unrelieved loss b/f	350,000
	Unrelieved loss c/f	260,000
2003	Assessment Year	
	Assessable profit	110,000
	Unrelieved loss b/f	260,000
	Unrelieved loss c/f	150,000
2004	Assessment Year	
	Assessable profit	50,000
	Unrelieved loss b/f	150,000
	Unrelieved loss c/f	100,000
2005	Assessment Year	
	Assessable profit	30,000
	Unrelieved loss b/f	100,000
	Unrelieved loss c/f	70,000

As a distributor of fertilizer, Mr Zobo is not engaged in agricultural trade or business as defined in PITA. The loss can be carried forward for a maximum of 4 years. Therefore, the unrelieved loss of ₦70,000 cannot be carried forward to 2006 assessment year.

If Mr Zobo had been engaged in animal husbandry, an example of agricultural trade or business, the unrelieved loss of ₦70,000 would have been carried forward to 2006 assessment year.

2006	Assessment Year	₦
	Assessable profit	60,000
	Unrelieved loss b/f	70,000
	Unrelieved loss c/f	10,000
	Total profit	Nil

Questions 15 – 17

Bassey – Computation of Total Income

		₦
2001	YOA	
	Professional income	250,000
	Trading profit	350,000
	Rental income	135,000
	Total income	735,000
2002	YOA	
	Prof. income	900,000
	Trading profit	250,000
	Total income	1,150,000
	Unrelieved trading loss c/f	950,000
2003	YOA	
	Prof. income	825,000
	Rental income	300,000
	Total income	1,125,000
	Trading profit	560,000
	Unrelieved loss b/f	950,000
	Unrelieved loss c/f	390,000

Question 18

Cater – Computation of Assessable Profit

		₦	₦
2005	(Penultimate Year)		
	Either preceding year basis (1/9/04 - 31/8/05)		480,000

Or current year basis (1/1/05 - 31/12/05)		
Profit (1/1/05 – 31/8/05) 8/12 x 480,000	320,000	
Loss (1/9/05 – 31/12/05) 4/7 x 140,000	80,000	240,000
whichever is greater		

Questions 19 – 22

FTC Ltd – Computation of Total Profits

		₦
2002	YOA (1/10/00 – 30/9/01)	
	Trade	500,000
	Transport	20,000
	Hotel	300,000
	Total profits	820,000
2003	YOA (1/10/01 – 30/9/02)	
	Trade	650,000
	Transport	140,000
	Total profits	790,000
	Hotel loss for the year c/f	600,000
2004	YOA (1/10/02 – 30/9/03)	
	Total profits (transport)	400,000
	Hotel:	
	Assessable profit	150,000
	Unrelieved loss b/f	600,000
	Unrelieved loss c/f	450,000
	Trade – loss for the year c/f	200,000

Note: A company is not entitled to current year loss relief.

Question 28 Chief Sabata

Unrelieved loss lapsed after 4 years:
Loss in 2011 assessment year (1/10/09 - 30/9/10)
Relieved in part in 2012 YOA (1/10/10 - 30/9/11)
Relieved in part in 2013YOA (1/10/11 - 30/9/12)
Relieved in part in 2014 YOA (1/10/12 - 30/9/13)
Relieved in part in 2015YOA (1/10/13 - 30/9/14)
Loss incurred in 2011 assessment year which could not be relieved after 2015 year of assessment must lapse.

Part II Short-Answer Questions

31. The only method of loss relief available to a company is carry forward loss relief.

32. (a) Current year loss relief
    (b) Carry forward loss relief
    (c) A combination of both (a) and (b) above

33. It can only be granted against future income from the same trade or business in which the loss was incurred.

34. There is no relief available for unrelieved losses in the year of cessation. Such losses must lapse. It cannot be carried backward and set off against previous years' profits.

14 Partnership Assessment

Part I Multiple-Choice Questions

1.	D	2.	C	3.	E
4.	C	5.	C	6.	C
7.	C	8.	D	9.	E
10.	B	11.	A	12.	D
13.	D	14.	B	15.	C
16.	E				

Workings

Questions 9 - 12

Partnership Computed Income

	₦	₦
Adjusted profit		266,000
Less:		
Salaries	216,000	
Interest on capital	450,000	666,000
Computed loss		400,000

Share of computed loss	
Titi (5/10 x 400,000)	200,000
Tata (3/10 x 400,000)	120,000
Timi (2/10 x 400,000)	80,000
	400,000

Computation of Assessable Income/(Loss) of each Partner for 2006 Assessment year

	Titi	Tata	Timi	Total
	₦	₦	₦	₦
Salaries	60,000	72,000	84,000	216,000
Interest on capital	100,000	150,000	200,000	450,000
Share of computed loss	200,000	120,000	80,000	400,000
Assessable income/(loss)	(40,000)	102,000	204,000	266,000

Question 13

Computation of Each Partner's Assessable Income

	Lion	Tiger	Total
	₦	₦	₦
2018 YOA (1/1/17 - 31/12/17)			
Adjusted profit			1,500,000
1st Period (1/1/17 - 31/3/17)			
Adjusted profit			
(3/12 x 1,500,000)			375,000
Apportioned as follows:			
Salaries (3 months)	60,000	90,000	150,000
Computed income (1:1)	112,500	112,500	225,000
Assessable income (A)	172,500	202,500	375,000
2nd Period (1/4/17 - 31/12/17)			
Adjusted profit			
(9/12 x 1,500,000)			1,125,000
Apportioned as follows:			
Salaries (9 months)	180,000	270,000	450,000
Computed income (60:40)	405,000	270,000	675,000
Assessable income (B)	585,000	540,000	1,125,000
Total assessable income (C) = (A) + (B)	757,500	742,500	1,500,000

Questions 14 - 16

Computation of Assessable Income of Each Partner

	Mbata	Dada	Oko	Apa	Total
	₦	₦	₦	₦	₦
Profit for the year ended 31/12/16					1,200,000
1st Period (1/1/16 - 30/6/16) Profit (6/12 x 1,200,000)	200,000	200,000	200,000	n/a	600,000
2nd Period (1/7/16 – 31/12/16) Profit (6/12 x 1,200,000)	n/a	300,000	180,000	120,000	600,000
Assessable income	200,000	500,000	380,000	120,000	1,200.000
Profit (1/1/17 – 31/12/17)		750,000	450,000	300,000	1,500,000

Part II Short-Answer Questions

17. Federal Capital Territory Internal Revenue Service. PITA defines the relevant tax authority of a partnership for a year of assessment as the tax authority of the territory in which the principal office or place of business of the partnership in Nigeria is situated on the first day of that year or is first established during that year.

18. Federal Capital Territory Internal Revenue Service. The tax authority of the territory in which the partnership is situated. Where the tax authority of a partner is not the same as that of partnership, the partnership's tax authority is to supply to that other authority particulars of that determination.

19. Federal Capital Territory, Abuja. The income of each partner from the partnership firm is deemed to be derived from the territory in which the principal office or place of business of the partnership is situated.

20. The income of the partnership is shared among the partners in their profit sharing ratio and the partners are assessed and charged to tax

individually. The tax assessment is made on the individual partners and not on the partnership firm itself.

21. The Tax Appeal Commissioners or court of competent jurisdiction in the territory in which the partnership has its tax authority.

22. When an individual becomes a partner in a partnership, he is treated as having commenced a trade, business, etc and the commencement rules are applicable to him except the nature of trade or business carried on by him before joining the partnership is the same as that carried on by that partnership.

23. When an individual ceases to be a partner in a partnership, he is treated as having ceased a trade, business, etc and the cessation rules are applicable to him except the nature of trade, business, etc carried on by him after leaving the partnership is the same as that carried on by that partnership.

24. He is deemed to be resident in the territory from which the income of the partnership is derived.

15 Estates, Trusts and Settlements

Part I Multiple-Choice Questions

1.	E	2.	A	3.	C
4.	D	5.	B	6.	D
7.	C	8.	C	9.	D
10.	C	11.	A	12.	A
13.	C	14.	D	15.	E
16.	C	17.	C		

Workings

Questions 12 - 16

OBB Estate
Computation of Assessable Income for 2014 Assessment Year

	₦	₦	₦
Business profit			500,000
Less capital allowances			55,000
			445,000
Gross rent		381,000	
Less expenses:			
Tenement rate	15,000		
Agent's commission	14,000		
Repairs and maintenance	30,000	59,000	322,000
Other income			268,000
Total income			1,035,000
Less:			
Fixed annuity to Kanu Heart Foundation		38,000	
Executor's remuneration		40,000	
Executor's admin. expenses		24,000	102,000
Computed income			933,000
Less ex-gratia payment to Imata			33,000
Remainder of computed income			900,000
Shared as follows:			
Imata (1/2 x 900,000)		450,000	
Amina (1/3 x 900,000)		300,000	750,000
Income assessable to tax in the name of the executor(1/6 x 900,000)			150,000

Assessable Income of Imata

	₦
Ex-gratia payment	33,000
Share of remainder of computed income	450,000
	483,000

Part II Short-Answer Questions

18. (a) Any expenses of the trustee or executor relative to the settlement, trust or estate which is authorized by the terms of the deed of settlement or trust or of the will, as the case may be.
    (b) Any annuity of fixed annual amount paid out of the income of the settlement, trust or estate in accordance with the provisions of the deed or will.

19. The trustee of a settlement or trust and the executor of an estate are responsible for the preparation of the account of the settlement, trust or estate

20. The accounts are prepared annually to 31st December and the last accounts are made up to the date on which the assets of the settlement, trust or estate are finally distributed.

21. False

22. (a) If the settlor or person creating the trust retains or acquires an immediately exercisable general power of appointment over the capital assets of the settlement or trust or over the income derived therefrom; or
    (b) If that settlor or person creating the trust makes use, directly or indirectly, by borrowing or otherwise, of any part of the income arising under the settlement or trust.

23. (a) Where the income is paid during the life time of the settlor; and
    (b) The child was an infant and unmarried at the time of payment.

    The income of the settlor's child shall not be deemed to be that of the settlor for any year of assessment if:

    (i) the income of the child during the year does not exceed ₦500;

(ii) the settlor is not resident in Nigeria during that year of assessment or is not in Nigeria for 183 days or more in any 12 month period commencing in the calendar year and ending either in the same year or the following year.

24. Oyo State

16 Tertiary Education Tax and National Information Technology Development Levy

Part I Multiple-Choice Questions

1.	C	2.	E	3.	E
4.	E	5.	C	6.	D
7.	C	8.	A	9.	C
10.	E	11.	E	12.	D
13.	B	14.	D	15.	C
16.	C	17.	E	18.	E
19.	B	20.	B	21.	B
22.	D	23.	E	24.	A
25.	A	26.	E	27.	C
28.	E	29.	E	30.	B

Workings

Questions 20 & 21

XYZ Ltd - Computation of Tax Liabilities for 2013 Year of Assessment

	₦	₦
Net profit per accounts		1,600,000
Less profit on disposal of fixed assets		30,000
		1,570,000

Add disallowable expenses:		
Depreciation	200,000	
Donations to social clubs	100,000	
General provision for bad debts	130,000	430,000
Adjusted/assessable profit		2,000,000
Less capital allowances		200,000
Total profit		1,800,000
Income tax liability (30% x 1,800,000)		540,000
Education tax (2% x 2,000,000)		40,000

Part II Short-Answer Questions

31. Five years in the first instance and may be reappointed for another four years and no more.

32. For the provision and maintenance of:
    (a) essential physical infrastructure for teaching and learning.
    (b) instructional material and equipment.
    (c) research and publication.
    (d) academic staff training and development.

33. The person guilty is liable:
    (a) for the first offence to a fine of ₦1,000,000 or imprisonment for a term of 6 months or both;
    (b) for a second and subsequent offence, to a fine of ₦2,000,000 or imprisonment for a term of 12 months or both.

34. The Federal High Court

35. The person guilty is liable:
    (a) for a first offence, to a fine of ₦200,000 or imprisonment for a term of one year or to both such fine and imprisonment; and
    (b) for a second and subsequent offences, to a fine of ₦500,000 or imprisonment for a term of three years or to both such fine and imprisonment.

36. Calculation of tertiary education tax

	₦
Total profit	500,000
Add:	
Capital allowances	55,000
Loss relief	65,000
Assessable profit	620,000
Tertiary education tax (2% x 620,000)	12,400

37. True

38. True

39. False

40. A demand note should be served on the company by the FIRS for the unpaid levy plus penalty and if payment is not made within two months of the demand, the company shall be guilty of an offence.

41. Either within eighteen months from the date of incorporation or six months from the end of the company's first accounting period, whichever is earlier.

42. Calculation of national information technology development levy

$$\frac{\text{Rate of NITDL}}{100 + \text{Rate of NITDL}} \times \text{Profit before tax}$$

$$\frac{1}{101} \times ₦3{,}720{,}000 = ₦36{,}831.68$$

17 Taxation of Specialized Companies

Part I Multiple-Choice Questions

1.	B	2.	B	3.	B
4.	A	5.	A	6.	D
7.	A	8.	D	9.	A

10.	E	11.	A	12.	E
13.	A	14.	C	15.	B
16.	D	17.	C	18.	C

Workings

Questions 13 - 17

Peacock Airline Limited
Computation of Income Tax Liability 2012 Year of Assessment

	₦	₦
Global income		80,000,000
Nigerian income:		
Income from cargo freight out of Nigeria		6,000,000
Income from passenger freight out of Nigeria		22,000,000
		28,000,000
Global adjusted profit:		
Net profit per accounts		57,000,000
Add disallowable expenses:		
Depreciation	2,000,000	
Donation to political party	100,000	
Other disallowable expenses	900,000	3,000,000
Global adjusted profit		60,000,000

$$\text{Adjusted profit ratio} = \frac{\text{Global adjusted profit}}{\text{Global income}} \times \frac{100}{1}$$

$$= \frac{60{,}000{,}000}{80{,}000{,}000} \times \frac{100}{1} = 75\%$$

$$\text{Depreciation ratio} = \frac{\text{Global depreciation}}{\text{Global income}} \times \frac{100}{1}$$

$$= \frac{2{,}000{,}000}{80{,}000{,}000} \times \frac{100}{1} = 2.5\%$$

For Nigerian tax purposes:	₦
Adjusted/assessable profit (75% x 28,000,000)	21,000,000
Less capital allowance (2.5% x 28,000,000)	700,000

Total profit	20,300,000
Income tax payable (30% x 20,300,000)	6,090,000
Minimum tax (2% x 28,000,000)	560,000

Note: Income tax payable by the company is ₦6,090,000 since the amount is higher than the minimum tax.

Question 18

MBA Unit Trust
Computation of Income Tax Liability

	₦	₦
Investment income		2,000,000
Less:		
Wages and salaries	800,000	
Manager remunerations	400,000	
Other expenses	115,000	1,315,000
Assessable profit		685,000
Less capital allowances		140,000
Total profit		545,000
Income tax liability (30% x 545,000)		163,500

Part II Short-Answer Questions

19. The full profit or loss arising from the carriage of passengers, mails, livestock or goods slipped or loaded into an aircraft in Nigeria, but does not include the profit or loss derived from passengers, mails, livestock or goods which are brought to Nigeria solely for transhipment or for transfer from one aircraft to another or in either direction between an aircraft and a ship.

20. The profit or loss of a foreign shipping or air transport company taxable in Nigeria is ascertained by applying
    (a) the adjusted profit ratio and
    (b) the depreciation ratio
    certified by the tax authority in the foreign company's country to the total sums receivable in respect of the carriage of passengers, mails, livestock or goods shipped or loaded in Nigeria.

21. This method can be applied if at the time of assessment the FIRS is not satisfied with the foreign company's tax authority's basis of computing and assessing profits or loss and the foreign tax authority's certification of the profit or loss ratio and the depreciation ratio.

22. Depreciation allowance is granted in lieu of capital allowance and is computed by applying the depreciation ratio to the total sums receivable in respect of the carriage of passengers, mails, livestock or goods shipped or loaded in Nigeria. The depreciation ratio is the ratio of depreciation for an accounting period to the total sums receivable in respect of the carriage of passengers, mails, livestock or goods.

23. CITA defines permanent establishment in relation to an insurance company as a branch, management or other fixed place of business in Nigeria, but does not include an agency in Nigeria unless the agent has and habitually exercises a general authority to negotiate and conclude contracts on behalf of such company.

24. The assessable profit is computed as investment income less management expenses and commissions.

25. True

26. The assessable profit is computed as the income accruing to the unit trust from all sources of its investment less management expenses, including the manager's remunerations.

27. The depreciation ratio is the ratio of depreciation for an accounting period to the total sums receivable in respect of the carriage of passengers, mails, livestock or goods.

28. The adjusted profit ratio is the ratio of profit or loss before depreciation of an accounting period to the total sums receivable in respect of the carriage of passengers, mails, livestock or goods.

29. The reserve for unexpired risks should not exceed 45% of the total premium for general insurance business other than marine insurance business and 25% of the total premium in the case of marine cargo insurance.

18 Pioneer Companies

Part I Multiple-Choice Questions

1.	E	2.	D	3.	A
4.	E	5.	C	6.	A
7.	B	8.	A	9.	E
10.	D	11.	E	12.	A
13.	A	14.	E	15.	C
16.	A	17.	D	18.	B
19.	C	20.	A	21.	C
22.	B	23.	A	24.	D
25.	E	26.	C	27.	D
28.	A	29.	E	30.	E
31.	A	32.	A	33.	E
34.	A	35.	D	36.	E
37	E	38.	E	39.	A
40.	E	41.	D	42.	E

Part II Short-Answer Questions

43. Industrial Development (Income Tax Relief) Act

44. The Industrial Development (Income Tax Relief) Act grants income tax relief or tax holiday to some companies regarded as pioneer companies. Such companies are exempted from payment of income tax for a period of three years. The period may be extended by two years at once or for one year and thereafter for another one year.

45. Industries which are engaged in the following:
    (a) Manufacture of refined petroleum products

(b) Manufacture of dairy products
(c) Manufacture of animal feeds
(d) Processing of cocoa

46. A pioneer certificate is a certificate given under the Industrial Development (Income Tax Relief) Act certifying among other things, a company to be a pioneer company.

47. (a) Particulars of the assets on which qualifying capital expenditure will be incurred by the company on or before production day and during a period of three years following production day and the place in which the assets are to be situated.
(b) In the case of a proposed company, the name, address, nationality of each promoter of the company.

48. Consolidated Revenue Fund of the Federation

49. The effective date is the date the application for the pioneer certificate was submitted to the Minister for Industries or the date the company was incorporated, whichever is the later.

50. The pioneer date if the pioneer company has been in operation for less than one year after the pioneer date or the date of the last anniversary of the pioneer date if the pioneer company has been in operation for not less than one year after the pioneer date.

51. The effective date of cancellation of the certificate is 1/6/05, the date of the last anniversary of the pioneer date, since the company has been in operation for more than one year after the pioneer date.

52. (a) Where the date of production day of a pioneer company is more than one year later than the estimated date given in the company's application for a pioneer certificate.
(b) Where the qualifying capital expenditure incurred by a pioneer company on or before the production day is less

than ₦50,000 in the case of an indigenous-controlled company or ₦150,000 in the case of any other company.

53. An indigenous-controlled company means any company in which:
    (a) the beneficial ownership of the whole equity capital of the company and of all other class of shares conferring voting rights in the company, is vested in persons who are citizens of Nigeria, otherwise than by naturalisation or registration; and
    (b) the persons mentioned in (a) control the composition of the board of directors of the company.

54. A production day certificate is a certificate issued to a pioneer company by the Industrial Inspectorate Division of the Federal Ministry of Industries certifying the day on which the trade or business of a pioneer company commenced.

55. The Industrial Inspectorate Division of the Federal Ministry of Industries

56. The production day is significant because it is the day on which the trade or business of a pioneer company commences. In other words, the tax relief period commences from the production day.

57. Certificate of qualifying capital expenditure is a certificate issued to a pioneer company by the FIRS certifying the amount of qualifying capital expenditure incurred by the company prior to its production day.

58. The sales proceeds is to be deducted from the total amount of qualifying capital expenditure incurred to determine the amount of qualifying capital expenditure to be certified.

59. The net loss of the pioneer period is available for relief in computing the total profits of the new trade or business after the pioneer period.

60. It is a trade or business of a pioneer company carried on by it during its tax relief period and which either ceases within that period or is deemed to cease at the end of that period.

61. Production day

62. On the first day following the end of its tax relief period.

63. The accounting periods of a pioneer company are as follows:
    (a) a period not exceeding one year commencing on its production day,
    (b) successive periods of one year thereafter, and
    (c) a period not exceeding one year ending at the date when its tax relief period ends.

64. If the profits are earned from any trade or business outside its pioneer enterprise (i.e. operations and activities not covered by the pioneer certificate).

65. If a pioneer company distribute any dividend to its shareholders in excess of the credit balance in the account maintained for exempted profits as at the date of such distribution.

66. On the day following the end of the tax relief period.

67. Capital allowances are claimable from the day following the end of its tax relief period.

68. The net loss is deemed to have been incurred on the day following the end of the tax relief period and will be taken into account in computing total profits of the first year of assessment of the new business.

69. False

70. False

19 Tax Returns, Assessments, Objections, Appeals and Collection

Part I Multiple-Choice Questions

1.	B	2.	B	3.	D
4.	D	5.	E	6.	B
7.	E	8.	D	9.	D
10.	B	11.	B	12.	E
13.	C	14.	C	15.	D
16.	D	17.	A	18.	C
19.	A	20.	C	21.	E
22.	D	23.	B	24.	C
25.	C	26.	D	27.	B
28.	A	29.	A	30.	E
31.	A	32.	A	33.	A
34.	B	35.	E	36.	E
37.	C	38.	D	39.	E
40.	A	41.	E	42.	E
43.	E	44.	D	45.	D
46.	B	47.	A	48.	B
49.	C	50.	D	51.	D
52.	E	53.	D	54.	D
55.	D	56.	D	57.	D
58.	C				

Part II Short-Answer Questions

59. The liquidator must make provision for full payment of any tax which maybe found payable by the company including any tax deduction made by the company under any laws in force in any part of Nigeria relating to the tax of individuals.

60. (a) The company will have to pay provisional tax.
(b) The company cannot be granted instalment payment facility.

61. Where the relevant tax authority suspects that
    (a) an offence involving non-disclosure of information or any irregularity or an offence in connection with or in relation to tax has been committed; and
    (b) evidence of the offence or irregularity can be found in the premises, office, etc of the taxpayer or in the residence of the principal officer, factor, agent or representative of the taxpayer.

62. A warrant

63. If the FIRS is satisfied that the delay in making the objection is due to the absent from Nigeria of the person in whose name the assessment is made.

64. When an aggrieved taxpayer has objected to his/its income tax assessment and has failed to reach an agreement with the relevant tax authority on amount of the tax chargeable, the tax authority will issue a notice of refusal to amend the assessment as desired by the taxpayer.

65. An assessment is deemed to be final and conclusive if no valid objection or appeal has been made within the time stipulated for giving notice of objection or appeal or where no due notice has been given of a further appeal against a decision of the Tax Appeal Tribunal or a Judge.

66. Power to distain

67. Proceeds of sale of any property distrained are to be used in the following sequence:
    (a) to pay the cost or charges of and incidental to the sale and keeping of the distress and disposal;
    (b) to pay the amount of tax due.

    The balance after the payment of (a) and (b) shall be payable to the taxpayer on demand being made by him or on his behalf within one year of the date of sale.

68. The assessment can be raised at any time and as often as may be necessary to recover the tax lost or underpaid.

69. A company is chargeable to tax
   (a) in its own name; or
   (b) in the name of any principal officer, attorney, factor, agent or representative of the company in Nigeria; or
   (a) in the name of a receiver or liquidator.

70. True

71. (a) Copy of memorandum and articles of Association and Certificate of Incorporation
   (b) Date of commencement of business and the company's accounting date.
   (c) Registered address of the company, name and addresses of the company's directors, auditors, bankers, etc.

72. False

73. False

20 Tax Clearance Certificate

Part I Multiple-Choice Questions

1.	C	2.	A	3.	C
4.	D	5.	D	6.	C
7.	A				

Part II Short-Answer Questions

8. A tax clearance certificate is a document issued by the tax authority to a taxpayer certifying that the tax assessed on the income of the person for the three years immediately preceding the current year of

assessment has been fully paid or that no tax is due on the income or that the person is not liable to tax for any of those years.

9. A fine of ₦50,000 plus double the tax payable by the taxable person or to three years' imprisonment or to both such fine and imprisonment.

21 Tax Evasion, Tax Avoidance, Tax Offences and Penalties

Part I Multiple-Choice Questions

1.	D	2.	B	3.	B
4.	A	5.	D	6.	E

Part II Short-Answer Questions

7. A fine of ₦500,000 in the case of a body corporate and ₦50,000 in the case of an individual.

8. The company is liable to pay a penalty of:
   (a) ₦25,000 in the first month in which the failure occurs and
   (b) ₦5,000 for each subsequent month in which the failure continues.

   Any director, manager, secretary, agent etc of the company who was a party to the offence being committed is equally liable to a fine of ₦100,000 or imprisonment for two years or both.

9. A fine of ₦20,000 and double the amount of tax undercharged or would have been undercharged as a result of the incorrect return.

10. A fine of ₦5,000 or to a maximum of 3 months' imprisonment or both.

11. A fine of ₦10,000 or to imprisonment of not less than 6 months or to both such fine and impridsonment.

12. Penalty of 10% per annum of the amount of tax unpaid and interest on annual basis at bank based lending rate on the tax due from the date when the tax becomes payable until it is paid.

13. A fine of ₦100,000 or 3 years' imprisonment or both.

14. A fine of ₦600 or 3 years' imprisonment or both.

15. A fine of ₦600 or 3 years' imprisonment or both.

16. Back-duty investigation

22 Presumptive Taxation and Tax Amnesty

Part I Multiple-Choice Questions

1.	B	2.	A	3.	D
4.	A	5.	A	6.	B
7.	D	8.	E	9.	A
10.	D	11.	B	12.	C
13.	E	14.	D	15.	E
16.	D	17.	D	18.	E
19.	B	20.	E	21.	B
22.	E	23.	A	24.	D
25.	A	26.	D	27.	A
28.	C	29.	E	30.	D
31.	A	32.	E	33.	B
34.	B	35.	E	36.	D
37.	D	38.	A	39.	E

23 Stamp Duties

Part I Multiple-Choice Questions

1.	D	2.	D	3.	C
4.	E	5.	D	6.	B
7.	D	8.	E	9.	B
10.	A	11.	D	12.	D
13.	D	14.	C	15.	A
16.	C	17.	A	18.	A
19.	A	20.	D	21.	D
22.	C	23.	C	24.	B

Part II Short-Answer Questions

25. Ad valorem duties

26. (a) Receipt
    (b) Affidavit, affirmation and statutory declaration
    (c) Letter or power of attorney

27. (a) Conveyance or transfer on sale of any property
    (b) Mortgage
    (c) Contract note for or relating to the sale or purchase of any stock or marketable security

28. Federal Capital Territory Internal Revenue Service

29. Commissioner of Stamp Duties

30. Adjudication

31. The instrument must be claimed by the owner within six months of its being left at office of the Commissioner. Otherwise a notice may be given in the Federal Gazette that the instrument will be destroyed if not claimed within two months of the publication of the notice.

After the said period, the instrument may be destroyed if it is not claimed.

32. The cancellation is done by the person writing on or across the stamp his name or initials, or the name or initials of his firm, together with the true date of his so writing, or otherwise effectively cancels the stamp and renders the same incapable of being used for any other instrument or for any postal; purpose or for payment of telegram.

    Where the person is an illiterate the mark of such person together with the true date of the marking thereof is written on or across the stamp.

33. A fine of ₦100

34. A penalty of ₦20 and as a further penalty, where the unpaid duty exceeds ₦20, an interest is paid on such duty at the rate of 10% per annum from the date the instrument was first executed up to the time when the amount of interest is equal to the unpaid duty.

    In the case of instrument subject to ad valorem duty, the fine is ₦20 and a further penalty equivalent to the unpaid duty unless there is a reasonable excuse for the delay in stamping.

35. On the average price of the stock on the date of the instrument.

36. The value of the money in dollars according to the current rate of exchange on date of the instrument.

37. (a) Minister of Finance in the case of Federal Government
    (b) Governor in the case of State Government

38. He shall be entitled to obtain judgment for the amount to which he has been penalized, together with cost, against the guilty person.

39. (a) Where the collection of duty or the stamping of instrument is impracticable or inexpedient, or

(b) Where such collection or stamping causes undue inconvenience to trade or business, or

(c) Where it is in the interest of Nigeria or of a State.

40. Charter party includes any agreement or contract for the charter of any ship or vessel or any memorandum, latter, or other writing between the captain, master or owner of any ship or vessel and any other person for or relating to the freight or conveyance of any money, goods, or effects on board of a ship or vessel.

41. Terms upon which a charter party may be stamped after execution:

(a) within seven days after the first execution thereof, on payment of the duty and a penalty of forty five kobo;

(b) after seven days but within one month after the first execution thereof on payment of the duty and a penalty of twenty Naira and shall not in any other case be stamped with an impressed stamp.

42. Where a charter party is first executed abroad without being duly stamped any party thereto may within ten days after it has been first received in Nigeria, and before it had been executed by any person in Nigeria, affix thereto an adhesive stamp demoting the duty chargeable thereon and at the same time cancel such adhesive stamp and the instrument when so stamped shall be deemed duly stamped.

43. An instrument is defined as every written document.

44. Fixed duties

24 Value Added Tax

Part I Multiple-Choice Questions

1.	C	2.	E	3.	B
4.	D	5.	A	6.	E
7.	D	8.	B	9.	A
10.	E	11.	A	12.	E
13.	E	14.	A	15.	B
16.	A	17.	A	18.	E
19.	E	20.	E	21.	A
22.	A	23.	E	24.	C
25.	A	26.	E	27.	A
28.	D	29.	B	30.	E
31.	E	32.	B	33.	C
34.	C	35.	D	36.	B
37.	A	38.	D	39.	A
40.	C	41.	D	42.	C
43.	C	44.	E	45.	C
46.	C	47.	B	48.	C
49.	A	50.	E	51.	A
52.	D	53.	A	54.	B

Workings

Question 29

CC Limited

Computation of VAT Payable to or Refundable by FIRS

	₦
VAT collected on sales (output tax) = 5% x 6,000,000	300,000
VAT paid on purchases (input tax) = 5% x 6,500,000	325,000
Net VAT refundable by FIRS	25,000

Question 30

	₦
Sales (15 crates @ ₦600 per crate)	9,000
Less trade discount (2% x 9,000)	180
Net sales	8,820
VAT (5% x 8,820)	441

Questions 31 - 34

Taxable Person	Sales Price (VAT Exclusive)	VAT Collected (Output tax)	VAT on Input (Input Tax)	Net VAT Payable to FIRS
	₦	₦	₦	₦
RM Supplier	52,500	2,625.00	0	2,625.00
Manufacturer	78,750	3,937.50	2,625.00	1,312.50
Wholesaler	94,500	4,725.00	3,937.50	787.50
Retailer	103,950	5,197.50	4,725.00	472.50
		16,485.00	**11,287.50**	**5,197.50**

Questions 35 - 37

Kaikai Limited
Computation of Value Added Tax Payable

	₦	₦
Output tax		
VAT collected on goods sold		1,250,000
VAT collected on services provided		24,000
		1,274,000
Input tax		
VAT paid on raw materials purchased	700,000	
VAT paid on goods purchased for resale	325,000	1,025,000
Net VAT payable		249,000

Question 50

	₦
Sales (excluding VAT)	500,000
Less cash discount (10% x 500,000)	50,000
	450,000
VAT (5% x 450,000)	22,500

Question 51

	₦
Sales (excluding VAT)	500,000
VAT (5% x 500,000)	25,000

Part II Short-Answer Questions

55. VAT is a tax charged on the supply of most goods and services (referred to as taxable goods and services). VAT is a tax on consumption which is collected at each point of sales of goods and services from production to consumption but eventually borne by the final consumer.

56. Withholding tax is not a separate type of tax rather it is an advance payment of income tax. Withholding tax deduction is made by the payer of the income when the income is paid or credited to the recipient. Withholding tax deduction is available as set off against the tax assessment of the relevant periods.

    VAT is a separate type of tax which is charged and payable on the supply of most goods and services. It is a tax on consumption or expenditure. The tax burden falls on the consumer while the manufacturers, wholesalers, retailers, etc are merely acting as agents of the FIRS for the collection of VAT.

57. Tax period means one calendar month commencing from the beginning of the month to the end of month.

58. A taxable person includes an individual or body of individuals, family, corporation sole, trustee or executor or a person who carries out in a place an economic activity, a person exploiting tangible or intangible property for the purpose of obtaining income therefrom by way of trade or business or a person or agency of government acting in that capacity.

59. Taxable goods and services are those goods and services which are not listed in the First Schedule to VAT Act as goods and services

exempted from VAT. In other words, the goods and services liable to VAT are known as taxable goods and services.

60. The value of taxable goods and services is determined in accordance with the provisions of VAT Act, that is:
    (a) if the supply is for a money consideration, its value shall be deemed to be an amount which with the addition of the tax chargeable is equal to the consideration.
    (b) if the supply is for a consideration not consisting of money, the value of the supply shall be deemed to be its market value.

61. The price of the goods imported plus:
    (a) all taxes, duties and other charges levied either outside or by reason of importation into Nigeria, other than the tax imposed by this Act
    (b) all cost by way of commission, parking, transport and insurance up to the port or place of importation (VATA 2004, s. 6).

62. (a) Medical and pharmaceutical products
    (b) Tractors, ploughs, agricultural equipment and implements purchased for agricultural purposes
    (c) All exports

63. (a) Services rendered by mortgage institutions
    (b) Plays and performances conducted by educational institutions as part of learning
    (c) All exported services

64. VAT is not charged on exempted supplies and the suppliers of such goods and services cannot obtain a refund of the VAT they have paid on inputs.

    VAT is charged on zero rate supplies at zero rate and the suppliers of such goods and services can get a refund of the VAT they have paid on inputs.

65. (a) To consider all the tax matters that require professional and technical expertise and make recommendations to the FIRS.
(b) To advise the FIRS on the duties specified in the VAT Act (i.e. assessment and collection of VAT and accounting for the tax so collected).

66. Government Ministries are required to register with the FIRS for VAT. Taxable persons are to show evidence of registration with the FIRS before being awarded contracts by Government.

67. Non-resident companies are required to register with the FIRS for VAT. While a non-resident company has to include VAT in its invoice, the person to whom the goods or services are supplied in Nigeria has an obligation to remit the tax to the FIRS in the currency of the transaction.

68. A penalty of ₦10,000 for the first month in which the failure occurs and ₦5,000 for each subsequent month in which the failure continues.

69. (a) Customer's name and address
(b) Date of supply
(c) Gross amount of transaction, tax charged and rate applied

70. VAT paid on purchases of goods and services is referred to as input tax, while VAT charged on sales of goods and services is referred to as output tax.

71. (a) Input tax on certain expenses which can be expended through the profit and loss account (income statement)
(b) Input tax on fixed assets which can be capitalized as part of the cost of the assets.

72. The net VAT payable to the VAT office is the excess of output tax over input tax.

73. The FIRS has to make a refund to the taxable person if input tax exceeds output tax.

74. 21st February, 2015.

75. The person to whom the goods services are supplied in Nigeria.

76. Best of judgment (BOJ) assessment

77.

	Offence	Penalty
a	Failure to notify the FIRS of any change of address within one month of such change.	Penalty of ₦5,000.
b	Failure to issue tax invoice for goods sold or services rendered	Liable on conviction to a fine of 50% of the cost of the goods or services for which the invoice was not issued.

78. A penalty of 5% per annum plus interest at the commercial rate of the amount of tax not remitted.

79. VAT is broad base. It is imposed on the supply of most goods and services. Agencies of Government, organizations and persons that are exempted from income tax are required to pay VAT on the taxable goods and services consumed by them. Consequently, the Federal Government is able to raise a substantial amount of revenue through the imposition of VAT.

80. VAT is disadvantageous because it is regressive. Nigeria has a single rate of VAT (5%) so both the rich and the poor buy from the same market and suffer the same rate of VAT. So the poor man feels the burden or pain of VAT more than the rich man.

81. It is difficult, if not impossible, for the FIRS to keep track of all the small businesses scattered all over the country. Many of them have

not even registered for VAT. Some are duly registered and have been collecting VAT without remitting to the FIRS.

82. VAT inclusive means that VAT is included or wrapped up in the price quoted. Therefore, VAT can be ascertained using the formula:

$$\frac{\text{Rate of VAT}}{100 + \text{Rate of VAT}} = \frac{5}{100 + 5} \times 240{,}000 = ₦11{,}428.57$$

83. Value Added Tax Act, Cap CI, LFN 2004

25 Capital Gains Tax

Part I Multiple-Choice Questions

1.	C	2.	E	3.	D
4.	D	5.	A	6.	B
7.	B	8.	B	9.	E
10.	D	11.	D	12.	D
13.	D	14.	A	15.	D
16.	A	17.	B	18.	D
19.	E	20.	B	21.	B
22.	A	23.	B	24.	E
25.	B	26.	E	27.	D
28.	C	29.	E	30.	E
31.	D	32.	B	33.	E
34.	E	35.	C	36.	E
37.	C	38.	E	39.	A
40.	E	41.	B	42.	B
43.	D	44.	D	45.	E
46.	B	47.	E	48.	A
49.	D	50.	E	51.	A
52.	C	53.	B	54.	E
55.	A	56.	A	57.	C
58.	E				

Workings

Questions 17 - 19
Mimiko LTD - Computation of CGT Payable for 2014 YOA

	₦	₦
Sale proceeds		1,750,000
Less:		
Cost of advertisement	35,000	
Cost of renovation prior to sale	150,000	
Sales agent's commission	87,500	272,500
Net sale proceeds		1,477,500
Less:		
Cost of acquisition	805,000	
Legal expenses on acquisition	40,250	845,250
Capital gain		632,250
Capital gains tax payable (10% x 632,250)		63,225

Question 20
Zambawa - Computation of CGT Payable for 2013 YOA

	₦	₦
Market value		1,500,000
Less allowable expenses:		
Cost of acquisition	750,000	
Cost of improvement	240,000	990,000
Capital gain		510,000
Capital gains tax payable (10% x 510,000)		51,000

Zambawa and his sister are connected persons, therefore, the transaction is deemed to be artificial or fictitious. The actual consideration (₦1,200,000) is considered to be inadequate, hence, the market value of the asset at the date of disposal (₦1,500,000) is used for the computation of capital gains tax.

Questions 22 - 25

Baba Ltd - Computation of CGT Payable for 2014 YOA

	₦	₦
Sale proceeds		2,000,000
Less incidental costs of disposal		100,000
Net sale proceeds		1,900,000
Less cost attributable to part sold:		
Cost of acquisition	2,600,000	
Professional fees	150,000	
Total cost of building	2,750,000	

Attributable cost = $\frac{A}{A + B} \times C =$

$\frac{2,000,000}{2,000,000 + 3,500,000} \times 2,750,000$	1,000,000
Capital gain	900,000
Capital gains tax payable (10% x 900,000)	90,000

Cost of part of building not disposed of =

Total cost of building	2,750,000
Less cost attributable to part of building disposed of	1,000,000
Cost of part of building not disposed of	1,750,000

Question 27

IBB Ltd - Computation of Capital Gains Tax Payable for 2014 YOA

	Building sold in April 2014		**Building sold in July 2014**	
	₦	₦	₦	₦
Sales proceeds		1,800,000		1,250,000
Less disposal expenses		180,000		125,000
Net sales proceeds		1,620,000		1,125,000
Less:				
Cost of acquisition	1,000,000			1,200,000
Cost of extension	100,000	1,100,000		
Capital gain/(loss)		520,00		(75,000)
Capital gains tax @ 10%		52,000		Nil

The loss of ₦75,000 incurred on the sale of one building is not deducted from the gain of ₦520,000 made on the sale of the other building. In other words, the capital gain of ₦520,000 is taxable, while there is no loss relief for ₦75,000.

Question 39

The full amount of the liability assumed by the purchaser of the asset is part of the consideration for the acquisition/disposal of the asset. Therefore, the consideration for acquisition is ₦400,000 + ₦600,000 = ₦1,000,000 provided that the purchaser has assumed liability for the debt.

Question 40

The chargeable gain is ₦660,000 – ₦580,000 = ₦80,000 and NOT ₦660,000 – ₦500,000 = ₦160,000. The chargeable gain is reduced so that it does not exceed the amount which would have accrued if the market value of the asset at the time of the creditor's acquisition was substituted for the amount of the debt discharged.

Question 41

XYZ Ltd - Computation of CGT Payable for 2017 Year of Assessment

	₦
Sales proceeds	9,650,000
Less disposal expenses	965,000
Net sales proceeds	8,685,000
Less:	
Cost of acquisition plus prof. charges	11,000,000
Capital loss	(2,315,000)
Capital gains tax @ 10%	Nil

The Capital Gains Tax Act does not make provision for loss relief.

Question 42

	₦
Proceeds	1, 300
Less cost of acquisition	350
Capital gains	950

Capital gains tax payable:	
Either 20% of capital gains (20% x ₦950)	190
Or ½ x (₦1,300 - ₦1,000) whichever is lower.	150

Question 44

Bayo - Computation of CGT Payable for 2018 Year of Assessment

	₦	₦
Proceeds		14,000,000
Less allowable deductions:		
Cost of acquisition	8,000,000	
Enhancement exp.(₦1,000,000 + ₦2,000,000)	3,000,000	11,000,000
Capital gain		3,000,000
Capital gains tax payable (10% x ₦3,000,000)		300,000

Question 45

Bayo - Computation of CGT Payable for 2018 Year of Assessment

	₦	₦
Market value		16,000,000
Less allowable deductions:		
Cost of acquisition	8,000,000	
Enhancement exp. (₦1,000,000 + ₦2,000,000)	3,000,000	11,000,000
Capital gain		5,000,000
Capital gains tax payable (10% x ₦5,000,000)		500,000

Question 46

Tom and Dick Computation of CGT Tax Payable for 2018 YOA

	₦	₦
Sale proceeds		10,000,000
Less sales agent's fee (5% x ₦10,000,000)		500,000
Net sale proceeds		9,500,000
Less:		
Cost of acquisition	7,000,000	
Enhancement exp. (₦500,000 + ₦800,000)	1,300,000	8,300,000
Capital gain		1,200,000
Capital gains tax payable (10% x ₦1,200,000)		120,000

Capital gains payable by:		
Tom (3/5 x ₦120,000)	72,000	
Dick (2/5 x ₦120,000)	48,000	120,000

Question 47

Amaka - Computation of CGT Payable for 2017 Year of Assessment

	Land at Awka Rd	Land at Enugu Rd
	₦	₦
Compensation/sales proceeds	1,900,000	10,000,000
Less incidental cost of disposal		2,000,000
Net sales proceeds		8,000,000
Less:		
Cost of acquisition	1,640,000	5,000,000
Capital gains	260,000	3,000,000
Capital gains tax at 10%	Nil	300,000

The capital gains of ₦260,000 is exempted from tax since it is as a result of compulsory acquisition of land by the federal government.

Question 48

Capital gain = 4/5 x (₦1,800,000 - ₦1,000,000) = ₦640,000
CGT payable = 10% x ₦640,000 = ₦64,000
Note that one fifth (1/5) of the building was used for private purposes.

Questions 49 & 50

Baba Ltd - Computation of CGT Tax Payable for 2010 YOA

	₦	₦
Sale proceeds		1,500,000
Less:		
Attributable cost = $\frac{A}{A+B} \times C$ =		
$\frac{1,500,000}{1,500,000 + 2,500,000} \times 3,000,000$		1,125,000
Capital gain		375,000
Capital gains tax payable (10% x 375,000)		37,500

Where:
A = the amount or value of the consideration for the part disposed of.
B = the market value of the part not disposed of.
C = the total cost of the asset.

Computation of CGT Tax Payable for 2018 Year of Assessment

Sale proceeds		3,500,000
Cost of part of building not disposed of in 2010:		
Total cost of building	3,000,000	
Less cost attributable to part of building disposed of	1,125,000	1,875,000
Capital gain		1,625,000
Capital gains tax payable (10% x 1,625,000)		162,500

Question 53
Feedwell Ltd - Computation of CGT for 2018 Year of Assessment

	₦	₦
Sale proceeds		1,800,000
Less cost of acquisition		1,000,000
Capital gain		800,000
Less capital gain rolled-over:		
Sale proceeds reinvested	1,800,000	
Less cost of old asset	1,000,000	
Capital gain rolled-over		800,000
Chargeable gain		Nil

Since the whole of the sale proceeds has been applied in acquiring another building, the capital gain of ₦800,000 is rolled-over so that no capital gains tax is payable in 2018 assessment year.

Question 54
Bebobsco - Computation of CGT for 2018 Year of Assessment

	₦
Sale proceeds	3,000,000
Less cost of acquisition of old asset	2,400,000
Chargeable gain	600,000
Capital gains tax payable (10% x 600,000)	60,000

Since the amount of the sale proceeds reinvested in acquiring the new plant and machinery (₦1,700,000) is less than the cost of the old asset (₦2,400,000), no roll-over relief is granted. In other words, none of the capital gain has been reinvested in the acquisition of the new asset, therefore, the whole amount of the capital gain is taxable.

Questions 55 & 56

Tata Ltd - Computation of CGT Payable for 2018 Year of Assessment

	₦	₦
Sale proceeds		2,600,000
Less cost of acquisition of old asset		1,600,000
Capital gain		1,000,000
Less capital gain rolled-over:		
Sales proceeds reinvested	2,200,000	
Less cost of old asset	1,600,000	
Capital gain rolled-over		600,000
Chargeable gain (i.e. capital gain not rolled-over)		400,000
Capital gains tax payable (10% x 400,000)		40,000

₦2,200,000 of the sale proceeds of ₦2,600,000 has been reinvested in the acquisition of another warehouse. The amount of proceeds/capital gain not reinvested is taxable in 2005 assessment year as calculated above.

Deemed or carrying cost of new warehouse

	₦
Cost of acquisition of new asset	2,200,000
Less capital gain rolled-over	600,000
Deemed cost of new asset	1,600,000

Question 57

Stone Ltd - Computation of CGT Payable for 2018 YOA

	₦
Sale proceeds	2,000,000
Less cost of acquisition	1,500,000
Capital gain	500,000

Instalments payable in 2018	
30/06/08	400,000
31/12/08	400,000
	800,000
Capital gains deemed accrued (800,000 x 500,000) / 2,000,000	200,000
Capital gains tax payable in 2018 (10% x 200,000)	20,000

Question 58

Okoro Ltd - Computation of Capital Gains Tax Payable for 2017 YOA

	₦
Sales proceeds	6,400,000
Less incidental cost of disposal	70,000
Net sales proceeds	6,330,000
Less:	
Cost of acquisition (see computation below)	5,520,000
Capital gains	810,000
Capital gains tax (10% x 810,000)	81,000

Computation of Cost of Acquisition

	₦
Deposit	1,200,000
Add instalments (24 instalments @ ₦200,000)	4,800,000
Hire purchase price	6,000,000
Less hire purchase interest (24 instalments @ ₦20,000)	480,000
Cash price	5,520,000

Part II Short-Answer Questions

59. A year of assessment with regards to capital gains tax begins from 1st January and ends on 31st December of the same calendar year.

60. There is a part disposal of assets:
    (a) where an interest or right in or over the assets is created by the disposal, as well as where it subsists before the disposal, and

(b) where, on a person making a disposal, any description of property derived from the assets remains undisposed of. (CGTA 2004, S.6{2}{b})

61. The cost attributable to the part disposed of an asset is calculated as:

$$\frac{A}{A + B} \times C$$

Where:

A = the amount or value of the consideration for the part disposed of.

B = the market value of the part not disposed of.

C = the total cost of the asset.

62. Chattel

63. Where the consideration exceeds ₦1,000, the capital gains tax chargeable shall not exceed half the difference between the amount of that consideration and ₦1,000.

64. Where it becomes necessary to determine which of two or more residences is an individual's main residence for any period, he may give a notice in writing to the relevant tax authority within two years from the beginning of that period choosing which of them is to be treated as his main residence. The notice may be varied by a further notice in writing to the relevant tax authority as regards any period beginning not earlier than two years before the giving of the further notice.

65. Within thirty days of service of the notice.

66. The gains accruing to the person are not subject to capital gains tax provided that the person had not:

(a) acquired the land at the time when he knew or might reasonably have known that it was likely to be acquired by the authority; or

(b) taken any steps by advertisement or otherwise to dispose of the land or to make his willingness to dispose of it known to the authority or others.

67. At a consideration equal to the amount of the consideration for which the asset was last disposed of by way of a bargain made at arm's length. Where the amount cannot be ascertained, the consideration is deemed to be the market value of the asset at the date of death.
No capital gains tax is chargeable on the gains which accrue on the disposal of assets on the date of the owner's death as stated above.

68. The chargeable gain deemed to accrue in each year of assessment is computed as:

$$\frac{\text{Amount of instalment (i.e. consideration payable in the year)}}{\text{Total consideration payable}} \times \text{Total chargeable gain}$$

The chargeable gain is deemed to accrue on the last day of that year of assessment and is taxable in that same year.

69. Transactions between connected persons are deemed to be artificial or fictitious if in the opinion of the relevant tax authority those transactions have not been made on terms which might fairly have been expected to have been made by persons engaged in the same or similar activities dealing with one another at arm's length.

70. Where the consideration for the acquisition/disposal is less than the market value of the asset, the consideration is deemed to be the market value.

71. The market value of any assets means the price which those assets might reasonably be expected to fetch on a sale in the open market (CGTA 2004, S. 21{1}).

72. The chargeable gains accruing on the disposal of any partnership assets are allocated to the partners. The partners are assessed and charged to tax individually.

73. (a) An ecclesiastical, charitable or educational institution of a public character.
(b) Any statutory or registered friendly society.
(c) Any co-operative society registered under the Co-operative Societies Law of any State.
(d) Any trade union registered under the Trade Unions Act.

74. C = the total cost of the asset.

75. Roll-over relief. The taxpayer can claim roll-over relief so that capital gains tax is not payable on the capital gain.

76. Roll-over relief is a relief claimable when a person carrying on a trade or business disposes of an eligible asset or receives compensation for the loss or destruction of an asset and reinvests the sale proceeds or compensation (in whole or part) in the acquisition of another asset of the same class for the purpose of the trade or business. The relief makes it possible to defer payment of capital gains tax on the old asset disposed of until a future date when the newly-acquired asset is eventually sold.

77. The relief makes it possible to exempt from capital gains tax the capital gains arising from the disposal of an asset until a future date when the new asset acquired in replacement of the old asset is eventually sold and not replaced. If the whole of the consideration (proceeds) is not reinvested, there will be restriction on the amount of the capital gains exempted from tax.

78. A person may be granted relief in respect of delayed remittance of gains if he claims that:
(a) he was unable to transfer those gains to Nigeria; and
(b) that the inability was due to the law of the country where the income arose, or to the executive action of its Government,

or to the impossibility of obtaining foreign currency in that territory; and

(c) the inability was not due to any want of reasonable endeavours on his part.

79. Registered shares or securities are situated where they are registered and, if registered in more than one register, where the principal register is situated.

80. True

81. Capital gains refer to the gains or profits arising from the disposal of capital assets such as building, land, plant and machinery, etc. It is the excess of the sale proceeds of an asset over the cost of the asset and other allowable expenditure.

82. Capital gains tax is a tax on gains arising from the disposal of chargeable assets (e.g. building, land, plant and machinery, etc).

83. A = the amount or value of the consideration for the part of asset disposed of.

26 Petroleum Profits Tax

Part I Multiple-Choice Questions

1.	C	2.	D	3.	A
4.	E	5.	B	6.	E
7.	E	8.	C	9.	A
10.	A	11.	C	12.	C
13.	C	14.	D	15.	E
16.	A	17.	B	18.	D
19.	C	20.	D	21.	C
22.	B	23.	E	24.	A
25.	D	26.	B	27.	E
28.	E	29.	B	30.	D

31.	E	32.	A	33.	B
34.	D	35.	A	36.	C
37.	C	38.	A	39.	D
40.	D	41.	D	42.	A
43.	B	44.	A	45.	D
46.	A	47.	D	48.	B
49.	A	50.	E	51.	E
52.	B	53.	C	54.	D
55.	C	56.	E	57.	A
58.	A	59.	C	60.	B
61.	E	62.	D	63.	B
64.	B	65.	E	66.	A
67.	B	68.	E	69.	B
70.	D	71.	B	72.	B
73.	E	74.	E	75.	A
76.	E	77.	C	78.	B
79.	C	80.	C	81.	D
82.	E	83.	C	84.	E
85.	C	86.	C		

Workings

Questios 45 & 46

Computation of Assessable Tax
for the Year ended 31st December, 2013

(a) Where an election has been made	₦
Adjusted profit	2,000,000
Less loss relief	-
Assessable profit	2,000,000
Less capital allowances	600,000
Chargeable profit	1,400,000
Assessable tax (85% x 1,400,000)	1,190,000
Unrelieved losses carried forward	300,000

(b) Where no election has been made	₦
Adjusted profit	2,000,000
Less loss relief	300,000

Assessable profit	1,700,000
Less capital allowances	600,000
Chargeable profit	1,100,000
Assessable tax (85% x 1,100,000)	935,000

Questions 47 - 49

Oguta Petroleum Ltd
Computation of Petroleum Investment Allowance for 2010

	Qualifying Expenditure	Petroleum Investment Allowance	
	₦	%	₦
Onshore	9,000,000	5	450,000
Offshore (up to and including 100 metres of water depth)	6,000,000	10	600,000
Offshore (between 100 and 200 metres of water depth)	5,000,000	15	750,000
	20,000,000		1,800,000

Computation of Annual Allowance

Year of Assessment	Qualifying Expenditure	Annual Allowance	
	₦	%	₦
2010 (1st Year)	20,000,000	20	4,000,000
2011 (2nd Year)	20,000,000	20	4,000,000
2012 (3rd Year)	20,000,000	20	4,000,000
2013 (4th Year)	20,000,000	20	4,000,000
2014 (5th Year)	20,000,000	19	3,800,000

Question 50

Calculation of Balancing Charge or Allowance

	₦
Cost of plant	1,500,000
Less capital allowances	900,000
WDV at date of disposal	600,000
Proceeds of disposal	1,650,000
Balancing charge	1,050,000

Balancing charge cannot exceed the capital allowances granted on the asset before disposal. Therefore, balancing charge is restricted to ₦900,000.

Question 51

Calculation of Balancing Charge or Allowance

Date of acquisition	01/05/2000
Date of disposal	30/12/2003
Annual allowance (20% x 10,000,000)	₦2,000,000
	₦
Cost of acquisition	10,000,000
Less:	
Annual allowance granted for 3 years	
(2000, 2001 and 2002 = 2,000,000 x 3)	6,000,000
WDV at disposal	4,000,000
Proceeds of disposal	3,500,000
Balancing allowance	500,000

Questions 52 - 54

Ogoni Petroleum Plc
Computation of Chargeable Profit for the Accounting Period ended 31st December, 2009

	₦	₦
Adjusted profit		50,000,000
Less losses brought forward		4,000,000
Assessable profit		46,000,000
Less capital allowances:		
Brought forward	31,000,000	
Annual allowance	9,000,000	
Balancing allowance	600,000	
Petroleum investment allowance	5,000,000	
	45,600,000	
Capital allowances restricted to:		
85% of assessable profit		
(85% x 46,000,000)	39,100,000	
Less 170% of PIA (170% x 5,000,000)	8,500,000	

Capital allowances relieved	30,600,000	30,600,000
Unrelieved capital allowances carried forward (45,600,000 – 30,600,000)	15,000,000	———
Chargeable profit		15,400,000

Questions 55 - 57

JJ Oil Ltd

Computation of Assessable Profit and Education Tax for 2010

	₦
Crude oil exported (350,000 barrels @ ₦800)	280,000,000
Crude oil locally disposed of (50,000 barrels @ ₦35)	1,750,000
Incidental income	1,500,000
	283,250,000
Less:	
Production and admin. expenses	42,275,000
	240,975,000
Education tax (2/102 x 240,975,000)	4,725,000
Adjusted/assessable profit	236,250,000

Question 58

Niger Delta Petroleum Limited
Computation of Adjusted Posted Price
and Value of Crude Oil Exported

Posted price at standard API gravity		$30.00
Standard API gravity	30°	
API gravity of crude oil exported	35°	
Increase in API gravity	5° @ $0.05	$0.25
Posted price per barrel in dollars		$30.25
Posted price per barrel in Naira	($1 = ₦105)	₦3,176.25
Value of crude oil exported (1,000 bbls @ ₦3,176.25)		₦3,176,250

Questions 59 & 60

Aziza Petroleum Ltd

Monthly instalment – March to August 2011		₦
Original estimated tax	=	36,000,000
Monthly instalment = 36,000,000/12	=	3,000,000
Total instalments paid before the revised estimated tax (N3,000,000 x 6 months)		18,000,000

Revised monthly instalments following the submission of revised estimated tax in September 2011:		
Revised estimated tax		45,600,000
Estimated tax already paid		18,000,000
Estimated tax outstanding		27,600,000
No. of months remaining (i.e. Sept. 2011 – Feb. 2012)	6 months	
Revised monthly instalment (27,600,000/6)		4,600,000

Part II Short-Answer Questions

87 Chargeable oil means casing head petroleum spirit and crude oil won or obtained by the company from such operations.

88. (a) Natural gas means gas obtained in Nigeria from boreholes and wells and consisting primarily of hydro-carbons.
 (b) Liquefied natural gas means natural gas in its liquid state at approximately atmospheric pressure.

89. Chargeable natural gas means natural gas actually delivered by such company to Nigeria National Petroleum Corporation under gas taken by or on behalf of the Government of the Federation in pursuance of Petroleum Act.

90. Posted price means the price f.o.b. at the Nigerian Port of export for crude oil of the gravity and quality in question which is from time to time established by the company, after agreement with the Government of Nigeria as to the procedure to be followed for the purpose, as its posted price for Nigeria.

91. Petroleum means any mineral oil or relative hydro-carbon and natural gas existing in its natural condition in Nigeria but does not include liquefied natural gas, coal, bituminous shares or other stratified deposits from which oil can be extracted by destructive distillation.

92. Petroleum operation means the winning or obtaining and transportation of petroleum or chargeable oil in Nigeria by or on behalf of a company for its own account or process, not including refining at a refinery in the operations of business carried on by the company engaged in such sale of or any disposal of chargeable oil by or on behalf of the company.

93. Casing head petroleum spirit means any liquid hydrocarbons obtained in Nigeria from natural gas by separation or by any chemical or physical process but before the same has been refined or otherwise treated.

94. Non-productive rent means and includes the amount of any rent as to which there is provision for its deduction from the amount of any royalty under a petroleum prospecting license or oil mining lease to the extent that such rent is so deducted.

95. Intangible drilling expenditure means all expenditure for labour, fuel, repairs, maintenance, hauling, supplies and materials (not being supplies and materials for well cement, casing or other well fixtures) which are for or incidental to drilling, cleaning, deepening or completing wells or the preparation thereof incurred in respect of:
    (a) Determinations of well locations, geological studies and topographical and geographical surveys preparatory to drilling;
    (b) Drilling, shooting, testing and cleaning wells;
    (c) Cleaning, draining and levelling land, road building and the laying of foundations;

(d) Erection of rigs and tankage assembly and installation of pipelines and other plant and equipment required in the preparation or drilling of wells producing petroleum.

96. The value of chargeable oil is the aggregate of:
 (a) The value of that oil as determined for the purpose of royalty;
 (b) Any cost of extraction of that oil deducted in determining its value; and
 (c) Any cost incurred by the company in transporting and storage of that oil between the field of production and place of disposal.

97. The value of chargeable natural gas is the sum of gross proceeds under individual gas sales contracts in the accounting period less the G-Factor Allowance applicable to individual gas sales contract at the appropriate rate percent of such proceeds.

98 G-Factor Allowance means gas production cost adjustment factor.

99. The expenses must be wholly, exclusively and necessarily incurred.

100. The first day of the company's first accounting period.

101. (i) Any loss on the disposal of such asset is deemed to be qualifying drilling expenditure incurred on the first day of the company's first accounting period.
 (ii) Any profit on the disposal of such asset is deemed to be income of the company's first accounting period.

102. (i) The company must have incurred qualifying capital expenditure in respect of the asset.
 (ii) The company must be the owner of the asset.
 (iii) The asset must be "in use" at the end of the accounting period.

103. Petroleum investment allowance

Qualifying Expenditure in respect of	%
Onshore operations	5
Operations in territorial waters and continental shelf areas up to and including 100 metres of water depth	10
Operations in territorial waters and continental shelf areas between 100 and 200 metres of water depth	15
Operations in territorial waters and continental shelf areas beyond 200 metres of water depth	20

104. Capital allowances and balancing charges are computed as if the asset was used wholly and exclusively for petroleum operations. The allowances and charges to be made in connection with petroleum operations will be restricted to what the FIRS considers to be just and reasonable having regards to all the circumstances.

105. The lower of:
   (a) The aggregate amount of the capital allowances computed; or
   (b) The sum equal to 85% of the assessable profits of the accounting period less 170% of the petroleum investment allowance computed for that period.

106. Section 22(1) of PPTA provides that a crude oil producing company which excuted a production sharing contract (PSC) with the Nigerian National Petroleum Corporation in 1993 is entitled to investment tax credit throughout the duration of the production sharing contract. On the other hand, the Deep Offshore and Inland Basin Production Sharing Contracts Act 1999 (Cap. D3, LFN 2004) stipulates that an investment tax credit is granted for PSC executed before 1st July, 1998, while an investment tax allowance is granted for PSC executed after 1st July, 1998.

107. Section 22(2) of PPTA provides that the investment tax credit available to the company is 50% flat rate of chargeable profit for the duration of the production sharing contract. On the other hand, the Deep Offshore and Inland Basin Production Sharing Contracts Act

1999 (Cap. D3, LFN 2004) stipulates that the investment tax credit shall be at a flat rate of 50% of the qualifying capital expenditure in the accounting period in which the asset was first used for the purpose of petroleum operations.
The investment tax credit is to be treated as a tax offset, i.e. it is to be deducted from the assessable tax to arrive at the chargeable tax.

108. The MOU accords a minimum guaranteed notional margin of \$2.50/bbl after tax and royalty to the oil company on its equity crude and a minimum of \$1.25/bbl after tax and royalty on the NNPC's crude which it lifts under the memorandum. The minimum guaranteed notional margin is premised on the fact that the technical cost (TC) of operation is not more than the notional technical cost which at present is \$4.00/bbl. Where the actual capital investment cost (T2) is greater than \$2.00/bbl on average, the minimum guaranteed notional margin will be increased to \$2.70/bbl for the company's equity crude and \$1.35/bbl for NNPC's crude.

109 In relation to PPT, when a company is resident in Nigeria it means the control and management of the business of the company are exercised in Nigeria.

110. (a) As a set off against the tax chargeable upon that company in respect of the income.
(b) Where the tax has been paid, the amount of the credit may be repaid to that company.
(c) The amount of credit may be carried forward against the tax chargeable upon that company of any subsequent accounting period.

111. It may appeal to the Federal High Court within 30 days after the date on which the decision was given. Further appeal shall lie to the Court of Appeal.

112. Chargeable tax.

113. The currency in which the transactions were effected.

114. The estimated tax for each year is payable in equal monthly instalments. The first monthly instalment is payable not later than the third month of the accounting period. Subsequent monthly instalments are payable not later than the last day of each month. The final instalment is payable within 21 days after the service of notice of assessment of tax for the accounting period.

115. Where any instalment is not paid on the due date a penalty of 5% of the amount of the instalment due shall be added to the instalment.

116. Fine of 200% of the tax not withheld or not remitted plus interest at the prevailing commercial rate.

117. Fine of ₦1,000 and triple the amount of tax for which the person assessable is liable under the Act or six months imprisonment or both.

118. Fine of ₦1,000 and double the amount of tax undercharged or would have been undercharged as a result of the incorrect amounts, schedules and statements.

119

Akwa Ibom Oil Company Limited
Computation of Royalty Payable

Water Depth	Rate (A)	Production in Barrels (B)	Realizable Price (C) $	Royalty Payable (A)x(B)x(C) $
201 - 500 metres	12%	18,000	79.1423	170,947.37
Inland basin	10%	28,600	79.1423	226,346.98
Royalty payable				397,294.35

120. Profit oil

121. Petroleum Profits Tax Act, Cap. P13, LFN 2004

122. Federal Inland Revenue Service.

Adjusted/assessable profit	2,350,000	1,070,000	3,420,000
Less capital allowances	89,000	70,000	159,000
Total profit	2,261,000	1,000,000	3,261,000
Income tax liability (30% x 3,261,000)			978,300
Less Commonwealth income tax relief			150,000
Final income tax liability			828,300
Education tax payable (2% x 3,420,000)			68,400

Computation of Commonwealth Income Tax Relief:

$$\text{Commonwealth rate of tax} = \frac{\text{Commonwealth tax}}{\text{Commonwealth income}} \times \frac{100}{1}$$

$$= \frac{350,000}{1,000,000} \times \frac{100}{1} = 35\%$$

Nigerian rate of tax = 30%

Since the Commonwealth rate of tax exceeds one-half of the Nigerian rate of tax, relief will be given at one-half of the Nigerian rate of tax. Thus Commonwealth income tax relief = ½ x 30/100 x 1,000,000 = ₦150,000.

Questions 25 - 28

Bobo Ltd

Computation of Double Taxation Relief for 2014 Year of Assessment

	₦
Nigerian profits	700,000
Foreign profits	500,000
Total profits	1,200,000
Income tax payable (30% x 1,200,000)	360,000
Credit allowable (double taxation relief):	
Either: foreign tax paid (40% x 500,000)	200,000
Or: tax credit computed by charging the doubly-assessed profit to tax at the Nigerian tax rate (30% x 500,000)	150,000
whichever is lower	

The final tax liability will be as follows:

Total tax liability	360,000
Less credit allowable (double taxation relief)	150,000
Final tax liability	210,000

Part II Short-Answer Questions

48. The Commonwealth rate of tax is determined by dividing the Commonwealth tax by the Commonwealth income.

49. The Commonwealth rate of tax.

50. The rate at which relief will be given shall be equal to the amount by which the Nigeria rate of tax exceeds one-half of the Commonwealth rates of tax.

51. As defined by the CITN, double taxation agreement is a bilateral agreement between two countries (or their governments) to eliminate or minimize the negative effects which double taxation could have on cross border transactions and movement of people, capital, commerce and technology between them.

52. (a) Avoidance of double taxation or to afford relief from double taxation.
    (b) Prevention of fiscal evasion and avoidance
    (c) Co-operation in tax matters in areas of exchange of information, non-discrimination and mutual agreement procedure.

53. (a) United Kingdom
    (b) France
    (c) Netherlands

54. No double taxation relief. No credit is allowable against foreign tax for any year of assessment if the taxpayer is not resident in Nigeria for that year (Note that this provision is not applicable to Commonwealth income tax relief).

55. The credit allowable under double taxation arrangement must not exceed:
    (a) the tax computed by charging the profits or income subject to Nigerian tax and foreign tax to tax at the Nigerian tax rate;
    (b) the total tax payable by the taxpayer for that year of assessment.

56. Commonwealth income tax relief can be given as a set off against the tax due or as a repayment out of the tax paid for that year of assessment.

57. Permanent establishment.

58. (a) A branch
    (b) An office
    (c) A factory

59. The profit of the Nigerian company attributable to the permanent establishment in United Kingdom may be taxed in that country.

60. International traffic is defined in the Nigerian double taxation agreements as any transport by a ship or aircraft operated by an enterprise of a contracting state, except where the ship or aircraft is operated solely between places in the other contracting state.

61. Where:
    (a) an enterprise of one country participates directly or indirectly in the management, control or capital of an enterprise of the other country, or
    (b) the same person participates directly or indirectly in the management, control or capital of an enterprise of one country and an enterprise of the other country, the enterprises involved are said to be associated.

62. A non-resident individual.

63. A non-resident company.

64. Nigerian company

65. Foreign company

66. (a) Where the branch is used solely for storage or display of goods and merchandise.
    (b) Where the branch is used solely for the collection of information.

67. (a) When the trade or business produces no assessable profits.
    (b) When the true amount of the assessable profit cannot be readily ascertained.

68. Turnkey project.

69. Tax heaven

70. Commonwealth income tax relief is given in a situation that a company which has paid or is liable to pay tax in Nigeria for any year of assessment on any part of its profit has also paid or is liable to pay tax in any country within the commonwealth or in the Republic of Ireland. The relief is used to reduce the tax paid or payable in Nigeria on that part of the company's profits which is liable to tax in Nigeria and in another Commonwealth country or in the Republic of Ireland

71. The Nigerian rate of tax is determined by dividing the tax chargeable for that year by the total profits or income of the company or the individual for that year.

72. False

73. Two methods:
    - Exemption method. The country of residence exempts from tax the income which has been taxed in the source country.

- Credit method. The tax paid in the source country is allowed as a credit against the tax charged in the country of residence on the same income.

28 Transfer Pricing, Thin Capitalization and Electronic Commerce

Part I Multiple-Choice Questions

1.	E	2.	E	3.	A
4.	D	5.	A	6.	D
7.	C	8.	A	9.	E
10.	D	11.	A	12.	B
13.	C	14.	A	15.	C
16.	A	17.	E	18.	D
19.	E	20.	A	21.	B
22.	A	23.	C	24.	D
25.	A	26.	E	27.	A
28.	A	29.	E	30.	A
31.	A	32.	A	33.	D
34.	D	35.	A	36.	D
37.	A	38.	E	39.	D
40.	A	41.	E	42.	E
43.	E	44.	A		

Part II Short-Answer Questions

45. Electronic commerce (e-commerce, ecommerce or e-comm)

46. It may be difficult for the tax authorities to identify, trace or verify many e-commerce transactions. Where products are delivered electronically (over the internet), they will escape indirect taxes (e.g. custom duties, VAT, etc) because these goods will not pass through convenient taxing points.

47. A situation whereby a company is financed with a much greater proportion of debt than equity.

48. Placing a limit on debt to equity ratio, e.g. 3:1, 2:1, 1.5:1 or restriction on deductibility of interest, e.g, interest allowable for tax purposes could be restricted to 30% of taxable profit before interest and taxes. Interest in excess of the prescribed level is disallowed as a deduction.

49. Each ultimate parent entity or a constituent entity of MNE group that is resident for tax purposes in Nigeria.

50. English Language

51. Base Erosion and Profit Shifting

52. Arm's length principle

53. connected (related or associated)

54. Controlled transaction

55. Independent enterprises or persons.

56. True

57. False

58. One per cent of the value of each controlled transaction for which the information or document was required in addition to ten thousand naira for each day in which the failure continues.

29 Merger, Acquisition, Tax Incentives and Tax Planning

Part I Multiple-Choice Questions

1.	A	2.	E	3.	E
4.	C	5.	C	6.	E
7.	A	8.	A	9.	D
10.	A	11.	D	12.	A
13.	B	14.	D	15.	B
16.	C	17.	A	18.	A
19.	B	20.	D	21.	A
22.	E	23.	D	24.	D
25.	E	26.	E	27.	D
28.	B	29.	D	30.	E
31.	D	32.	B	33.	E
34.	B	35.	E	36.	D
37.	A	38.	E	39.	E
40.	B				

Part II Short-Answer Questions

41. Yes. CITA provides that no merger, take-over, transfer or restructuring of the trade or business carried on by a company shall take place without having obtained the Federal Inland Revenue Service's direction and clearance with respect to any tax that may be due and payable under the Capital Gains Tax Act.

42. The income must be put in a reserved fund to be used within five years for the building expansion of new hotels, conference centres and facilities for purpose of tourism development.

43. The company is allowed investment tax relief for each year expenditure is incurred on each such facility at the following rate of the expenditure:

(a) no facilities at all 100%
(b) no electricity 50%
(c) no water 30%
(d) no tarred road 15%

44. (a) A Nigerian company which engages in manufacturing and earns less than ₦1 million turnover per annum is assessable to tax at the rate of 20% instead of 30% in the first five years.
(b) Capital allowances claimable by a manufacturing company in a year of assessment are not restricted to $66^{2}/_{3}$% of the year's assessable profits.

45. (a) Interest on loan for agricultural trade or business is exempted from tax subject to the conditions stipulated in CITA.
(b) A company carrying on agricultural trade or business is exempted from payment of minimum tax.

46. The moratorium must not be less than eighteen months and the rate of interest on the loan should not be more than the base lending rate at the time the loan was granted.

47. Third Schedule

Table of Tax Exemption on Interest on Foreign and other Loans

Payment Period including Moratorium	Grace Period	Tax Exemption Allowed
Above 7 years	Not less than 2 years	100%
5 - 7 years	Not less than 18 months	70%
2 - 4 years	Not less than 12 months	40%
Below 2 years	Nil	Nil

48. Gas utilization is defined in CITA as the marketing and distribution of natural gas for commercial purposes and includes power plant,

liquefied natural gas, gas to liquid plant, fertilizer plant, gas transmission and distribution pipelines.

49. The company may be granted an initial tax free period of three years, which may be renewed for an initial period of two years if the performance of the business is satisfactory.

50. The tax free period starts on the day the company commences production as certified by the Ministry of Petroleum Resources

51. (a) An annual allowance of 90% with 10% retention for investment in plant and machinery.
    (b) An additional investment allowance of 15% which shall not reduce the value of the asset.

52. Executive Order No. 007 of 2019 (Companies Income Tax {Road Infrastructure Development and Refurbishment Investment Tax Credit Scheme} Order, 2019.

53. The profit of an export oriented undertaking is exempted from tax for the first three consecutive years of assessment provided the conditions stipulated in CITA are met.

54. True

55. False

56. Tax planning involves taking conscious efforts to consider the tax that will be payable by a taxpayer at a future date and how such tax can be minimized (ICAN).

57. True

30 Tax Implications of Leasing

Part I Multiple-Choice Questions

1.	E	2.	C	3.	D
4.	E	5.	A	6.	D
7.	B				

Part II Short-Answer Questions

8. Finance lease

9. Operating lease

10. Sale and leaseback

31 Taxation of Non-Governmental Organisations (NGOs)

Part I Multiple-Choice Questions

1.	A	2.	E	3.	A
4.	D	5.	D	6.	B
7.	C				

32 Tax Audit and Investigation

Part I Multiple-Choice Questions

1.	E	2.	C	3.	A
4.	D	5.	A	6.	C
7.	E	8.	D	9.	B

10.	D	11.	D	12.	D
13.	E	14.	B	15.	B
16.	D	17.	E	18.	C
19.	C	20.	A	21.	C
22.	D	23.	A	24.	C
25.	D	26.	C	27.	B
28.	A	29.	E	30.	D
31.	A	32.	C	33.	D
34.	E				

Personal Income Tax in Nigeria

3rd Edition

Offiong U. Bassey

This book provides a comprehensive and up-to-date treatment of personal income tax in Nigeria and is particularly relevant for:

- students reading Financial Studies, Accountancy, Taxation and related courses in the Nigerian universities and polytechnics at undergraduate and postgraduate levels;
- students preparing for professional examinations such as ATSWA, TTS, ICAN, CITN, ANAN, ICPAN, CICMA and other examinations of comparable standards;
- members of staff of the FIRS and State tax authorities;
- tax practitioners, accountants, lecturers and others who may wish to acquire a good knowledge of the law and practice of personal income tax in Nigeria for whatever reason.

The book contains several worked examples together with discussion questions, problems and case studies drawn from the past examination papers of the Institute of Chartered Accountants of Nigeria (ICAN) and the Chartered Institute of Taxation of Nigeria (CITN) to assist the students in their preparation for future examinations. Definitions of terms relating to personal taxation are provided in the glossary at the end of the book.

Contents

PART 1 **INTRODUCTION TO TAXATION AND NIGERIAN TAX SYSTEM**

Chapter 1 Introduction to Taxation
Chapter 2 Background of Nigerian Tax System
Chapter 3 National Tax Policy
Chapter 4 Administration of Personal Income Tax

PART 2 **LIABILITY TO PERSONAL INCOME TAX IN NIGERIA**

Chapter 5 Persons and Income Chargeable
Chapter 6 Residence and Relevant Tax Authority

PART 3 **INCOME FROM EMPLOYMENT**

Chapter 7 Reliefs and Tax Exempt Deductions

Chapter 8 Employment Income
Chapter 9 Pay As You Earn (PAYE)

PART 4 INCOME FROM PROPERTY, SAVINGS AND INVESTMENTS

Chapter 10 Investment Income
Chapter 11 Withholding Tax

PART 5 INCOME FROM TRADE, BUSINESS, PROFESSION AND VOCATION (SELF-EMPLOYMENT)

Chapter 12 Ascertainment of Income
Chapter 13 Basis of Assessment
Chapter 14 Capital Allowances
Chapter 15 Total Income and Loss Reliefs
Chapter 16 Partnership Assessment

PART 6 RETURNS, ASSESSMENTS, COLLECTION, OBJECTIONS, APPEALS, OFFENCES AND PENALTIES

Chapter 17 Returns, Assessments and Collection Procedures
Chapter 18 Objections and Appeals
Chapter 19 Tax Clearance Certificate
Chapter 20 Tax Evasion, Tax Avoidance, Artificial Transactions and Back Duty Investigation
Chapter 21 Tax Offences and Penalties
Chapter 22 Presumptive Taxation
Chapter 23 Tax Amnesty

PART 7 MISCELLANEOUS

Chapter 24 Estates, Trusts and Settlements
Chapter 25 Double Taxation Relief
Chapter 26 Federal Capital Territory Internal Revenue Service

References
Appendices
Glossary
Index

Companies Taxation in Nigeria
3rd Edition
Offiong U. Bassey

This book gives a full coverage of companies income tax, pioneer industries, tertiary education tax, national information technology development levy, stamp duties, value added tax, capital gains tax, double taxation, tax incentives, tax planning, tax audit and investigation, tax implications of mergers and acquisitions, transfer pricing, e-commerce and other advanced topics in Nigerian Taxation.

The book is useful to a wide range of readers particularly:

- students reading Financial Studies, Accountancy, Taxation and related courses in the Nigerian universities and polytechnics at undergraduate and postgraduate levels;
- students preparing for professional examinations such as ATSWA, TTS, ICAN, CITN, ANAN, ICPAN, CICMA and other similar examinations;
- members of staff of the Federal Inland Revenue Service;
- tax practitioners, accountants, lecturers and others who may wish to obtain a good grounding in companies taxation for whatever purpose.

The book contains a large number of worked examples together with discussion questions, problems and case studies drawn from the past examination papers of the Institute of Chartered Accountants of Nigeria (ICAN) and the Chartered Institute of Taxation of Nigeria (CITN) to assist the students in their preparation for future examinations. Definitions of terms relating to companies taxation are provided in the glossary at the end of the book.

Contents

PART 1 **FEDERAL INLAND REVENUE SERVICE AND TAX ADMINISTRATION**

Chapter 1 Federal Inland Revenue Service and Tax Administration

PART 2 **COMPANIES TAXATION**

Chapter 2 Profits Chargeable
Chapter 3 Ascertainment of Profits
Chapter 4 Computation of Income Tax Payable
Chapter 5 Tertiary Education Tax
Chapter 6 National Information Technology Development Levy
Chapter 7 Withholding Tax

Chapter 8 Basis of Assessment
Chapter 9 Capital Allowances
Chapter 10 Total Profits and Loss Relief
Chapter 11 Taxation of Specialized Companies
Chapter 12 Taxation of Pioneer Companies
Chapter 13 Returns, Assessments and Collection Procedures
Chapter 14 Objections and Appeals
Chapter 15 Tax Clearance Certificate
Chapter 16 Tax Offences and Penalties

PART 3 STAMP DUTIES AND VALUE ADDED TAX

Chapter 17 Stamp Duties
Chapter 18 Value Added Tax

PART 4 CAPITAL GAINS TAX

Chapter 19 Capital Gains Tax

Part 5 INTERNATIONAL TAXATION

Chapter 20 Double Taxation Relief
Chapter 21 Taxation of Non-Residents
Chapter 22 Multinational Transfer Pricing and Thin Capitalization
Chapter 23 Tax Implications of Electronic Commerce

PART 6 MISCELLANEOUS

Chapter 24 Tax Incentives
Chapter 25 Tax Planning
Chapter 26 Tax Implications of Merger and Acquisition
Chapter 27 Tax Implications of Leasing
Chapter 28 Tax Implications of the Adoption of the IFRS
Chapter 29 Taxation of Non-Governmental Organizations (NGOs)
Chapter 30 Tax Audit and Investigation

References
Appendices
Glossary
Index

Petroleum Profits Tax in Nigeria

3rd Edition

Offiong U. Bassey

This book provides a comprehensive introduction to petroleum profits tax in Nigeria for the benefit of students reading Accountancy, Taxation and related courses in the Nigerian universities and polytechnics and students preparing for professional examinations. The book will also be of great assistance to members of staff of the FIRS, lecturers, professional accountants, tax practitioners, etc.

The book contains several multiple-choice and short-answer questions together with discussion questions and problems drawn from the past examination papers of the Institute of Chartered Accountants of Nigeria (ICAN) and the Chartered Institute of Taxation of Nigeria (CITN) to assist the students in their preparation for future examinations. Answers are also provided to enable the students to verify whether they have solved the questions and problems correctly.

Contents

Chapter 1	Introduction
Chapter 2	Administration
Chapter 3	Ascertainment of Profits
Chapter 4	Classifications of Costs
Chapter 5	Loss Relief
Chapter 6	Capital Allowances
Chapter 7	Ascertainment of Tertiary Education Tax, Assessable Tax, Chargeable Tax and Royalties
Chapter 8	Production Sharing Contract and Investment Tax Credit
Chapter 9	Memorandum of Understanding
Chapter 10	Persons Chargeable
Chapter 11	Accounts and Returns
Chapter 12	Assessments
Chapter 13	Objection and Appeal
Chapter 14	Collection, Recovery and Repayment of Tax
Chapter 15	Offences and Penalties
Chapter 16	Miscellaneous Provisions
Summary	
Bibliography	
Appendix I	Multiple-Choice and Short-Answer Questions
Appendix II	Discussion Questions and Problems
Appendix III	Solutions
Index	

Taxation & Advanced Taxation

Offiong U. Bassey

This book is specifically written for students preparing for the examinations of the Institute of Chartered Accountants of Nigeria (ICAN). The book provides answers to several questions drawn from the past examination papers of the Institute of Chartered Accountants of Nigeria and the Chartered Institute of Taxation of Nigeria (CITN) to enable the students to know what the examiners are looking for and to assist them in their preparation for future examinations. The book is equally useful to students preparing for other professional examinations of comparable standards and students reading Accountancy, Taxation and related courses in the Nigerian universities and polytechnics. The book will also be of tremendous assistance to lecturers who are preparing students for various examinations in Taxation.

Contents

Chapter 1	Introduction to Taxation and Nigerian Tax System
Chapter 2	Administration of Personal Income Tax
Chapter 3	Federal Inland Revenue Service (Establishment) Act, 2007
Chapter 4	Persons and Income Chargeable
Chapter 5	Residence and Relevant Tax Authority
Chapter 6	Employment Income and Pay As You Earn
Chapter 7	Investment Income and Withholding Tax
Chapter 8	Ascertainment of Profits
Chapter 9	Basis of Assessment
Chapter 10	Capital Allowances
Chapter 11	Loss Reliefs
Chapter 12	Partnership Assessment
Chapter 13	Estates, Trusts and Settlements
Chapter 14	Computation of Companies Income Tax
Chapter 15	Tertiary Education Tax and Information Technology Development Levy
Chapter 16	Taxation of Specialized Companies
Chapter 17	Pioneer Companies
Chapter 18	Tax Returns, Assessments and Collection Procedures
Chapter 19	Tax Objections and Appeals
Chapter 20	Tax Clearance Certificate
Chapter 21	Tax Evasion, Tax Avoidance, Tax Offences and Penalties
Chapter 22	Stamp Duties

Chapter 23	Value Added Tax
Chapter 24	Capital Gains Tax
Chapter 25	Petroleum Profits Tax
Chapter 26	Accounting for Taxes
Chapter 27	Double Taxation Relief and Taxation of Non-residents
Chapter 28	Transfer Pricing, Thin Capitalization and Electronic Commerce
Chapter 29	Tax Implications of Mergers and Acquisitions
Chapter 30	Tax Incentives
Chapter 31	Tax Planning
Chapter 32	Tax Audit and Investigation

Mail Order

If this book is not available in your local bookshop, you can order for it from the publisher and necessary arrangement will be made to deliver it to you. Direct your order to:

The Marketing Manager
Best Brain Bookshops
P. O. Box 6461
Marina, Lagos
Nigeria

Or

E-mail: bassey64@yahoo.com
Or

Call: 08091091666, 08025294928, 08036722720